NATURE AND MOTION
IN THE MIDDLE AGES

STUDIES IN PHILOSOPHY
AND THE HISTORY OF PHILOSOPHY

General editor: Jude P. Dougherty

**Studies in Philosophy
and the History of Philosophy**   **Volume 11**

Nature and Motion in the Middle Ages .

by James A. Weisheipl, O.P.
edited by William E. Carroll

THE CATHOLIC UNIVERSITY OF AMERICA PRESS
Washington, D.C.

Copyright © 1985
The Catholic University of America Press
All rights reserved
Printed in the United States of America

Library of Congress Cataloging in Publication Data

Weisheipl, James A.
  Nature and motion in the Middle Ages.

  (Studies in philosophy and the history of
philosophy ; v. 11)
  Reprint of essays originally published 1954–1981.
  "Selected bibliography of the works of James A.
Weisheipl, O.P.": p.
  1. Physics—Philosophy—Addresses, essays,
lectures.   I. Carroll, William, 1943–
II. Title.   III. Series.
B21.S78 vol. 11   [QC6.2]   100 s   [530'.01]   84-12129
ISBN 0-8132-0599-9

Table of Contents

Acknowledgments

The editor thanks Father James Weisheipl, O.P., for his permission to edit this collection of his essays. Without his encouragement and support this book would not be possible. The editor acknowledges with special gratitude the assistance provided by Paul Pearson and Eric Reitan in the final preparation of the text for publication. For permission to publish essays which first appeared elsewhere, the editor thanks the publishers and editors listed below:

"The Concept of Nature," *The New Scholasticism* 28 (1954), 377–408.

"Natural and Compulsory Movement," *The New Scholasticism* 29 (1955), 50–81.

"The Principle *Omne quod movetur ab alio movetur* in Medieval Physics," *Isis* 56 (1965), 26–45.

"The Specter of *motor coniunctus* in Medieval Physics," *Studi sul XIV secolo in memoria di Anneliese Maier,* edited by A. Maierù and A. P. Bagliani (Rome: Edizioni di Storia e Letteratura, 1981), 81–104.

"Motion in a Void: Aquinas and Averroes," *St. Thomas Aquinas 1274–1974: Commemorative Studies,* edited by A. Maurer (Toronto: Pontifical Institute of Mediaeval Studies, 1974), I, 467–88.

"The Celestial Movers in Medieval Physics," *The Thomist* 24 (1961), 286–326.

"The Commentary of St. Thomas on the *De caelo* of Aristotle," *Sapientia* 29 (1974), 11–34.

"Classification of the Sciences in Medieval Thought," *Mediaeval Studies* 27 (1965), 54–90.

"The Evolution of Scientific Method," *The Logic of Science,* edited by V. E. Smith (New York: St. John's University Press, 1964), 59–86.

"The Relationship of Medieval Natural Philosophy to Modern Science: The Contribution of Thomas Aquinas to Its Understanding," *Manuscripta* 20 (1976), 181–96.

Editor's Introduction

The systematic study of the sensible world, the science which Aristotle called physics and which later came to be known as natural philosophy, has occupied some of the greatest minds of the West. The enterprise has not been easy. From the beginning Aristotle had to counter the ancient dichotomy between Parmenides (all change is illusion) and Heraclitus (everything is flux) as well as the Platonic view that scientific knowledge of the evanescent world of sense experience was not possible. Indeed, the questions concerning the reality and intelligibility of change, which Aristotle discusses in the opening books of the *Physics,* and the questions concerning the nature of science and the requirements for demonstrative knowledge, which he examines in the *Posterior Analytics,* continue to inform our discussions of these subjects. It is to Aristotle that we owe the first sustained defense of the integrity and autonomy of the science of physics. And in the Latin Middle Ages, with the rediscovery and translation of Aristotle's treatises on the natural sciences, Albert the Great, Thomas Aquinas, and others labored mightily to understand, explain, and build upon Aristotle's insights.

In the modern and contemporary world the study of physics, in the Aristotelian sense, has declined. The reasons for this decline, which in many respects has been precipitous, are several. Many thinkers argue that since the time of Galileo and Newton, with the advent of the "scientific revolution" and the rise of "modern science," the physics we associate with Aristotle and the Latin scholastics is irrelevant: it has been overthrown and replaced by a new science. There are other thinkers who would deny that there is any real distinction between metaphysics and natural philosophy, and thus they make the latter but a part of the former. If natural philosophy is taught at all it is found in departments of philosophy, and is usually considered separate from, if not wholly irrelevant to, the natural sciences. Furthermore, the claims which Aristotle and his medieval commentators made for science (*scientia*)—in its strictest sense—as knowledge of what is necessarily the case through proper causes have been rejected as naive and unfounded by many modern philosophers of science. In

ix

the face of such criticism, the study of natural philosophy would at best become the study of the history of ideas about our understanding of the sensible world. In fact, there is a tendency to view the study of Aristotelian physics through the Middle Ages as an archaeological excursion in which we examine the fossils of an extinct species. Such an investigation is neither without interest nor without importance, but for the natural philosopher it is always a preliminary task.

As Aristotle often observes, the source of many disagreements is to be found in a failure among disputants to discuss the same thing in the same respect. Such a failure has been especially evident in the history of science. Terms such as "nature," "motion," "cause," "physics," "science," and the like have been and are used in many senses. And any discussion of nature and motion in medieval thought is compromised from the start if we do not understand how these words are used. Such a "tyranny of terms" has taken a heavy toll in the usual understanding, or rather misunderstanding, of the history of science.

The essays collected in this volume illustrate the work of a distinguished scholar, Father James Weisheipl, O.P., whose writing and teaching have resulted in important additions to our understanding of nature and motion. Weisheipl's meticulous attention to texts and his skills as historian, philosopher, and theologian are evident in all his work. In his analysis of medieval physics we discover a cogent argument that St. Albert and St. Thomas are the surest guides to a sound interpretation of Aristotle and to a good understanding of nature and motion.

In many ways the first essay in this book, "The Concept of Nature," sets the theme for the entire work. Indeed, Weisheipl's analysis of the Aristotelian understanding of nature in the Latin Middle Ages informs all of his later writings. In the three decades since he first published this essay, Weisheipl has broadened and deepened our understanding of nature, motion, and a whole range of related topics in natural philosophy. His contributions in this respect start with a study of Aristotle's definition of nature: "a principle or cause of motion and rest in those things in which it exists *per se* and not incidentally." For Aristotle, this internal source of consistent activity and rest distinguishes all things natural from those of chance and from those of art. The source of a thing that comes to be through art is always external to that thing. And chance is the unintended, unexpected, unpredicted, and therefore, in a sense, the irrational that happens in the world. We see at once not only the distinctions among nature, art, and chance, but also the connection between nature and motion. It was a common expression in the Middle Ages that to be ignorant of motion was to be ignorant of nature. The essays in this volume exhibit Weisheipl's careful explanation of the distinctions among nature, art, and chance, his probing discussion of the understanding and misunderstandings of Aristotle's exposition of nature, and his systematic presentation of the ideas of motion in medieval and early modern thought.

Nature, as Aristotle defines it, has two distinct senses: (1) the active principle that is "form," and (2) the passive principle that is "matter." The significance of this twofold sense of nature was not lost on the Latin scholastics who spoke of nature in two wide senses: as "form" or *natura secundum principium activum seu formale,* and as "matter" or *natura secundum principium passivum, receptivum seu materiale.* The natural philosopher does not properly concern himself with those things which come into existence by art or by chance; that is, he does not study their coming into existence *as* works of art or *by* chance. He does study, however, both the active principle (form) and the passive principle (matter) of all natural things: that is, he seeks to discover the intrinsic sources of motion and rest in things. But since no passive principle can be actualized without some extrinsic, efficient cause acting for a definite purpose, the natural philosopher must also study the efficient and final causes of all natural things, in addition to their formal and material causes.

Weisheipl, following in the tradition of St. Thomas, shows that the source of much of the misunderstanding of the Aristotelian explanation of nature, especially concerning the distinction between natural and violent motion, stems from a failure to distinguish principle from cause. This failure led many commentators on Aristotle, both in the Middle Ages and more recently, to search for an extrinsic efficient cause, a *motor coniunctus,* to account for naturally moving bodies. Weisheipl explores this and related problems in the third, fourth, and fifth essays. Especially important in this respect is his analysis of the meaning of *Omne quod movetur ab alio movetur.* Many recent historians of science find this principle, viz., everything that is moved is moved by another, to represent a fundamental discontinuity between Aristotelian and modern physics. For Weisheipl, such is not the case, and his exposition of the principle and the history of its interpretation is one of his major contributions to the history of medieval science.

Weisheipl argues that modern physics has its origins not in the overthrow of Aristotelian physics but rather in the tremendous expansion of what Aristotle, Aquinas, and others recognized as intermediate sciences (*scientiae mediae*): sciences which, in this instance, employ mathematical principles in understanding the quantitative features of the cosmos. Although the mathematician differs from the physicist or natural philosopher in that he abstracts from sensible matter and from motion, considering quantity (discrete and continuous) as such, still principles derived from mathematics can be used in the study of the world of sense experience, the world of physical quantity. Mathematical astronomy, optics, and harmonics are examples of such intermediate sciences which Aristotle and Aquinas recognized. Weisheipl's recent work on Galileo and inertia, the essays on the classification of the sciences in the Middle Ages, on the evolution of the scientific method, and on the relationship between medieval natural philosophy and modern science describe continuities in the history of science and also disclose some of the distinctive features of at least the modern physical sciences.

There is some repetition in the essays in this book. Except for the first two, they were not explicitly written to be part of one book. Nevertheless, there is a unity throughout these essays in that Weisheipl, as noted above, returned frequently to the same themes in his analysis of nature and motion in the Middle Ages. The material is not easy, and has often been misunderstood. And thus, in retaining passages of certain essays which restate, in one form or another, what is found elsewhere in the book, I have followed the principle: *repetitio est mater studiorum*. Father Weisheipl, like Thomas Aquinas, uses repetition as a means to broaden, deepen, and reinforce his analysis.

As Weisheipl points out in the final essay in this book, many contemporary philosophers fail to distinguish between natural philosophy and metaphysics on the one hand, or natural philosophy and modern mathematical physics on the other: some reduce natural philosophy to metaphysics, others think that modern science has replaced natural philosophy. The essays in this volume offer a corrective to such views. With St. Albert and St. Thomas, Weisheipl affirms the autonomy of the study of nature as a science distinct from metaphysics and theology, as well as from mathematics and the intermediate sciences. And Weisheipl's work offers eloquent testimony both to the insights of these two medieval interpreters of Aristotle and to the living tradition of natural philosophy.

Cornell College   WILLIAM E. CARROLL

I

THE CONCEPT OF NATURE

Words can exercise a very strong tyranny over the mind, unless one realizes that words are merely a feeble medium in which to communicate our thoughts and our experience of reality. Words are symbolic, not immediately of things, but of ideas; and those ideas ultimately involve a highly complex human experience of a reality which cannot be fully comprehended. There is, however, a common tendency, unconscious of course, to substitute words for the reality, thinking that in knowing the right word or phrase, we thereby know the reality we are talking about. This tendency is particularly dangerous in a philosophical tradition, in which words are carefully selected and definitions canonized. When such scientific terms and definitions are employed without sufficient analysis of meaning they deceive us into thinking we understand reality, while actually they are an impediment to true understanding. Modern philosophers, for the most part, shy away from traditional terminology for fear of being misunderstood or not understood at all. They tend to coin their own words, free of undesired implication, or juxtapose unexpected phrases to jolt the reader into seeing the meaning intended. Logical positivism has at least this merit that it insists on a careful analysis of meaning as a necessary factor in philosophical and scientific understanding.[1]

The term "nature" has particularly suffered great abuse. In medieval thought the term was used in many senses, but each sense was clearly specified. Renaissance philosophy regarded nature as something divine and self-creative; it distinguished *natura naturata,* or the complex of observable changes and processes, from *natura naturans,* or the immanent force which animates and directs them. The Aristotelians whom Bacon, Boyle, and Newton attacked seemed to have avoided scientific research, claiming "nature" as a sufficient ex-

---

[1] Cf. A. Whitehead, *Modes of Thought* (Cambridge, Eng., 1938), pp. 1–171; also *Process and Reality* (New York, 1941), pp. 16–20.

1

planation of physical phenomena. While today the term has been applied in so many different senses, it seems to have no specific implication at all; much less is it an explanation. Therefore it is important that we analyze carefully the concept of nature to see its precise meaning.

In contemporary usage the term "nature" is on the whole most often used in a collective sense for the sum total or aggregate of natural things. We often speak of nature in the sense of the "universe" or "cosmos," meaning by that the whole of natural reality outside the mind. This sense implies a bifurcation of mind and external reality, which can be misleading. But the important point is that this notion of "nature" signifies something global and self-contained; it is a *nomen absolutum*. Even when we refer to the "nature" of man, of law, or of any other reality, our reference is usually to its essence in the static sense of what makes it to be what it is. In other words, "nature" in its ordinary use is by no means a functional term but rather a static and self-contained one. It is synonymous with "essence," or *quod quid est*. At the same time, this is not the only sense in which the word is used in modern languages. There is another sense, which we recognize to be its original and, strictly, its proper sense: when it refers not to a collection, but to a *principle*, or *source*. We often say that a man has an affectionate or quarrelsome nature, meaning that the man's own temperament in some way accounts for his expression of affection or irascibility. We say it is the nature of water to flow downhill, the nature of dogs to bark. In this sense the word "nature" refers to something intrinsic which is responsible for the behavior. This is more clearly implied in the common distinction between natural behavior, that is, behavior resulting from something intrinsic to the thing itself, and compulsory, which arises from external constraint contrary to its proper activity. "Nature" as used in this sense of an intrinsic source is a *relative* term, that is, it is spoken of and thought of always in relation to a characteristic behavior or property. There is a great difference between these two senses. The absolute term merely connotes existence. The relative term, on the other hand, always implies source and responsibility. Although both senses are used in English, it is easy to see that the relative use of the term is prior and logically, as well as etymologically, would antecede its use in the absolute sense.[2]

Early Greek philosophy employed the term φύσις, from which we derive our word "physics" and its variants, only in the relative sense of a source, or ἀρχή. Not until relatively late is the term employed in the

[2] Cf. R. G. Collingwood, *The Idea of Nature* (Oxford, 1945), pp. 43–48.

secondary sense of an aggregate of natural things, that is, more or less synonymously with the word κόσμος.[3] The term φύσις originally seems to have meant the process of generation, but the existing fragments of the pre-Socratics invariably employ the term to signify the "source" of the process. The Ionians, for example, were principally concerned with finding the original material "out of which" the entire universe is formed, an original source which would explain the evident phenomena of various movements in the universe. The single element of fire, air, or water was regarded by the Ionians as the true "nature" of things; it was the ultimate reality responsible for activity. Empedocles, realizing the insufficiency of a single element, regarded the four elements as the true nature of things. He makes a point of insisting that only those four elements should be called φύσις and reprimands his contemporaries who apply the term even to mixtures of these elements.[4] It is very important to remember that the pre-Socratic problem was the search for an ultimate explanation of sensible phenomena, and not merely a question of the "one" or the "many." The ultimate "one" postulated by the Ionians was not a static substratum but a source, a φύσις from which flows movement and sensible reality. Although the term was applied to a great many things, the essential connotation remained the same, namely, a material source of changing phenomena.[5]

[3] For example Gorgias, the famous Sicilian of the late fifth century, wrote a treatise entitled *PERI TOÛ MÊ 'ONTOS, Ê PERI PHÛSEÔS;* from what Sextus tells us, it is clear that φύσις means not a principle but merely the world of nature; for Gorgias maintained: (1) that nothing exists; (2) if anything exists, it is incomprehensible; (3) if it is comprehensible, it is incommunicable. Cf. H. Diels, *Fragmente der Vorsokratiker,* 5th ed. (Berlin, 1934–38), 82B, frag. 3. References to Diels abbreviated to *Vorsok.*

[4] Diels, *Vorsok.,* 31B, frag. 8.

[5] Over the past forty years a strong controversy has raged concerning the principal meaning of φύσις among the pre-Socratics. Cf. summary in A. Mansion, *Introd. à la Physique Aristotélicienne,* 2d ed. (Louvain, 1945), pp. 59–63; also bibliography in W. A. Heidel, "Perì phúseos, A Study of the Conception of Nature among the Presocratics," *Proceed. of the Am. Acad. of Arts and Sciences* 45, no. 4, p. 96, note 69. The main point of the controversy seems to be whether the term primarily signified the eternal primary material of which the world is made (Burnet, *Early Greek Philosophy,* 4th ed. [London, 1945], pp. 10–11; Appendix, pp. 363–64) or the universal process of growth (W. A. Heidel, *op. cit.;* W. B. Veazie, "The Word PHUSIS," *Archiv für Gesch. d. Philos.,* Bd. 33, H. 1/2 [1926], 3–22). Mansion attempts to harmonize the opposing positions by insisting that "pour les penseurs antérieurs à Socrate la φύσις cosmique englobait l'ensemble des phénomènes naturels, dont le monde est le théatre avec la réalité matérielle primitive, source et origine de ces phénomènes" (*op. cit.,* p. 63). It would seem that the difficulty depends upon accepting or rejecting Aristotle's claim (*Metaph.* V, 4, 1014b17), that the term originally signified the process of birth, and then transferred to designate the source of this process. If Aristotle's claim is correct, then φύσις is a *relative term* designating the "source" but always connoting "movement"; this is not a compound sense, but a single relative sense. Then, too, although the pre-Socratics considered this source (φύσις) to be "ageless and deathless," as Burnet points out (*op. cit.,* p. 10), it would seem

In a very famous passage of the *Laws* Plato accuses his predecessors and contemporaries of impiety and of leading young men away from the gods.[6] All other philosophers, he says, teach that this beautiful universe, the regularity of celestial movements, and the human soul arise "not because of mind, nor because of any god, nor by art, but as we may say, by *nature* and *chance*."[7] Plato recognizes that all things which come about in the universe are the result either of art (τέχνη), nature (φύσις), or chance (τύχη).[8] But the ancient philosophers and even his own contemporaries attribute the origin of the universe and its phenomena to nature, a blind material element which operates by chance. He asks how was it that "nature" in the first place acquired movement and force to produce the order of the universe? How, he asks, can soul be a result of material φύσις, since intelligence must be anterior in order to direct growth and order?[9] If φύσις means the "first source," then the term should be applied not to fire, air, or earth but to Soul.[10] For Plato it is Soul (God) which is the first source of all being and becoming, the ruler of the heavens, the lawgiver.[11] The ancient philosophers, who attribute all phenomena to nature, derogate from the rights of God, Who is the true Nature, unseen by the senses of the body, but perceived by the intellect.[12] In his explanation of the material world Plato gives to art a preeminence over nature and chance. That is to say, Plato insists that the material universe is a product of the *art* of God.[13]

Plato, however, does not use the term φύσις consistently throughout his works, for sometimes he opposes the two classes of being, φύσις and intelligence,[14] and sometimes he attributes the traditional role of φύσις to Soul, maintaining that the use of the term to designate material elements must be absolutely condemned.[15] In fact, it must be

---

that this eternal and absolute characteristic of φύσις is a subsequent attribute of the One, which was called nature.

[6] Plato, *Laws* X, 884A–913D.

[7] *Laws* X, 889B. Cf. Aristophanes, "Zeus is dethroned and Vortex reigns in his stead" (*Clouds* 828); see also Diogenes IX, 31–34, Diels, *Doxographi Graeci* (Berlin, 1929), pp. 142–43; and Burnet, *Early Greek Philosophers*, pp. 338–39, 341–47.

[8] *Laws* X, 888E. Plato implies that this division was employed also by his adversaries; cf. also 889C.

[9] *Laws* 891B–892A.

[10] *Ibid.*, 892C.

[11] *Ibid.*, 896D–897C.

[12] *Ibid.*, 898D–E.

[13] Aristotle himself employed this explanation in his early work *De philosophia*, where he represents the world as produced "by the very perfect art of God." V. Rose, *Fragmenta*, Biblioth. Teubneriana (Leipzig, 1886), frag. 21.

[14] Cf. *Ap.* 22C.

[15] *Laws* X, 892B–C.

admitted that Plato did not develop a doctrine of nature; rather he replaces the theory of nature by a theory of Soul.[16] His concern is to show that all material reality proceeds from divine intelligence, which necessarily must be anterior to the world. Furthermore, in the course of developing his arguments against his adversaries, he shows that all corporeal movement without exception depends upon the influences and direction of the Soul which permeates space.[17] Therefore, for Plato it is not nature which is primary in the explanation of physical reality but the divine Soul which produces the world and directs movement by *art*.

Undoubtedly Aristotle had in mind Book X of the *Laws* when he developed his own doctrine of nature in Book II of the *Physics*. The threefold division of causes into nature, art, and chance is Plato's point of departure for attacking his adversaries. This same threefold division is Aristotle's starting point for rehabilitating the naturalist theories of the pre-Socratics in face of Plato's criticism. Whereas Plato, insisting on the priority of Soul, had rejected the idea of nature and attributed most of the characteristics of φύσις to Soul, Aristotle tried to maintain both the priority of Soul and the reality of "nature."

Before analyzing Aristotle's idea of nature, one should consider the passage in Book V of the *Metaphysics* where he discusses the various meanings of the word φύσις.[18] In this philosophical lexicon, probably an earlier work than Book II of the *Physics*,[19] Aristotle intends to explain the various senses in which the word is used. Realizing that different senses of the same word are somehow related, he attempts to show the primary sense of the word and how other senses are related to it. He lists six principal meanings of the term φύσις; these he reduces to one which is the primary and strict sense.[20] For Aristotle the primary and strict sense of the term φύσις is a formal, or active, principle of movement and rest in all corporeal reality.

(1) Aristotle tells us that the word originally meant "the genesis of growing things—the meaning which would be suggested if one were to pronounce the *v* in φύσις long." That is to say, the word is probably

[16] A. Mansion, *op. cit.*, p. 83.

[17] *Laws* X, 899Dff.

[18] Arist., *Metaph.* V, 4, 1014b17–1015a19.

[19] This is the opinion of Zeller and Jaeger; cf. Zeller, *Die Phil. d. Griechen* (Leipzig, 1879), II, 2, 157. But W. K. C. Guthrie has presented some strong arguments in favor of a very late composition; cf. *Classical Quarterly* 27 (1933), 162–71; 28 (1934), 90–98.

[20] Arist., *Metaph.* V, 4, 1014b17–1015a19. St. Thomas very frequently lists and discusses the analogy of these different senses, especially *In V Metaph.*, 5, nn. 808–26; *In III Sent.*, d. 5, q. 1, a. 2; *Sum. cont. gent.* IV, c. 35; *De Unione verbi Incarnati*, n. 1; *Summa theol.* I, 29, 1 ad 4.

derived from φύω which has υ long in most of its forms, so that the connotation of φύσις is that of a process. It is impossible to convey this sense in English, but there is a similarity in Latin for it seems that *natura* originally signified *nativitas*.[21] For Aristotle, then, φύσις originally meant the process of growing.[22]

(2) From the activity of growth, the word was transferred to signify the active principle of growing things. St. Thomas explains this by saying that "active powers are customarily named from the activities."[23]

(3) Then the term was extended to signify "the source of the primary movement in each natural object which is in it in virtue of its own essence [οὐσία],"[24] that is, it signifies *the active principle of movement in all natural things*. That Aristotle means here the *active* source of each body's characteristic movement is clear from his example of growing things.[25]

(4) But this sense of φύσις, as we have seen, was first applied to "the primary material out of which any natural object is made."[26] Aristotle notes that some have called it fire, others earth, others air, others water, others something else of the sort, and some named it more than one of these, and others all of them.[27]

(5) But φύσις was soon applied also to the form and total composition of natural objects. We have seen that the earliest philosophers

[21] "Fundamentally *natura* signified 'birth' (as in Terence, *Ad.*, 126, 902), i.e., the process by which living objects come into being." *Hasting's Encyclopedia of Religions and Ethics* (Edinburgh, 1917), IX, 244b.

[22] Burnet, however, doubts (*op. cit.*, pp. 10–12; 363–64) that φύσις ever had this meaning, as he has been unable to find this exclusive sense in any of the pre-Socratic fragments. He is followed in this by Lovejoy in the *Philosophical Review* 18 (1919), 369ff., as well as by Sir David Ross (*Aristotle's Metaphysics* [Oxford, 1924], I, 296–98) and by R. G. Collingwood (*The Idea of Nature* [Oxford, 1945], pp. 80–81). This specialized difficulty must be left to the scholars. But it must be admitted that the word at least had this connotation, as we can see from Plato's use of γένεσις in *Laws* X, 892C and Aristotle's strange arguments from Antiphon, in *Phys.* II, 1, 193a12–17, 193b8–13. Considering the origins of human language there is no reason to suppose that such a connotation is not indicative of the original sense Aristotle mentions.

[23] ". . . quia virtutes agentes ex actibus nominari consueverunt." *In III Sent.*, d. 5, q. 1, a. 2; cf. *In V Metaph.*, 5, n. 809.

[24] Arist., *Metaph.* 1014b19–20.

[25] Cf. also St. Thomas: "Inde ulterius processit nomen naturae ad significandum principium activum cuiuslibet motus naturalis." *In III Sent.*, d. 5, q. 1, a. 2; "Et haec est definitio posita in II Physicorum." *In V Metaph.*, 5, n. 810.

[26] Arist., *Metaph.* 1014b27–28.

[27] *Ibid.*, 1014b32–35.

wanted to restrict the term φύσις to the elements, but Empedocles, quoted by Aristotle on this point, acknowledges that men give the name even to mixtures.[28] It is really this sense of φύσις that Aristotle develops in his philosophy of nature. The background of this must be understood in the light of his frequent attack on the pre-Socratics in that they considered only matter to be "substance," failing to distinguish between "first matter" and the material substance.[29] As the pre-Socratics were unable to explain essential changes, the immutable matter was "substance," to which they applied the idea of φύσις; the composition (form), although theoretically only a mixture, was nevertheless called φύσις by ordinary men.[30] Aristotle's explanation of substantial change allows him to justify and to develop this common use of "nature" as the specifying form of bodies which manifest characteristic activities.

(6) Finally "by an extension of meaning from this sense of φύσις every essence in general has come to be called a nature."[31] This is the static sense of nature as "the essence, which the definition signifies,"[32] or "the informing specific difference in each and every thing."[33] In this transferred sense φύσις is a *nomen absolutum*, quite different from the preceding uses. In his *Commentary on the Metaphysics* St. Thomas lists this not among the principal significations of the word but as an extension "secundum quamdam metaphoram."[34]

Considering these various senses, Aristotle concludes, "It is plain that nature in the primary and strict sense is the essence of things which have in themselves, as such, a source of movement."[35] But matter, too, can be called nature, "because it is qualified to receive this."[36]

[28] Diels, *Vorsok.*, 31B, frag. 8. For the exegesis of this passage cf. Burnet, *op. cit.*, pp. 205–6, note 4.
[29] Cf. Arist., *Metaph.* I, 3, 983b6–19; 7, 988a18–b22; VII, 3; cf. also St. Thomas, *In VII Metaph.*, 2, nn. 1281–93, where he develops this idea very clearly.
[30] Diels, *Vorsok.*, 31B, frag. 8. St. Thomas explains: "Decipit autem antiquos philosophos hanc rationem inducentes, ignorantia formae substantialis. . . . Forma autem substantialis non est sensibilis nisi per accidens; et ideo ad eius cognitionem non pervenerunt. Sed totum subiectum, quod nos ponimus ex materia et forma componi, ipsi dicebant esse primam materiam, ut aerem, aut aquam, aut aliquid huiusmodi. Formas autem dicebant esse, quae nos dicimus accidentia. . . ." VII *Metaph.*, lect. 2, n. 1284.
[31] Arist., *Metaph.* 1015a11–12.
[32] Cf. St. Thomas, *Sum. cont. gent.* IV, 35.
[33] Boethius, *De Duab. Nat.*, PL 64, 1341.
[34] *In V Metaph.*, 5, n. 823; but in parallel places St. Thomas lists all the senses together as analogically similar.
[35] Arist., *Metaph.* 1015a13–15.
[36] *Ibid.*, 1015a15–16.

In the *Metaphysics* Aristotle presents all of this without proof or elaboration. He is concerned only with classifying the various meanings of the term "nature" and in pointing out the primary meaning. However, Aristotle's own position in the history of Greek thought is very clear from this passage. It is mainly in Books II and VIII of the *Physics* that he justifies and elaborates his conception of nature as an intrinsic principle of movement.

The Aristotelian conception of nature must be understood in contrast to art and chance. We have already seen that this tripartite division was commonplace at the time of Plato. By art is meant any production by human intelligence, anything produced by the human mind acting upon reality.[37] By this is meant not only pictures, statues, machines, and other works of craftsmanship but every result of human interference, such as pushing, pulling, throwing, twirling, holding, and so forth. In other words, a stone which is thrown into the air would not be considered to move upward naturally but would be considered to be the result of "art." This means, not that every human action on the physical world is "artistic," or "intelligent," but that there are phenomena in the world which *can be accounted for* as the work of human activity. Besides the result of human activity, there are many phenomena which are the result of mere *chance*, or accident. Chance is the irrational element in the world. Certainly after a chance event has occurred the phenomenon can be explained rationally as the concurrence of such and such a factor. But the event itself is unpredictable; it is the unexpected, the unintended. Just as in human experience many things happen merely by chance, so too in the physical world many events are the result of two factors, each of which has its own history. But every result of chance presupposes factors which have an individual history, a makeup and intelligibility which are proper to each. That is to say, just as not every phenomenon can be explained by human control, so neither can every phenomenon be explained by chance. For chance is not a thing but a concurrence; and every concurrence involves things.[38] Therefore some agent other than

---

[37] Plato seems to have been the first to apply "art" to the activity of divine intelligence in the world. But in the present context Aristotle means to discuss only the work of human intelligence.

[38] Chance plays a very large role in the Aristotelian view of the universe, but Aristotle is careful to point out that chance as such is the *meeting* of particular bodies, and indeed, the meeting of *individual* bodies. That is to say, such a meeting is not within the intentionality of any particular body (cf. *Phys.* II, 5–6). Thus he defines chance as a "causa per accidens" (*Phys.* II, 5, 197a5–6), meaning that the event is *not intended* by either factor. St. Thomas insists that nowhere within the whole physical universe is there a cause which *per se* intends the chance event, *concursus;* cf. *Sum. cont. gent.* III, 86; c. 93; *Sum. theol.* I, 115, 6; 116. Chance is not to be understood here as "probability."

"art" or "chance" is necessarily operative in the universe; for convenience this agency may be called *nature*.

From what has been said it is clear that human activity in the world and chance both presuppose phenomena which cannot be accounted for by either of them. Human activity presupposes not only the existence of things and phenomena upon which to work but even a qualitative differentiation which must be acknowledged. For example, an artist cannot make a statue out of air, nor can an aviator fly through the earth. There are, in other words, objective phenomena which must be recognized before they can be utilized by man. The results of chance also presuppose the concurrence of qualitatively different phenomena each with its own characteristics, and functioning according to its own determined laws. It is only the simultaneity of definite factors which results in an explosion, the birth of a monster, or a devastating cyclone. Chance results are irrational precisely because they involve the meeting of qualitatively different phenomena, each acting according to its own laws.

The fundamental assumption in the Aristotelian conception of nature is that natural phenomena, that is, those arising from neither art nor chance, are intelligible; there is a regularity, a determined rationality, about these phenomena which can be grasped. This must be the basic assumption of all science, for without it science itself is impossible.

When the great variety of "natural" phenomena has been classified scientifically, their individual characteristics and laws noted, we are still left with the question of their radical source, the ultimate accountability of all such phenomena. Even the action and reaction of various elements, the variation of circumstances, the intricate dependencies and interplay of everything from electrons to cosmic rays still leave the question of *source* unanswered. What is the source of any of this activity? It does not make much difference what name is applied. The important thing is that we must in the last analysis acknowledge a certain *internal spontaneity* in all things from the smallest to the largest in the universe. When one considers, for example, the great variety of activities proper to chemical elements, electrons, and other physical bodies, the phenomena of illumination and ultraviolet rays, one can only say that they proceed automatically and spontaneously from the bodies themselves. There can be no other "source" for characteristic activities except internal spontaneity. Obviously these phenomena are not the result of chance; this is precluded by a regularity and constancy which can even be measured. Nor can it be said that such movement is acquired from something else, for experience shows that even the transmission of activity depends essentially on the internal disposition and "willingness" of each body in view of its proper activity; thus not all bodies can be acted upon in the same way. Therefore, we must admit that in each physical reality there is something ultimately *given* in experience, which is none other than the spontaneous manifestation of its characteristics and proper activities. There is nothing "behind" this spontaneity, as far as the body is concerned; it is just "given" in experience. All the factors involved in the event must be considered, the circumstances of variation, intensity, prevention, and so forth, but in the last analysis there is the spontaneity "given," as from the body itself. Together with this spontaneity there are also certain receptivities for external influence, receptivities which are compatible with the spontaneous characteristics of each body. To both of these intrinsic sources, the spontaneous and the receptive, Aristotle gives the name *nature,* which he defines as "the principle of movement and rest in those things to which it belongs properly (*per se*) and not as concomitant attribute (*per accidens*)."[39]

Fundamentally this is Aristotle's procedure, but more specifically, he draws a comparison between natural and artificial bodies.[40] Natural bodies come into being through natural agencies; artificial bodies are produced by man. Moreover, the essential difference between them is that natural bodies *do* something: some grow and decay, others move and manifest activities, and so forth. But artificial compositions merely exist as an expression of an idea. Whatever "activity" there is about an artificial composition is the result, not of the artistic as such, but of the natural elements of which it is composed; or it is the result of calculated compulsion. For example, a painting falls to the ground, burns, or decays, not because it is a painting, but because of the materials of which it is made. Everyone realizes that the movement of a watch or mechanical doll comes about not spontaneously but from a spring which is wound by the user. Therefore, Aristotle concludes that the difference between natural and artificial things is that natural things have within themselves an intrinsic source of movement and rest, "in virtue of itself and not in virtue of a concomitant attribute."[41]

For Aristotle, then, nature is this intrinsic source of characteristic movement. Things "have a nature" or are "natural" which have such a

---

[39] This definition (*Phys.* II, 1, 192b21-3) is repeated, more or less complete, in various works of Aristotle: *Phys.* III, 1, 200b12–13; VIII, 3, 253b5–6; 4, 254b16–17; *De caelo* I, 2, 268b16; III, 2, 301b17–18; *De anima* II, 1, 412b15–17; *Gen. an.* II, 1, 735a3–4; *Metaph.* VI, 1, 1025b20–21; IX, 8, 1049b8–10; XII, 3, 1070a7–8; *Eth. Nic.* VI, 4, 1140a5–6; *Rh.* I, 10, 1369a35–b1.

[40] Arist., *Phys.* II, 1, 192b8–32.

[41] Arist., *Phys.* II, 1, 192b22–23.

principle. He insists that "each of them is a substance, for each is a subject; and nature always implies a subject in which it inheres."[42] Aristotle's point is that if we wish to understand natural phenomena, we must admit an internal spontaneity (nature) within concrete bodies for their characteristic behavior.[43] He is not appealing to an abstraction,[44] nor to anything outside the acting body. He is insisting that we see spontaneous activity and all we can say is that it *is* spontaneous; the source of characteristic spontaneity he calls "nature." Therefore he says, *that* such a reality exists is obvious, and it would be absurd to attempt any "proof."[45]

It has been shown that bodies in the universe manifest not only a certain "spontaneity" for characteristic behavior but also certain "receptivities" for external influence. This leads Aristotle to point out that "nature" is used in two senses: as an *active* (spontaneous) principle and as a *passive* (receptive) principle.

In Book II of the *Physics* Aristotle is merely concerned with showing that the ancient use of φύσις should be applied not only to the "matter" out of which things are made but also, and more properly, to the "form" of the thing itself. The ancients rightly attributed φύσις to matter, but as they were unable to account for intrinsic change, "matter" for them meant the "substance" which was conceived as an *active* principle of behavior. Aristotle, relying on his doctrine of potency and act, insists that the true "matter" is antecedent to substance; this "matter" is purely *passive*, being a pure potentiality for being (substance). Employing the analogy of art, he says, "We should not say that there is anything artistic about a thing, if it is a bed only potentially, not yet having the form of bed; nor should we call it a work of art."[46] Similarly in natural products, "what is potentially flesh or bone has not yet its

---

[42] *Ibid.*, 192b33–34. The punctuation here used is that of Hamelin (Aristote, *Physique* II, pp. 40–41) and Mansion (*op. cit.*, p. 100) which is suggested by the paraphrase of Themistius and Philoponus. This seems to be clearer than the usual reading given by Bekker, Didot, and Ross: "Each of them is a substance; for it is a subject, and nature always implies a subject in which it inheres" (Ross trans., *Basic Works*, p. 236). On the basis of this usual punctuation, also employed by William of Moerbeke, St. Thomas finds it necessary to give this interpretation: "Et talia sunt omnia subiecta naturae: quia natura est subiectum, secundum quod natura dicitur materia; et est in subiecto, secundum quod natura dicitur forma" (*In II Phys.*, 1, n. 6). But it seems that Aristotle does not have this in mind, for he has not yet shown that nature can be said of both matter and form; this he does in 193a9–21.

[43] A. Mansion, *op. cit.*, p. 100.

[44] "Thus in the second sense of 'nature' it would be the shape or form (not separable except in statement) of things which have in themselves a source of motion." Arist., *Phys.* II, 1, 193b3–5.

[45] Arist., *Phys.* II, 1, 193a2–8.

[46] Arist., *Phys.* II, 2, 193a33–35.

own 'nature' and does not exist 'by nature,' until it receives the form specified in the definition, which we name in defining what flesh or bone is."[47] That is to say, nature as an *active* and spontaneous principle, which the ancients attributed to matter, properly applies to "form"; if the term is applied to "matter," it connotes passivity.

The scholastics developed to a considerable extent this twofold sense of nature as an active and as a passive principle. Nature as matter, or *natura secundum materiam*,[48] signified not only the pure potentiality of the first matter but all passivities of bodies which require a natural agent to actualize them. Nature as form, or *secundum principium formale*, signified the active and spontaneous source of all characteristic properties and behavior; ultimately this active principle was considered to be the "substantial form" which functions through active qualities.[49] Thus in scholastic terminology nature as "matter" is equivalent to *principium passivum, receptivum*, and *materiale;* while nature as "form" is equivalent to *principium activum*, or *formale*.[50] These two senses of "nature" in scholastic philosophy must be explained briefly.

St. Thomas lays down the general principle that natural bodies have within them a principle of movement precisely to the extent to which they have motion: inasmuch as they spontaneously *move*, they have an "active" principle; and inasmuch as they must *be moved*, they have the "passive" principle, which is matter.[51] Experience alone can

[47] *Ibid.*, 193a36–b2.
[48] St. Thomas, *In II Phys.*, 1, n. 4.
[49] Cf. St. Thomas, VII *Metaph.*, lect. 8, n. 1448; II *Sent.*, dist. 14, q. 1, a. 5 ad 2.
[50] The equivalence of *principium materiale* and *passivum* on the one hand and *principium formale* and *activum* on the other is very clear in St. Thomas: "Habet enim huiusmodi motus in mobili *principium*, non solum *materiale et receptivum*, sed etiam *formale et activum*" (*De pot.*, 5, 5); ". . . non est naturalis propter *activam inclinationem formalis principii* in corpore caelesti ad talem motum, sicut est in elementis" (*ibid.*, ad 12). "Non autem potest esse quod motus caelestis sequatur *formam* caelestis corporis sicut *principium activum* . . . sed solum *ratione principii passivi, quod est materia*" (*Sum. cont. gent.* III, 23). ". . . contrarietas motuum naturalium consequitur proprietatem *principiorum activorum sive formalium*, ad quae consequitur motus; non autem contrarietatem *principiorum passivorum sive materialium*" (*In I De caelo*, lect. 6, n. 13; cf. III, 7, nn. 5–9). "Non enim oportet ad motum naturalem quod semper principium motus, quod est in mobili, sit *principium activum et formale;* sed quandoque est *passivum et materiale*" (*In VII Metaph.*, 8, n. 1442z). This equivalence was also common to the fourteenth-century scholastics, as Walter Burley testifies: "Primo quod cum dicitur quod naturalia inquantum huiusmodi habent in seipsis principium motus et status, ibi hoc nomen principium accipitur communiter *pro principio secundum materiam, idest, pro principio passivo*, et *pro principio motus secundum formam, idest, pro principio activo*" (Burlaei, *In Physicas Arist. Expositio et Quaestiones* [Venetiis, 1501], Lib. II, fol. 36r col. 1).
[51] "Et ideo dicendum est quod in rebus naturalibus eo modo est principium motus, quo eis motus convenit. Quibus ergo convenit movere, est in eis principium activum motus; quibus autem competit moveri, est in eis principium passivum, quod est materia." *In II Phys.*, 1, n. 4.

indicate whether bodies spontaneously act or are being acted upon by an external force.

I. NATURE AS PASSIVE PRINCIPLE

Some of the medieval writers, notably St. Albert, thought that "nature" always implies some *active* source, and that the term "natural" should be restricted to those phenomena which proceed more or less actively from the body. Since for St. Albert the movement of the heavens is caused by separated intelligences, such movement was considered the work not of nature but of intelligence.[52] Even substantial change, according to him, is "natural" in view of a certain incomplete active principle, an *inchoatio formae*, which assists the external agent.[53] St. Albert, however, does distinguish between "form" as the perfect active principle and "matter" as a passive potentiality, having only the beginning of form and requiring an external mover to actualize it fully.[54]

St. Thomas, however, rejects the *inchoatio formae* as an impossibility.[55] He insists that for natural phenomena it is not necessary that all movement proceed from an active principle; natural receptivity itself is sufficient to render the motion "natural."[56] Consequently the celestial movements are natural because the heavenly bodies have a natural potentiality for being moved by spiritual beings. That is, if they are moved by intelligences, then it is natural to the celestial bodies to be moved.[57] And substantial generation is natural, because the pure potentiality of first matter is intrinsically capable of *being moved*.

Every body which is *acted upon* is in some sense passive, but this

---

[52] St. Albert, *In II Phys.*, tr. I, cap. 2 (ed. Borgnet).

[53] "Dicunt ergo quidam quod etiam in huiusmodi mutationibus [substantialibus] principium activum motus est in eo quod movetur; non quidem perfectum, sed imperfectum, quod coadiuvat actionem exterioris agentis. Dicunt enim quod in materia est quaedam inchoatio formae, . . . et ab hoc principio intrinseco generationes corporum simplicium naturales dicuntur." St. Thomas, *In II Phys.*, 1, n. 3. The *quidam* here refers to St. Albert and St. Bonaventure; cf. St. Albert, *In II Phys.*, tr. I, cap. 9; *Sum. theol.*, P. 2, tr. I, q. 4, n. 2, a. 1, p. 82; St. Bonaventure, *In II Sent.*, d. 18, a. 1, a. 3; and Giles of Rome, *In Phys.* II, lect. 1, dub. 9.

[54] Cf. *In VIII Phys.*, tr. II, cap. 4. He defines the passivity of nature as "illud quod habet in se susceptivam et passivam potentiam recipiendi formam, sec. quam movet motor suus per inchoationem ipsius formae in ipso." *Ibid.*

[55] Cf. *In II Phys.*, 1, n. 3; *In VII Metaph.*, 8, n. 1442a–z.

[56] "Non enim oportet ad motum naturalem, quod semper principium motus, quod est in mobili, sit principium activum et formale; sed quandoque est passivum et materiale." St. Thomas, *In VII Metaph.*, 8, n. 1442z.

[57] "Et sic etiam motus localis corporum caelestium est naturalis, licet sit a motore separato, inquantum in ipso corpore caeli est potentia naturalis ad talem motum." St. Thomas, *In II Phys.*, 1, n. 4.

passivity is not to be identified with "nature" as a passive principle. Three passivities must be distinguished: (i) for compulsory movement; (ii) for artistic formation; and (iii) for natural production. A stone which is thrown into the air has a certain passivity for this motion, but as the motion itself is not natural,[58] neither is the potentiality. When an artist chooses his material, he must choose something suitable with which to work, as not all materials present the same possibilities. But since such potentialities are realized by art and not by nature, they are not properly called "natural."[59] In the strict sense, a "natural" potentiality is one which *intrinsically tends* toward perfect realization, and which can be actualized by a natural agent.[60] In other words, nature as a passive principle essentially implies an intrinsic *intentionality* of final realization, a receptivity which tends toward the *good* of the whole. That is to say, it implies, first of all, the order of final causality. The actualization of a natural potentiality is not to be conceived as something superadded, like the addition of a number. Rather the potentiality itself intrinsically tends toward, aims at, realization, just as the mind essentially tends toward knowledge. The scholastic philosophers called this an "appetite" and a "desire" for realization, which realization is its assimilation to being and perfection. Secondly, nature as a passive potentiality implies a capacity for realization by natural agencies, that is, agencies which are neither "art" nor "chance." Nothing in the universe is isolated and self-sufficient; everything depends upon innumerable external factors for its coming into being and for its very survival. It is to these receptivities for external influence that the idea of nature as a passive principle applies.

All such passive potentialities, obviously, must be actualized by external agencies. It is in this sense that Aristotle expressed the well-known axiom that "whatever is moved is moved by something else."[61]

---

[58] This question is taken up in Chapter II.

[59] "Et propter hoc factiones rerum artificialium non sunt naturales: quia licet principium materiale sit in eo quod fit, non tamen habet potentiam naturalem ad talem formam." St. Thomas, *In II Phys.*, 1, n. 4.

[60] "Differentia tamen est inter materiam naturalium et artificialium: quia in materia rerum naturalium est [1] *aptitudo naturalis ad formam*, et [2] *potest reduci in actum per agens naturale;* non autem hoc contingit in materia artificialium." St. Thomas, *In VII Metaph.*, 8, n. 1442z. (Italics mine.)

[61] The point is that this axiom applies only to nature as a *passive* principle. Sometimes this phrase is interpreted as "Everything that is in motion must be moved by something else," in the sense that every motion here and now requires a mover for the preservation of movement (Ross's trans. of 241b24). Sir David Ross, among many others, interprets Aristotle as meaning all motion requires actual contact with the mover for the duration of the motion; cf. *Aristotle's Physics* (Oxford, 1936), comm. on 266a10–11

When Aristotle discusses the causes of motion in Book VIII of the *Physics*,[62] he considers three classes of movement: living, compulsory, and spontaneous. The movement of living things is easy enough to explain, for living things move themselves, as we can see; therefore, they are the cause of their own motion (254b14–24). Compulsory motion is also easily accounted for, since it is derived from the agent which imparts compulsion—for example, the boy who throws the ball (254b24–33). But the greatest difficulty is presented in explaining the *cause* of spontaneous movement. "It is in these cases that difficulty would be experienced in deciding whence the motion is derived, e.g., in the case of light and heavy things" (255a1–2). Obviously such bodies do not move themselves, that is, they cannot be the cause of their own motion, for this is the prerogative of living things (255a5–19). But Aristotle shows that although inanimate bodies spontaneously manifest their proper activities unless an obstacle intervenes, they first have to be generated (moved) from potentiality. For example, hydrogen exists potentially in water and must be generated by some agency before it can manifest the characteristic behavior of hydrogen. Thus inasmuch as each natural reality was at one time not yet actually existing, it had to be brought into actual being by an external agent. Aristotle's explanation depends upon his theory of intrinsic change: substantial natures are generated (moved) from pure potentiality into the full reality of a substance by an adequate agency. When such bodies are generated (moved), they must be moved by something else. But once such natures are actually existing, they spontaneously manifest their characteristic behavior unless externally impeded. However, every formal nature still has innumerable secondary receptivities whereby it depends upon and is woven into the whole fabric of the universe. Even these receptivities, by which every body is "open" to the universe, require external influence to achieve fulfillment.

Briefly, then, nature as a passive principle involves two factors. It essentially implies intentionality of ends, which are necessary for the good of the whole being. And it presupposes natural agencies which can actualize it.

(pp. 721–22), 266b27–267a20 (pp. 725–26). Philosophically there is no need for a constant physical mover to account for motion; nor is this what Aristotle himself intends to say, as will be explained. We are not here discussing nature "inquantum agit in virtute Dei" (*Sum. cont. gent.* III, 66; cf. 67). That is a different question altogether. St. Thomas acknowledges that "non est contra rationem naturae [i.e., ut principium activum] quod motus naturalis sit a Deo sicut a primo movente." *Sum. theol.* I-II, 6, 1 ad 3.

[62] *Phys.* VIII, 4, 254b14–256a2.

II. NATURE AS ACTIVE PRINCIPLE

In the proper and strict sense of the term, "nature" signifies an active principle of spontaneous behavior. It is a matter of experience that each physical reality in the universe steadfastly insists on being itself; it behaves in a characteristic way and, in a sense, refuses to behave in any other way. In other words, every physical reality manifests determined properties and behavior; and it is through such characteristics that different realities can be recognized. This is the very foundation of physical science. The human intellect, however, has no direct or *a priori* knowledge of "essences" or "natures"; it must carefully examine the sensible characteristics and behavior of natural bodies in various settings.[63] Since every physical unit operates not in a void but always in an actual environment, the qualitative characteristics of the actual environment must be taken into consideration when accounting for the various natural phenomena, for even the same reality will act differently in different environments. However, neither the environment nor the proximity of sociable or unsociable factors should be confused with the actual spontaneity the body manifests under those circumstances. There is always the danger of thinking that we have found the explanation of a natural phenomenon when we have merely discovered a secondary factor. Apart from the natural receptivities each body has for external influence, there remains the fundamental spontaneity by which the body acts in its own right, acts as itself.

Aristotle's definition of nature as a *principle* must be understood in the strict sense of a relative term.[64] That is to say, "nature" is not some complete entity within physical bodies which springs forth now and then in its performance. *It neither is, nor can be known as, a complete entity.* Our knowledge of it involves the experience of sensible manifestations and the realization that certain characteristic manifestations are spontaneously "given" in reality. Indeed, "natures" exist only in the concrete, existing individual, so that our knowledge of nature in general or any particular nature involves the actual experience of innumerable individual phenomena; and in no way can our "concept" of nature be separated from these personal experiences.[65] "Unde," St.

---

[63] "Natura enim uniuscuiusque rei ex eius operatione ostenditur." St. Thomas, *Sum. theol.* I, 76, 1; cf. *Sum. cont. gent.* III, 69.

[64] "Ponitur autem in definitione naturae *principium*, quasi genus, et non aliquid absolutum, quia nomen naturae importat habitudinem principii." St. Thomas, *In II Phys.*, 1, n. 5.

[65] "De ratione autem huius naturae est quod in aliquo individuo existat, quod non est absque materia corporali; sicut de ratione naturae lapidis est quod sit in hoc lapide, et de ratione equi est quod sit in hoc equo, et sic de aliis. Unde natura lapidis, vel cuius-

Thomas says, "deridendi sunt qui volentes definitionem Aristotelis corrigere, naturam per aliquid absolutum definire conati sunt, dicentes quod natura est *vis insita rebus,* vel aliquid huiusmodi."[66] John Philoponus, considering Aristotle's definition to be rather a description *per effectum,* thought it should be corrected to "life or a force radicated in bodies, forming and directing itself."[67] St. Albert[68] and Roger Bacon[69] also defined nature as a *vis insita rebus.* In the latter half of the fifteenth century Basil Valentinus, a Benedictine alchemist, introduced an *archaeus* into the known alchemical elements by which the ruler of the universe determined the phenomena of chemical changes; other alchemists introduced a "celestial virtue."[70] Even at the time of J. B. van Helmont (1577–1644) the *archaeus* continued to be invoked as the seminal efficient cause which accounted for the figure, motion, and so forth of chemical elements.[71] Aristotelians of the seventeenth century referred to "nature" as a *virtue* or as an *occult specific quality.*[72] While it is true that "nature" is a kind of force, or power, this way of speaking too easily conveys the idea of a little imp contained within bodies, which accounts for the various phenomena. In a precise analysis of meaning it is more accurate to say that our concept of nature is a reflexive realization that certain phenomena are spontaneously "given" as from the body itself.

---

cumque materialis rei, cognosci non potest complete et vere, nisi secundum quod cognoscitur ut in particulari existens." St. Thomas, *Sum. theol.* I, 84, 7.

[66] *In II Phys.,* 1, n. 5.

[67] Ioannis Philoponi, *In Arist. Physicorum libros tres priores,* Comm. in Arist. Graeca, XVI (Berlin, 1887), Lib. II, cap. 1, p. 197:33–35.

[68] St. Albert: "Est enim natura vis insita rebus naturalibus ex similibus secundum naturam similia procreans." *In II Phys.,* tr. I, cap. 7 (ed. Borgnet, t. III, 103b); also cap. 5, p. 101a.

[69] Roger Bacon, *Quaestiones supra libros quatuor Physicorum,* Lib. II, q. 7 (*Opera Hactenus Inedita,* fasc. VIII, ed. Delorme [Oxford, 1938], pp. 58–59; q. 8, pp. 59–60; *et passim*).

[70] W. C. Dampier, *A History of Science,* 4th ed. (Cambridge, 1949), p. 114. Dampier (*loc. cit.*) erroneously refers to Basil Valentinus as a Dominican monk. There can be little doubt that he was a Benedictine monk of Erfurt. Cf. Sudhoff in *Die deutsche Literatur des Mittelalters: Verfasserlexikon,* Bd. I (Berlin, 1933), pp. 176–77; Herman Kopp, *Die Alchemie in älterer und neuerer Zeit* (Heidelberg, 1882). The oldest known MS of Valentinus (Oxford, Ash. 1447) refers to him as "monachi Germani," which would not be accurate if he were a Dominican friar. Cf. *Catalogue of the Ashmolean Manuscripts,* 1447 (IX, 3): "Medicina catholica Basilii Valentini monachi Germani, chymiatri summi, ab ipso lapis ignis vocata cum quibusdam aliis medicinis et experimentis."

[71] Cf. A. Crombie, *Augustine to Galileo* (London, 1952), pp. 355–57. "The seminal efficient cause archaeus containeth the Types or Patterns of things to be done by itself, the figure, motion, houre, respects, inclinations, fitnesses, equalizings, proportions, alienation, defect, and whatsoever falls under the succession of dayes, as well as in the business of generation, as of government." J. B. van Helmont, *Oriatrike,* chap. 4, quoted by Dr. Crombie, *op. cit.,* p. 356.

[72] Cf. I. Newton, *Opticks* (London, 1704), pp. 375–78; R. Boyle, *A Free inquiry into the received Notion of Nature, Works* (London, 1744), IV, 358–424.

Collingwood describes Aristotle's nature as a world of self-moving, living things.[73] But this is to confuse the spontaneity of nature with the prerogative of living bodies. Aristotle himself was careful to point out the essential difference between living and nonliving things.[74] The fundamental attribute of living things is that they *move themselves*, that is, they themselves are the *cause* of their own motion. The soul of living things is the sufficient mover, the *causa efficiens*, of such activities as flying, walking, swimming, digestion, reproduction, and growth. But there are other characteristics of each and every living body of which the soul is not the "mover" but merely the spontaneous source—for example, the color and size of the creature,[75] its position on the earth and its falling down,[76] the chemical processes of metabolism, and the throbbing of life itself.[77] In other words, when discussing the characteristics of living things, two aspects must be carefully distinguished: (i) those characteristics which arise spontaneously from the very existence of the being, given the necessary environment; (ii) those phenomena which are actively caused by it. Nature as an active principle is not the "mover," or the "efficient cause," of natural phenomena but only the "given" spontaneous source which was begotten by some effective agency.

For St. Thomas the "formal principle" of every physical being is truly an *active principle* of characteristic behavior, but not the *motor* or *principium motivum*. The reason for this is obvious. If the essential characteristic of a living thing is to *move itself*, then self-movement cannot be the property of a nonliving thing. That is, an inanimate being cannot be the cause of its own activity. In a very technical sense, the "efficient cause" (if one raises the question) of spontaneous phenomena is the agency which brought such a being into existence. In other words, whatever agency produces a physical body must also be acknowledged as the agency responsible for all the inseparable and spontaneous characteristics of that body. But physical bodies not only exist, they also manifest activity and movement. Therefore, St. Thomas very frequently insists that "in heavy and light bodies nature is a formal principle of movement, for just as the other attributes follow upon substantial form, so too does place, and consequently motion toward place; not that the natural form is a mover, but the

[73] R. Collingwood, *Idea of Nature, op. cit.,* pp. 82–85.
[74] Cf. Arist., *Phys.* VIII, 4; *De anima* I, 3, 5, etc.
[75] St. Thomas, *In II De anima,* 8, n. 332.
[76] St. Thomas, *In VIII Phys.,* 7, n. 3.
[77] St. Thomas, *In De motu cordis,* nn. 7–8, *Opuscula Omnia* (Paris, 1949), t. I, 67–68.

mover is the progenitor which produced such a form, upon which such motion follows."[78]

From this it is clear that Aristotle did not explain natural motion by the constant exerted efficiency of a mover, as is often thought.[79] Aristotle insists that "it is not the action of another body that makes one of these bodies move up and the other down; nor is it constraint, like

---

[78] *In II Phys.*, 1, n. 4 (text below); cf. *In I De caelo*, 18, n. 1; II, 2, n. 6; III, 7, nn. 5–9; *In II Phys.*, 5, n. 5; IV, 12, n. 9; VIII, 8, nn. 5–7; *Sum. cont. gent.* III, 82, 84; *De pot.*, q. 5, a. 5.

The text of *In II Phys.*, lect. 1, n. 4 is given in all printed editions, including the Leonine, as follows: "In corporibus vero gravibus et levibus est principium formale sui motus (*sed huiusmodi principium formale non potest dici potentia activa, ad quam pertinet motus iste, sed comprehenditur sub potentia passiva: gravitas enim in terra non est principium ut moveat, sed magis ut moveatur*): quia sicut alia accidentia consequuntur formam substantialem, ita et locus, et per consequens moveri ad locum: non tamen ita quod forma naturalis sit motor, sed motor est generans, quod dat talem formam, ad quam talis motus consequitur."

At first sight the phrase in parentheses seems to contradict the doctrine expounded in the text. The phrase in question actually disrupts the smooth flow of thought in St. Thomas's reasoning. The Leonine editors admit that the text in question is not to be found in any of the codices: "Haec omnia, quae parenthesi clausimus omittuntur a codicibus. Et revera non videntur necessario postulari a contextu, et iis omissis, ratio quae immediate ponitur, *quia sicut alia*, melius cohaeret cum praecedentibus, ad quae referri debet, nempe *In corporibus vero*, etc." (*Opera Omnia*, ed. Leonine, t. II, p. 56a, note a). This passage is really taken from St. Thomas's *Commentary on the Metaphysics* V, 14 (n. 955), probably in answer to Scotus's position (cf. Venice ed. of St. Thomas's commentary, 1595, fol. 31a). In this passage St. Thomas is discussing the different senses of *potestas*. The first sense expresses a "principium motus et mutationis in alio inquantum est aliud," that is, an *efficient cause* (cf. also *In IX Metaph.*, 7). In Aristotelian terminology an efficient cause is frequently called *potentia activa;* as has been explained, "nature" is not an efficient cause, although it is an *active* and *formal principle.* A careful reading of the collated text of this passage of the *Commentary on the Metaphysics* will show the precise point St. Thomas has in mind:

Est enim quoddam principium motus vel mutationis in eo quod mutatur, ipsa scilicet materia vel aliquod principium formale, ad quod consequitur motus, sicut ad formam gravis vel levis sequitur motus sursum aut deorsum. Sed huiusmodi principium non potest dici potentia activa, ad quam pertinet motus iste. Omne enim quod movetur ab alio movetur. Neque aliquid movet seipsum nisi per partes, inquantum una pars eius movet aliam, ut probatur in 8 Phys. Natura igitur, secundum quod est principium motus in eo in quo est, non comprehenditur sub potentia activa, sed magis sub passiva. Gravitas enim in terra non est principium ut moveat, sed magis ut moveatur. Potentia igitur activa motus oportet quod sit in alio ab eo quod movetur, sicut aedificativa potestas non est in aedificato, sed magis in aedificante.

The meaning of the passage, then, is that nature as a formal principle is not a *potentia activa* or *effectiva.* Therefore even the phrase inserted in the parentheses above does not contradict our exposition, for nature as a formal, or active, principle is not an efficient cause.

The above text of the *Commentary on the Metaphysics* has been collated with the following MSS: Brit. Museum, Add. 18,375; Vat. lat. 767; Vat. lat. 768; Vat. lat. 769; Vat. Pal. lat. 1063; and MS Leonina (s. xiv). Sincere gratitude is due to Father A. Dondaine, O.P., for valuable aid in checking this passage as well as others in the course of our study.

[79] P. Hoenen, *Cosmologia*, 4th ed. (Rome, 1949), p. 494; Liberatore, *Institutiones Philosophicae, Cosmologia*, n. 99 (Prati, 1881), p. 95; H. Butterfield, *The Origins of Modern*

the 'extrusion' of some writers."[80] Commenting on this passage, St. Thomas says there are some who postulate a *per se* mover to account for the movement of bodies even after such bodies already exist; this Aristotle is denying, for light bodies are moved upward and heavy bodies downward by the progenitor inasmuch as it produced that type of body in the first place.[81] In a secondary sense whatever deflects the normal path of motion or whatever removes an obstacle to spontaneous movement can also be called an accidental cause of the movement.[82] The important point is that once a particular body is in existence, there is *no need* for an agent constantly acting upon it to account for its activity. The body itself *acts*.

Nor can the "form" be said to be the "mover accompanying the bodies which it moves."[83] For Aristotle as well as for St. Thomas the form is *not the mover* but the *source* of necessary and spontaneous movement. Avicenna in his *Sufficientia*[84] and Algazel's paraphrase, *Maqâcid el-falâcifa*,[85] propound the theory that in natural movement the form is the mover of the body which it informs. In a certain sense Averroes too follows this opinion.[86] But the Aristotelian answer to this

---

Science (London, 1951), pp. 3–4; W. C. Dampier, *op. cit.*, p. 131; A. C. Crombie, *Augustine to Galileo*, p. 82.

[80] Arist., *De caelo* I, 8, 277b1–2; the reference is to the atomists Leucippus and Democritus, who postulate the vortex (δίνη) to account for motion.

[81] "Per quod quidem intelligendum est quod removet exteriorem motorem, qui per se huiusmodi corpora moveat postquam sunt formam specificam sortita. Moventur enim levia quidem sursum, gravia autem deorsum a generante quidem, inquantum dat eis formam quam consequitur talis motus; sed removente prohibens, per accidens et non per se. *Quidam vero posuerunt quod postquam speciem sunt adepta huiusmodi corpora indigent ab aliquo extrinseco moveri per se: quod hic Philosophus removet.*" *In I De caelo*, 18, n. 1 (italics mine).

[82] Cf. *In VIII Phys.*, 8, n. 7: "sicut si sphaera, idest pila, repercutiatur a pariete, per accidens quidem mota est a pariete, non autem per se; sed a primo proiiciente per se mota est. Paries enim non dedit ei aliquem impetum ad motum, sed proiiciens: per accidens autem fuit, quod dum a pariete impediretur ne secundum impetum ferretur, eodem impetu manente, in contrarium motum resilivit. Et similiter ille qui divellit columnam, non dat gravi superposito impetum vel inclinationem ad hoc quod sit deorsum: hoc enim habuit a primo generante, quod dedit ei formam quam sequitur talis inclinatio. Sic igitur generans est per se movens gravia et levia, removens autem prohibens per accidens."

[83] Hoenen, *Cosmologia*, pp. 497–502; Crombie, *Augustine to Galileo*, p. 82.

[84] Cf. H. A. Wolfson, *Crescas' Critique of Aristotle* (text, trans. and commentary) (Cambridge, 1929), pp. 672–75; also Carra de Vaux, *Avicenne*, pp. 184–85. The late fourteenth-century Jewish philosopher Crescas also follows the Arabian tradition; cf. *Critique (Or Adonai)*, ed. Wolfson, prop. XVII, pp. 296–99.

[85] *Algazel's Metaphysics*, ed. J. T. Muckle (Toronto, 1933), pp. 30–31; 99–102. Concerning the nature of the *Maqâcid*, cf. D. Salman, "Algazel et les Latins," *Arch. d'hist. doctr. et litt. du M. A.* 10 (1935), 103–27.

[86] Averroes, *Phys.* VIII, 4, comm. 29–32; theory proposed and refuted by St. Thomas, *In III De caelo*, 7, nn. 8–9. See also Ernest A. Moody, "Galileo and Avempace," *Journal of the History of Ideas* 12 (1951), 163–93, 375–422.

theory is obvious: if the natural form moves the body which it informs, then what is the difference between living and nonliving things? For Aristotle and St. Thomas no such distinction can be drawn in nonliving things between form as mover and body as moved, for each nonliving thing is a single continuous whole, without parts; only by part moving part can the living organism exercise self-motion.[87]

Thus nature as an active principle differs both from life and from pure inertia; it partakes of the activity of living things inasmuch as natural bodies have within themselves an active source of spontaneous activity, and it partakes of the passivity of potentiality inasmuch as such activity is the result of having been brought into existence by some external agency. Because natural spontaneity is not to be confused with life, St. Thomas sometimes refers to nature as a *principium passivum*.[88] But in every one of these passages St. Thomas is merely insisting that this principle (nature) should not be considered as a *principium motivum* (*efficiens*), or *causa se movens*.

The linguistic inadequacies of expressing both the natural spontaneity of physical bodies and the obvious fact that they are not living produced considerable confusion among later scholastics. Duns Scotus, following Avicenna, describes nature as an active principle which in a sense moves itself to activity.[89] Domingo de Soto (1494–1560) insists that in no sense can nature be called an "active principle," for this is the prerogative of living things.[90] By the seventeenth century John of St. Thomas (1589–1644) could refer to the "celebrated difficulty" of whether natural bodies are moved by an intrinsic active or passive principle.[91] But the difficulty was more verbal than real. Even Domingo de Soto proposed the now-common distinction among Thomists, that the nature of inanimate things is a *principium* "*quo*" of their activities, while the cause of the nature is the *principium* "*quod*."[92]

---

[87] Cf. Arist., *Phys.* VIII, 4, 255a5–19; St. Thomas, *In VIII Phys.*, 7, nn. 6–8; *In VII Phys.*, 1, n. 2. The basic error of Avicenna is his conception of form as a *thing* in its own right; cf. St. Thomas, *Sum. theol.* I, q. 110, a. 2; *Sum. cont. gent.* III, c. 68; also P. Hoenen, *De Origine Formae Materialis* (Rome, 1932). In animate activity the whole subsistent being is responsible for the subsequent movement, which it accomplishes through the various organic parts. Since inanimate things have no organic parts, they cannot move themselves.

[88] St. Thomas, *In VIII Phys.*, 8, n. 7; *In I De caelo*, 3, n. 4; II, 2, n. 6; 3, n. 2; III, 7, nn. 8–9.

[89] Joannis Scoti, *Comm. in II Sent.*, d. 2, q. 10.

[90] Domingo de Soto, *Super Octo Physicorum quaestiones*, 2d ed., Salamanca, 1551, super II, q. 1, fol. 31v–34r; cf. super VIII, q. 3, fol. 104r–v.

[91] Joannis a S. Thoma, *Cursus philosophicus*, Phil. nat., I P., q. IX, a. 2, ed. Reiser (Rome, 1933), t. II, p. 184b; q. 23, a. 1, p. 461a.

[92] "Mens igitur Aristotelis est quod principium naturalis motus elementorum est

Nature is a source not only of activity but also of rest.[93] This should be understood not as the mere absence of activity but as the positive possession of fulfillment. In other words, all movement essentially implies the attainment of something; it necessarily implies some kind of aim to be attained.[94] This is not to say that absolute *rest* exists in the universe. Constant movement is an evident phenomenon of experience. But to every particular movement there corresponds some finality attained, even if it is only the self-preservation of the individual. Strictly speaking, movement for its own sake is inconceivable, for the very reality of movement consists in some "otherness" to be attained, some achievement through activity. Therefore "nature" cannot be the source of mere activity, but it must primarily aim at some achievement acquired through movement. In other words, just as all movement implies some "aim," the spontaneous source of movement necessarily has some aim in view.[95] As we shall see, it was this consideration which led the ancients to postulate celestial movers for the heavenly bodies, which move locally without attaining any internal finality. The "rest" of which Aristotle speaks must be taken in the wide sense of the possession of fulfillment, whether of characteristic attributes or of internal finality acquired through activity. This internal finality and fulfillment may be described aptly by Whitehead's expression as "self-enjoyment."

---

duplex: aliud *quo,* et aliud *quod;* principium *quo* principale est forma ipsa substantialis; minus autem principale et instrumentale, est gravitas et levitas; principium autem *quod* est generans." De Soto, *Quaest. super VIII Phys.,* q. 3, *ed. cit.,* fol. 104r, col. 2; cf. J. a S. Thoma, *op cit.,* q. 23, a. 1 ad 3; *ed. cit.,* p. 458a; C. Alamanno, *Summa philosophiae,* P. II, q. 34, a. 2 ad 4 (Paris, 1890).

[93] Arist., *Phys.* II, 1, 192b20. Some of the ancient commentators, notably Alexander and Porphyry (according to Simplicius, *Commentaria in Arist. de Physico* [Venetiis, 1546], Lib. II, fol. 42v–43r), Simplicius himself (*ibid.*), and Philoponus (*In Physica,* ed. Vitelli [Berlin, 1887], t. XVI, 198–99) were more or less embarrassed with this part of Aristotle's definition, since there is no rest to celestial motions. But St. Thomas points out that Aristotle only wishes to say that "nature" is responsible for rest as well as for activity in those bodies which naturally come to rest. Cf. *In II Phys.,* 1, n. 5.

[94] If there were no aim whatever, the body could not move at all, for the aim is the reason for the movement. Since motion is not an end in itself, St. Thomas insists that "natura nunquam inclinat ad motum propter movere, sed propter aliquid determinatum quod ex motu consequitur." *De pot.,* 5, 5; cf. *Sum. cont. gent.* III, 23.

[95] This is not to say that inanimate beings have consciousness or knowledge of their aim. While it is true that such terms as "aim," "desire," "appetite," "intentionality," etc. are primarily used in the context of human activity, the *analogical* use of these terms with regard to inanimate movement does not mean to imply consciousness of aim in the bodies themselves. However, this aim does imply a Supreme Intelligence which directs natural things. "Tendunt enim in finem sicut directa in finem a substantia intelligente, per modum quo sagitta tendit ad signum directa a sagittante" (St. Thomas, *Sum. cont. gent.* III, 24). The scholastic terminology was commonly attacked in the seventeenth century by such men as Bacon, Boyle, etc. as the expression of animism and an-

The Aristotelian conception of active nature is remarkably similar to Whitehead's description of nature as "life."[96] Whitehead is fully aware of the essential difference between animate and inanimate reality. However, he sees such a vast similarity that he considers the notion of "life," in the wide sense of the term, as the key to understanding the whole of reality. Against a background of a temporal advance and essential interconnectedness of physical reality each unit manifests a similarity to organic life. This analogy consists in three aspects, which Whitehead terms "creative activity," "aim," and "self-enjoyment."[97] By creative activity is meant the spontaneous and novel production of an event, so that every being, in a sense, creates from within its own structure and activity. "It is the clutch at vivid immediacy" and the principle of novelty.[98] By "aim" Whitehead means "the exclusion of the boundless wealth of alternative potentiality, and the inclusion of that definite factor of novelty which constitutes the selected way of entertaining those data in that process of unification."[99] That is, every body intrinsically aims at a particular way of enjoyment, utilizing the environment for its proper fulfillment. Finally, "self-enjoyment" is the organic unity and self-identity of the individual "arising out of this process of appropriation."[100] Whitehead strongly objects to the lifeless and inert character of the Newtonian-Humean universe. He insists that "nature is full-blooded; real facts are happening."[101] Thus Whitehead has reintroduced into philosophy spontaneous activity and finality, the two essential elements in the Aristotelian conception of nature.

Nature, then, as an active principle involves two essential factors. It is essentially a source of spontaneous activity and characteristics; conceptually it is the reflexive realization that certain characteristic manifestations of every physical body are spontaneously "given" in reality. And this implies an intrinsic finality, or aim, which is the fulfillment and "self-enjoyment" of the individual. Just as intentionality of purpose and passivity characterize the idea of nature as a passive principle, so intentionality and intrinsic spontaneity characterize the idea of nature as an active principle.

---

thropomorphism; this was due to a misconception of *analogical usage*—a human necessity.

[96] Cf. *Modes of Thought*, Part III, "Nature and Life," pp. 173–232.

[97] *Ibid.*, p. 208.

[98] *Process and Reality*, p. 160.

[99] *Modes of Thought*, pp. 207–8.

[100] *Ibid.*, pp. 205–6.

[101] *Modes of Thought*, p. 197; see also pp. 173–201, and his *Science and the Modern World* (Cambridge, 1946), pp. 49–141.

II

NATURAL AND
COMPULSORY MOVEMENT

The concept of nature which has been expounded[1] necessarily implies a selection or determination of activities which are conducive to the well-being of the individual. Nature as an active principle is a spontaneous source of purposeful activities, determined characteristics which are for the fulfillment of the individual. Thus carbon does not act in the same way as, let us say, helium. Likewise the "natural" receptivities of any physical being are only those which are conducive to the well-being of the whole, as was explained. Thus if nature both as an active and as a passive principle has a determined "aim," that is, intrinsic intentionality of purpose, there necessarily follows a distinction between those activities within the ambit of intentionality and those which are not. That is to say, there necessarily follows a distinction between "natural" and non-natural activity. In this sense, "natural" activity would be any characteristic behavior spontaneously produced by the body in a particular environment, or at least one for which the body has a connatural receptivity in its favor. Conversely, non-natural activity would be all movements which are foisted upon it from without. These non-natural movements may be the result of chance, human control, or violent force. The essential characteristic of non-natural or compulsory movement is that there is no intrinsic intentionality of that activity on the part of the being itself.

Whenever the notion of "aim" is introduced, such a distinction between natural and non-natural activity necessarily follows. Thus, although A. N. Whitehead attacks the Aristotelian distinction as an unfortunate and hasty classification,[2] his own principles of philosophy

---

[1] See Chapter I above.

[2] "The greatest curse to the progress of science is a hasty classification based on trivialities. An example of what I mean is Aristotle's classification of motions into violent and natural." A. Whitehead, *Essays in Science and Philosophy* (London, 1948), pp. 174–75.

demand this distinction. Whitehead maintains the essential self-identity of each individual reality in the universe and the self-identity of different types. He insists that each unit of reality, which spontaneously creates its activity, *aims* at producing its own individual and typical "self-enjoyment." By *aim* Whitehead explicitly acknowledges "the exclusion of the boundless wealth of alternative potentiality, and the inclusion of that definite factor of novelty which constitutes the selected way of entertaining those data in that process of unification."[3] That including of definite factors in the process of unification is what Aristotle calls "natural movement." Those potentialities which are intrinsically excluded, but which result from an external intrusion, are called non-natural by Aristotle.

This distinction between natural and non-natural movement would have no meaning in a world of complete inertia, that is, in a world where intrinsic intentionality of purpose is excluded—really or philosophically. The relevance of this distinction lies properly in the order of final causality. When final causality is denied, the distinction ceases to have any meaning.

Pierre Duhem's monumental studies on the precursors of Galileo are designed to prove a thesis which has subsequently found favor among many historians of modern science. Duhem maintains that it was the overthrow of the Aristotelian distinction between natural and compulsory movement by means of the theory of impetus which led to the principle of inertia, the cornerstone of modern physics.[4] Anneliese Maier, however, maintains that Duhem has exaggerated the role of impetus and has partly misrepresented the historical problem.[5] In fact, Maier maintains that the theory of impetus is a natural development of Aristotelian doctrine, and that this theory is very different from the principle of inertia proposed in the seventeenth

---

[3] A. Whitehead, *Modes of Thought* (Cambridge, Eng., 1938), pp. 207–8.

[4] P. Duhem, *Études sur Léonard de Vinci*, 3 vols. (Paris, 1906, 1909, 1913); *Système du Monde*, 5 vols. (Paris, 1913–17); "Physics—History of," *Catholic Encyclopedia* (New York, 1911), XII, 47–67. Cf. also R. Dugas, *Histoire de la Mécanique* (Neuchatel, 1950), pp. 19–104; H. Butterfield, *The Origins of Modern Science* (London, 1951), pp. 1–14; P. Hoenen, *Cosmologia*, 4th ed. (Rome, 1949), pp. 482–508; E. Whittaker, *A History of the Theories of Aether and Electricity* (London, 1951), I, 1–6; R. Masi, "Nota sulla storia del principio d'inerzia," in *Rivista di Filosofia Neoscolastica* 40 (1948), 121ff.

[5] "Duhem hat in grossangelegten Untersuchungen, die freilich der Nachprüfung im einzelnen nicht immer standhalten, den Ursprung der Geschichte der Theorie verfolgt, und das Verdienst, als erster auf sie hingewiesen und sie herausgestellt zu haben, wird ihm immer bleiben. Aber in der Beurteilung ihrer Bedeutung ist er, wenn nicht zu einer Überschätzung, so doch mindestens zu einer falschen Einschätzung gekommen. Die scholastische Naturphilosophie stellt im Vergleich zu der physikalischen Vorstellung der Neuzeit eine so heterogene Gedankenwelt dar, dass wir sie nur von ihren eigenen Voraussetzungen aus begreifen können." *Zwei Grundprobleme*, II Abschnitt: *Die Impetustheorie*, 2d ed. (Rome, 1951), pp. 113–14.

century.[6] Without delving into this vast subject, it is important to consider briefly the theory of impetus and the principle of inertia in order to see more clearly the significance of "natural" motion.

I. THE THEORY OF IMPETUS

The problem of explaining the movement of projectiles and every "non-natural" motion inevitably arises in an attempt to maintain the reality of nature as a source of determined behavior. The difficulty is to explain the continuation of such motion after it has left the source of projection. If the upward movement of a stone is not due to the stone itself but to the hand which threw it, what is responsible for the continued movement after it has left the hand? The principle of sufficient reason demands that *something* be responsible. It is obvious that the stone does not move itself upward, for this is a property of living things only. The stone does not move upward spontaneously, for this movement is contrary to its "nature." The hand which threw it does not continue the movement, for the stone is no longer in contact with the hand. Since something must be responsible for the continuation and none of these possibilities are admissible, the problem arises of finding the explanation.

Aristotle himself saw the difficulty, but his solution, which is subject to some misunderstanding, was later found to be erroneous. However, it is important to know not only precisely what Aristotle maintained but also *why* he maintained it, for in this lies the validity of Aristotle's position.

Aristotle considers the problem in three brief passages;[7] and in all of these passages his insistence is that not even violent movement can take place unless the natural is presupposed. In Book VIII of the *Physics* Aristotle proposes the problem and suggests two solutions: that of Plato and his own. For Plato bodies have only one proper movement, namely, motion to their proper place in the Receptacle. Even this movement is explained by the shape of the elementary bodies and the shaking of the Receptacle by the Soul.[8] All other movements take place by collision and mutual replacement, ἀντιπερίστασις, that is, the air or water pushed in front of the projectile gathers in behind it and so pushes it on.[9] Aristotle objects that

[6] A. Maier, *op. cit.*, pp. 113–14; cf. *Die Vorläufer Galileis im 14. Jahrhundert* (Rome, 1949).
[7] Arist., *Phys.* IV, 8, 215a1–18; VIII, 10, 266b27–267a22; *De caelo* III, 2, 301b17–33.
[8] Cf. Plato, *Timaeus* 49A–53A; 57B–58C. See also F. Cornford, *Plato's Cosmology* (London, 1937).
[9] "And, indeed, with respect to all the motions of water, the falling of thunder, and

in this explanation only motion itself is conferred by the mover, in which case "all the things moved would have to be in motion simultaneously and also to have ceased simultaneously."[10] He insists that the only way to explain the continuation of movement in the projectile is to say that the mover gives not only motion but also a power of moving (δύναμις τοῦ κινεῖν ἐγγίγνεται) to the "air or to water or to something else of the kind, naturally adapted for imparting and undergoing motion."[11] Movement is thus retarded when the motive force imparted decreases until finally "one part of the medium no longer causes the next to be a mover but only causes it to be in motion."[12]

In Book III of the De caelo Aristotle shows why this power of moving must be given to the medium. Since projectile motion is "violent" and violence implies "a source of movement in something other than itself or in it qua other,"[13] the source of such motion cannot be in the body itself. To attribute this motive force to the body would be to give it an internal principle, while violence is always from without. Furthermore, that external source of violent motion must be naturally adapted to producing the motion, otherwise the same problem arises as with the projectile itself. But air and water, according to Aristotle's doctrine, are naturally both "heavy and light," depending upon the actual environment. Thus the motive power can be given to the medium; the air "qua light produces upward motion, being propelled and set in motion by the force."[14] Therefore, in Aristotle's view, the upward movement of the projectile is possible because the medium is naturally endowed with this function of upward and downward motion; and he insists that "if the air were not endowed with this function, constrained movement would be impossible."[15]

This same idea lies behind the passage in Book IV of the Physics.[16] He argues against the existence of a void by insisting that violent

---

the wonderful circumstances observed in the attraction of amber, and the Herculean stone,—in all these, no real attraction takes place at all; but as a vacuum can nowhere be found, the particles are mutually impelled by each other; hence, as they all individually, both in a separate and mingled state, have an attraction for their own proper place, it is by the mutual intermingling of these affections, that such admirable effects present themselves to the view of the accurate investigator." Plato, Timaeus 80C; cf. 59A, 79B, C, E.

[10] Arist., Phys. 266b34–267a2.
[11] Ibid., 267a4–5; see 267a8–9.
[12] Ibid., 267a9–10.
[13] De caelo III, 2, 301b18–19.
[14] Ibid., 301b24–25.
[15] Ibid., 301b29–30.
[16] Phys. IV, 8, 215a13–18.

motion cannot arise from a source internal to the projectile but must be caused by an external medium. Since in a void there is no medium, Aristotle concludes that even violent motion would be impossible if actual space were a void.

The important point to notice is that Aristotle appeals to air to explain projectile motion, not because all movement must be *ab alio*, but because such movement is "violent" and *therefore* must be from an extrinsic source. Aristotle defines violent movement as "that whose moving principle is outside, the thing compelled contributing nothing."[17] This is the fundamental reason for appealing to an external source, such as the air. It is this idea of an "extrinsic," "non-natural" source which lies behind the scholastic development of impetus.

The Christian scholar John Philoponus of Alexandria (sixth century) seems to have been the first to show that the medium cannot be the cause of projectile motion.[18] If it is really the air which carries the stone or the arrow along, as Aristotle claims, then why must the hand touch the stone at all, or why must the arrow be fitted to the bowstring? One can beat the air violently and still not move the stone. Furthermore, a heavier stone can be thrown farther than a very light one, but if air is the cause of this motion, a very light stone should obviously travel farther. Then, too, why is motion deflected when two bodies collide and not when they merely pass each other? In fact, Philoponus points out, the air—and every medium—offers resistance to motion, so that instead of being a cause, it is rather an obstacle. Therefore, he concludes that violent motion cannot be explained by the Aristotelian theory. "On the contrary, it is necessary that a certain incorporeal motive power [κινητικήν τινὰ δύναμιν ἀσώματον] be given to the projectile through the act of throwing." In other words, Philoponus insists that it is not to the medium that the thrower gives the motive power but to the projectile itself. This, Duhem says, is the language of "common sense."[19] However, Philoponus points out that this motive "energy" (ἐνέργεια) is only borrowed and is decreased by the natural tendencies of the body and the resistance of the medium.

Unfortunately, Simplicius (d. 549) did not bother to present Philoponus's position clearly, but in two of his "Digressiones contra Ioannem grammaticum,"[20] he attacks the denial of what he thinks to

---

[17] Arist., *Eth. Nic.* III, 1, 1110b15; cf. 1110a2; *De caelo* III, 2, 301b18–19.
[18] Ioannis Philoponi, *In Arist. Physicorum libros quinque posteriores commentaria,* ed. Vitelli, Comm. in Arist. Graeca, XVII (Berlin, 1888), Lib. IV, cap. 8, pp. 636–42.
[19] P. Duhem, *Le Système du Monde,* I, 383.
[20] After VIII *Phys.,* comm. 8 and comm. 12, Simplicii *Commentaria in octo libros Physicorum* (Venice, 1546), 2a pars, fol. 51v–54v; fol. 57v–59r.

be the fundamental principle involved, namely, the denial of "whatever is moved must be moved by something else in contact with it." He himself develops a peculiar theory whereby the projectile and the medium alternately act upon one another until the *vis motrix* is exhausted. He confesses that he is insisting upon this for two reasons: whatever is moved must be moved by something else, and the two must be in contact.[21] Medieval knowledge of Philoponus was largely limited to the report of Simplicius.

It is not clear what influence, if any, Philoponus's theory had on the formation of the scholastic notion of impetus. Duhem believes that it came through the *Theorica planetarum* of the Spanish-Arabian astronomer Alpetragius (Al-Biṭrûjî),[22] which work was translated into Latin by Michael Scot in 1217.[23] But Maier has shown that Duhem quotes from the printed edition of 1531 in which the theory of Philoponus is very clear, but the Scot translation of the pertinent passage has no connotation whatever of an impetus theory.[24] Pines, discussing the Arabic theories of impetus, suggests that it may have been through Avicenna's commentary on the *Physics*.[25] But the Latin version, known as the *Sufficientia*, contained only the first four books, and the single vague reference in Book II, chapter 8, can be understood in an Aristotelian sense.[26] Maier believes that the scholastics developed the theory independently, mainly through their discussions of instrumental causality in the sacraments and reproduction.[27]

Although the Aristotelian theory was generally accepted in the thirteenth century, the reason for accepting it is clear: violent motion cannot be accounted for by an internal, innate source.[28] St. Thomas,

---

[21] *Ibid.*, fol. 91ra.

[22] Duhem, *Études sur Léonard de Vinci*, II, 191ff.; III, 23; also R. Dugas, *Histoire de la Mécanique*, p. 47. The title, *Theorica planetarum*, was given to this work by Calonymos ben David, whose translation from the Hebrew was printed in Venice in 1531, fol. 277–303. Today the work is more correctly known as *De motibus celorum*.

[23] Cf. C. Haskins, *Studies in the History of Mediaeval Science*, 2d ed. (Cambridge, Mass., 1927), pp. 272–98. A critical edition of the Latin translation of Michael Scot has been edited by F. Carmody, *De Motibus Celorum* (Berkeley, 1952).

[24] A. Maier, *Zwei Grundprobleme*, pp. 127–29. See Scot's trans., VIII, 11, ed. Carmody, p. 93.

[25] S. Pines, "Les précurseurs musulmans de la théorie de l'impetus," *Archeion* 21 (1938), 298ff.

[26] Cf. A. Maier, *Zwei Grundprobleme*, pp. 129–33.

[27] *Ibid.*, pp. 133–34.

[28] Cf. St. Albert, *In Phys.*, VIII, tr. IV, cap. 4; *In Phys.*, IV, tr. II, cap. 5; *In De caelo*, III, tr. I, cap. 7; St. Bonaventure, II *Sent.*, dist. 31, a. 1, q. 1; Roger Bacon, *Quaestiones super libros Physicorum*, Lib. VII, ed. Delorme (*Opera Hactenus Inedita*, fasc. XIII [Oxford, 1935]), pp. 338–47. "Non est autem intelligendum quod virtus violenti motoris imprimat lapidi qui per violentiam movetur, aliquam virtutem per quam moveatur, sicut

discussing reproduction, points out the essential difference between natural and non-natural motive forces: "virtus quae est in semine a patre, est *virtus permanens ab intrinseco, non influens ab extrinseco,* sicut virtus moventis quae est in proiectis."[29] Since violent motion is always alien and borrowed, it lasts only as long as the force remains, being resisted by the natural forces of the body.[30]

The scholastic theory of impetus seems to have been first suggested by the Franciscan Francis de Marchia. While discussing sacramental causality, he raises the question of impetus.[31] After a long and careful discussion of the Aristotelian theory, he concludes that projectile motion cannot be explained by the air but must be explained by a *virtus derelicta in lapide a motore.*[32] However, he is careful to point out that this force is not permanent or innate; it is rather an "accidental and extrinsic force," a "certain extrinsic form."[33] Therefore, this accidental force is alien and repugnant to the natural inclination of the body; it is, indeed, a "violent" and non-natural source of movement.[34]

Jean Buridan, twice rector of the University of Paris between 1328 and 1340, reached the same conclusions, but it is most probable that he did so independently of de Marchia's teaching. In his *Quaestiones*

---

virtus generantis imprimit genito formam, quam consequitur motus naturalis: *nam sic motus violentus esset a principio intrinseco, quod est contra rationem motus violenti.*" St. Thomas, *In III De caelo,* lect. 7, n. 6 (emphasis mine).

[29] *De anima,* 11 ad 2.

[30] "Instrumentum intelligitur moveri a principali agente, quamdiu retinet virtutem a principali agente impressam; unde sagitta tamdiu movetur a proiciente, quamdiu manet vis impulsus proicientis." St. Thomas, *De pot.* III, 11 ad 5; cf. *Sum. cont. gent.* III, c. 24: "Sicut enim sagitta consequitur inclinationem ad finem determinatum ex impulsione sagittantis, ita corpora naturalia consequuntur inclinationem in fines naturales ex moventibus naturalibus, ex quibus sortiuntur suas formas et virtutes et motus." A. Rozwadowski, basing himself on the last three cited texts (*De anima,* 11 ad 2; *De pot.* III, 11 ad 5; *Sum. cont. gent.* III, c. 24), tries to show that St. Thomas held the theory of impetus in the same sense in which it was later expounded by Jean Buridan and his school. Cf. "De Motus Localis Causa Proxima secundum Principia S. Thomae," *Divus Thomas* (Piacenza) 42 (1939), 104–13. Duhem thinks that in these passages St. Thomas is using a popularly expressed similarity. Father M.-D. Chenu rejects Rozwadowski's thesis as a forced reading. Cf. "Aux origines de la 'science moderne,'" in *Revue des Sc. Phil. et Théol.* 29 (1940), 217, note. A careful consideration of the above-quoted texts will show that they are all perfectly consistent with the Aristotelian theory, and there is no reason to suppose that St. Thomas held the impetus theory which was developed later. However, the theory of impetus is a clear development of his principles.

[31] Text edited from the MSS by Maier, *Zwei Grundprobleme,* pp. 166–80.

[32] *Ibid.,* line 305, p. 174.

[33] Cf. *ibid.,* lines 313–59, pp. 175–76.

[34] "Movens enim sive agens non confert ipsi mobili passo vim [sive] perfectionem aliquam naturalem sive [sibi?] intrinsecam, nec etiam confert vim sive perfectionem aliquam accidentalem et extrinsecam sibi convenientem, sed magis dispositionem sibi convenientem auferre, dando enim quod sibi disconveniens est et contra eius naturalem inclinationem aufert quod conveniens est." *Ibid.,* lines 336–43.

super octo libros Physicorum[35] and in his *Quaestiones de Caelo et Mundo*,[36] he considers the Platonic and Aristotelian theories of projectile motion, but both seem to offer great difficulty. He points out that the Aristotelian theory cannot account for the rotational movement of a grindstone or a disk, for the motion continues even when a covering is placed close to the bodies, thus cutting off the air. Furthermore, a stone can be thrown farther than a pebble, while violent beating of the air will not move the stone. Therefore, he concludes that the mover must impress a certain *impetus* upon the body itself by which it continues to move until overcome by the resistance of the air and natural gravity.[37] And like de Marchia he insists that the impetus is "sibi [corpori] violentus et innaturalis, quia suae naturae formali disconveniens et a principio extrinseco violenter impressus, et quod natura ipsius gravis inclinat ad motum oppositum et ad corruptionem ipsius impetus."[38]

Albert of Saxony and Marsilius of Inghen likewise teach that a certain force is given to the body by which it moves, but they insist that this "accidental and extrinsic force" is violent and therefore continually decreases until finally it is destroyed.[39] This became the common "Aristotelian" teaching throughout the fifteenth and sixteenth centuries. Since the theory of impetus is actually consistent with the principles of Aristotle, later scholastics such as Laurence Londorius, the first rector of St. Andrew's, Augustine Nipho, Cardinal Cajetan, Alexander Piccolominus, and Scaliger interpreted Aristotle's words in a wide sense consistent with the theory. Thomists such as Capreolus and Domingo de Soto claimed it as the "opinion of St. Thomas."[40] Some writers of the sixteenth century, however, conceived the impetus as a

---

[35] Paris 1509, Lib. VIII, q. 12; this question about which we are concerned was critically edited by Maier, *op. cit.*, pp. 207–14.

[36] Edited by Ernest A. Moody (Cambridge, Mass., 1942), Lib. II, qq. 12–13, pp. 176–84; Lib. III, q. 2, pp. 240–43.

[37] "Ideo videtur mihi dicendum, quod motor movendo mobile imprimit sibi quendam impetum vel quandam vim motivam illius mobilis ad illam partem ad quam motor movebat ipsum, sive sursum sive deorsum sive lateraliter vel circulariter, et quanto motor movet illud mobile velocius tanto imprimet ei fortiorem impetum. . . . Sed per aerem resistentem et per gravitatem lapidis inclinantem ad contrarium eius ad quod impetus est natus movere, ille impetus continue remittitur." *Ibid.*, lines 124–32, p. 211; cf. *Quaestiones de Caelo et Mundo*, Lib. II, q. 13, line 34 (p. 183)–line 7 (p. 184); Lib. III, q. 2, lines 18–39 (p. 243).

[38] *Quaest. sup. oct. lib. Physicorum*, Lib. VIII, q. 12, ed. Maier, *op. cit.*, lines 198–202.

[39] Cf. Marsilius of Inghen: "Et si quaeras quare impetus sic ultra non sufficit movere, respondetur quod hoc est, quia est violentus corporibus motis, quae ipsum continue remittuntur et tandem corrumpunt." Text ed. Maier, lines 141–43, p. 283.

[40] Capreoli, *Defensiones theologiae d. Thomae*, Sent. II, dist. 6, q. 1, a. 3; Domingo de Soto, *Super octo libros Physicorum quaestiones* (Salamanca, 1551), Lib. VIII, q. 3, fol. 103vff.

mover.[41] Against such a conception, Domingo de Soto argues that the impetus cannot be a *mover,* the *efficient cause* of violent motion, for this would be to conceive the body as living. Rather it is the *instrument* of the agent who is the efficient cause.[42] He points out the analogy between impetus and nature, for just as the "cause" of natural activity is the progenitor and not "nature," so too the "cause" of violent motion is the agent and not the "impetus."[43] Thus impetus is a foreign and borrowed quality which automatically acts without being a "mover," a quality which necessarily diminishes due to the opposing natural forces.

From this it is clear that the theory of impetus is strictly an Aristotelian development. Not only was it developed within the framework of Aristotelianism, but it follows from Aristotle's principles and is consistent with experience. It safeguards the distinction between natural and compulsory motion, for the impetus always remains an alien and extrinsic quality, even though foisted upon the projectile, while nature is a permanent and radical source of characteristic behavior. Furthermore, the theory embodies the principle of finality, for nature intrinsically strives towards its own fulfillment and, therefore, strives to overcome the alien force; the only finality involved in impetus is that which is given by the extrinsic source of projection. This is very different from the principle of inertia, which not only eliminates the distinction between natural and compulsory motion but destroys the notion of finality as well.

II. THE PRINCIPLE OF INERTIA

During the sixteenth century a new philosophical spirit emerged, anti-Aristotelian in character. This spirit seems to have originated among logicians who wished to replace traditional logic with mathematics.[44] But with Cardano, Benedetti, Telesio, Bruno, and Galileo,

---

[41] E.g., Girolamo Cardano: "Cum supponitur quod omne quod movetur ab alio movetur, verissimum est. Sed illud quod movet est impetus acquisitus, sicut calor in aqua, qui est ibi praeter naturam ab igne inductus et tamen igne sublato manum tangentis exurit." *De subtilitate rerum,* Lib. XXI (Lyon, 1551), p. 90.

[42] "Impetus ergo quia non est suppositum, non agit, sed est virtus agentis, puta motoris." Domingo de Soto, *op. cit.,* fol. 104v–105r.

[43] ". . . pro coperto reliquisse ex analogia gravium et levium, quae est prima ratio affirmandi huiusmodi impetum. Nempe quod sicut generans grave tribuit illi naturalem qualitatem, quae est gravitas, qua illud permovet usque ad centrum, sic et proiciens impingat proiecto quo illud eminus moveat." *Ibid.,* fol. 104v. See our previous chapter.

[44] Although there were earlier works of this nature, Peter Ramus (1515–1572) exercised the most noticeable influence, mainly through his *Dialecticae institutiones.* His best-known followers were Sturm in Germany, Arminius in Holland, du Naniel in Belgium,

this spirit appeared in natural philosophy as well. Particularly in questions of projectile motion the new scientists took occasion to attack
Aristotle.[45] In their minds the scholastic theory of impetus was conceived in a *quantitative* manner; and it is this new theory which has
become known as the principle of inertia.[46]

Giovanni Benedetti (1530–1590) had already insisted that every
body, naturally falling or projected, tends to move in a straight line.
But it was Galileo (1564–1642) who first formulated the principle of
inertia. In his *Discourses on the Two New Sciences*, the Third Day, he
assumes that the momentum of a given body falling down an inclined
plane is proportional only to the vertical distance and independent of
the inclination; from this he concludes that a body falling down one
plane would acquire momentum which would carry it up another to
the same height. The fact that the descent and ascent of a pendulum
are exactly equal regardless of the length of the cord and of the
weight of the bob are adduced to confirm his view.[47] The momentum
of such a falling body is accelerated by gravity; as it rises it is retarded
and eventually overcome by an equal gravity. But if a body moved
along a horizontal plane where all causes of acceleration or retardation were absent, its motion would be perpetual and uniform. Thus
Galileo says, "Any velocity once received by a body is perpetually
maintained as long as the external causes of acceleration or retardation are removed, a condition which is found only on horizontal
planes."[48] On the Fourth Day Galileo considers the movement of projectiles. He imagines a perfectly round body projected along a horizontal plane where all adverse forces are removed. He concludes that
according to his previous arguments the velocity of the projectile
would remain uniform and perpetual if the plane were extended to

---

and Temple in England.

[45] Cf. Bernardino Telesio, *De rerum natura iuxta propria principia*, 2d ed. (Naples,
1570), Lib. I, cap. 46, fol. 32v; Giordano Bruno, *Camoeracensis Acrotismus, seu Rationes
articulorum adversus Peripateticos Parisiis propositorum, Opera Omnia Latina* (Naples, 1879),
I, 138. Even in his youthful work *De Motu* (ca. 1590) Galileo begins the chapter on
projectiles as follows: "Aristoteles, sicut fere in omnibus quae de motu locali scripsit, in
hac etiam quaestione vero contrarium scripsit." Ed. Nazionale, *Opera Omnia*, I, 307.

[46] Cf. A. Maier, *op. cit.*, pp. 303–14; also *Die Vorläufer Galileis in 14. Jahrhundert*,
pp. 132–54.

[47] Cf. Galileo, *Discorsi e Dimostrazioni Mathematiche intorno a Due Nuove Scienze attenenti
alla Meccanica, et ai Movimenti Locali*, Giornata Terza, *Opere di Galileo Galilei* (Padua,
1744), III, 96.

[48] ". . . velocitas gradus, quicunque in mobili reperiatur, est in illo suapte natura
indelebiter impressus, dum externae causae accelerationis, aut retardationis tollantur,
quod in solo horizontali plano contingit. . . . Ex quo pariter sequitur, motus in solo
horizontali esse quoque eternum: si enim est aequabilis, non debilitatur, aut remittitur,
et multo minus tollitur." *Discorsi*, Giornata Terza, prob. IX, prop. 23, Scholium, *ed. cit.*,
p. 123.

infinity.[49] Thus the *impeto* as such is a uniform velocity in a straight line which is accelerated or retarded only by extrinsic forces; were it not for these forces, the velocity would remain constant perpetually.

For Galileo the *impeto*, or *momento*, is not a quality by which motion takes place, as was held by the scholastics, but the *quantity of motion* measured by the mass times the velocity (mv). Rather than an alien source of violent motion, it is the measure of all motion. By considering only the quantitative aspect of motion he reduces both "natural" and "violent" motion to the same category of impetus, so that the distinction ceases to have meaning. The important point to notice is that Galileo is concerned not with explaining the existence of motion but only with the *change* or cessation of motion. For him it is not the continuation of motion which needs to be explained but change of direction and velocity. Motion which does not involve change of direction or velocity is thus called "inertial motion"; and the resistance to this change is commonly called the "force" of inertia.

About the same time Isaac Beeckman, the close friend of Descartes, expressed the principle of inertia clearly when he wrote in his *Journal*, "A thing once moved would not come to rest but for some external impediment."[50] Christian Huygens had a clearer idea of the principle and formulated it as a "hypothesis" for his work on the pendulum.[51] Descartes (1596–1650), however, extended the principle to cover the whole of natural philosophy by making it "the first law of nature."[52] The principle of inertia reached its classical formulation in Isaac Newton's *Principia:* "Every body continues in its state of rest or of uniform motion in a straight line, unless it is compelled to change that state by forces impressed upon it."[53]

The principle of inertia is, indeed, as Whitehead calls it, "the first

---

[49] "Mobile quoddam super planum horizontale projectum mente concipio omni secluso impedimento: iam constat ex his, quae fusius alibi dicta sunt, illius motum aequabilem, et perpetuum super ipso plano futurum esse, si planum in infinitum extendatur." *Ibid.*, III, 141.

[50] "Omnis res semel mota nunquam quiescit nisi propter externum impedimentum." Quoted by Maier, *Zwei Grundprobleme*, p. 311.

[51] "Si gravitas non esset, neque aer motui corporum officeret, unumquodque eorum, acceptum semel motum continuaturum velocitate aequabili, secundum lineam rectam." *Horologium Oscillatorium* (Paris, 1673), Part II, Hypothesis I.

[52] "Prima lex naturae: quod unaquaque res quantum in se est, semper in eodem statu perseveret; sicque quod semel movetur, semper moveri pergat." *Principia Philosophiae* (1644), P. II, art. 37, *Oeuvres*, ed. Adam-Tannery, VIII, 62.

[53] "Corpus omne perseverare in statu suo quiescendi vel movendi uniformiter in directum, nisi quatenus illud a viribus impressis cogitur statum suum mutare." *Philosophiae Naturalis Principia Mathematica*, Law I. The first edition of this work was printed in London, 1687; modern English trans. of the 2d ed., F. Cajori (Berkeley, 1947). For the background of Newton's 2d ed., *ibid.*, pp. 628–32.

article of the creed of science."[54] But the numerous and varied studies, criticisms, and justifications of this principle show that its meaning is not as clear as one might hope.[55] Einstein's criticism of the Newtonian formulation and the "unification of inertia and gravitation" in relativity physics have obscured even more the meaning of the principle.[56] It is clear that the Galilean and Newtonian theory established an entirely new outlook on nature, but as Whitehead points out, "it is noticeable that no reason was produced in the 17th century for the Galilean as distinct from the Aristotelian position."[57] Since the principle of inertia played such an important role, it is necessary to consider not only its relation to Aristotelian natural philosophy but also the meaning and logical foundation of the principle.

It is clear that the doctrine of inertia had its rise in the science of mechanics. Mechanics in its proper sense is a practical science of determining the amount of force to be applied in order to produce a certain effect. This is clear in such elementary problems as the lever, equilibrium, displacement, and so forth, in which the resistance afforded by a body is taken into account (force of inertia) or the irrelevant state of a body is disregarded (principle of inertia).[58] In this sense the principle was not first discovered by Galileo but was already recognized by Stevinus, da Vinci, and Archimedes. However, it is one thing to justify the principle in mechanics, and quite another to establish it as "the first law of nature."

Foundation of the Principle

What is the logical foundation for the principle of inertia? Is it self-evident that every body continues in its state of rest, or of uniform motion in a straight line, except so far as it may be compelled by force to change that state? Usually the proposition is stated as immediately evident. It is pointed out that a block of wood thrown along a rough road slides only a short distance, along a floor a longer distance, and along ice still farther. "From examples like these, it is reasoned that if friction could be eliminated entirely, which cannot actually be done, a body once set into motion on a level surface would continue to move indefinitely with undiminished velocity; thus uniform motion is a

[54] *Essays in Science and Philosophy* (London, 1948), p. 171.
[55] Cf. G. Whitrow, "On the Foundations of Dynamics," *British J. for the Phil. of Sc.* 1 (1950), 92ff.; R. J. Nogar, "Toward a Physical Theory," *The New Scholasticism* 25 (1951), 397–438.
[56] Cf. A. S. Eddington, *Space, Time, and Gravitation* (Cambridge, 1920), pp. 136–51; *The Nature of the Physical World* (London, 1947), pp. 115–39.
[57] *Science and the Modern World* (Cambridge, 1946), p. 60.
[58] This point is explained at length below.

natural condition."[59] But such reasoning neither proves the proposition nor manifests its self-evidence. The fact that a body continues longer over a smooth surface does not prove that, were the surface infinitely smooth, it would continue indefinitely.[60] Nor is this self-evident. It assumes that the body itself is a null factor and that external factors can be excluded to render the motion uniform. In actual experience there is no manifestation of the first assumption, for in all evident phenomena such motion is resisted, and this resistance is relative to the body.[61] In other words, actual experience is against such an assumption. Relativity physics denies the second assumption, for bodies are always in a gravitational field—and indeed, constitute it; thus the motion would be not uniform but accelerated.[62] It seems clear, then, that the usual examples given to display the "self-evidence" of this principle are unsatisfactory.

In the early days of modern science it was thought that the principle of inertia was philosophically demonstrated and experimentally verified.[63] In Descartes' system the principle is founded on the conservation of momentum. He alleged that in the beginning God created not only matter but also a determined *quantitas motus*, which could neither be augmented nor decreased.[64] This he thinks is necessary, for

---

[59] *Physics*, E. Hausmann and E. P. Slack, 3d ed. (New York, 1948). "Intuitively, also we recognize that were it not for disturbing and extraneous forces, especially friction, this constant speed in a straight line might be maintained forever." H. B. Lemon, *From Galileo to the Nuclear Age* (Chicago, 1946), p. 6.

[60] This argument by extrusion can be answered on experimental grounds. Increasing the smoothness of two surfaces in contact does not reduce their friction indefinitely, for a point is reached where further polishing increases the friction. Cf. Fred. Palmer, "Friction," *Scientific American* 184 (1951), 54–59.

[61] Jean Buridan suggested that since the heavenly bodies do not offer resistance (an Aristotelian doctrine, cf. *De caelo* II, 1, 283b26–284a25) the original impetus given to them by God would be sufficient to keep them moving forever. "Posset dici quod non apparet necessitas ponendi huiusmodi intelligentias, quia diceretur quod Deus quando creavit mundum, unumquemque orbium caelestium movit sicut sibi placuit et movendo eos impressit sibi impetus moventes eos absque hoc quod amplius moveret eos, nisi per modum generalis influentiae, sicut ipse concurrit coagendo ad omnia quae aguntur. . . . Et illi impetus impressi corporibus caelestibus non postea remittebantur vel corrumpebantur, quia non erat inclinatio corporum caelestium ad alios motus, nec erat resistentia quae esset corruptiva vel repressiva illius impetus. Sed hoc non dico assertive, sed ut a dominis theologis petam quod in illis doceant me, quomodo possunt haec fieri." *QQ. in VIII Physicorum*, q. 12, ed. Maier in *Zwei Grundprobleme*, lines 170–84; also in *QQ. de Caelo et Mundo*, Lib. II, q. 12, ed. Moody, pp. 180–81.

[62] Eddington says pointedly that the teacher "glosses over the point that if there were no interference with the motion—if the ice were abolished altogether—the motion would be by no means uniform, but like that of a falling body." *Space, Time, and Gravitation*, p. 136.

[63] Cf. H. Poincaré, *Science and Hypothesis* (London, 1905), pp. 94–95.

[64] "Deum esse primariam motus causam: et eandem semper motus quantitatem in universo conservare." *Prin. Phil.*, P. II, art. 36, *ed cit.*, VIII, 61.

otherwise God would have to continue creating motion; and this is contrary to His immutability! Throughout the entire universe the "quantity of motion" remains constant, so that when one body is at rest, another is in motion; when one moves twice as fast, another moves half as fast as previously.[65] Descartes determined the "quantity of motion" to be measurable as the product of the mass moved into the velocity with which it is moved, that is, Galileo's momentum, mv. Change, then, was to be explained as the transference of momentum from one body to another through impact. Since the quantity of motion in the universe (mv) must be constant, *id quod movetur, quantum in se est, semper moveri.*[66] Thus for Descartes the principle of inertia was based upon the conservation of momentum (mv), and conservation was thought necessary because of the immutability of God.

Leibniz (1646–1716), however, pointed out that momentum is not constant in the universe, for it cannot be shown that every body imparts the same quantity of motion to some other body.[67] Furthermore, Leibniz maintained that it is not momentum which accounts for movement but rather a certain *vis viva, lebendige Kraft,* which is measured not by mv but by mass times the velocity squared (mv^2). He maintained that it was *vis viva* which accounted for motion in the world and which, furthermore, remained constant throughout the universe.[68] Leibniz is really pointing out here the difference between momentum and what has become known as energy. The important

---

[65] "Ita scilicet ut putemus, cum una pars materiae duplo celerius movetur quam altera, et haec altera duplo maior est quam prior, tantundem motus esse in minore quam in maiore; ac quanto motus unius partis lentior sit, tanto motum alicuius alterius ipsi aequalis fieri celeriorem." *Ibid.,* p. 61.

[66] *Prin. Phil.,* P. II, art. 37, *ed cit.,* VIII, 62. Spinoza's presentation of Descartes' argument, *more geometrico demonstratum,* shows clearly the supposed logical foundation of the principle of inertia. "(Propositio XIX: Unaquaeque res, quatenus simplex et indivisa est, et in se sola consideratur, quantum in se est, semper in eodem statu perseverat.) Demonstratio: cum nihil sit in aliquo statu, nisi ex solo Dei consursu (per prop. 12. part. I); et Deus in suis operibus sit summe constans (per Coroll. Propos. 20. part. I); si ad nullas causas externas, particulares scilicet, attendamus, sed rem in se sola consideramus, affirmandum erit, quod illa, quantum in se est, in statu suo quo est, semper perseverat. Q.E.D." Spinoza, *Renati Des Cartes Principiorum Philosophiae More Geometrico Demonstratae, Opera,* ed. Van Vloten and Land (The Hague, 1914), IV, 159.

[67] Principally in his *Système nouveau de la nature,* ed. by C. J. Gerhardt, *Die philosophischen Schriften von G. W. Leibnitz* (Berlin, 1890), IV. For the controversy between the followers of Descartes and Leibniz on this point, cf. H. W. B. Joseph, *Lectures on the Philosophy of Leibniz* (Oxford, 1949), pp. 27–54.

[68] ". . . eandem motricis potentiae summam in natura conservari." Leibniz called this active force *vis viva* because it seemed to multiply itself in the square of the velocity. Prof. Joseph points out that the importance of the squared velocity for Leibniz was that it led to some reality beyond mere mechanics; Leibniz was fully aware that a velocity could not be really (physically) squared, but that it was a mental process which yielded a

point is that Leibniz bases the principle of inertia on the conservation of energy, instead of on Descartes' momentum.[69] However, as Leibniz denies any *real* interaction between the unextended monads which make up the real world, the conservation of energy is a *phenomenological principle* which depends upon "pre-established harmony" in which God alone is the true cause. In the *Discours de Métaphysique*, § 18, Leibniz says:

Although all the particular phenomena of nature can be explained mathematically or mechanically by those who understand them, yet nevertheless, the general principles of corporeal nature and even of mechanics are rather metaphysical than geometrical and belong rather to certain forms or indivisible natures, as the causes of what appears, than to corporeal or extended mass.[70]

Descartes realized that his doctrine of conservation seemed to preclude every activity of the soul upon the body. To reconcile the conservation of momentum in the world and the activity of the soul on the pineal gland, Descartes maintained that the soul cannot give momentum to the body but only change of direction. In answering this "ingenious" distinction, Leibniz points out that even change of direction requires a force, but he acknowledges the impossibility of the soul's acting upon the body even to change the direction of the "animal spirits"—"a thing which appears as inconceivable as to say that it gives them movement, at least unless one has recourse, as I do, to the pre-established harmony."[71] For Leibniz the phenomenological world may be described through mechanical laws, but the real world and even the foundation of mechanical laws are to be found in the realms beyond mechanics. Furthermore, the conservation of *vis viva* in the world depends upon the will of God.

Even Isaac Newton insisted that mechanical laws applied in the universe *as though* bodies themselves were the *cause* of such motion.[72] Newton tried to distinguish very carefully between the mathematical principles which could describe the activity of nature and the "metaphysical reality" about which he would make no "hypotheses" but in which he firmly believed. Under the direct influence of Henry More's Platonism and Jacob Boehme's mysticism he attributed the real cause

---

number corresponding to a physical effect. Therefore, the reality which could not be attained in Cartesian mechanics had to be sought in his "metaphysical" monads. Cf. Joseph, *op. cit.*, pp. 41–61.

[69] Cf. Leibniz, Letter to Volder, *Philosophische Schriften*, II, 170.

[70] Leibniz, *Philosophische Schriften*, IV, 444.

[71] Leibniz, *Système nouveau, Phil. Schriften*, IV, 497.

[72] See my "Space and Gravitation," *The New Scholasticism* 29 (1955), 175–223.

of material effects to God, Who operates through space, His "Sensorium."[73] Prof. Snow summarizes Newton's philosophy as follows: "While the motion of matter follows the general laws of mechanics, the real or final cause of motion does not, but a Divine Providence creates, conserves, and regulates motion, in order that 'bodies may not go off their course'."[74] Newton, however, did believe that the first two laws of motion were substantiated by Galileo's work on the inclined plane and by Huygens's work on the pendulum.[75]

In the seventeenth century, therefore, the principle of inertia was thought to rest on conservation of momentum or energy. This latter principle was thought to be based upon: (i) certain experimental phenomena, namely, the inclined plane and the pendulum; and (ii) upon "metaphysical" (or theological) considerations. But it is clear that the experiments on the inclined plane and on the pendulum are strictly mechanical in the proper sense of the word; they neither manifest the self-evidence of the principle of inertia nor demonstrate it. Much less do these experiments establish it as a universal law of nature. It is true that the so-called principle is *involved* in these and other experiments, as will be shown later, but this is not to establish it as the first law of nature. It should not be necessary to consider the "metaphysical" (or theological) arguments which were adduced in defense of the principle, as hardly anyone today relies upon them, at least in the present context.

When Immanuel Kant tried to establish the universality of Newtonian physics in the face of Hume's skepticism, he reduced the principles of mathematics and natural philosophy to *a priori* judgments or conditions of the mind. Thus he believes the principles of inertia and conservation to be universally valid, because they are demanded by the law of causality, an *a priori* necessity which the mind imposes on events. But by the law of causality Kant means that "every change must have a cause"; this cause not only is extrinsic but must act con-

---

[73] The most extensive study of Newton's personal philosophy has been made by A. J. Snow in his *Matter and Gravity in Newton's Physical Philosophy* (London, 1926). Arguing against Descartes, Henry More insisted that although the material effects of nature are mechanical, the real cause must be immaterial and spiritual—by penetrating matter, it is the source of motion, of cohesion, or separation of parts of bodies; it is the directing force of all motion, animate and inanimate. (Cf. More, *Immortality of the Soul*, Bk. I, chap. ii, arts. 11–12.) More attributed "spiritual substance" to God, the angels, the mind of man, and space, the extension and "sensorium" of God. (Cf. More, *Enchiridion Metaphysicum*, chap. 28, par. 2; chap. 8; also preface to the *Immortality of the Soul*.)

[74] A. J. Snow, *op. cit.*, p. 210. The phrase "final cause" is used in the accepted seventeenth-century sense of "metaphysical"; ever since Francis Bacon relegated the study of final causes to metaphysics, the phrase had become identical with metaphysical among English writers.

[75] Cf. Newton, *Principia*, Scholium to Definitions, *ed. cit.*, pp. 21–28.

tinually upon the body whenever there is a change of *state,* that is, a change from rest to motion or a change in velocity.[76] In other words, Kant's idea of causality presupposes the validity of the principle of inertia, as his very concept of causality implies.[77]

With the development of thermodynamics in the last century and the universal application of the conservation of energy by Helmholtz (1821–1894), it was generally believed that the principle of inertia had universal validity.[78] But Poincaré pointed out that the laws of thermodynamics are valid only in a particular set of phenomena and cannot be extended to the whole universe by giving the laws an absolute meaning.[79] Poincaré himself believed that the principle of inertia is neither imposed on the mind *a priori* nor universally demonstrated. But he adds, "This law, verified experimentally in some particular cases, may be extended fearlessly to the most general cases; for we know that in these general cases it can neither be confirmed nor contradicted by experiments."[80]

From these considerations the following points seem to emerge. (i) *The principle of inertia is not self-evident.* While it is true we may conceive or imagine a being with uniform motion in a straight line, unable to change except by an external agent, no such being can possibly exist in the world we know. (ii) *The principle is not demonstrated as a universal law of nature.* Philosophical reasoning does not demonstrate it, for the data of human experience are contrary to the statement of the principle; the various branches of physical science which "involve" the principle cover only particular phenomena, that is, limiting cases, and therefore cannot manifest it for the whole of natu-

---

[76] Cf. *Kritik der reinen Vernunft,* B. II, Kap. II, sect. 3, 3A.

[77] It may be pointed out that in Kant's scheme of the sciences there is no room for natural philosophy in the Aristotelian sense of the word. By "pure natural science" Kant understands the application of mathematics to phenomena, or what the Aristotelian would call mathematical physics. (Cf. Kant, *Prolegomena,* § 14.) Thus it is not surprising that his concept of causality should be that of the mathematical physicist, which concept implies the principle of inertia. Cf. Josef Schmucker, "Der Einfluss des Newtonschen Weltbildes auf die Philosophie Kants," in *Philosophisches Jahrbuch* 61 (1951), 52–58.

[78] Cf. Hermann von Helmholtz, "On the Conservation of Force," in *Harvard Classics* (Scientific Papers), XXX, 181–220; see also Ernst Mach's *History and Root of the Principle of the Conservation of Energy* (Chicago, 1918). Mach however believes that the principle has a more universal, i.e., nonmechanical, validity than Helmholtz maintained (cf. pp. 38–39; 59–74). For Mach the principle of conservation is based on the theorem of excluded perpetual motion; this in turn he derives from another form of the causal principle, viz., "it is not possible to create work out of nothing." But a careful study of Mach's arguments will show that this statement is to be understood in a mathematical, and not a philosophical, context.

[79] H. Poincaré, *Science and Hypothesis,* pp. 129–35.

[80] *Ibid.,* p. 97.

ral reality. (iii) *The principle is not even demonstrated in any of the existing branches of physical science.* While it is true that the principle seems to be "involved" in many particular cases, so that we can say with Poincaré that it is "verified experimentally in some particular cases," there is no actual proof of it as a "law." Rather than proving the principle, the mechanical and mathematical science of nature *assumes* it. Yet there is a necessity in this: the mathematical sciences must assume it, if they are to remain mathematical. But this necessity of assuming it can be brought out only by explaining the actual meaning of the principle of inertia.

Meaning of the Principle

When discussing the meaning of this "principle," care must be taken not to confuse it with secondary factors, which, although very important in mathematical physics, do not express the essential meaning of the principle. For example, the fundamental idea of the principle should not be confused with a "force of resisting" an external deterrent to the actual course of a body. Certainly every natural body in a gravitational field will have a *vis resistendi*, but this is not what is meant by the "law" of inertia. Nor should the law be limited to the particular phrase "uniform motion," that is, motion in a "straight line."[81] Although this aspect of Newton's formulation has important consequences in *determining* the motion of a body, the essential idea is that a body once moved continues to move—whether with uniform or with accelerated motion is of secondary importance, as far as understanding the principle is concerned. Relativity physics has brought out very clearly the ambiguity of this part of Newton's proposition; since all measurements of moving bodies depend upon the position and condition of the observer, how are we to know whether the motion is uniform or accelerated? Nevertheless, the essential idea implied in the principle of inertia remains even in relativity physics.

It is commonly claimed that the greatest triumph of the seventeenth century was to rid the celestial spheres of spiritual movers and to effect the unification of celestial and terrestrial mechanics. As Prof. Butterfield puts it, "The modern law of inertia, the modern theory of motion, is the greatest factor which in the seventeenth century helped to drive the spirits out of the world and open the way to a universe

---

[81] Strictly speaking uniform motion and motion in a straight line are identical in the language of physics inasmuch as any change in either requires an external agent. But for the sake of clarity both expressions are frequently used in this chapter as though they were distinct.

that ran like a piece of clockwork."[82] An examination of how this was done and what it means will lead to a clarification of the concept of inertia.

In the Aristotelian philosophy of nature a distinction is drawn between celestial and terrestrial bodies. The distinction fundamentally lies in the different ways the two are moved: terrestrial bodies naturally come to rest, the celestial do not. As was pointed out previously, nature as an active principle necessarily involves some *finality*, "for since nature always tends determinately towards one [perfection], not being indifferently suited to many, it is impossible that a given nature aim at motion for its own sake."[83] With regard to motion in place a given nature tends toward a suitable place, a congenial environment, in which it is relatively at rest. But we see that the heavenly bodies move continually without a particular place in which to rest. Even if it could be shown that the celestial motions are gradually coming to rest, such a rest would not be a good thing for either the planet or the universe, so that this cessation of movement could not be called the natural aim of celestial motion. Whether the earth is considered to be one of the moving planets or not does not alter the case: bodies on this earth must have a determined place for survival, while planetary bodies move continuously in their orbits.[84] Since celestial bodies have no intrinsic finality accruing to them in rest, St. Thomas concludes that their motion arises not from an intrinsic *active* (formal) principle but from an intrinsic *passive* (material) principle, which needs to be continually moved by some noncorporeal being.[85] This was the real basis for distinguishing the two classes of bodies—a functional division. All the other properties attributed to the heavenly bodies are secondary. They were thought to be "ingenerable and incorruptible,"

---

[82] *Origins of Modern Science* (London, 1951), p. 7; see also C. Singer, *A Short History of Science* (Oxford, 1943), pp. 212–17.

[83] "Cum enim natura semper in unum tendat determinate, non se habens ad multa, impossibile est quod aliqua natura inclinet ad motum secundum se ipsum." St. Thomas, *De pot.*, 5, 5.

[84] "Caelum autem non pervenit suo motu in aliquid *ubi*, ad quod per suam naturam inclinetur, quia quodlibet *ubi* est principium et finis motus." *Ibid.;* cf. *Sum. cont. gent.* III, c. 23; *In II De caelo*, lect. 18, n. 1.

[85] "Unde non potest esse suus motus naturalis quasi sequens aliquam inclinationem naturalis virtutis inhaerentis, sicut sursum ferri est motus naturalis ignis." *De pot.*, 5, 5; cf. ad 12; II *Phys.*, lect. 1, n. 4. Whether the heavenly bodies are animated, as Aristotle believed, or moved extrinsically by God or angels does not affect the immediate point, for in any of these cases continual motion can be explained, for the finality is in the mover. But St. Thomas insists, *"Non autem esset via solvendi, si moverentur per solum naturae impetum, sicut corpora gravia et levia." In II De caelo*, lect. 18, n. 1.

because no generation or corruption was observed.[86] They were thought to be of a different element to account for this.[87] This teaching was the general, although not the universal, opinion of medieval philosophers.[88]

From the earliest days of astronomy men have tried to determine the relative positions, periods, and velocities of the heavenly bodies. The astronomers assumed the motion of the planets and attempted no explanation of why they moved; this was the task of philosophers. Even Copernicus did not attempt to explain why the planets moved as they do; he merely assumed that this was their nature.

Descartes, however, believed that a completely mechanical explanation of the universe was possible, and he sought a physical cause to keep the heavenly bodies in motion. This cause he found in vortices, a subtle material fluid which whirled around carrying the heavier bodies with it.[89] The Cartesian vortices were proposed as a causal explanation of both terrestrial gravitation and celestial movement.[90] Johannes Kepler (1571–1630) discovered his three famous laws from the observational data amassed by Tycho Brahe; they are strictly empirical laws, in so far as one may call an astronomical law empirical. Nevertheless, he tried to find some physical force emanating from the sun which could supply the planet's motion in an elliptic path. In the introduction to his *Astronomia Nova* of 1609 Kepler proposes the hypothesis that the sun propagates into the depths of the universe a

[86] Cf. St. Thomas, *In I De caelo*, lect. 7, n. 6.

[87] Cf. St. Thomas, *In I De caelo*, lect. 4.

[88] Even in the thirteenth century there were some who dispensed with the need for angels to move the heavenly bodies and who explained this motion as "a natural inclination to move in circular motion." An *active* inclination toward such motion would dispense with a continual mover, as has been explained. Notably Robert Kilwardby, O.P., defends this position of *quidam* in his response to the forty-three questions sent by the master general, John of Vercelli, in 1271. Cf. text of q. 2, n. 3 from Bordeaux MS 131 published by M.-D. Chenu: "Aux origines de la 'science moderne,'" 211–12; also "Les réponses de S. Thomas et de Kilwardby à la consultation de Jean de Verceil," in *Mélanges Mandonnet* (Paris, 1930), I, 191–222. Fr. Daniel Callus, O.P., has pointed out that this idea can be traced to the earliest days of Aristotelianism in Oxford; some sixty years before Kilwardby, John Blund expounded the same doctrine in his unpublished *De anima*, collated by Fr. Callus. Cf. D. A. Callus, "The Treatise of John Blund On the Soul," in *Autour d'Aristote: Receuil d'Études de Philosophie Ancienne et Médiéval Offert à Monseigneur A. Mansion* (Louvain, 1955), pp. 471–95. This theory was not unknown in the fourteenth century, for Jean Buridan and Albert of Saxony defend it as a probability (cf. above, note 61). Likewise Copernicus tends to explain the circular movement of the earth and other planets by a natural inclination of the form; cf. *De Revolutionibus Orbium Caelestium*, Lib. I, cap. iv and viii, ed. Thorn, pp. 14–15, 21–24.

[89] Cf. Descartes, *Principia Philosophiae*, III, art. 53–157, *ed. cit.*, pp. 106–202.

[90] Cf. Letter LXI, *Oeuvres*, I, 314; Letter CLXXIX to Mersenne, *Oeuvres*, II, 635; *Prin. Phil.*, P. IV, art. 24, p. 214.

species immateriata of itself.[91] Giovanni Borelli (1608–1679) followed
Kepler in the view that the planets need a force emanating from the
sun to push them around in their orbits, and he added that it if were
not for this centrifugal force, the planets would fall into the sun by the
effect of gravity, which he described as a *natural instinct* in bodies to
fall towards the sun.[92] But all such attempts to find a physical cause
impelling the celestial bodies lacked astronomical verification, as they
arose mainly from a philosophical desire to unite all physical
phenomena in a mechanical explanation of movement.

The great triumph of Newton was that he reached the goal which
eluded his contemporaries. The cornerstone of his success was the
principle of inertia. Two concepts were very much to the fore during
the latter part of the sixteenth and early part of the seventeenth
centuries: the concepts of centrifugal force and attraction. Giambat-
tista Benedetti, Borelli, Descartes, Hooke, and Huygens had established at great length that the motion of a stone in a sling naturally
tends to move along the tangent to the circle described, so that it is the
tension in the cord, curbing this tangential motion, which keeps the
stone in the arc.[93] The notion of attraction had become popular with
the publication of Sir William Gilbert's *De Magnete* in 1600. It was
these two ideas that Newton united in his famous proof that the earth
attracts the moon in the inverse proportion of its distance, as was
required by Kepler's three laws.[94] Since the earth's circumference and
the distance of the moon were known, the orbital velocity of the moon
could easily be calculated on the basis of the lunar month. The problem was to find out how much the moon would fall were there no
centripetal force holding it in its orbit; or in other words, how much
force was needed to counteract the velocity of the moon. Newton
found that it would fall 15½ Paris feet per minute, which corre-
sponded to Huygens's figures for the movement of the pendulum.[95]

[91] *Opera Omnia Kepleri*, ed. Frisch, III, 156.
[92] Cf. A. Armitage, "Borelli's Hypothesis and the Rise of Celestial Mechanics," *Annals of Science* 6 (1948–50), 268–92. This article explains admirably the development of celestial mechanics up to Newton's formulation.
[93] Cf. A. Armitage, *art. cit.*, p. 275.
[94] Newton, *Principia Mathematica*, Bk. III, prop. IV, Theorem 4, ed. Cajori, pp. 407–9; for the derivation of the inverse square law from Kepler's third law, cf. Max Born, *Natural Philosophy of Cause and Chance* (Oxford, 1949), Appendix 2, p. 129.
[95] "And therefore the force by which the moon is retained in its orbit becomes, at the very surface of the earth, equal to the force which we observe in heavy bodies there. And therefore (by Rule 1 and 2) the force by which the moon is retained in its orbit is that very same force which we commonly call gravity." *Ibid.*, ed. Cajori, p. 408. Cf. also F. Cajori, *A History of Physics* (New York, 1916), pp. 56–62.

Thus Newton maintained that the attraction, varying inversely as the square of the distance, held good universally, allowing for minor discrepancies.

It is easy to see how important the principle of inertia is in this demonstration. Newton assumes that the moon does move; he assumes moreover that it would move at a constant rate at a tangent to the circle were it not for the attracting force. The point is to find two quantities which will equate: in this case it is the velocity of the moon and the rate of supposed fall. (The applicability of this equation to terrestrial gravitation establishes the universal law.) In every equation something must be considered irrelevant, that is, something must be assumed as not affecting the quantities. In the present case it is the actual movement of the moon or the observer. Newton assumes that the moon would move with uniform motion in a straight line, *so that motion does not have to be considered in the equation.* Once the quantities are obtained it is as though the bodies were at rest. In other words, the argument begins with considering the velocity (and mass, which is measured through acceleration), but once the quantities have been obtained it is no longer a question of the actual motion but only of the proportionality of these quantities. Thus it must be assumed that every body continues in its state of rest, or of uniform motion in a straight line, except so far as it may be compelled by force to change that state. That is to say, uniform motion, rest, and even actual movement can be considered null factors in the equation, for they do not affect the case. Only new quantities, such as those which change the velocity or direction, have meaning and so must be considered in devising an equation. Thus inertial motion, or an inertial system, is one in which certain factors are disregarded.

But at this point the question arises as to what is meant by uniform motion in a straight line. Does not this statement presuppose an absolute frame of reference in which it has meaning? But if all measurements of time and space are relative to the observer, who may or may not be moving in an inertial system, then there are factors which are not null but definite quantities which must enter into the equation. How are we to know that a certain system is inertial? In the Newtonian theory this may be answered in two ways: (i) it moves with uniform motion if it is not affected by external forces; or (ii) it is an actual fact that we can choose a series of coordinates with reference to which bodies at rest remain at rest and bodies in motion continue in uniform rectilinear motion. With regard to the first Einstein answers that "it involves an argument in a circle: a mass moves without acceleration if it is sufficiently far from other bodies; we know that it is sufficiently far from other bodies only by the fact that it moves without acceleration."[96] With regard to the second Einstein showed that there is no reason to give preference to an inertial system over one moving with accelerated motion.[97] By identifying inertial and gravitational mass and by showing how a field may be regarded as both inertial (uniform) and gravitational (accelerated), Einstein established his principle of equivalence, that is, a physical event described in an inertial system may be described equivalently in a non-inertial system. In formulating his general theory of relativity, Einstein carries the equivalence of systems to an extreme limit: "All Gaussian four-dimensional co-ordinate systems are equally applicable for formulating the general laws of Physics."[98] It is clear, then, as Sir Edmund Whittaker says, "What Einstein's theory really does is to abolish the old idea of gravitation altogether, and to replace it by *the idea of inertial frameworks.*"[99] In other words, although relativity physics disagrees as to what is inertial motion, that is, as to *what* may be regarded as a null factor, the ultimate agreement lies in the acceptance of something as irrelevant and null in the equating of quantities. It is this acknowledgment of the irrelevance, the nullity, of certain factors which constitutes the principle of inertia.

The basis for the principle of inertia lies, therefore, in the nature of mathematical abstraction. The mathematician must equate: a single quantity is of no use to him. In order to equate quantities he must assume the basic irrelevance or nullity of other factors, otherwise there can be no certainty in his equation. The factors which the mathematician considers irrelevant are, as we have seen, motion, rest, constancy, and unaltered directivity; it is only the *change* of these factors which has quantitative value. Thus for the physicist it is not motion and its continuation which need to be explained but change and cessation of motion—for only these have equational value. The principle of inertia which is necessitated by every equation must exclude the vitality of real existence, spontaneity, motion, and finality. In other words, the logical function of inertia in mathematical abstraction necessarily relinquishes the reality and spontaneity of nature.

To return to the question of spiritual movers, it is clear that the

---

[96] A. Einstein, *The Meaning of Relativity* (London, 1950), p. 57. Cf. also A. Eddington, *Space, Time, and Gravitation*, pp. 136–37.

[97] Cf. A. Einstein, *The Theory of Relativity*, 8th ed. (London, 1924), pp. 59–79; see also L. Silberstein, *The Theory of Relativity*, 2d ed. (London, 1924), pp. 294–312.

[98] E. Freundlich, *Einstein's Theory of Gravitation* (London, 1924), pp. 45–61; also essay by Prof. H. L. Brose, *ibid.*, p. 127.

[99] E. Whittaker, *From Euclid to Eddington* (Cambridge, 1949), p. 115. (Italics mine.)

principle of inertia has not done away with their need. It would be more accurate to say that mathematical physics is not concerned with who or what moves the heavenly bodies. A spiritual force moving the planets would be of no use to the mathematician, for he could never get two quantities to equate. But neither is it true to say that the principle of inertia has done away with their need. In the early part of the seventeenth century physicists tried to find a physical cause to explain the movement; Newton merely disregarded the question and looked for two quantities which could be equated. In Newtonian physics there is no question of a cause, but only of differential equations which are consistent and useful in describing phenomena.[100]

From what has been said it is clear that the principle of inertia, the foundation of mathematical physics, is neither self-evident nor demonstrable in any way. The logical basis of the principle lies in the nature of mathematical abstraction, which must leave out of consideration the qualitative and causal content of nature. That is to say, mathematical physics can never attain the ultimate reality of "nature," its spontaneity and intentionality, its qualitative characteristics and causal dependencies—all of which are given in human experience. Furthermore, since mathematical physics abstracts from all these factors, it can say nothing about them; it can neither affirm nor deny their reality, although a mathematician can be led to believe in a reality wider than his abstractions. If, therefore, the concept of nature, as expounded, is justified in human experience, so too is the distinction between natural and compulsory movement. Since these realities are of no use to the mathematician as such, he must reduce whatever he can to the common factor of quantity. But to the natural philosopher, who embraces the *whole* of human experience, the distinction between natural and compulsory motion is of utmost importance. The two pictures of the universe afforded by mathematical abstraction and philosophical experience, far from being incompatible, are the necessary binoculars of physical knowledge.

---

[100] "When we say force is the cause of motion, we are talking metaphysics; and this definition, if we had to be content with it, would be absolutely fruitless, would lead to absolutely nothing. For a definition to be of any use [in mathematical physics] it must tell us how to measure force." H. Poincaré, *Science and Hypothesis*, p. 98.

III

GALILEO AND THE
PRINCIPLE OF INERTIA

For close to three centuries undergraduates have been introduced to physics by being told in brief how Galileo almost single-handed overturned the antiquated Aristotelian view of the universe and established the principles of modern science. The very first principle, the beginner is told, is the principle or the "law" of inertia. This principle, being the most fundamental, the most universal, and the most certain law in the whole of modern science, ought to be memorized in the immortal words of Isaac Newton: "Every body perseveres in its state of rest or of uniform motion in a straight line, unless it is compelled to change that state by forces impressed upon it."[1] This law, as Whitehead put it, "is the first article of the creed of science, and like the Church's creed it is more than a mere statement of belief, it is a paean of triumph over defeated heretics."[2] The defeated heretics, Whitehead explained, are "the Aristotelians who for two thousand years imposed on dynamics the search for a physical cause of motion."[3]

Being the very first article of the creed of science, the principle of inertia cannot possibly be proved. Not only can it not be proved, but it must be accepted on faith. It is, in fact, contrary to everything the student has ever experienced. The only kinds of motion in a straight line the student has experienced are the rising and falling of bodies, and these are neither uniform nor perpetual, while the only motions

[1] "Corpus omne perseverare in statu suo quiescendi vel movendi uniformiter in directum, nisi quatenus illud a viribus impressis cogitur statum suum mutare." Isaac S. Newton, *Philosophiae Naturalis Principia Mathematica*, Lex I. The first edition of this work was printed in London in 1687; modern English trans. of the second edition (from Latin here cited, London, 1713) by F. Cajori (Berkeley, 1947). For background of the three editions, see I. Bernard Cohen, *Introduction to Newton's 'Principia'* (Cambridge, Mass., 1971).

[2] A. N. Whitehead, *Essays in Science and Philosophy* (New York, 1968), pp. 234–35.

[3] *Ibid.*, p. 235.

that might be uniform and perpetual are celestial, but these are not in a straight line. The student, however, is told to have faith, memorize the first law of motion, and learn to see how it must be the foundation for the second and third laws of motion; these latter have tremendous ramifications and can be tested in countless ways. Then at last he will have to concede that the first law of motion is indeed true or, at least, holds "as though it were true," and about this there can be no doubt. Whitehead was indeed correct when he called the law of inertia "the first article of the creed of science," for it must be believed on faith in science. It is the glory of the seventeenth century to have discovered this law, hidden from ages past.

It is always the prerogative of the victors to write the history of the struggle, and to rewrite the history of the heretics. This, no doubt, has many advantages. For one, it simplifies the story and shows the inevitability of the outcome. But we must remember that the victors of the scientific revolution in the seventeenth century were not Galileans, or even Cartesians, but Newtonians. That is, the Newtonian victors see Copernicus, Galileo, and even Kepler as so many preludes to Newton or as the first light of the scientific revolution, much as Protestants see (or used to see) Wycliff as the morning star of the Reformation. Then, too, we must remember that this revolution in science came upon the heels of a deeper reformation in religion. While this sequence, no doubt, had nothing to do with the triumph of "modern science," it has a great deal to do with the historians of that scientific conflict.

In this paper I wish to focus attention on the so-called principle of inertia and its antecedents, particularly in respect to Galileo's *Dialogue concerning the Two Great Systems of the World* (1632) and to a lesser extent his *Discourses on the Two New Sciences* (1638).

The historical question, as Stillman Drake puts it, is "whether and to what extent Galileo is entitled to credit for the anticipation of Newton's first law of motion."[4] Drake and just about everyone else would concede that "technical priority for the first complete statement of the law of inertia belongs to Descartes, who published it in 1644, two years after Galileo's death, supported by a philosophical argument." Drake, of course, rejects the philosophical argument proposed by Descartes or anyone else. On the other hand, Alexandre Koyré insists that it was Pierre Gassendi who "won for himself the everlasting glory of having been the first to publish—if not the first to

---

[4]Stillman Drake, *Galileo Studies* (Ann Arbor, 1970), p. 241, revised from "Galileo and the Law of Inertia," *American Journal of Physics* 32 (1964), 601–18.

state—a correct formulation of the principle of inertia."[5] Then, too, since the work of I. Bernard Cohen, no one today would press the prior use by Kepler of the term "inertia" or *vis inertiae* in this context, since we know that Newton explicitly rejected Kepler's concept of inertia and intended something quite different.[6] In other words, historians of science today fully appreciate the role of Descartes in the formation of Newton's ideas and credit him, however differently intended, with the actual wording of the law.[7] But the battle still goes on among historians of science as to how much Galileo himself anticipated the concept behind the words of Gassendi, Descartes, and Newton. The actual question, as we shall see, is really much larger than what Stillman Drake might have had in mind when he formulated the historical question as he did. It really has to do with the so-called precursors of Galileo and the controversy initiated by Pierre Duhem at the turn of this century.

In this paper I would like to do two things. The first is to consider, however briefly, six modern historians of science in chronological order concerning Galileo and the principle of inertia. The six historians I wish to consider are William Whewell, Ernst Mach, Pierre Duhem, Alexandre Koyré, Anneliese Maier, and Stillman Drake. This is not difficult and it is most illuminating. The second is more difficult: I would like to cut through some of the more common misconceptions of most historians and present what might be a more modest view of the matter.

I

William Whewell (1794–1866)

The Reverend William Whewell, an Anglican clergyman ordained during the reign of George IV (1826), doctor of divinity, and master of Trinity College, Cambridge, for twenty-five years before his death in 1866, was one of the first historians of modern science, at least in the English language. A most remarkable scientist in his own right, he reformed education in science and mathematics and contributed substantially to the terminology as well as to the theory of science; an exceptional linguist, notably in Greek and German, he wrote a history

[5] Alexandre Koyré, *Galileo Studies*, trans. John Mepham (Atlantic Highlands, New Jersey, 1978), pp. 244–45; cf. note 21 on p. 270.
[6] See I. B. Cohen, *Introduction to Newton's 'Principia,'* pp. 27–29; *Newton and Kepler* (London, 1971), and elsewhere.
[7] I. B. Cohen, *Introduction*, p. 28, note 4.

of science and later a philosophy of science that influenced a century of undergraduates. For thirty years Whewell worked on a three-volume *History of the Inductive Sciences from the Earliest to the Present Time*, which first appeared in 1837, dedicated to Sir John Herschel. No less a man than A. N. Whitehead was brought up on Whewell's *History* in its third edition.

Within the three-volume *History*, Whewell devoted less than 130 pages to the period of "first awakening" of science among the Greeks, from the pre-Socratics to Ptolemy and the Arabs. It should come as no surprise that he devoted less than 70 pages to the Middle Ages, the period of "its midday slumber."[8] After this "stationary period" of dogmatism and mysticism, Whewell begins to see light in the new humanism of the Renaissance and the Copernican prelude to the age of Galileo. For Whewell, the passage from Greek antiquity to the new age of science was "a passage from astronomy to mechanics, a transition from the *formal* to the *physical* causes; from time and space to force and matter; from phenomena to causes"—or, as we might say, from kinematics to dynamics.[9] Thus "if the Greeks had not cultivated conic sections, Kepler could not have superseded Ptolemy; [and] if the Greeks had cultivated dynamics, Kepler might have anticipated Newton."[10]

Whewell devoted twelve pages to the earliest attempts to discover "the first law of motion."[11] Here the stage is set with Aristotle's disastrous division of motions into "natural" and "violent." "But the most common mistake of this period [before Newton] was, that of supposing that as force is requisite to move a body, so a perpetual supply of force is requisite to keep it in motion."[12] For this reason Johannes Kepler sought in vain for physical forces from the sun to keep the planets in motion, and Descartes looked to his vortices, just as Aristotle had to look to the air to keep the projectile in motion. Even Galileo was slow to see "that the distinction of natural and violent motions was altogether untenable; [and] that the velocity of a body in motion increased or diminished [solely] in consequence of the action of extrinsic causes," and not as the consequence of motion itself or the

---

[8] William Whewell, *History of the Inductive Sciences from the Earliest to the Present Time*, 3d ed. (New York, 1875), 1:50.

[9] "Dynamics," for Whewell, is the science which treats of the motion of bodies; "statics" is the science which treats of the pressure of bodies which are in equilibrium, and therefore at rest. See *ibid.*, 1:311, note.

[10] *Ibid.*, 1:311.

[11] *Ibid.*, 1:319–30.

[12] *Ibid.*, 1:320.

nature of the body.[13] That is to say, without the action of extrinsic causes, the motion of all bodies would go on forever in a straight line with uniform velocity.

Whewell was reluctant to say who first announced this law of motion in a general form. But he is certain that Galileo asserted the true law only in his 1638 *Discourses on the Two New Sciences* (which, he admitted, may have been written earlier), and then only when he treated of projectiles. The crucial passage for Whewell comes on the Fourth Day when Whewell quotes Salviati as saying: "Conceive a movable body upon a horizontal plane, and suppose all obstacles to motion be removed; it is then manifest, from what has been said . . . that the body's motion will be uniform and perpetual upon the plane, if the plane is infinitely extended."[14]

The upshot of all this is that, according to Whewell, Galileo only slowly and intermittently perceived the law of inertia and expressed it clearly only in the *Discorsi* of 1638 in the context of projectile motion, when he dispensed with a cause to keep the body in motion.[15] One hundred years later A. N. Whitehead was sufficiently moved by Whewell to insist that the principle of inertia was already implied in Galileo's *Dialogo* of 1632 when he explained why loose things on earth are not left behind as the earth moves.[16] Similarly Stillman Drake rallies to the defense of Galileo at this precise point, when he expresses exasperation and impatience over Ernst Mach's attempt to find the law in the writings of Galileo.[17]

Ernst Mach (1838–1916)

Ernst Mach once said, "One can never lose one's footing, or come into collision with facts, if one always keeps in view the path by which

---

[13] *Ibid.*, 1:322.

[14] *Ibid.*, 1:323; cf. trans. by Crew and de Salvio: "Imagine any particle projected along a horizontal plane without friction; then we know, from what has been more fully explained in the preceding pages, that this particle will move along this same plane with a motion, which is uniform and perpetual, provided the plane has no limits." Galileo, *Dialogues concerning Two New Sciences* (New York, 1954), p. 244.

[15] Whewell, *History* 1:322. Whewell's principal biographer admits that "his assessment of the importance of contributions of such major figures as Galileo and Descartes suffers from a heavy intrusion of religious and philosophical biases." R. E. Butts, *Dictionary of Scientific Biography* (New York, 1973), 10:293b.

[16] "It has been stated by Whewell that in his *Dialogues on the Two Principal Systems of the World* Galileo does not enunciate the first law of motion, and that it only appears in his subsequent *Dialogues on Mechanics*. This may be formally true so far as a neat decisive statement is concerned. But in essence the first law of motion is presupposed in the argumentation of the earlier dialogues. The whole explanation why loose things are not left behind as the Earth moves depends upon it." A. N. Whitehead, *Essays*, p. 235.

[17] S. Drake, "Galileo and the Concept of Inertia," *Galileo Studies*, pp. 241–42.

one has come."[18] For more than thirty years, Ernst Mach labored over the seven editions of his ponderous *Science of Mechanics* after its first appearance at Prague in 1883. His dense account of Galileo's search for the principle of inertia has frustrated more than one reader, but his point seems to be that "Galileo discovered the so-called law of inertia quite incidentally," and even then it played no prominent part in his thought.[19] Agreeing with the pioneer work of his contemporary Emil Wohlwill concerning Galileo and the Curia,[20] Mach argued that "the predecessors and contemporaries of Galileo, nay, even Galileo himself, only very gradually abandoned the Aristotelian conceptions for the acceptance of the law of inertia,"[21] and even then Galileo always gave preferential treatment to the uniformity and perpetuity of circular motion.

For Mach the crucial insight came to Galileo when he chanced to combine two important images: the acceleration of a falling body, and an ideal body rolling uniformly *ad infinitum* along a horizontal plane. Thus in the absence of a new force, a moving body "preserves its direction and velocity unaltered,"[22] while in the presence of a force the state of a body is altered. Both Ernst Mach and Emil Wohlwill were unwilling to grant that Galileo had a clear and distinct conception of the law of inertia from the beginning of his search. Stillman Drake, on the other hand, insists that from the beginning "Galileo was in possession of the law of inertia," even though he did not provide a clear and complete statement of it.[23]

What all of these historians are agreed upon is that Galileo had no real precursors for his perception of the law, regardless of when he perceived it. It fell to a young Frenchman at the turn of this century to discover "les précurseurs parisiens de Galilée." This man was Pierre Duhem.

Pierre Duhem (1861–1916)

A born historian and philosopher of science, Pierre Duhem prided himself in being first and foremost Professor of Theoretical Physics at

[18] E. Mach, *History and Root of the Principle of the Conservation of Energy*, trans. P. Jourdain (Chicago, 1911), p. 17.
[19] E. Mach, *The Science of Mechanics: A Critical and Historical Account of Its Development*, trans. Thomas J. McCormack, 6th ed. (Chicago, 1960), p. 171.
[20] See *ibid.*, pp. 155, 169.
[21] *Ibid.*, p. 169.
[22] *Ibid.*, p. 171. While Mach agreed that Galileo had some presentiment of the principle of inertia and even formulated it in part on certain occasions, he insisted that Galileo always gave preferential treatment to the uniformity and perpetuity of circular motion, and was thus handicapped from start to finish.
[23] S. Drake, "Galileo and the Concept of Inertia," p. 241.

the University of Bordeaux for more than 20 years before his untimely death of a heart attack in 1916, at the age of 55. He was then working on a monumental *Le système du monde*, a history of cosmological systems from the pre-Socratics to Copernicus in twelve volumes. Duhem completed ten of the volumes before his death, the first five being published by him and the remaining five by his daughter in the 1950s.

While working on *L'évolution de la méchanique* (1903), the first of his many works on the history of science, Duhem suspected that Leonardo da Vinci might have had some influence on Galileo's notion of *impeto* and projectile motion.[24] Consequently he undertook serious study of Leonardo and his sources over the next ten years. By the time his third volume of *Études sur Léonard de Vinci* appeared in 1913, he was fully convinced that Jean Buridan and his disciples in early fourteenth-century Paris were the true "precursors of Galileo" inasmuch as they developed a doctrine of *impetus* to explain continued motion of projectiles contrary to Aristotle.[25]

As Duhem interpreted the medieval scene, Aristotle distinguished between natural and violent motions and in both cases required the continued causality of a mover to account for motion. In the case of natural motions, it was the nature of the body itself. In the case of violent motion, as when a projectile is hurled in the air, it must be the air that forces the body along. But, as Duhem explained to his readers, Aristotle noted two possible views: one of ἀντιπερίστασις, which claimed that the forced air in front of the projectile moves behind to fill the vacancy; the other his own, which gave to the medium, such as air, the power to move and carry the projectile along until that power is exhausted.[26]

For Duhem, it was the Parisian master Jean Buridan who in the early fourteenth century proposed an entirely new theory, whereby an *impetus* is given not to the air but to the projectile itself, causing it to move, though separated from the thrower, until overcome by contrary forces. This un-Aristotelian theory of *impetus*, according to Duhem, was accepted by Buridan's disciples Albert of Saxony (founder of the University of Vienna), Marsilius of Inghen (first rector of

---

[24] See P. Duhem, *The Evolution of Mechanics*, trans. Michael Cole, introd. by editor G. Æ. Oravas (Alphen aan den Rijn, 1980), pp. ix–xxxiii. See also W. A. Wallace, *Prelude to Galileo: Essays on Medieval and Sixteenth-Century Sources of Galileo's Thought* (Dordrecht and Boston, 1981), esp. "Pierre Duhem: Galileo and the Science of Motion," pp. 303–19.

[25] Vol. 3 of *Études sur Léonard de Vinci* (Paris, 1913) was subtitled "Les Précurseurs parisiens de Galilée."

[26] P. Duhem, *Études*, 3.

the University of Heidelberg), and Nicole Oresme (the most illustrious of Buridan's disciples and bishop of Lisieux). These fourteenth-century Parisians, according to Duhem, were known to Galileo, who twice referred to them as *Doctores Parisienses* in his early writings,[27] which Favaro entitled *Juvenilia*.[28] Duhem realized that John Philoponus in the sixth century had a similar view, but he was unknown to Buridan. Moreover it was Buridan who suggested that God could have given such an *impetus* to celestial bodies at the beginning of time, and Oresme who first used *impetus* to explain acceleration of falling bodies and even worked out the rate of speed proportioned to the distance covered. In fact, according to Duhem, Oresme worked out a pre-Cartesian coordinate system for plotting the distance and time of uniformly difform motion. These Parisian masters, therefore, were the direct influences on Galileo and other seventeenth-century pioneers of modern science.[29]

With the discovery of these "precursors of Galileo" Duhem turned his attention to writing a complete history of cosmological systems from the pre-Socratics to Copernicus according to his own theory of physical science, which was basically a "saving of the appearances," in the tradition of Plato, Simplicius, Osiander, and Poincaré.[30] Despite his early death at the age of 55 in 1916 and his exclusion from the power circles of Paris, Duhem created an entirely new field of investigation, called the history of medieval science. This new area of study is now recognized in almost every center of learning in the Western world, even though Duhem's central thesis was far from welcome among his contemporaries or our own.

One of the first to reject the search for predecessors was Antonio Favaro, the learned editor of the complete works of Galileo sponsored

[27] On this see William A. Wallace, "Galileo and the *Doctores Parisienses*," in *Prelude to Galileo*, pp. 192–252, revised and enlarged with appendix from earlier version in *New Perspectives on Galileo*, ed. R. E. Butts and J. C. Pitt (Dordrecht and Boston, 1978), pp. 87–138.

[28] *Le Opere di Galileo Galilei*, ed. Antonio Favaro, 20 vols. in 21 (Florence, 1890–1909; repr. 1968), vol. 1, pp. 15–177 (= *Juvenilia*).

[29] Duhem even suggested the volume from which Galileo had extracted his information about the *Doctores Parisienses*, namely, the collection of works edited by George Lokert, publ. at Paris in 1516, and again in 1518. Duhem, *Études*, 3:583.

[30] P. Duhem, *To Save the Phenomena: An Essay on the Idea of Physical Theory from Plato to Galileo*, trans. E. Doland and C. Maschler (Chicago, 1969); originally appeared as five articles in the *Annales de philosophie chrétienne*, 1908. Duhem's historical studies, and not his Catholicism, served as a basis for his personal philosophy of science, which conceived all scientific theories as conventional constructs and approximations of the real world; it was somewhat similar to the *commodisme* of Henri Poincaré. See Duhem's *The Aim and Structure of Physical Theory*, trans. Philip P. Wiener (Princeton, 1954), and especially the foreword by Louis de Broglie.

by the Italian government (1890–1909). For Favaro, the search for any precursor was an appalling indignity to all fathers of modern science, especially to Galileo, Descartes, and Newton.[31] In this overall attack on Duhem's medievalism and continuity thesis, Favaro was not alone. In fact, he voiced the sentiments of most of his contemporaries around the time of the First World War. But an entirely new approach to the problem was suggested by Alexandre Koyré in the 1940s and 1950s.

Alexandre Koyré (1892–1964)

A Russian Jew, whose parents emigrated to Germany and then to Paris at the turn of this century, Alexandre Koyré was trained in philosophy. He became an apostle of Platonism, an authority on Hegelian phenomenology, Russian rationalism, and modern pantheism. In his shocking studies on Galileo, meticulously scholarly and surprisingly unorthodox, he maintained not only that Galileo never arrived at the idea of Newtonian inertia but that it was philosophically impossible for him to have done so. In his *Galileo Studies* (*Études galiléennes*), first published in Paris (1939/40) and translated into English in 1978, he concentrated on Galileo's law of falling bodies in relation to Newtonian inertia. Koyré had in mind not only the common opinion that Galileo understood the law of inertia, at least sometimes, but also Duhem's efforts to trace Galileo's antecedents back to the scholastic Aristotelians of the fourteenth century. For him, Galileo could not have been further from modern physics—which Koyré considered "the most distinctive triumph of European intelligence"[32]—than when he spoke of the finite cosmos.[33]

Koyré's thesis concerning the principle of inertia at the dawn of modern science can be summarized in three points:

1. The crux of the scientific revolution was the geometrization of physical quantity in the manner of Archimedes and the displacement of the finite Aristotelian universe with infinite geometrical space in the manner of Euclid and Plato. The first to understand this new conception fully was Isaac Newton, but Galileo and Descartes had their part to play in the drama.[34]

---

[31] A. Favaro, "Galileo Galilei e i Doctores Parisienses," *Rendiconti della R. Accademia dei Lincei* 27 (1918), 3–14; and his earlier review of Duhem's book, "Léonard da Vinci a-t-il exercé une influence sur Galilée et son école?" *Scientia* 20 (1916), 257–65.

[32] Charles Gillispie, "Koyré, Alexandre," *New Catholic Encyclopedia* (New York, 1974), 16:240b.

[33] See also A. Koyré, *From the Closed World to the Infinite Universe* (Baltimore and London, 1957), esp. pp. 88–109.

[34] See Charles C. Gillispie, "Koyré, Alexandre," in *Dictionary of Scientific Biography*

2. Galileo's geometrization of bodies, as early as 1604, disengaged falling bodies from Aristotelian "natures" and "proper places" and led to the law of uniform acceleration in falling bodies as proportional to elapsed time. But since Galileo's finite cosmos was bounded by circular motion, he could not have conceived uniform motion in a straight line *ad infinitum*, as is required for the law of inertia.

3. Descartes, unable ever to conceive correctly the law of falling bodies, understood perfectly the law of inertia as an indifference to rest or uniform motion in a straight line *ad infinitum* in Euclidean space, unless changed by forces impressed from without.

In other words, Koyré considered infinite space and uniform motion in a straight line to be essential to the Newtonian concept of inertia, which Galileo never attained. But Koyré granted to Galileo the fundamental ingredient of modern physics, namely, the concept of "motion," not as a *process* dependent on causes, but as a *state* (*status*), in itself indifferent to bodies and purpose, geometrically relative only to other bodies in space. As Charles Gillispie noted, in a single sentence found in one footnote in an early work of Koyré one can find an anticipation of his lifework: "All the disagreement between ancient and modern physics may be reduced to this: whereas for Aristotle, motion is necessarily an *action*, or more precisely an actualization (*actus entis in potentia inquantum est in potentia*), it became for Galileo as for Descartes a *state*."[35] Thus for Koyré, if there were to be any precursors for Galileo, they would have to be sought among the Platonists of old, not among Aristotelians of the Middle Ages.

It remained to Anneliese Maier, however, to reconsider Duhem's continuity thesis in detail and to take into consideration the novel position of Koyré.

Anneliese Maier (1905–1971)

Anneliese Maier was a professional philosopher well trained at the University of Berlin in eighteenth-century German thought when she arrived in Rome in 1936, in search of unpublished letters of Leibniz, then being collected for publication by the Prussian Academy of Science. A young woman around 30, she found not only letters but a new career and a home, for all practical purposes, in the Vatican Library

---

7:482b–490, esp. 485b–487a.
    [35] A. Koyré, "Remarques sur les paradoxes de Zénon" (orig. German in *Jahrbuch für Phil. u. Phänomenologische Forschung*, 1922), trans. in *Études d'histoire de la pensée philosophique* (Paris, 1961), p. 30, note 1; see C. C. Gillispie, *Dictionary of Scientific Biography* 7:485b.

under the paternal eye of Msgr. Auguste Pelzer. After studying the philosophy of seventeenth-century science in *Die Mechanisierung des Weltbildes* (1938), she was encouraged to move into medieval science and examine the thesis of Pierre Duhem. From her earliest and most famous study, *Die Impetustheorie* (1940), to her last work on the subject, her views remained essentially unchanged; they only got clearer and stronger. They can perhaps be summarized in three propositions:

1. Galileo was the first to transform an untenable scholastic theory of impetus in *De Motu Antiquiora* (ca. 1590) into a metaphysically new concept of motion in the *Dialogo* (1632) that is logically equivalent to the law of inertia. Galileo accomplished this "years before Descartes formulated his law of conservation or Isaac Beeckman wrote his *Journal*."[36]

2. The late scholastic theory of *impetus*, according to which the imparted force would decrease to extinction, depends upon certain "absurdities of Aristotle," principally on *Omne quod movetur ab alio movetur:* "Every motion requires a particular mover that is connected with it and is its direct cause."[37]

3. The metaphysical difference between the two notions (scholastic vs. scientific) is that the medieval scholastics thought of "motion" as a *process* involving a mover and resistance, whereas Galileo and the moderns think of "motion" as a *state* (a *status*, in Newtonian language) needing no cause and no resistance.[38]

Miss Maier was particularly concerned not about the mathematical formulation of the law of inertia but about its metaphysical status as a principle involving an entirely new concept of "motion" discovered by Galileo as he developed his doctrine of projectile motion in the *Dialogue*, the Second Day. For her the novelty lies in Galileo's thinking of violent motion impressed on a projectile moving along a horizontal plane as no longer subject to intrinsic, automatic decrease either by itself (as for Francis de Marchia's *impetus*) or by contrary forces, such as *gravitas* (as for Buridan and his disciples). A perfectly smooth ball rolling along a frictionless, horizontal plane would have no natural tendency to move downward or upward or to stop. "Hence," Galileo says, "it necessarily follows that in the case of motion which neither

---

[36] A. Maier, "Galilei und die scholastische Impetustheorie," *Ausgehendes Mittelalter,* vol. 2 (Rome, 1967), pp. 465–90, trans. S. D. Sargent, *On the Threshold of Exact Science* (Philadelphia, 1982), p. 106.

[37] A. Maier, "'Ergebnisse' der spätscholastischen Naturphilosophie," *Scholastik* 35 (1960), 161–88, trans. by S. D. Sargent, *op. cit.*, p. 148.

[38] A. Maier, *ibid.*, trans. Sargent, pp. 157–63, etc.

approaches nor recedes from the center, the moving object experiences neither repulsion nor attraction; there is, consequently, no reason why the force impressed upon it should decrease."[39] The point is that "the precursors of Galileo in the fourteenth century" discovered by Duhem thought of the projectile as having "a power of moving" (vis movendi) impressed upon it by the thrower, but a power that would be overcome by contrary forces such as "gravity," "obstacles," or just plain "fatigue" (fatigabilitas). For Galileo and the moderns, on the other hand, a quantity of "motion" (impeto) once in the body is considered a fixed "state of being" that remains permanent until overcome by forces outside the body. Such a state of being is oblivious to its causes, finality in natural place, or the nature of the body. The state of "being in motion" simply is a fact and no questions are asked about how it got that way. For Miss Maier, the principal obstacle to such a modern conception was the Aristotelian notion of "motion" as a process (actus entis in potentia), needing to be preserved by a mover in actual contact (omne quod movetur ab alio movetur), so that when the mover stops, the motion stops as well. The rejection of Aristotle's axiom Omne quod movetur ab alio movetur was, for Anneliese Maier, the great achievement of the scientific revolution accomplished by Galileo in the Dialogo of 1632.

However much Anneliese Maier admired late medieval natural philosophy, and however much she thought fourteenth-century scholastics might have anticipated Galileo (if they had rejected Aristotle's "absurdities"), the fact is that, for all her pioneering work, she never found any precursors of Galileo.[40] For her, there never were any "Vorläufer Galileis im 14. Jahrhundert." They were too Aristotelian. They were too much attached to two fatal ideas: (i) the unnaturalness of impetus, meaning that it will wear off because of contrary natural forces, and (ii) the need for a continual mover for all motion, because "whatever is moved, is moved by another." Therefore the scholastics were incapable of perceiving the very first law of modern science.

Stillman Drake (1910–)

Understandably Stillman Drake is gratified with Miss Maier's rehabilitation of Galileo as the first light of modern science, although he

---

[39] Sargent's translation of Galileo's Italian in Maier, "Galilei und die scholastische Impetustheorie," p. 489, *On the Threshold of Exact Science*, p. 121.

[40] This is developed by Miss Maier especially in her " 'Ergebnisse' der spätscholastischen Naturphilosophie"; a full but faulty translation of this appeared in *Philosophy Today* 5 (1961), 92–107, under the title "Philosophy of Nature at the End of the Middle Ages," and was better, but only partly, translated by Sargent, *op. cit.*, pp. 144–70.

is uncomfortable with the "metaphysical" baggage this experimental-ist is expected to carry. For Drake, Miss Maier showed that Galileo had no precursors and that he reached the vision of inertia, at least im-plicitly, by his own genius. But she did not answer Koyré's basic claim that Galileo never allowed for the possibility of inertia in a straight line *ad infinitum*, since his was a finite universe bounded by celestial bodies moving with "circular inertia," that is, perpetual uniform mo-tion in a circle.

In various studies dealing with Galileo, "circular inertia," and the law of inertia, Drake maintains that Galileo was really condescending to his Aristotelian readers when he rhapsodized about circular motion and praised the perfection of circles over every other figure. For Drake these rhapsodies were simply a rhetorical device to win over unsuspecting readers filled with Aristotelian notions.[41] But Galileo's meticulous measurements of free-fall down various inclined planes, for Drake, is a real "demonstration" of the extrapolated conclusion that a body once moved along any horizontal plane, neutral to gravity or levity, would continue *ad infinitum* in a state of uniform motion.[42] Koyré simply misunderstood Galileo's rhetorical strategy in the *Dialogo* and created a myth about "circular inertia," which has nothing to do with Galileo at all.

More important for our purpose, Drake argues that Galileo's own conception of inertia originated in his youthful intuition of *motus neuter* as a motion that is neither "natural" nor "violent" but a real motion between the two tendencies, and one that can be preserved forever without change, even in a straight line.[43] Both the terminology and the concept of a neutral motion can be found in Galileo's *De Motu Antiquiora* (ca. 1590). This notion was more fully developed in Galileo's mature works and became what Drake calls "a restricted law of inertia."[44] For Drake there are two essential notions that constitute the law of inertia:

[41] See especially Drake's "Galileo and the Concept of Inertia" and "The Case against 'Circular Inertia,'" in *Galileo Studies*, pp. 240–78, and elsewhere.

[42] S. Drake, *Galileo at Work: His Scientific Biography* (Chicago, 1978), pp. 123–33.

[43] "Galileo's restricted inertial concept had its roots in *De motu*, though it had not been stated there in 1591. Rather Galileo at first had demonstrated only that a body sup-ported on a horizontal plane could in principle be set in motion by any force however small." Drake, *Galileo at Work*, p. 128.

[44] "Galileo formulated at most a restricted law of inertia, applicable only to terrestrial bodies. . . . Galileo's restricted law of inertia, applying only to heavy bodies near the surface of the earth, was in a sense all that was needed or justified in physics up to the time of Newton's discovery of the law of universal gravitation." S. Drake, *Galileo Studies*, p. 255.

1. a body's *indifference* to motion or to rest, as when Galileo writes to Mark Welser concerning sunspots in 1612: "To some movements [physical bodies] are *indifferent*, as are heavy bodies to horizontal motion, to which they have neither inclination . . . nor repugnance. And therefore, all external impediments being removed, a heavy body on a spherical surface concentric with the earth will be indifferent to rest or to movement toward any part of the horizon."[45]

2. a body's *continuance* in the state it is once given, as when Galileo writes in the same letter: "It will remain in that state in which it has once been placed; that is, *if placed in a state of rest*, it will *conserve that;* and *if placed in movement* toward the west, for example, it will *maintain itself in that movement.*"

This essential core of the inertial concept, explicitly conceived as *indifference* to motion or rest and *continuance* in the state it is once given, is, according to Drake, "original with Galileo," and "not derived from, or even compatible with, impetus theory, which assumed a natural tendency of every body to come to rest."[46] The association of these two concepts, far from being rooted in "rotary motion" or "circular inertia," was, in Drake's opinion, linked in Galileo's mind "by the unifying concept of 'neutral' motion which had first led him to an inertial principle."[47] Drake therefore concludes that Galileo always had "a restricted law of inertia" from his earliest days, and that the notion of "*ad infinitum* in a straight line" is not as essential to the law of inertia as Koyré would have it.

In this survey of historians of science from William Whewell to Stillman Drake, we have seen a great diversity of opinions concerning Galileo and the principle of inertia, presumed to be the cornerstone of modern physics. Everyone from Whewell to Drake agrees that Galileo, at least in some of his works, perceived some form of the inertial principle, at least implicitly. Even Koyré granted the case for "circular motion" while denying that Galileo could ever conceive of perpetual rectilinear motion in his closed world. Everyone except Pierre Duhem thought the idea was original with Galileo, and even he thought it was the un-Aristotelian scholastics of the fourteenth century who opened the way. In other words, all of these historians are unanimous in seeing a radical incompatibility between Aristotle's de-

---

[45] Letter of Galileo addressed to Welser, August 14, 1612, trans. S. Drake, *Discoveries and Opinions of Galileo* (New York, 1957), p. 113; also quoted in Drake, "Galileo and the Concept of Inertia," p. 251.

[46] *Ibid.*

[47] *Ibid.*

mand for causes of motion and Galileo's (and modern science's) rejection of efficient causes. From the philosophical point of view perhaps Anneliese Maier's statement of the problem is typical: Aristotle's principle "Everything that is moved, is moved by another" had to be rejected to allow for the modern principle of inertia. On this score even the two Catholic historians we have considered, Pierre Duhem and Anneliese Maier, agree with all the others that this principle must go: it is contrary to modern science!

II

To resolve this problem we must examine three philosophical issues: First, Aristotle's view of projectile motion; second, impetus among the scholastics; and finally Galileo's principle of inertia. In each of these our concern is principally with the efficient causality involved. We begin with Aristotle's presumed demand for an efficient cause to keep motion going.

Aristotle and Projectiles

There is little need to recall the popular conception or rather misconception of Aristotle's concept of motion. It is briefly expressed by A. C. Crombie when he reduces the whole medieval corpus of Aristotelian "mechanics" to

the principle that local motion, like other kinds of change, was a process by which potentiality towards motion was made actual. Such a process necessarily required the continued motion of a cause and when the cause ceased to operate, so did the effect. All moving bodies which are not alive thus received their motion from a mover distinct from themselves and the mover necessarily accompanied the body it moved.[48]

This popular view is more succinctly stated by E. J. Dijksterhuis when he presents what he thinks is Aristotle's view:

Every motion (*motus*) presupposes a mover (*motor*): *omne quod movetur ab alio movetur.* This *motor* must either be present in the *mobile* or in direct contact with it; *actio in distans* is excluded as inconceivable; a *motor* must always be a *motor conjunctus.*[49]

From this view it follows that (i) all substantial forms are movers, i.e., efficient causes of their own motion, (ii) projectiles are necessarily carried by the air or medium, and (iii) intelligences or God must

[48] A. C. Crombie, *From Augustine to Galileo* (London, 1957), p. 82; also p. 244.
[49] E. J. Dijksterhuis, *The Mechanization of the World Picture*, trans. by C. Dikshoorn (Oxford, 1961), p. 24.

produce the rotation of the spheres. Why the third conclusion must follow is never explained, but that is not our present concern.

My concern here is only secondarily with the first conclusion: All substantial forms or "natures" are efficient causes of their own motion. This understanding of Aristotle is really not Aristotle's but Avicenna's.[50] If all substantial forms were the efficient cause of their own motion, what would be the difference between living and nonliving things? Animals are defined as living things that move themselves. When Aristotle defines "nature" as "the *principle* and *cause* of motion and rest, etc." (*Phys.* II, 1, 192b21–23), he clearly means that every "nature" is at least a *principle* (ἀρχή), but it can also be a *cause* (αἰτία), as in animals that move themselves by parts, as in running, flying, swimming, and the like. In all other cases, even in animals that move themselves, all other motions come from "nature" as from a *principle*, a source, of motion, as falling down, floating, growing up, being alive with blood circulating, and possessing specific traits.

My principal concern in this paper is with Aristotle's explanation of how projectiles can continue to move after leaving the hand of the projector (*proiciens*). Invariably Aristotle discussed this problem as a type of "violent" or "compulsory" motion as opposed to "natural" motion, which is from "nature."[51] Clearly activities (*motus*) can be related to "nature" in various ways: according to nature (*secundum naturam*), above nature (*super naturam*, e.g., grace), outside nature (*extra naturam*), beyond nature (*supra naturam*, e.g., miracles), incidental to nature (*praeter naturam*), incidental to the intention of nature (*praeter intentionem naturae*), or finally against or contrary to nature (*contra naturam*). The peculiarity of "violent" motion is that it is imposed upon the patient, *nil conferente vim passo* (*Eth. Nic.* III, 1, 1110a2–3). Obviously if a motion is imposed contrary to the inclination of that nature, it must be "from another" (*ab alio*).

In *Physics* VIII, 4, discussing whether everything that is moved is moved by another, Aristotle lists violent motion as the clearest case where all such motions are "from another." By definition they are imposed from without. The second case for Aristotle is self-movers (animals which move themselves), where we can see one part, an arm or a leg, moved "by another." For Aristotle, such animals are very

[50] See my "Aristotle's Concept of Nature: Avicenna and Aquinas," in *Approaches to Nature in the Middle Ages*, ed. L. D. Roberts (Binghamton, 1982), pp. 137–60; also Chapter V below.

[51] Aristotle, *Physics* IV, 8, 215a1–18; VIII, 10, 266b27–267a22; *De caelo* III, 2, 301b17–33. For further discussion of this see Chapter II above.

different from living plants or animals that do not move themselves but cling to other things. Finally, there are all those other movements that are neither violent nor animate of the self-moving type; these are called "natural" because they are produced by "nature" without an apparent "mover." These, Aristotle says, "present the greatest difficulty" (254b33).

What is conspicuous about all of these "natural" motions of our experience is that they derive from "natures" that themselves must be brought into existence by substantial generation. Therefore, Aristotle argued, all natural motions, such as the falling of heavy bodies and the rising of light, flowing from natures that must themselves be generated "by another," must be credited to the "generator" (*generans*) of that nature. Obviously some "nature" may be prevented by some obstacle from doing what it is supposed to do "naturally"; one who removes such an obstacle (*removens prohibens*) would be no more than a "mover" accidentally (*per accidens*). The real "mover" *per se* responsible for the natural downward movement would be none other than the *per se generans*. It is entirely in this sense that Aristotle concluded that all motions, even "natural" ones, are "from another" (*ab alio*).

Aristotle's view is most clearly stated by St. Thomas when he says:

> In heavy and light bodies there is a formal principle [*principium formale*] of their movement, because just as other accidents are consequent upon the substantial form, so also is place [*locus*] and consequently motion to place [*moveri ad locum*], not however such that the natural form is the mover [*motor*], but the *motor* is the *generans* which gave such a form upon which such motion follows.[52]

To put the matter most simply, in *Physics* VIII, 4, Aristotle established the principle *Omne quod movetur ab alio movetur* by induction from the three types of movement found in nature: forced, animate, and natural. (i) Forced motions are clearly imposed from outside the body, *ab alio*. (ii) Animate local motions arise from within only when one part is moved by another, *ab alio*. (iii) Natural motions spring spontaneously and inevitably from the "nature" that is generated by another (*ab alio*), unless it is impeded by some obstacle. Therefore the *per se* efficient cause of the body having that "nature" is the *per se* cause of the motions that necessarily follow upon it. There is no such thing

---

[52] St. Thomas, *In II Phys.*, lect. 1, n. 4: "In corporibus vero gravibus et levibus est principium formale sui motus, quia sicut alia accidentia consequuntur formam substantialem, ita et locus, et per consequens moveri ad locum; non tamen ita quod forma naturalis sit motor, sed motor est generans, quod dat talem formam, ad quam talis motus consequitur." Cf. *In VIII Phys.*, lect. 8, n. 7.

as a conjoined "mover" to account for the downward fall of a heavy body.[53]

Since the movement of the projectile is, by definition, "violent," it must be *ab alio* all the way. After it leaves the hand of the thrower (*proiciens*), it requires "the continued motion of a cause" not because it is a "process" but because it is "violent," and therefore *ab alio*. Aristotle designated the intermediate air as the cause of the continued motion of the projectile because it is the only thing around, as far as he could see, that could serve as a mover in contact.

In discussing this problem Aristotle noted two views: the view called ἀντιπερίστασις, or mutual replacement of air, often attributed to Plato (*Ti.* 59A), and his own. Both views agree that the projectile's motion is "violent" and therefore imposed *ab alio*, the projectile itself contributing nothing. They differ in that the former credits the principal agent with giving only "motion" (*moveri*) to the intermediate medium, whereas Aristotle would have the agent give both "motion" (*moveri*) and "the power to move" (*posse movere* or *potentia movendi*) to the medium.[54] That is, Aristotle would make the medium a "mover" as well as "moved" (*movens motum*) rather than just something moved (*moveri*). His objection to ἀντιπερίστασις is that if only *moveri* were given to the medium, then it would cease when the agent stops, whereas in Aristotle's own view the agent gives the "power to cause motion" to the medium so that the projectile is "moved by another" (*movetur ab alio*), an intermediary, until "the preceding [part of air] transmits to the [next] no power to cause motion but only causes it to be in motion" (267a10–11). In either view, however, violent motion would be impossible in a void, since there would be no medium to transmit the mover's action.[55]

Impetus and the Scholastics

What Pierre Duhem thought was a simple, unanimous opinion of "impetus" in the fourteenth century, turns out after the research of Anneliese Maier to be multiple and complex. For our purpose the consideration of three different views will suffice: those of Francis de Marchia, Jean Buridan, and Domingo de Soto.

---

[53] See Chapter V below. Note that in Latin the immediate, proper act of every *ens mobile* is always expressed in the passive voice, viz., *moveri*. The active voice, *movere*, is always transitive and requires an object distinct from itself that is moved (*motum ab alio*).

[54] See Arist., *Phys.* IV, 8, 215a14–19; VIII, 10, 267a3–21; *An. post.* II, 15, 98a25–28. St. Thomas, *In VIII Phys.*, lect. 22, esp. nn. 3–4; *In II Post. Anal.*, lect. 17, n. 5.

[55] Arist., *Phys.* IV, 8, 215a14–19; see St. Thomas, *In IV Phys.*, lect. 11, n. 6. But if natural motion is possible in a void, as Thomas thinks, there is no reason why a projectile moved by "impetus" could not also move therein; see Chapter VI below.

Pierre Duhem did not know of Francis de Marchia, who apparently was the first scholastic to propose a theory of impetus in the Latin West. He was first noted by the Polish Vincentian Konstanty Michalski in 1927[56] and further discussed by Anneliese Maier in her now-famous *Die Impetustheorie* of 1940.[57] An Italian Franciscan theologian, he lectured on the *Sentences* at Paris along Scotist lines in the academic year 1319–20. Preliminary to discussing the causality of the sacraments in Book IV, he parenthetically raised the problem of projectile motion and argued on the basis of ordinary experience that the force (*vis*) required to continue motion must be in the projectile rather than in the medium of air. Such an impulse in the projectile, for him, was not motion itself but an unnatural, accidental quality productive of motion, a *virtus motiva* and *causa effectiva* of continued motion,[58] which lasted only for a time until eliminated. Many today follow Miss Maier in describing de Marchia's impetus as "self-expending" in contrast to Buridan's, which is gradually overcome by contrary forces, such as gravity.[59] In any case, this unnatural moving force was seen to be the true efficient cause of continued motion after the projectile left the hand of the thrower.

About twenty years later and apparently with no dependence on Francis de Marchia, Jean Buridan lectured on Aristotle at Paris in the Faculty of Arts. With no hesitation and from early on, he rejected Aristotle's view of projectile motion on the basis of common experience (*propter multas experientias*). He argued that the moving force, which he called *impetus*, had to be in the projectile itself and not in the medium. For him impetus was a qualitative power, a *virtus movens*,

---

[56] C. Michalski, "La physique nouvelle et les différents courants philosophiques au XIVe siècle" (1927), *Bulletin de l'Académie Polonaise des Sciences et des Lettres*, Classe d'histoire et de philosophie (Cracovie, 1928), 1–71; repr. *Opuscula Philosophica: La Philosophie au XIVe Siècle*, ed. Kurt Flasch (Frankfurt, 1969), pp. 207–77. On the career of Konstanty Michalski (1879–1947), see the obituary by Francesco Corvino in *Rivista Critica di Storia della Filosofia* 14 (1959), 206–20.

[57] A. Maier, *Die Impetustheorie*, in *Zwei Grundprobleme der scholastischen Naturphilosophie*, 3d ed. *Studien zur Naturphilosophie der Spätscholastik* (Rome, 1968), 2:113–314, and addenda, 360–93.

[58] Michalski quotes Francis de Marchia's Commentary on the *Sentences* IV, q. 1, in Paris MS, BN lat. 15852, fol. 168r (*op. cit.*, ed. Flasch, pp. 253–55); see text edited by A. Maier, *op. cit.*, pp. 166–80. De Marchia even claims this as one of the advantages of his theory over that of Averroes: "quoniam ponendo virtutem istam esse formaliter in lapide moto salvatur quod ipse lapis movetur aliquo modo per se, non per accidens ad motum aeris" (*ibid.*, p. 173.252–55).

[59] See Marshall Clagett, *The Science of Mechanics in the Middle Ages* (Madison, 1959), p. 520. Even Francis de Marchia speaks of impetus as a "virtus neutra non habens contrarium," so that one would not expect it to be overcome by contrary forces such as gravity, nature, resistance and the like. On this see Ernest A. Moody, "Galileo and Avempace," *Journal of the History of Ideas* 12 (1951), 392–94.

which was gradually overcome by the "nature" of the body, gravity and the like. It was the power to move the body attributed by Aristotle to the medium now transferred to the projectile as a *motor coniunctus*.[60] Nevertheless Buridan insisted that this force was "unnatural," "violent," and "foreign," violently imposed by an extrinsic cause, only to be overcome by the natural forces within the body and eventually eliminated.[61]

Thomists, however, had difficulty with impetus conceived as an "efficient cause," a *motor* within an inanimate body. John Capreolus, Domingo de Soto, John of St. Thomas, and many others had no difficulty in accepting impetus as a non-natural force within the projectile, but they could not accept impetus as an efficient cause, a *causa motiva*, a *motor*, moving the body as though the projectile were a self-mover, like a bird flying through the air.[62] For Capreolus (d. 1444) the one and only efficient cause of such motion is the thrower (*proiciens*); impetus can be no more than a "detached instrumental cause" of the thrower.[63] The Spanish Thomist Domingo de Soto (1494–1560) saw a clear analogy between the efficient causality of the *generans* producing "nature," whence comes "natural" motion, and the *proiciens* producing "impetus," whence comes "violent" motion. And just as "nature" in a heavy body is an innate *principle* of downward motion, and *not* an efficient cause, so "impetus" imposed on a body would be an alien, borrowed *principle* of upward motion, and *not* an efficient cause.[64] It

---

[60] Text of Buridan's *Physics* VIII, q. 12, ed. Maier, *loc. cit.*, pp. 207–14. Thus Buridan says: "ille impetus est *una qualitas innata movere corpus*, cui impressa est, sicut dicitur quod qualitas impressa ferro a magnete movet ferrum ad magnetem" (ed. Maier, p. 214.230–32); but throughout, Buridan conceives impetus as a *causa movens efficiens*.

[61] "Ad primam difficultatem potest dici, quod grave proiectum sursum bene movetur a principio intrinseco sibi inhaerente, et tamen dicitur moveri *violenter*, ex eo quod illud principium, scil. ille impetus, est *sibi violentus et innaturalis*, quia suae naturae formali *disconveniens et a principio extrinseco violenter impressus*, et quod *natura ipsius gravis inclinat ad motum oppositum* et *ad corruptionem* ipsius impetus" (ed. Maier, p. 213.196–202).

[62] See J. A. Weisheipl, "Natural and Compulsory Movement," *Nature and Gravitation*, pp. 43–44. J. Capreoli, *Defensiones theologiae d. Thomae*, Sent. II, dist. 6, q. 1, a. 3; Domingo de Soto, *Super octo libros Physicorum quaestiones* (Salamanca, 1551), Lib. VIII, q. 3; Joannis a S. Thoma, *Naturalis philosophiae* II, q. 23, aa. 1–2.

[63] See Johannis Capreoli, *Defensiones theologiae d. Thomae*, Sent. II, dist. 6, q. 1, a. 3 (ed. Paban and Pègues, Tours, 1902, pp. 397a–404a). Throughout this refutation of Gregory of Rimini Capreolus quotes Thomas at great length to show "quamvis forma naturalis sit principium motus, non tamen est motor" (Thomas, *In II Sent.*, dist. 14, q. 1, a. 3) by showing that natural bodies are not self-movers: "Et ideo quae moventur naturaliter, non movent seipsa: non enim grave movet se ipsum deorum; sed generans, quod dedit ei formam" (*Contra gentiles* II, c. 47). So likewise the projectile does not move itself, but is moved by the one who threw it.

[64] ". . . pro coperto reliquisse ex analogia gravium et levium, quae est prima ratio affirmandi huiusmodi impetum. Nempe quod sicut generans grave tribuit illi naturalem qualitatem, quae est gravitas, qua illud permovet usque ad centrum, sic et proi-

was this view of impetus that Capreolus and De Soto called "the opinion of St. Thomas."[65]

The Thomistic view has the double advantage of retaining the distinction between living and nonliving things in terms of causality and of preserving the distinction between "natural" and "violent" motions. The latter distinction is essential for Aristotelian physics, although it is inimical to the Newtonian concept of inertia, which abolishes such a distinction,[66] although Galileo himself acknowledged it.

Galileo and the Principle of Inertia

At the outset we should acknowledge that the beginnings of a new idea are never as clear as the final articulation and appreciation. One cannot expect Galileo's perception of inertia, for example in his letter of 1612, to have the same geometrical clarity as Descartes' *Principia Philosophiae* of 1644, or Newton's *Principia Mathematica Philosophiae Naturalis* of 1687 or 1713. Newton's *Principia* is thoroughly non-Aristotelian; Descartes' *Principia* is manifestly anti-Aristotelian; but Galileo's new principles were conceived in a context of Aristotelian naturalism. What I hope to show is that while the ultimate formulation of the principle of inertia in classical physics is Newtonian, its origins lay in the innocent concept of *motus neuter*, already noted by Stillman Drake.

At the term of this seventeenth-century development there is Newton's formulation, which should be kept firmly in mind: "Every body perseveres in its state of rest or of uniform motion in a straight line, unless it is compelled to change that state by forces impressed upon it."

In this formulation, it would seem, two original ideas are assumed and one ancient idea affirmed. First, a three-dimensional body (*corpus*) is conceived as a *corpus mathematicum* completely devoid of "nature" in the Aristotelian sense, or of anything that would affect the presence or absence of motion. Second, the state of moving uniformly in a straight line (*status movendi uniformiter in directum*) is conceived as

---

ciens impingat proiecto quo ipsum eminus moveat." Domingo de Soto, *Super octo libros Physicorum quaestiones* (Salamanca, 1551), Lib. VIII, q. 3, fol. 104v–105r.

[65] Capreolus, *ibid.;* de Soto, *ibid.,* fol. 103vff.

[66] Failing to understand this, Allan Franklin misunderstands Galileo: "Galileo's impetus does not contain the idea of motive force or a cause of motion that is included in the medieval view. . . . it is close to the idea of conservation of momentum and inertia, although as we shall see later Galileo does not arrive at a clear or correct statement of these principles." A. Franklin, *The Principle of Inertia in the Middle Ages* (Boulder, 1976), p. 54.

equivalent to the absence of motion, or equal to a state of rest (*status quiescendi*). Third, responsibility for any change of state (*nisi cogitur statum illum mutare*) is to be placed or found in outside forces impressed upon it (*a viribus impressis*).

These three concepts, it would seem, are essential for the formation of a new science of motion, a *nuova scienza del movimento*, notably the practical science of "mechanics." If such a science is to be founded on sound mathematical laws, identifiable quantities must be formulated in mathematical equations in which one side is equal to the other. The first presupposition of such a science is that $0 = 0$ and that anything new comes from without. Thus the "body" in question must be, to begin with, as nude as a mathematical body, devoid of all causal or quasi-causal factors. Moreover, if it is to be a mathematics of motion, some body in motion must be in a state equivalent to rest. This is possible only if a certain kind of motion, clearly specified, is taken as the equivalent of "no motion," or "zero." Newton sensibly took "moving uniformly in a straight line" as that kind of motion; he might have taken uniformly accelerated motion, as long as it was taken as zero. Since some such understanding must be taken as a point of equivalence, the Newtonian law of inertia is an inevitable fiction of imagination required for a mathematics of motion. The universality of the mechanics proposed determines the universality of the presupposition created for mathematics. As Newton proposed a universal mechanics, his first presupposition had to be universal: *omne corpus*. This was also true of Descartes, who proposed this principle as "the first law of nature." But Galileo originally suggested this idea in the limited mechanics of falling bodies and applied it to rotational motion.

Descartes the mathematician had no difficulty in thinking of the universe as a machine, created by God in the beginning with a fixed "quantity of matter" and a fixed "quantity of motion" (*quantitas motus*) that could only be transferred from one body to another by collision. Galileo, however, was too much the realist to think that real bodies are entirely devoid of "nature" or characteristics that would affect motion. Moreover, Galileo always acknowledged the difference between "natural" and "violent" motion; between these he recognized another kind of motion that was "neutral," neither violent nor natural. It was this kind of motion that Galileo expanded into his germinal notion of inertia.

Already in 1964 Stillman Drake argued (i) that Galileo really had a "restricted law of inertia," contrary to Koyré; (ii) that it had "nothing to do with the question of projectile motion," contrary to Duhem; and (iii) that he discovered it as early as 1590 in his novel concept of a motion that he called "neutral" (*motus neuter*).[67] In his unpublished treatise *De Motu Antiquiora* (ca. 1590) Galileo perceived what Drake calls "the essential core of the inertial concept": a body's indifference to motion and rest, and its continuance in the state it is once given.[68] This special kind of motion, according to Drake, between "natural" and "violent" was "Galileo's first essential step toward the concept of inertia."[69] But Drake goes on to say, "This idea is, to the best of my knowledge, original with Galileo."[70]

Actually the concept of intermediate or "neutral" motion comes up in Galileo's *Physical Questions* (*Juvenilia*), which are earlier than *De Motu*, when Galileo quotes St. Albert on the movement of fire in its natural place; since such a movement is neither "natural" nor "violent," it is a different kind of motion.[71] In *De Motu* Galileo spoke in this way of rotational movement around the center and even of a pinwheel with its upward and downward movements.[72] His more common use of this idea was in his work on inclined planes, where it applies to the case of a ball rolling along a plane perfectly horizontal to the earth, for such a movement is neither up nor down.[73] Drake

---

[67] S. Drake, "Galileo and the Law of Inertia," *American Journal of Physics* 32 (1964), 601–8; later expanded and revised as "Galileo and the Concept of Inertia," *Galileo Studies*, pp. 240–56. It is to the later edition that we refer.

[68] *Ibid.*, p. 251. Galileo: "On a perfectly horizontal surface, a ball would *remain indifferent and questioning between motion and rest*, so that any the least force would be sufficient to move it, just as any little resistance, even that of the surrounding air, would be capable of holding it still. From this we may take the following conclusion as an indubitable axiom: *That heavy bodies, all external and accidental impediments being removed, can be moved in the horizontal plane by any minimal force.*" *Galileo on Motion and on Mechanics*, trans. I. E. Drabkin and S. Drake (Madison, 1960), p. 171.

[69] *Ibid.*, p. 249. From his earliest writings Galileo presupposed Aristotle's division of motions into "natural" and "violent," defining them as follows: "There is natural motion when bodies, as they move, *approach* their *natural places*, and forced or violent motion when they *recede from* their *natural places.*" *Galileo on Motion and Mechanics*, p. 72. This defines only rectilinear motion; it was the intermediate kind that Galileo conceived as "neutral" (*neuter*) or "indifferent" (*indifferens*).

[70] Drake, *ibid.*, p. 251. Unfortunately for Drake this idea goes back to Albertus Magnus, at least, and to Mutio Vitelleschi and Ludovico Rugerio, at the latest. See William A. Wallace, *Galileo's Early Notebooks: The Physical Questions* (Notre Dame, 1977).

[71] The Latin passage from Galileo's *De Motu* is quoted by W. Wallace in his "Galileo and Albertus Magnus," repr. in *Prelude to Galileo*, p. 270. The Latin text of Albert referred to is his paraphrase *De caelo* I, tr. 1, cap. 4: ". . . quia nos videmus in molare molendini, quod habet duos *motus* accidentales; unum quidem, qui est ascendere sursum, et alterum, qui est revolvi circa centrum, quo tenetur super molarem inferiorem, et *ille videtur esse medius inter naturalem et illum qui est ascendere sursum*, quia circulari motu movetur ad inferiorem molarem et elevatur secundum aliquid ab ipso, quia aliter non contereretur grana" (ed. Colon. V/1:13.11–19). For the example of fire revolving around the top of a furnace, see *ibid.*, p. 13.2–6.

[72] See Drake, *Galileo Studies*, pp. 249–50; Wallace, *Prelude to Galileo*, pp. 313–14.

[73] *Galileo on Motion and Mechanics*, pp. 72, 171; see also note on p. 171. See also Drake, "Galileo and the Concept of Inertia," pp. 249–51.

thus sees the two essential ingredients of the inertial concept fully developed in Galileo's letter of August 14, 1612, to Mark Welser on sunspots:

All external impediments being removed, a heavy body on a spherical surface concentric with the earth will be *indifferent to rest or movement* toward any part of the horizon. And it will *remain in that state* in which it has once been placed; that is, if placed in a state of rest, it will conserve that; and if placed in movement toward the west, for example, it will maintain itself in that movement.[74]

While Drake would like to have the idea of indifferent or "neutral" motion originate with Galileo, the truth is that the passage referring to St. Albert (*De caelo* I, tr. 1, c. 4) was developed earlier by at least two professors at the Collegio Romano, Vitelleschi and Rugerius.[75] Since such a motion is neither according to nature nor against nature, it should more properly be called *praeter naturam*. The case of projectile motion was worked out by Galileo within the context of "natural" and "violent" motion, just as it was by earlier scholastics. It would seem that here Galileo merely took over the idea of *impeto*, as Duhem had suspected.

From this study of Galileo and the principle of inertia, it should be clear that the principle *Omne quod movetur ab alio movetur* has been misunderstood by most modern historians, including Anneliese Maier. What is at stake here is rather the concept of "nature," for if there is no "nature" there cannot be natural or violent motions; nor can there be an intermediate motion called "neutral," which Galileo always acknowledged. Galileo's concept of "neutral" motion must be universalized by extrapolation to create a mechanics of nature which is consistent with human experience.

It seems that there is a twofold continuity to be affirmed. First, there is a continuity between traditional Aristotelian physics and modern science which is greater than what Anneliese Maier and most other historians suspect. Second, the continuity between mathematical constructs (as in Ptolemaic and Copernican astronomy and modern physics) and Aristotelian realism is greater than Duhem and other philosophers of science would lead us to believe. If the principle of inertia is an inevitable hypothesis demanded by mathematical ab-

---

[74] Galileo, *Letter on Sunspots* (1613), trans. S. Drake, *Discoveries and Opinions of Galileo*, p. 113; see Drake's note 8, *ibid.*, pp. 113–14.
[75] On this see William A. Wallace, "Galileo and Scholastic Theories of Impetus," in *Studi sul XIV secolo in memoria di Anneliese Maier*, ed. A. Maierù and A. Paravicini Bagliani (Rome, 1981), pp. 275–97, esp. 292–95; repr. in *Prelude to Galileo*, pp. 320–40.

straction, as I propose here and elsewhere,[76] then it is a matter not simply of "saving the appearance" of reality but of devising the best human and practical means possible to understand the world of nature. In this Galileo was certainly a pioneer.

[76] Chapter II above. A paradigm of the relation between mathematical physics and philosophical physics today could very well be the classical relation between mathematical astronomy (e.g., Ptolemy's *Almagest*) and physical astronomy (e.g., Ptolemy's *Planetary Hypotheses*). Ptolemy, it would seem, saw not only compatibility but also a real continuity, though not identity, between these two branches. For him it was more than just "saving the appearances" or devising "constructs"; it was an attempt to understand this universe in some intelligent way, using all the best tools available. In the Middle Ages Albert the Great may not have known Ptolemy's *Planetary Hypotheses* directly, but somehow he knew its essentials, and always considered the astronomy of Ptolemy and Aristotle together to be more consistent with observation than the thoroughly concentric system of Al-Biṭrûjî, *De motibus celorum*, ed. F. J. Carmody (Berkeley, 1952); cf. B. R. Goldstein, *Al-Bitruji: On the Principles of Astronomy*, 2 vols. (New Haven, 1971). Albert's source might have been Jābir ibn Aflah, *Astronomia, libri IX* (ca. 1150), trans. into Latin by Gerard of Cremona; or possibly Ibn al-Haytham, *Liber de mundo et caelo*, translated in the thirteenth century. A good beginning has been made in this avenue of research by Betsey P. Buchwald, "The Astronomy of Albertus Magnus" (Ph.D. thesis, University of Toronto, 1983), esp. pp. 248–309.

IV

THE PRINCIPLE *OMNE QUOD MOVETUR AB ALIO MOVETUR* IN MEDIEVAL PHYSICS

The problem we wish to consider in this paper can be expressed very simply. The solution to the problem, however, is far from simple, both scientifically and historically. The problem is simply this: What is the meaning of the basic principle of medieval physics, *Omne quod movetur ab alio movetur,* literally, "Whatever is moved is moved by another"?[1]

The importance of this principle in medieval thought is most easily recalled in Aristotle's proof of a First Mover in the *Physics* and *Metaphysics,* and in St. Thomas's first proof for the existence of God in the *Summa theologiae, Summa contra gentiles,* and *Compendium theologiae.* Aquinas's first proof has been quoted, paraphrased, amplified and condensed, accepted and rejected, and even misunderstood so many times that we may sometimes feel uncertain as to what it really does mean. At the risk of quoting what is already well known, let us recall the argument from the *Summa theologiae:*

It is certain to the intellect and obvious to the senses that something is moved in this world. But whatever is moved is moved by another; for nothing is moved except insofar as it is capable of possessing the term to which it is moved, while a thing moves another inasmuch as it is actually effective. To move means to draw something from potentiality to actuality, and nothing can be drawn from potentiality to actuality except by something active; just as

---

[1] The meaning of this axiom was heatedly debated in the 1920s and 1930s in the context of its theological implications; see, for example, Johann Stufler, S.J., "Der hl. Thomas und das Axiom: Omne, quod movetur ab alio movetur," *Zeitschrift für katholische Theologie* 47 (1923), 369–90; Gallus M. Manser, O.P., *Das Wesen des Thomismus,* 2d ed. (Freiburg i. Schweiz, 1935), pp. 312–22, 549–71. It is clear that modern scholastics, while conceding the significance of the axiom, interpret it in a variety of ways, often diametrically opposed to one another. A diversity of medieval interpretations is now beginning to be appreciated; see Roy R. Effler, O.F.M., *John Duns Scotus and the Principle "Omne quod movetur ab alio movetur"* (St. Bonaventure, N.Y., 1962).

an actually hot body, like fire, makes wood, which is potentially hot, to be actually hot, thereby moving and changing it. It is not possible that a thing be both actual and potential possessor of the same term, but only of different terms; for what is actually hot cannot at the same time be potentially hot, although it can be potentially cold. Therefore it is impossible that anything be at the same time and in the same respect both mover and moved, or that it move itself. Thus whatever is moved is moved by something else. Consequently if that by which a thing is moved is itself moved, then it too must be moved by another, and that by another. But this cannot go on indefinitely, for then there would be no original mover, nor consequently any other mover, since dependent movers do not move except insofar as they have been moved by the original mover, even as a baton moves only because the hand moves it. Consequently one must arrive at some First Mover which in no way is moved; this all men understand to be God.[2]

In this presentation of the case a number of problems arise with regard to the principle *Omne quod movetur ab alio movetur.* The first problem is whether the principle is actually demonstrated or whether it is self-evident once the terms are understood, a principle *per se notum sapientibus* perhaps.[3]

In the passage quoted above, Aquinas shows the truth of the principle by explaining the terms *moveri* and *movere.* "To be moved" (*moveri*) is a passive capacity for someone else's action. "To move" (*movere*), on the other hand, is a transitive verb designating an agent's activity on a recipient. Thus the active voice *movere* signifies a movement, or change, precisely as produced by an agent, while the passive voice *moveri* signifies that same movement, or change, precisely as it is taking place in the recipient. As explained in Aristotle's *Physics* III, 3, the one reality of motion belongs to both agent and patient, but in different ways. Motion belongs to the recipient as an actuality existing in it, perfecting it, for it is the recipient which undergoes change. But the same motion belongs to the agent as the actuality produced by the agent, caused by it, for it is the agent which is responsible for the change. Thus the process of constructing a building belongs both to the builders and to the building, but it is the builders who *build* and the building which *is built.* Once the terms *moveri* and *movere* are

---

[2] *Sum. theol.* I, q. 2, a. 3.

[3] In Aristotelian thought there are various kinds of principles. The basic distinction between principles of being (or things) and principles of thought was frequently employed by Aristotle himself. Principles of thought include not only definitions but also true premises, of which some must be proved by prior principles, others are immediately evident, and still others are immediately evident and absolutely first. See *Posterior Analytics* I, 2. The schoolmen, following a suggestion of Boethius (*De hebdomadibus,* PL 64, 1311), distinguished between principles immediately evident to everyone (*omnibus*) and those immediately evident to experts learned in a discipline (*sapientibus,* or *doctis*). See St. Thomas, *In Boethium De hebdomadibus,* lect. 1; *In I Post. Anal.,* lect. 5, n. 7.

understood, then it is evident that "to be moved" cannot be the same as "to move," otherwise a thing would be moved and not moved at the same time under the same aspect. Thus if anything is to be moved at all, then it must be moved by something other than itself. That is, nothing can move itself. In other words, if "to be moved" is a passive capacity for someone else's action, then someone else must do the acting. This clarification of terms in St. Thomas's argument is essentially the same as Aristotle's procedure in *Physics* VIII, 5. Although Aquinas says that the proposition must be proved (*probanda*),[4] it would seem that a clarification of terms such as this is not necessarily a demonstration in the strict sense of the term.

Aristotle, however, justifies the principle *Omne quod movetur ab alio movetur* with two additional arguments, which might be called "proofs" in the wide sense. In *Physics* VIII, 4, he establishes it—to use the words of Aquinas and Albertus Magnus[5]—*per inductionem*. Aristotle shows that in all cases of violent motion, as when a discus is thrown or trees are blown down, the mover is obviously extrinsic; in all cases of natural motion, as coming-to-be, growing, ripening, and falling, the mover is also extrinsic, although this is less obvious; and in all animate motions, as walking, talking, and scratching, the mover is distinct from the part moved. Consequently everything that is moved is moved by another. We shall come back to this later. For the present it is sufficient to note that this induction is not strictly demonstration.

Finally, in *Physics* VII, 1, Aristotle shows that if anything is assumed to move itself, as Plato assumes, then it is really moving itself not *primo* and *per se* (καθ' αὑτὸ καὶ πρῶτον) but only by reason of parts, which is not self-movement *primo* and *per se*. Here Aristotle simply shows that it is impossible for anything to move itself *primo* and *per se* because "to move" is not the same as "to be moved."[6] As soon as it is shown that "to move" and "to be moved" are distinct actions requiring distinct parts, then it is clear that the mover does not move itself. Rather, the part that is moved is moved by a part distinct from itself, that is to say, by another.

---

[4] *Sum. cont. gent.* I, c. 13: "In hac autem probatione sunt duae propositiones proban-dae, scilicet quod omne motum movetur ab alio, et quod in moventibus et motis non sit procedere in infinitum." Aquinas goes on to say that Aristotle proves (*probat*) the first proposition in three ways, the ways described in the paper.

[5] *Ibid.*, par. 8; Albertus Magnus, *Lib. VIII Phys.*, tr. I, c. 1, ed. A. Borgnet (Paris, 1890), III, 484a.

[6] According to the text, Aristotle's argument rests on the impossibility of a "first part" in motion, since motion is infinitely divisible; therefore there cannot be a first moving part by which a body could move itself. This Aquinas considers to be a true demonstration *propter quid*, because it expresses the real reason why a thing cannot move itself: "sed videtur dicendum quod non sit demonstratio *quia*, sed *propter quid;* continet enim

Without attempting to give a definitive answer to our first problem, we perhaps can say that the principle *Omne quod movetur ab alio movetur* is not demonstrated strictly speaking. Rather it seems to be an axiom, or principle *per se notum sapientibus*, requiring sense experience and a careful analysis of the terms.[7] Once the terms are understood in their technical sense, the proposition seems to be immediately evident. In any case, since this point is not essential to our paper, it is true to say that in the late Middle Ages the principle was used axiomatically in philosophical argumentation, even without proper clarification and justification. For this reason the principle has been and still is frequently misunderstood.

Incidentally—and here, I think, we come to the Gordian knot—we are not saying that "whatever moves or whatever is in motion is moved by another." A proposition such as this is neither self-evident nor true. It is not true to say that whatever moves (*omne movens*) is also moved, for clearly the *primum movens* is not moved; that is the whole point of the argument. Nor can one say that everything that is now in motion (*omne in motu*) is being moved here and now by something else. In the first place, this is contrary to the grammar of the text. In the second place, this proposition is not at all evident to the senses or to reason. St. Thomas never said, *Omne movens ab alio movetur;* nor did Aristotle. The Greek verb κινούμενον in Aristotle's text is middle and passive in form, and it means "is being moved," a sense clearly expressed in the Latin passive *movetur.*[8] Certainly the active sense of *movens* is out of the question. Nor did St. Thomas—or Aristotle, for that matter—ever maintain that everything that is in motion must be here and now moved by something, as some imagine. This interpretation is grammatically impossible and philosophically absurd. It is precisely this bad grammar and bad philosophy which have given rise to misunderstanding concerning the principle *Omne quod movetur ab alio movetur.*

The second problem which arises out of St. Thomas's first proof concerns the word *movetur.* What does St. Thomas intend to include in this term? According to Aristotle, motion (κίνησις or *motus*) strictly so-

---

causam quare impossibile est aliquod mobile movere seipsum." *In VII Phys.,* lect. 1, n. 6.

[7] In Aquinas's view such evident principles are "derived" from principles commonly known to all, but this is not to say that they are "demonstrated" merely because learned terms are reduced to simpler and better-known terms. The usual example of a principle *per se notum sapientibus* is rather striking. "Alia vero animi conceptio est communis solum doctis, quae derivatur a primis animi conceptionibus, quae sunt omnibus hominibus communes; et huiusmodi est 'incorporalia non esse in loco,' quae non approbatur a vulgo, sed solum a sapientibus." *In Boeth. De hebdomad.,* lect. 1.

[8] For the Greek text see note 19.

called is found only in three categories, namely, "quantity" (growing
and shrinking), "quality" (intension and remission), and "where"
(various types of locomotion). If *movetur* means to be moved by these
motions and not by any other kind of change, one will conclude either
to an animated material substance causing motion or to a separated
immaterial substance, which will not necessarily be God as St. Thomas
understands him. In this case the existence of God is, strictly speaking, not demonstrated. Therefore, St. Thomas must have intended
the verb *movetur* to be taken in the widest possible sense of any change
whatever produced by another. Consequently *movetur* must include
every coming into being, even of the whole substance whether it be
physical or spiritual.

But then a third problem arises from the example of the hand
moving the baton and from St. Thomas's frequent reference to the
whole universe as the instrument of the First Cause.[9] Does Aquinas
mean that the whole universe is like a pencil or baton in the hand of
God? This example of strict instrumental causality implies that not
only the First Mover but also every intermediate mover is here and
now moving the instrument to produce the desired effect, namely,
motion. In this case, it would seem that every physical motion would
require "a particular mover bound to it and generating it directly," to
use the phrase of Anneliese Maier.[10] This interpretation, however, not
only eliminates the concept of nature and the concept of secondary
causality in physics but is contrary to the grammar of the axiom and
contrary to St. Thomas's expressed view of the matter.

I

In medieval physics there were three highly controversial problems
which involved the principle *Omne quod movetur ab alio movetur.* These
were the problem of the natural fall of heavy bodies, the problem of
projectile motion, and the problem of celestial motion. I am not saying that these were the only problems of physics which involved the
Aristotelian principle. By no means is this so. Since everything in
nature is in some way *moved,* there is always the scientific problem of
seeking its true physical causes. St. Thomas begins his treatise *De motu
cordis* by saying, "Since everything which is moved must have a mover,
there is the problem of what moves the heart and what type of motion

---

[9] *Sum. theol.* I, q. 19, a. 4; q. 22, a. 2; q. 103, a. 5 ad 2; *Sum. cont. gent.* II, cc. 22–23; III,
cc. 64–70; etc.
[10] Anneliese Maier, " 'Ergebnisse' der spätscholastischen Naturphilosophie," *Scholastik*
35 (1960), 170.

does the heart have."[11] In fact, the principle *Omne quod movetur ab alio movetur* is so fundamental and universal in Aristotelian natural philosophy that it must be recognized as one of the first principles of the entire science of nature. In the eyes of modern historians of science this was the most basic and most erroneous principle in Aristotelian physics. Thus while recognizing the universality of this principle in ancient and medieval Aristotelianism, we wish to limit our discussion to three problems in medieval physics: the natural motion of heavy bodies downward, the unnatural motion of projectiles, and the perpetual motion of rotating spheres. Modern historians of science concentrate on these three problems in order to evaluate the Aristotelian principle by modern concepts of gravitational motion and the law of inertia.

Modern historians are surprisingly at one in their interpretation and evaluation of Aristotelian physics. Following an earlier tradition, historians like Pierre Duhem,[12] Sir David Ross,[13] Father Peter Hoenen,[14] Alistair C. Crombie,[15] Marshall Clagett,[16] Eduard J. Dijksterhuis,[17] and Anneliese Maier[18] interpret the Aristotelian principle to mean that everything that is moving must be moved by something here and now conjoined to the moving body. In the Oxford translation of Aristotle's works, Hardie and Gaye always render the classical axiom as "Everything that is in motion must be moved by something."[19] According to Ross, Aristotle tacitly assumes

that one body can be in movement as a result of the influence of another only so long as the other body is continuing to act on it, and is in fact still in contact with it. He [Aristotle] has in fact no concept of the First Law of Motion, that if a body has once been set in motion it will continue to move till it is acted on by some fresh force.[20]

---

[11] *De motu cordis ad mag. Philippum*, in *Opera Omnia* (ed. Parma, 1875), XVI, 338a.

[12] Pierre Duhem, *Le Système du monde*, I (Paris, 1913), pp. 174–75.

[13] W. D. Ross, *Aristotle's Physics* (Oxford, 1936), pp. 88–94; comm. on 266a10–11 (pp. 721–22), 266b27–267a20 (pp. 725–26).

[14] Peter Hoenen, *Cosmologia*, 4th ed. (Rome, 1949), pp. 497–502.

[15] Alistair C. Crombie, *Augustine to Galileo* (London, 1952), p. 82; *Medieval and Early Modern Science*, 2 vols. (Garden City, N.Y., 1959), Vol. 1, pp. 69–70, 76–78, 114–15; Vol. 2, pp. 47–48.

[16] Marshall Clagett, *The Science of Mechanics in the Middle Ages* (Madison, 1959), pp. 424–26.

[17] E. J. Dijksterhuis, trans. C. Dikshoorn, *The Mechanization of the World Picture* (Oxford, 1961), pp. 24–31.

[18] Maier, *art. cit.*, 161–87; *Studien zur Naturphilosophie der Spätscholastik*, Vol. 1 (Rome, 1949), pp. 54–72, 132–33; *Studien*, Vol. 2 (Rome, 1951), pp. 114–19; *Studien*, Vol. 3 (Essen, 1943), pp. 143–57, 181–88, 220–23; *Studien*, Vol. 4 (Rome, 1955), pp. 227–30.

[19] The Greek text reads: Ἅπαν τὸ κινούμενον ὑπό τινος ἀνάγκη κινεῖσθαι (*Phys.* VII, 1, 241b34; cf. alternative VII, 1, 241b24).

[20] Ross, *op. cit.*, comm. on 266a10–11 (p. 722).

Since motion is by definition a continuous actualization of potentiality, Mr. Crombie conceives this to be a process which necessarily requires the continued operation of a cause in such a way that when the cause ceases to operate, so does motion.[21] Crombie goes on to explain, "All moving bodies which were not alive thus received their motion from a mover distinct from themselves and the mover necessarily accompanied the body it moved." Professor Clagett explains the mind of Aristotle in the same way:

> The first point to recognize is that for Aristotle motion is a process arising from the continuous action of a source of motion or "motor" and a "thing moved." The source of motion or motor is a force—either internal as in natural motion or external as in unnatural motion—which during motion must be in contact with the thing moved.[22]

Professor Dijksterhuis gives the same explanation:

> Aristotelian physics is based on the axiom that every motion (*motus*) presupposes a mover (*motor*): omne quod movetur ab alio movetur. This *motor* must either be present in the moving body or be in direct contact with it; action at a distance is excluded as inconceivable: a *motor* must always be a *motor conjunctus*.[23]

Modern historians, however, experience some difficulty in identifying the *motor coniunctus,* the *agens proximum* of freely falling bodies. They readily point out that for Aristotle the celestial spheres are moved by intelligent souls and that projectiles are moved by the medium, both of which agents are clearly distinct from the body moved. But the accompanying mover of a freely falling body is less easy to discover in Aristotle. Dijksterhuis is of the opinion that "Aristotle does not make any unambiguous statement about this, and Scholasticism therefore had to study this problem anew."[24] According to Dijksterhuis the scholastics finally decided that the *agens proximum* of natural motion downward or upward must be the substantial form.[25] Ross, Hoenen, Crombie, Clagett, and Maier do not hesitate to imagine the substantial form as the immediate, conjoined mover of natural bodies in Aristotelian physics. In this view the substantial form is the mover, and matter is that which is moved. Duhem, however, sensed the inappropriateness of this way of speaking; he insisted that "the Stagirite intended the form to be moved together with the matter."[26]

---

[21] Crombie, *Augustine to Galileo*, p. 82.
[22] Clagett, *op. cit.*, pp. 425–26.
[23] Dijksterhuis, *op. cit.*, p. 24.
[24] *Ibid.*, p. 26.
[25] *Ibid.;* also p. 177.
[26] Duhem, *op. cit.*, p. 208.

Consequently Duhem preferred to explain Aristotle's doctrine exclusively in terms of natural place enticing bodies not yet in it, a kind of extrinsic form desired by bodies which must move toward it.[27] Giving in fact an explanation of the final cause of natural locomotion, Duhem did not identify the efficient mover supposedly responsible for the downward movement of heavy bodies and the upward movement of light. Contemporary authors, however, do not sense any inappropriateness in identifying substantial form as the *motor coniunctus*, the efficient cause of natural motion in Aristotelian physics. They are content to imagine substantial form and primary matter as two distinct and independent substances, one as mover, the other as moved. This view they attribute to Aristotle and to medieval scholasticism! More important, they seem to be unaware of the insuperable difficulty presented when we come to explain the difference between living and nonliving things, for living things are precisely those things which are able to move themselves (*se moventes*), that is, to be an efficient cause of some of their motions. It will hardly do to say that Aristotle thought of inanimate bodies as "self-movers."

A similar awkwardness is noticed in the explanation of Aristotelian dynamics. Modern historians explain that the velocity of a moving body in Aristotle's physics is in direct proportion to the power of the accompanying mover and in inverse proportion to the resistance offered by the medium. Mr. Crombie explains the mind of Aristotle as follows:

With falling bodies the force or power causing the movement was the weight, and so it followed from the above principles that in any given medium the velocity of a falling body was proportional to its weight and further, that if a body were moving in a medium which offered no resistance its velocity would be infinite.[28]

Suddenly and without warning we are presented with a new factor, resistance from a medium, such as air. Matter, which "is moved" by the substantial form, drops from the picture completely without explanation. Apparently this matter offers no resistance to the *motor coniunctus*. But since it is assumed that Aristotle demanded resistance for the very possibility of motion, the medium is introduced to provide resistance and the possibility of motion. We are now talking not

[27] *Ibid.*, p. 209: "Ce corps, étant en puissance de quelque chose, peut, à l'égard de ce quelque chose, être considéré comme une matière; ce dont il est en puissance, ce dont il est privé peut, à l'égard de ce corps, être regardé comme une forme; voilà pourquoi on peut dire que lorsqu'il est porté vers son lieu naturel, il est porté vers sa forme."

[28] Crombie, *Augustine to Galileo*, p. 83; *Medieval and Early Modern Science*, Vol. 2, pp. 47–49.

about motions as they actually occur in the universe but about the very possibility of motion. Thus it is said that the velocity of a freely falling body must be in direct proportion to the power of the accompanying mover and in inverse proportion to the resistance offered by the medium.[29]

Modern historians discussing the Aristotelian concept of motion inevitably argue the case in terms of acceleration, as though Aristotle had identified motion with acceleration or, what is worse, with velocity itself. For Aristotle speed is not motion but a property of motion. While Aristotle had a great deal to say about "motion," "being moved," and the like, he had notoriously little to say about acceleration. He noted that in *natural* terrestrial motions a body "seems always to be moving with a quickening velocity, whereas what is *forced* against its nature is always losing velocity."[30] He further noted that only rotational motion can be uniform, for natural rectilinear motions "are never uniform as they pass from the beginning to the end, for in them the mobile moves more rapidly in proportion as it is further from the position of rest."[31] Aristotle was fully aware that in all natural local motion there was acceleration the closer the body got to its goal,[32] but he never conceived of this as a special problem needing a special solution in terms of new movers. For him it was sufficient that a body "be moved by another" in the first place and that, if the motion is natural, it will be accelerated by nature, by φύσις.[33] Aristotle's concern, at least in the *Physics,* was much wider than a concern over natural acceleration—which to him posed no problem. His concern was with the basic question of "being moved" in the first place, whether in natural generation, in unnatural (forced, or mechanical) motions, or in uniform celestial motions. Aristotle was clearly intent upon showing that in all three types of motion the body was or is moved by another; he does this in order to establish the activity of the First Mover. Modern historians, however, are anxious to evaluate all this in terms of the modern problem of acceleration and gravitational forces, thus restricting the wider Aristotelian concern.

In *Physics* VII, 5, Aristotle did indeed discuss certain proportions of velocity which would follow from doubling the force exerted on a body and from decreasing its resistance by one-half. But modern historians see in this a universal law of Aristotelian dynamics, so that in all motions, both mechanical and natural, velocity is thought to be

[29] *Ibid.*
[30] Aristotle, *Phys.* V, 6, 230b24–25.
[31] *Phys.* VIII, 9, 265b12–14.
[32] *De caelo* I, 8, 277a27–33.
[33] James A. Weisheipl, O.P., *Nature and Gravitation* (River Forest, Ill., 1955).

inversely proportional to resistance, whether that resistance comes
from a solid body being moved mechanically or from a natural
medium such as air. Generally the universal law of Aristotelian dynamics is symbolized by

$$v = f \times \frac{F}{R} \text{ or } v = f \times \frac{W}{R}$$

(in which F = moving force, R = resistance, v = velocity, f = constant
of proportionality, and W = weight). In all such cases the moving
force must be divided by resistance.[34] Thus resistance is thought to be
an essential factor for all motion, and without resistance of some kind,
velocity is said to be infinite, that is, instantaneous (in instanti). But all
modern historians agree that for Aristotle motus in instanti is impossible. Therefore they conclude that in Aristotelian physics motion in a
void is absolutely impossible.

These views of modern historians of Aristotelian physics are fully
expressed by Anneliese Maier in her explanation of the principle
under discussion. For Miss Maier the principle, which she phrases as
Omne quod movetur ab aliquo movetur, means that "every movement
requires a particular mover bound to it and generating it directly, and
every normal, successive motion taking place requires a resistance
which opposes the moving force and which is overcome by that force,
since without resistance there would be no motus, but mutatio, i.e., an
instantaneous change of place."[35] She goes on to explain that adher-
ence to this erroneous principle prevented Aristotelian scholastics
from discovering the principle of inertia, which states that a body
once set in motion will continue in rectilinear motion forever unless
deterred by another body. Thus, according to Maier, the scholastics
not only failed to anticipate the principle of inertia but were prevented from doing so because they adhered to the erroneous principle Omne quod movetur ab alio movetur.[36]

From what has been said of natural movement downward and upward, it is not surprising that modern historians explain the impetus
theory of the fourteenth century in terms of a motor coniunctus, an
immediate efficient cause accompanying the moving body until it is
overcome by the natural forces of the body. Impetus is thus conceived

[34] Op. cit., p. 30. On this Dijksterhuis says: "In the above formulation of the fundamental law of dynamics a peculiarity of Aristotelian thought, which later seriously
impeded the growth of classical mechanics, is clearly revealed, namely the tendency to
divide the moving force by anything that may be considered as resistance, and never to
subtract the latter from the former."

[35] Maier, art. cit., p. 170.

[36] Ibid., pp. 169–70, 177–80.

of as a mover, an efficient cause, the immediate agent of compulsory movement. Explaining the fourteenth-century theory of impetus, Dijksterhuis says, "It was assumed that the *proiciens* imparted this power to the *mobile*, for which it formed the *motor conjunctus*."[37] The difference between such an impetus and substantial form is that impetus will eventually be overcome and eliminated by the contrary tendencies of substantial form. But both are said to be movers accompanying the body in motion. Both are said to require resistance.

Jean Buridan had suggested in his questions on the *Physics*, q. 12, that God could have given such an impetus to the celestial spheres at the time of creation, thus eliminating the need for continual movement by intelligences. Buridan went on to say that "these *impetus* which God impressed on celestial bodies have not been diminished or destroyed in the passage of time, because in celestial bodies there was no inclination to other motions, nor any resistance which could destroy or restrain these *impetus*."[38] Duhem, Crombie, and Dijksterhuis see in this statement a foreshadowing of Galileo's principle of inertia. But surely, if their interpretation of Aristotelian dynamics is correct, then there should be no motion at all, not even for Buridan, since celestial bodies in the traditional view never provided any resistance, whether moved by God immediately or by intelligences or by impetus. Something is wrong somewhere!

From what has been said it would seem that we need to reconsider Aristotelian physics, particularly in the Middle Ages. What is needed is a reconsideration of the principle *Omne quod movetur ab alio movetur* along more historical and scientific lines.

II

In the first place we must keep in mind that there were many interpretations of Aristotle in the Middle Ages. Not everyone who commented on the works of Aristotle, nor everyone who quoted him enthusiastically, should be classified as an Aristotelian. It is well known that many did not fully appreciate what has been called Aristotle's fundamental discovery in natural philosophy, namely, the reality of pure potentiality as a passive principle of change, a principle called πρώτη ὕλη, "first matter." Without this basic philosophical insight, the radical oneness of individuals is always in jeopardy. With this insight, however, there is no insolvable problem about the substantial unity of

---

[37] Dijksterhuis, *op. cit.*, p. 179.
[38] Jean Buridan, *QQ. in lib. Phys.*, q. 12, ed. Maier (*Studien*, Vol. 2, p. 212), lines 179–82.

individuals, the unicity of substantial form, the possibility of fundamental change, and a host of related questions disputed in the Middle Ages. The failure to achieve this insight is plainly manifest in the conception of "form" as an accompanying mover and "matter" as a separate part moved. This conception is nowhere to be found in the works of Aristotle, as Duhem and Dijksterhuis have admitted. However, it did exist among some interpreters of Aristotle in the Middle Ages.

Avicenna's *Sufficientia*[39] explained natural motion to the Latins in terms of a natural inclination to a natural place. The rising of light bodies and the falling of heavy bodies comes about necessarily from the essence of the body. "However," Avicenna remarked, "it is absolutely impossible for an essence of a thing to cause its own motion unless it be a mover through its own form and a moved through its own subject [*nisi sit ipsamet movens per suam formam et mota per suum subiectum*]."[40] As Avicenna was never able to explain natural generation of forms from the potentiality of matter but had to appeal to an external *dator formarum*,[41] he could speak of forms as natural movers and subjects as matter moved. He saw no incongruity in speaking of inanimate bodies moving themselves through form, *elevando et movendo se*, as one Latin passage expressed it.[42] For Avicenna celestial motions are produced both by the natural inclination of the body and by the intelligent soul animating it.[43] Both of these views, of course, could also be read in Algazel's paraphrase, *Maqâcid el-falâcifa*.[44]

It was Averroes, however, who most influenced Latin interpretations of Aristotle's natural philosophy. Like Avicenna, Averroes conceived the form of heavy bodies, *gravitas*, to be the accompanying mover of downward natural movement and "matter" to be the body moved. However, his very detailed explanation rests on two assumed requirements for all motion: first, that some mover must accompany a body in motion, and second, that the mover must encounter resistance.

---

[39] Avicenna, *Opera philosophica* (ed. Venice 1508), fol. 13r–36v.

[40] *Ibid., Sufficientia*, Lib. II, cap. 1, fol. 24ra. See Harry A. Wolfson, *Crescas' Critique of Aristotle* (Cambridge, Mass., 1929), pp. 673–75; also Bernard Carra de Vaux, *Avicenne* (Paris, 1900), pp. 184–85.

[41] On this see St. Thomas, *De pot.*, q. 3, a. 8; q. 6, a. 3; *Sum. theol.* I, q. 45, a. 8; *In II Sent.*, d. 1, q. 1, a. 3 ad 5; a. 4 ad 4; *In VII Metaph.*, lect. 7, nn. 1430–31; lect. 8, nn. 1438–42.

[42] Avicenna, *op. cit., Metaphysica*, tr. 6, cap. 3, fol. 93ra.

[43] See Harry A. Wolfson, "The Problem of the Souls of the Spheres from the Byzantine Commentaries on Aristotle through the Arabs and St. Thomas to Kepler," paper read at Dumbarton Oaks in May 1961, offprint, pp. 82–83.

[44] *Algazel's Metaphysics*, ed. J. T. Muckle (Toronto, 1933), pp. 30–31, 99–102.

In his commentary on *De caelo* III, comm. 28,[45] Averroes compares natural and violent motions. Not only does violent, or unnatural, motion arise from an outside projector, but its entire production is foreign and alien to the body being imposed upon. The originator of this violent motion is the original *proiciens*, but the continuator of this alien motion—for both Aristotle and Averroes—is the medium, which has been given power to continue this motion. Similarly the original cause of natural gravitational motion is the generator of the heavy body, who in generating the form inevitably confers natural motion and all other natural accidents consequent upon that form. Thus the *generans* is the *motor extrinsecus* of natural movement by means of the form given. But Averroes goes on to assume that some intrinsic mover (*motor intrinsecus*) must continue to produce motion after the natural body has been separated from its extrinsic progenitor. Since this natural motion arises from the form, Averroes thinks that this intrinsic form is the immediate mover in natural motions. Consequently the natural movement of nonliving things is somewhat similar to self-movement in animals. But there is an essential difference: the animal soul is a self-mover *per se*, the natural form is a self-mover *per accidens*. True self-movement requires a real distinction between mover and part moved; this is the case in animals, which move their arms and legs *per se*. The natural form, however, is not distinct from matter in this way. Hence the natural form must move the medium, which in turn moves the entire body, much like a rower in a boat who is moved by his own rowing. Consequently Averroes concludes to the indispensability of the medium for natural motion.[46] Obviously without a resisting medium there is nothing for the rower to row against.

In his commentary on the *Physics* IV, comm. 71,[47] Averroes discusses the possibility of movement in a vacuum. He insists that for all movement the moving force must meet some resistance in order to have a determined velocity. Since no resistance can arise from the matter of a natural body moved by its form, there must be resistance from some medium such as air or water. Since resistance is necessary for motion, there can be no motion in a void. Then Averroes raises an objection presented by Avempace, that the proportion of velocity depends not on resistance but on time. Avempace does not think that absence of

---

[45] Averroes, *Opera* (ed. Venice 1574), t. V, fol. 197rb–199ra.

[46] *Ibid.*, fol. 199ra: "Et cum ita sit, lapis igitur non movet essentialiter nisi aerem in quo est, et movet se, quia hoc quod movet se sequitur motum aeris, sicut de homine cum navi. Et cum ita sit, aer igitur et aqua sunt necessaria in motu lapidis, et hoc est illud quod promisimus declarare hic in expositione Physicorum, sed iste locus est convenientior."

[47] Averroes, *Opera* (ed. Venice 1562), t. IV, fol. 158v–162ra.

resistance would produce instantaneous change, since celestial motions are devoid of resistance, yet they require time for their different velocities. Averroes dismisses Avempace's position as mathematically erroneous, since Avempace talks about velocity in terms of adding or subtracting amounts of motion, whereas Averroes conceives of velocity as inversely proportional to resistance, that is, as a divisor. Thus if resistance is zero, then velocity would be infinite, that is, instantaneous, which for Averroes is impossible.

Averroes recognized three possible sources of resistance: an independent obstacle, as in displacement of bodies; natural resistance of a body to compulsory motion; and the medium through which a body moves. The sum of these resistances divides the moving force and renders motion possible. Thus in a vacuum there could be no natural successive motion; since there is no medium, there is no resistance against which to act.

Averroes dismisses Avempace's point about the lack of resistance in celestial bodies by pointing to the real distinction between the celestial body and the soul, and the proportion between them. Hence for Averroes there is a kind of resistance in celestial bodies to their proportionate movers. In elementary bodies, where matter is not a *res in actu* but only *in potentia*, the form needs a medium upon which to act.[48]

The position of Averroes can be summed up as follows: every movement taking place in the universe, whether natural or violent or celestial, requires an accompanying mover, intrinsic in the case of natural and celestial motion, extrinsic in the case of projectiles. Thus everything moved (*omne motum*) requires an immediate mover. Thus *omne motum* is equivalent to *omne in motu*. Moreover every motion presupposes resistance either from the body itself or from some medium. Thus velocity is directly proportional to the moving force or weight, and inversely proportional to resistance; where there is no resistance, there can be no successive motion.

Clearly the position attributed by modern historians to Aristotle is, in fact, the position of Averroes. Our concern here is not to evaluate Averroes' interpretation of Aristotle. Rather it is to compare medieval views of *Omne quod movetur ab alio movetur.* It cannot be denied that many schoolmen accepted the interpretation of Averroes. In particular it was accepted by Peter of Auvergne, Godfrey of Fontaines, Peter

---

[48]*Phys.* IV, comm. 71, *ed. cit.,* fol. 161vb: "Manifestum est quod ista resistentia invenitur inter motorem et rem motam quando res mota fuerit distincta per se, sicut est dispositio in corporibus caelestibus. In elementis vero res mota est in potentia et motor in actu, cum sit composita ex prima materia et formis simplicibus, et motor est forma et res mota est materia; et quia haec corpora non distinguuntur in rem motam et motorem in actu, impossibile est ea moveri sine medio."

Olivi, Duns Scotus, and by the bulk of beginners' manuals popular in the fourteenth and fifteenth centuries.[49] However, Averroes' interpretation was explicitly rejected on all essential points by St. Thomas Aquinas and to a lesser degree by Albertus Magnus[50] and even by Siger of Brabant, the eminent founder of Latin Averroism.[51] The cornerstone of St. Thomas's explanation of the axiom is the concept of nature. Aristotle had defined nature ($\phi\acute{v}\sigma\iota\varsigma$) as "the principle [$\dot{\alpha}\rho\chi\acute{\eta}$] of movement and rest in those things to which it belongs *per se* and not as something concomitant."[52] Moreover Aristotle had shown that not only is the traditional notion of form $\phi\acute{v}\sigma\iota\varsigma$ but also the potentiality for this form is $\phi\acute{v}\sigma\iota\varsigma$.[53] That is, both matter and form are natures, form as the active principle of motion, matter as the passive principle for receiving motion and form. Medieval scholastics in general, and St. Thomas in particular, developed to a great extent this twofold meaning of nature: "form" as an active and formal principle,

---

[49] For example, the anonymous beginners' manual published by Marshall Clagett (*op. cit.*, pp. 445–62) states: "the intrinsic form of a moving body is called the intrinsic motor of the moving body; from this it is evident that natural motion by form and by intrinsic motor are identical, since the intrinsic form and the intrinsic motor by which a moving body is moved are the same thing" (p. 445).

[50] Albert strongly insists that the "mover" in natural motions is the generator of the form and nothing else. "Et ideo dicendum videtur quod id quod movetur ad locum, et non movetur per se, movetur a generante aut removente prohibens, sicut dictum est in 8° Physicorum. Sed quando movetur a generante, non movetur aliter ab ipso nisi quia dat ei suam formam, et quia formam, dat ei consequentia omnia formam illam, sicut saepe diximus." *Lib. III De caelo*, tr. I, cap. 7, ed. Borgnet, IV, 255a. However, he clung to the instrumentality of the medium simply on the authority of Aristotle: "Sed in istam opinionem ego nulla ratione consentio, eo quod Aristoteles egregius Philosophus expresse dicit, quod aer deservit ad motum localem per modum instrumenti." *Ibid.*, p. 254b.

[51] See fragments edited by Albert Zimmermann, *Die Quaestionen des Siger von Brabant zur Physik des Aristoteles* (Cologne, 1956), p. 31. For example, in the Borghese fragment (MS Vat. Borgh. 114) of Book II, q. 2, Siger explicitly rejects the Averroist doctrine of self-movement *per accidens* through a resisting medium: ". . . sed grave movet se per accidens ita, sicut movet se nauta per accidens eo quod movet navem per se. Ita dicit COMMENTATOR. Et modum dat dicens quod grave medium movet se per se, et medio impulso ab ipso movetur per accidens ipsum grave. *Hoc autem non videtur esse verum.* Unde habet grave quod moveat medium? Nam medium movere non est nisi ex moveri ipsius gravis. Sic enim movent motores corporei, quod eorum impulsionem naturaliter et tempore praecedit moveri ipsorum. *Propter hoc dicendum est aliter.* Debetur intelligere, quod quando admotum est impedimentum gravis detinens ipsum superius, adhuc non est grave deorsum distantia media impediente. Est ergo deorsum in potentia. Sed potentia est accidentalis" (p. 31). Italics mine.

[52] *Phys.* II, 1, 192b21–23. This definition is repeated more or less complete in various works of Aristotle: *Phys.* III, 1, 200b12–13; VIII, 3, 253b5–6; VIII, 4, 254b16–17; *De caelo* I, 2, 268b16; III, 2, 301b17–18; *De anima* II, 1, 412b15–17; *Gen. an.* II, 1, 735a3–4; *Metaph.* VI, 1, 1025b20–21; IX, 8, 1049b8–10; XII, 3, 1070a7–8; *Eth. Nic.* VI, 4, 1140a5–6; *Rh.* I, 10, 1369a35–b1.

[53] *Phys.* II, 1, 193a9–b21; II, 2, 194a12–25.

"matter" as a passive and potential principle.[54] Nature as matter, or *natura secundum materiam*, came to signify not only the pure potentiality of first matter but all passivities of bodies which require a natural agent[55] to actualize them. Nature as form, or *secundum principium formale*, signified the active and spontaneous source of all characteristic properties and behavior; ultimately this active principle was considered to be the substantial form which functions through active qualities.[56] Thus in scholastic terminology nature as "matter" is equivalent to *principium passivum, receptivum*, and *materiale*, while nature as "form" is equivalent to *principium activum et formale*, and *activa inclinatio formalis principii*. This identification of form with *principium activum* is consistent throughout the works of Aquinas.[57] Nevertheless, Aquinas does not identify *principium activum* with a *movens* or a *motor coniunctus*. The word *principium*, St. Thomas insists,[58] must be taken strictly; it is not a cause or a mover. A formal principle (*principium*, ἀρχή) is simply a spontaneous source of all that comes from it naturally, that is, all characteristic attributes and activities. Once it is brought into being, it immediately (*statim*) and spontaneously manifests characteristic behavior, unless accidentally impeded from doing what comes naturally. Thus, *qui dat formam, dat consequentia ad formam*.[59] For this reason Aquinas, following Aristotle, always says that the only *per se* cause of those motions is the generator of the body; the *per accidens* cause is whatever removes an impediment to natural, spontaneous motions.[60]

---

[54] See Chapter I above.

[55] Natural and artificial products were distinguished on the basis of the natural and artistic (human) agencies required to actualize the passivity. This difference in agency indicated a difference in the "matter" of natural and artificial things, inasmuch as the matter of artificial things does not have a "natural aptitude" for an artificial form. A clear explanation is given by St. Thomas, *In VII Metaph.*, lect. 8, n. 1442z; *In II Phys.*, lect. 1, n. 4.

[56] St. Thomas, *In VII Metaph.*, lect. 8, n. 1448; *In II Sent.*, dist. 14, q. 1, a. 5 ad 2.

[57] For example, Thomas, *De pot.*, q. 5, a. 5: "Habet enim huiusmodi [elementaris corporis] motus in mobili principium, non solum materiale et receptivum, sed etiam formale et activum. Formam enim ipsius elementaris corporis sequitur talis motus, sicut et aliae naturales proprietates ex essentialibus principiis consequuntur; unde in eis generans dicitur esse movens in quantum dat formam quam consequitur motus." Also ad 12; *Sum. cont. gent.* III, c. 23; *In II Sent.*, d. 14, q. 1, a. 1 ad 1; d. 18, q. 1, a. 2; *In III Sent.*, d. 3, q. 2, a. 1 ad 6; d. 22, q. 3, a. 2, sol. 1; *In I De caelo*, lect. 16, n. 13; *In III De caelo*, lect. 7, nn. 5–9; *In VII Metaph.*, lect. 8, n. 1442z.

[58] *In II Phys.*, lect. 1, n. 5: "Ponitur autem in definitione naturae *principium*, quasi genus et non aliquid absolutum, quia nomen naturae importat habitudinem principii."

[59] *In III De caelo*, lect. 7, n. 8. This principle is found throughout St. Thomas's writings on the subject.

[60] *In VII Phys.*, lect. 8, n. 8: "Quaedam enim sunt quae moventur secundum naturam, non tamen a seipsis, sicut gravia et levia, et haec etiam ab aliquo moventur, ut ostensum est, quia aut moventur per se a generante, quod facit ea esse gravia et levia, aut

Speaking of the natural, spontaneous motion of heavy and light bodies, Aquinas consistently and repeatedly says:

In heavy and light bodies there is a formal principle of their motion, because just as other accidents flow from substantial form, so too place, and consequently movement toward place; not however that the natural form is a *motor;* rather the *motor* is the *generans,* which gave such a form from which motion follows.[61]

St. Thomas emphatically denies that the form is an accompanying mover or the efficient cause of natural motion. The reason for this is twofold: first, Aristotle clearly demonstrated that nothing can move itself *primo* and *per se;* second, there is an obvious difference between living and nonliving things. Living things can indeed move themselves to certain activities, but not to all. An animal can move itself from place to place, but it cannot move its heart to beat, any more than it can move itself to have a heart, arms, and legs. Thus it is the nature of a living form which spontaneously and necessarily provides a heart and motion of the heart, if there is no impediment. This nature, then, is not the efficient cause or mover of the heart's motion.[62]

---

moventur per accidens ab eo quod 'solvit,' idest removet ea quae impediunt vel removent naturalem motum." See *Sum. theol.* I, q. 18, a. 1 ad 2, and q. 105, a. 2.

[61]*In II Phys.,* lect. 1, n. 4: "In corporibus vero gravibus et levibus est principium formale sui motus, quia sicut alia accidentia consequuntur formam substantialem, ita et locus, et per consequens moveri ad locum; non tamen ita quod forma naturalis sit motor, sed motor est generans, quod dat talem formam, ad quam talis motus consequitur." (On the textual difficulty of this passage in the Leonine edition, see Chapter I above, note 78.) See also *In II Phys.,* lect. 5, n. 5; *In IV,* lect. 12, n. 9; *In VIII,* lect. 8, nn. 5–7; *In I De caelo,* lect. 18, n. 1; *In II,* lect. 2, n. 6; *In III,* lect. 7, nn. 5–9; *Sum. cont. gent.* III, c. 23; *De pot.,* q. 5, a. 5; *De verit.,* q. 24, a. 1; *De motu cordis;* and additional references above in note 57. St. Thomas's view is expressed with particular clarity in *De verit.,* q. 22, a. 3: "In rebus corporalibus . . . formae earum non possunt esse moventes, quamvis possint esse motus principium, ut quo aliquid movetur; sicut in motu terrae gravitas est principium quo movetur, non tamen est motor." Of course, St. Thomas does not intend by this position to dispense with the universal causality of God in all natural actions, no more than does this universal causality dispense with nature as an active principle. Thus Aquinas says, *De pot.,* q. 3, a. 7: "Non ergo sic est intelligendum quod Deus in omni re naturali operetur quasi res naturalis nihil operetur, *sed quia in ipsa natura vel voluntate operante Deus operatur;* . . . sicut dicitur in IV Phys., quod generans movet grave et leve inquantum dat virtutem per quam consequitur talis motus. Et hoc modo Deus agit omnes actiones naturae, quia dedit rebus naturalibus virtutes per quas agere possunt, non solum sicut generans virtutem tribuit gravi et levi, et eam ulterius non conservat, *sed sicut continue tenens virtutem in esse,* quia est causa virtutis collatae, non solum quantum ad fieri sicut generans, sed etiam quantum ad esse, ut sic possit dici Deus causa actionis inquantum causat et conservat virtutem naturalem in esse." (Italics mine.)

[62]*De motu cordis,* ed. Parma, XVI, 359a; "Motus sursum est naturali igni, eo quod *consequitur formam eius; unde et generans quod dat formam est per se movens secundum locum.* Sicut autem formam elementi consequitur aliquis motus naturalis, sic nihil prohibet alias formas sequi alios motus naturales; videmus enim quod ferrum naturaliter

In plain English we can say that for St. Thomas the form simply *moves;* it is not a *mover.* But since that form had to be generated in the first place, that is, "moved to be," the "mover" in all natural motions is the progenitor. Thus what is "being moved" is nature in the passive sense of matter, not the body already in existence. When nature in the passive sense "was moved" in the generation of a new substance, it was moved by something else: *Omne quod movetur ab alio movetur.* Once the new substance is generated, however, its formal principle no longer needs to be moved (*moveri*); it already has everything it needs to do whatever comes naturally, according to St. Thomas, even falling downward or rising upward. A natural body is, as it were, an instrument of its progenitor, even after a particular progenitor has ceased to exist, for everything a natural body does naturally, it does in virtue of what it received in the first place.[63]

Commenting on Averroes' reasons for considering the natural form a mover, St. Thomas remarks in his commentary on *De caelo:*

Both arguments stem from the same error. [Averroes] thought that the form of heavy and light bodies is an active principle of motion after the manner of a mover needing some resistance contrary to the tendency of form, and that motion is not immediately due to the agent who conferred the form. But this is absolutely false. The form of heavy and light bodies is a principle of motion not as a generator of motion but as a means by which the mover moves, just as color, a principle of sight, is a means by which something is seen. . . . Thus movement of heavy and light bodies does not come from the generator by the intervention of another moving power [*mediante alio principio movente*]. Nor even is there any need to look for resistance here other than that which exists between generator and generated. Thus it follows that air is not required for natural motion of necessity [*ex necessitate*], as in the case of violent motion, since that which moves naturally has a force [*virtutem*] imparted to it which is a source of motion. Consequently there is no need for a body to be moved by

movetur ad magnetem, qui tamen motus non est ei naturalis secundum rationem gravis et levis, sed secundum quod habet talem formam. Sic igitur et animal inquantum habet talem formam quae est anima, nihil prohibet habere aliquem motum naturalem; *et movens hunc motum est quod dat formam.* . . . *Sic igitur motus cordis est naturalis quasi consequens animam, inquantum est forma talis corporis, et principaliter cordis.* . . . sicut Philosophus dicit VIII Phys., motum gravium et levium esse a generante, inquantum dat formam, quae est motus principium." (Italics mine.)

[63] Because of this original *movetur* and continued activity in virtue of what was received, it is most proper to speak of all nature in the passive voice as opposed to true self-movers (souls) and movers of other things (*potentiae activae*). Compare the use of passive voice in text from *De veritate* and *De potentia* in note 61 above, and in note 62. For this reason Aquinas can say, "Potentia igitur secundum quod est principium motus in eo in quo est, non comprehenditur sub potentia activa, sed magis sub passiva," *In V Metaph.,* lect. 14, n. 955. In other words, in Aquinas's terminology *potentia activa* is not the same as *principium activum et formale.* See my explanation in Chapter I, note 78.

any other force impelling it, as though it were a case of violent motion, having no implanted force from which motion springs.[64]

In this passage St. Thomas explicitly denies three points: (1) that the natural form is a *motor coniunctus*, (2) that there need be any continual mover to explain natural motions, and (3) that there need be any resisting medium for natural motions.

The question of a resisting medium was discussed thoroughly by St. Thomas in his commentary on the *Physics*,[65] as Dr. Moody has already noted.[66] After noting the objections of Avempace and Averroes' attempt to refute them, St. Thomas calls Averroes' refutation frivolous (*frivola*). Even if there were no medium, there is still the quantitative distance to be covered by a moving body. Because of this distance to be covered, time is required; therefore this motion has a determined velocity. Consequently for St. Thomas the velocity of a moving body is determined not by resistance but by the time required to cover a given distance. Thus even if there were no resisting medium, as in a void, a body would fall at a determined rate because of the time required to cover that particular distance. On this point St. Thomas agrees with Avempace against Averroes. For Averroes, as we have seen, there could be no motion at all in a void because there would be nothing against which the moving form could row its boat.

While we are on the question of the vacuum, let us consider it for a moment. The point under discussion in Aristotle's *Physics* IV, 6–9, is not whether a vacuum is possible, but whether the void posited by Leucippus and Democritus to explain motion is the real reason why natural bodies move as they do. Leucippus and Democritus had posited the reality of nonbeing, the empty, to allow for the movement

---

[64] *In III De caelo*, lect. 7, n. 9: "Utrumque autem ex eadem radice erroris procedit. Existimavit [Averroes] enim quod forma corporis gravis et levis sit principium activum motus *per modum moventis*, ut sic oporteat esse aliquam resistentiam ad inclinationem formae, et quod motus non procedat immediate a generante qui dat formam. Sed hoc est omnino falsum. Nam forma gravis et levis *non est principium motus sicut agens motum, sed sicut quo movens movet;* sicut color est principium visionis, quo aliquid videtur. . . . Sic igitur *motus gravium et levium non procedit a generante mediante alio principio movente; neque etiam oportet aliam resistentiam quaerere in hoc motu,* quam illam quae est inter generans et genitum. Et sic relinquitur quod *aer non requiratur ad motum naturalem ex necessitate,* sicut in motu violento. Quia id quod naturaliter movetur habet sibi inditam virtutem, quae est principium motus; unde *non oportet quod ab alio impellente moveatur,* sicut id quod per violentiam movetur, quia nullam virtutem inditam habet, ad quam sequatur talis motus." (Italics mine.)

[65] *In IV Phys.*, lect. 12, nn. 8–14.

[66] Ernest A. Moody, "Galileo and Avempace," *Journal of the History of Ideas* 12 (1951), 163–93, 375–422.

of solid atoms.[67] Accordingly, the void is a cause of motion by allowing room for movement. St. Thomas believes that "Aristotle argues against them as though the whole cause of velocity depended on the medium; . . . we are thus given to understand that they attributed the entire cause of motion to the medium and not to the nature of bodies."[68] This accounts for the facetiousness of some of the arguments in these chapters.

Some of the commentators, including Averroes, made too much of Aristotle's arguments against a void, failing to see the point of this discussion in Book IV. The point is that the void posited by Leucippus and Democritus cannot account for the motions we witness in the universe. Averroes and many after him took the opposite position from that of Leucippus and Democritus. The atomists said there could be no motion without a void; Averroes said there could be no motion in a void simply because there would be no resistance. Resistance, therefore, becomes the essential element in Averroist dynamics. This, as we have seen, is entirely rejected by St. Thomas.

Celestial motion, on the other hand, presents a special problem to St. Thomas.[69] Since nature as an active principle is always determined to a specific goal, "it is impossible that any nature intend motion for the sake of motion."[70] Therefore "celestial motion cannot arise spontaneously from the form of celestial bodies as from an active principle" similar to natural forms of terrestrial bodies, which act in order to possess a goal attained.[71] But if there can be no active principle of perpetual motion, then celestial bodies can have only a passivity to be moved by something else. In this matter, St. Thomas notes, it makes no difference whether we conceive the celestial bodies to be moved by intelligent souls conjoined to them, as Aristotle thought, or by intellectual substances entirely distinct, like angels. In either case the only "nature" celestial bodies can have is a passive, receptive, material one, *ratione principii passivi, quod est materia*, needing to be moved by another. St. Thomas sees no other way of explaining perpetual mo-

---

[67] For the pertinent texts, translation, and comment, see G. S. Kirk and J. E. Raven, *The Presocratic Philosophers* (Cambridge, 1962), pp. 404–9.

[68] *In IV Phys.*, lect. 12, n. 10. "Et ideo contra eos Aristoteles argumentatur, ac si tota causa velocitatis et tarditatis esset ex parte medii; . . . per hoc dat intelligere quod totam causam motus ponebant ex parte medii, et non ex natura mobilis."

[69] See Chapter VII below.

[70] "Impossibile est igitur quod natura intendat motum propter seipsum," *Sum. cont. gent.* III, c. 23, par. 6. "Impossibile est quod aliqua natura inclinet ad motum secundum seipsum," *De pot.*, q. 5, a. 5.

[71] *Sum. cont. gent.* III, c. 23; *De pot.*, q. 5, a. 5; *In II De caelo*, lect. 18, n. 1; *Resp. ad XLII art.*, a. 5.

tion.[72] "Hence, unless the celestial bodies are moved by God, they must either be animated and moved by their proper souls or be moved by angels, *quod melius dicitur.*"[73] In this paper I am not trying to evaluate St. Thomas's arguments for angelic movers of the heavens. I am merely trying to explain *movetur* in St. Thomas's view. It should be clear that for St. Thomas *movetur* refers exclusively to nature as a passive and material principle of motion and rest. It does not refer to nature as an active and formal principle of motion and rest, except in the sense that it too had "to be moved," generated, produced in the first place. In order to prove the existence of God one would have to go beyond the physical order of terrestrial and celestial movements to determine whether separated substances are in any sense *moventur*, that is, brought into being or moved intellectually. This is not our concern here. My only point is that *movetur* always means passivity for someone else's action, and not the fact that something is here and now in motion.

Until the early fourteenth century all violent motions, being *a principio extrinseco nil conferente vim passo*, were generally explained in terms of an extrinsic mover continuing to exert force.[74] In the case of projectiles, which are no longer in contact with the original mover, an explanation was sought in the surrounding medium, such as air. Plato had explained continued movement of projectiles by mutual replacement (ἀντιπερίστασις), that is, the air pushed in front of the projectile gathers in behind it and so pushes it on.[75] Aristotle objected that in Plato's explanation only motion is conferred on the air and not the power to move as well. In Aristotle's explanation both movement and power to move are given to the medium. Aristotle could not conceive this power being given to the projectile because the power "to move" must be distinct from the body "moved."

However, around 1320 a Franciscan, Francesco Rossi (de Marchia), proposed a new theory while lecturing on Book IV of the *Sentences* at Paris. While discussing sacramental causality, he raised the question of impetus in order to show that both the sacraments and the projectile

---

[72] "Non autem esset via solvendi, si moverentur per solum naturae impetum, sicut corpora gravia et levia." *In II De caelo,* lect. 18, n. 1.

[73] *Resp. ad XLII art.,* a. 5.

[74] Despite various attempts to prove the contrary, it must be admitted that Aquinas did not teach a doctrine of impetus like that proposed by de Marchia and Buridan. Rather he followed the view of Aristotle on projectile motion. This is rather surprising, since his doctrine of sacramental causality contained all the essential principles for the analogy with projectile motion. In other words, the new doctrine of impetus was seen to be consistent with the principles of Aquinas by such Thomists as Capreolus, Domingo de Soto, and others.

[75] Plato, *Timaeus* 80C; see also 59A, 79B, C, E.

have a certain residing force within by which something is produced. After a long and careful discussion of the Aristotelian theory, he concluded that projectile motion cannot be explained by the air but must be explained by a *virtus derelicta in lapide a motore.*[76] In order to indicate the unnatural and alien character of this force, de Marchia called it "an accidental and extrinsic force," "a certain extrinsic form." De Marchia conceived this *virtus derelicta* in projectiles and in the sacraments not as *motores coniuncti* but simply as instrumental powers separated from the true cause which conferred the *virtus.*

Buridan developed the theory of impetus in his commentaries on Aristotle. Like de Marchia he insisted that the impetus given to a projectile is violent, unnatural, extrinsic in its nature, and destined to be diminished and extinguished by the natural forces of the body. Similarly, Buridan conceived impetus not as a *motor coniunctus* but simply as a vehicle by which the mover achieves his goal. Later scholastics, such as Capreolus and Domingo de Soto, saw even more clearly that impetus cannot be considered an accompanying mover, an efficient cause of projectile motion, for this would be to conceive the body as a self-mover. Rather it is the instrument of the agent who is the only true mover. De Soto points out the analogy between impetus and nature as a formal principle, for just as the "mover" or "cause" of natural motion is the progenitor and not nature, so too the "mover" or "cause" of violent motion is the agent and not impetus.[77]

Considering, however, the widely accepted notion of form as an accompanying mover, it is not surprising that many scholastics in the late Middle Ages came to consider impetus as a "mover accompanying the projectile." This, as we have seen, is the interpretation given to it by modern historians of medieval science. The fundamental error, we suggest, lies in the failure to distinguish a "principle" from a "cause." We can agree that the projectile "is moved." Indeed, the ball "is thrown." But, we suggest, the ball is thrown by the boy, not by the force impressed.

Some years ago Sir Edmund Whittaker published a critique of Aquinas's arguments for the existence of God in the light of modern scientific theory. For him,

the first proof, or the proof from motion, is open to the objection, first brought against it by Duns Scotus and William of Ockham, that the principle

---

[76] Text edited by Maier, *Studien*, Vol. 2, pp. 166–80.
[77] Domingo de Soto, *Super libros Physicorum quaestiones*, Lib. VII, q. 3 (Salamanca, 1551), fol. 104v–105.

omne quod movetur ab alio movetur, on which the whole argument depends, is irreconcilable with sound dynamical science, and is therefore false.[78]

However, Sir Edmund interprets this axiom to mean that whatever is in motion must be kept in motion by another,[79] which we have seen is not the meaning of the principle. He does, however, point out the absurdity of speaking of position *B* as a "perfection" not yet possessed by a star in position *A*.[80] And he does point out the impossibility of calling an impulse given the star in the beginning a "mover" and an *aliud*.[81] He has in fact criticized the Averroist and late Averroist view on sound Thomistic grounds. What Sir Edmund failed to see was that even in the principle of inertia we admit that bodies "are moved" and indeed "by another"; that is the point of the phrases "put into motion" and "unless acted upon by another body." More important, Sir Edmund failed to see that a body in natural motion does not need other forces to move it, since it already has everything it needs to move *in virtute primae agentis;* it already has, for Aristotle and many schoolmen, everything it needs even to accelerate naturally. As far as the actual motion is concerned, neither the principle of inertia nor the Aristotelian principle demands that there be movers to account for motion. The only basic difference is that the principle of inertia demands additional force to account for acceleration. Aristotle and his medieval followers on this point saw no need for additional movers to account for acceleration; the original mover and the nature (φύσις) of the body were thought to be enough.

This is not to suggest that Aristotelian physics is in any way similar to modern dynamics. Not at all. The "natural way" and the "mathematical way," to use Newton's felicitous expressions, are two radically different approaches to the world of nature. What I am suggesting is that the principle *Omne quod movetur ab alio movetur,* understood as Aquinas understood it, is still philosophically correct today. Its philosophical validity in no way undermines modern laws of dynamics; on the other hand, its validity in no way validates those laws. But the Averroist interpretation, presented by modern historians of science as the "Aristotelian view," did not have to wait until the seventeenth century to be discredited; it was already discredited in the thirteenth on strictly Aristotelian grounds.

---

[78] Edmund Whittaker, *Space and Spirit: Theories of the Universe and the Arguments for the Existence of God* (Hinsdale, Ill., 1948), pp. 45–46.

[79] *Ibid.,* p. 51.

[80] *Ibid.,* pp. 133–35.

[81] *Ibid.,* pp. 136–37.

V

THE SPECTER OF *MOTOR CONIUNCTUS* IN MEDIEVAL PHYSICS

A small error in the beginning proves to be a big one in the end, since, as Aristotle points out,[1] a principle of reasoning though small in structure is great in power. The error in question is expressed in the various understandings and translations of the Aristotelian axiom: *Omne quod movetur ab alio movetur.* A mistranslation invariably implies a misunderstanding of this fundamental principle of Aristotelian physics. A literal translation is simply the Latin and English passive voice: "Everything that is moved is moved by another." This is the proper translation of the Greek middle voice in the text: ἅπαν τὸ κινούμενον ὑπό τινος ἀνάγκη κινεῖσθαι. Invariably, however, modern translators render this phrase as "Everything that is in motion must be moved by something";[2] "Everything that is in movement is necessarily moved by something";[3] "Whatever is in motion is put in motion by another";[4] or even "If a thing is in motion it is, of necessity, being kept in motion by something"[5]—and this is taken to mean "Everything which is in motion is being moved by another."[6]

It has been argued that the literal translation of the subject phrase *Omne quod movetur* in the passive sense of being formally moved makes the principle purely tautological and an analytic proposition in the modern sense.[7] Therefore Effler takes Aristotle's principle to mean that everything here and now moving is being moved by something other than itself here and now. It may be argued, however, that the point of the axiom is precisely the *ab alio.* Consequently the literal

---

[1] Aristotle, *De caelo* I, 5, 271b12–13.
[2] Oxford trans. of *Physics* VII, 1, 241b24 by R. P. Hardie and R. K. Gaye.
[3] P. Duhem's translation in *Le système du monde,* I, p. 174.
[4] English *Sum. theol.* of St. Thomas, I, q. 2, a. 3.
[5] Loeb translation by P. H. Wicksteed and F. M. Cornford.
[6] R. Effler, *John Duns Scotus and the Principle "Omne quod movetur ab alio movetur"* (St. Bonaventure, 1962), pp. 35, 167, *et passim.*
[7] *Ibid.,* pp. 34–35.

sense of the axiom is not tautological, since what the principle denies is that an inanimate body is moved *a seipso*. This is made clear in Aristotle's very next sentence: "For if it does not have within itself the principle of its motion, it is evidently moved by another."[8] The crucial word here is ἀρχή, *principium*, for Aristotle is discussing in this passage the explanation of natural motion in terms of φύσις, which is defined as the ἀρχή or *principium*, the source, of motion in those things in which it is *per se* and not as a concomitant attribute.[9] The small error in the beginning which proves so big in the end is the failure to understand the precise meaning of *principle* as distinct from a *cause*. This failure has led many modern commentators—and some scholastics—into error and has created the specter of a *motor coniunctus* even in the free fall of heavy bodies and the rising of light.

E. J. Dijksterhuis embraces this specter when he says: "Every motion (*motus*) presupposes a mover (*motor*): *omne quod movetur ab alio movetur*. This *motor* must either be present in the *mobile* or be in direct contact with it; *actio in distans* is excluded as inconceivable; a *motor* must always be a *motor conjunctus*."[10] Similarly A. C. Crombie promulgates this myth of a *motor coniunctus* when he insists that the whole corpus of Aristotelian "mechanics" that came down to the thirteenth century was expounded by the principle explained in the *Physics*, "the principle that local motion, like other kinds of change, was a process by which a potentiality towards motion was made actual. Such a process necessarily required the continued motion of a cause and when the cause ceased to operate, so did the effect. All moving bodies which were not alive thus received their motion from a mover distinct from themselves and the mover necessarily accompanied the body it moved."[11] The myth therefore of a *motor coniunctus* is read into the Aristotelian principle *Omne quod movetur ab alio movetur* through a mistranslation and misunderstanding of the axiom. But the root of the misunderstanding is the failure to understand the nature of a principle, as distinct from an efficient cause, of motion.

Aristotle did not take this axiom to be self-evident or something imposed *a priori*. He actually proves it both by induction and by demonstration: by induction when he shows that there is no other explanation, by demonstration when he shows that all homogeneous bodies are infinitely divisible and therefore lack a *first*, which could be a

---

[8] Arist., *Phys.* VII, 1, 241b25–26.

[9] Arist., *Phys.* II, 1, 192b21–23.

[10] E. J. Dijksterhuis, *The Mechanization of the World Picture*, trans. by C. Dikshoorn (Oxford, 1961), p. 24.

[11] A. C. Crombie, *From Augustine to Galileo* (London, 1957), p. 82, also p. 244.

mover. To understand Aristotle's proofs we must examine the actual teaching of Aristotle.

First it should be noted that the Greek equivalent of the phrase *motor coniunctus* is nowhere found in Aristotle. The notion, however, could be said to be found in Aristotle in two cases: (1) the case of living things that move themselves by parts, and (2) the case of celestial spheres, which for him were animated by a separated substance which acts both as a form (an *anima*) and as an efficient cause of movement. Thus the notion of a substantial form of inanimate bodies being a *motor coniunctus* or a *causa efficiens motus* is entirely foreign to Aristotle's own philosophy.

The Aristotelian explanation of natural inanimate motion was fully espoused by Albertus Magnus and Thomas Aquinas. But this was against a doctrine of *motor coniunctus* already promulgated by Avicenna and Averroes. The failure of Duns Scotus to follow the Aristotelian line, however, and his reluctance to accept a distinct *motor coniunctus* in natural inanimate motions caused him to pursue an entirely different course that ended in the rejection of the principle as he understood it. After explaining Aristotle's views and the supporting views of Albert and Thomas, we will consider briefly the introduction of the *motor coniunctus* in Avicenna and Averroes. Then we will see how Duns Scotus rejected the specter of the *motor coniunctus* as well as the motion principle.

1. ARISTOTLE AND NATURAL MOTION

In explaining things which move essentially as distinct from accidentally, Aristotle explains that some derive their motion from themselves, while others derive their motion from something else.[12] Those bodies that derive their motion from something else may be moved either naturally or unnaturally and violently. Aristotle considers it obvious that all animals which move themselves from place to place do so by their own power and causality through the movement of their various parts, as in crawling, walking, flying, and the like. Not all animals, of course, move themselves locally; the lowest kinds of animals are devoid of this special power of movement, and anchor themselves to other natural things. Aristotle is most explicit in saying that self-movement (*a seipsis*) "is a characteristic of life and peculiar to living things,"[13] by which he means to refer to animals that move

---

[12] Arist., *Phys.* VIII, 4, 254b12–13.
[13] Arist., *Phys.* VIII, 4, 255a6.

themselves. On the other hand, for him the most obvious cases of motions that are derived *ab alio* are all cases of violent motion in both animate and inanimate things.[14] Such are cases in which heavy bodies are thrown upward and light bodies forced downward. "The fact that a thing that is in motion derives its motion from something is most evident in things that are in motion unnaturally, because in such cases it is clear that the motion is derived from something other than the thing itself."[15] However one may explain the continuation of violent movement (Aristotle notes two explanations), the *cause* responsible for the projectile's movement is obviously the projector of the body in the first place; thus the boy who hits the ball is responsible for breaking the window. What Aristotle calls the "greatest difficulty" is the causal explanation of natural motions that are not animals moving themselves. He explicitly cites the "case of light and heavy things."[16] But this same difficulty also arises in explaining the causes responsible for the other types of "natural motion" noted in Book V, namely, growing and shrinking in the category of quantity and alterations in the category of the third species of quality. These motions include the process of growth, nutrition, and the generation of seed, as well as all the vital signs manifest in plants and animals, such as budding and the heartbeat. In other words, once a natural thing exists, it does certain things automatically and *naturally*, as from φύσις, an intrinsic principle of characteristic motion and rest. One may legitimately ask what the efficient cause of such characteristic motions and rest is, but one is immediately faced with the problem that these are not living things that move themselves by parts.

The solution Aristotle sees to the problem rests with the "fact that the term 'potentially' is used in more than one sense."[17] For this reason it is "not evident whence such motions as the upward motion of fire and the downward motion of earth are derived." Earth and fire are not living things that move themselves by parts. Here Aristotle distinguishes two basic senses of the word *potential.* One who does not yet have a science, say geometry, possesses that science "potentially" in a different sense from one who while already possessing that knowledge is not actually exercising it. It is one thing not yet to have the science; quite another to have it and not use it. Thus a light body can be said to possess downward movement "potentially" in a way different from that of a heavy body already constituted, but prevented

[14] 254b20–33.
[15] 254b24–26.
[16] 255a2.
[17] 255a30–31.

from downward movement. That is to say, a body that is actually light is doubly in "potentiality" to downward movement. It first has the radical potentiality to becoming a heavy body; then once constituted, it has the additional potentiality for downward movement. In other words, all generable bodies have the radical potentiality for coming-into-being. This is called first potentiality. Once the new substance is generated from the radical "potentiality" of its matter, it is totally "capable" of the natural movement proper to it. This is called second potentiality or potentiality to second act. The body may, however, be prevented from attaining this second act or actual downward movement because of some impediment.

Anneliese Maier has rightly noted that for Aristotle there are only two possible efficient causes of natural motion in inanimate bodies: the *generans,* which is the *per se* efficient cause of all the motions consequent upon the nature generated, and the *removens prohibens* or *removens impedimentum,* which is the *per accidens* cause of that actual motion.[18] Whatever removes an impediment, such as the column that supports the weight, cannot be anything more than a *per accidens* cause of the falling weight, since all it did *per se* was to remove the impediment to a fall that the weight was capable of having in its own right. Therefore the whole burden of efficient causality for that motion rests with the generator which begot that nature in the first place. Aristotle recognizes no other efficient *causes* of natural motions, except perhaps the causality of celestial bodies which concur in the production of substantial forms in the terrestrial world. Very often it is the sun itself that produces the new substantial form from the potentiality of matter. In every case, for Aristotle, it is the *generans* of the nature that is the *per se* efficient cause of motion and rest, as it is of everything else the body does or has naturally. At no time does Aristotle consider the substantial nature itself to be the efficient cause of natural inanimate motions or rest, even though every nature is a principle of natural motion and rest.

This brings us to the important distinction in Aristotle's philosophy between a *principium* and a *causa,* an ἀρχή and an αἰτία. Simply speaking, a "principle" is that from which anything flows in any way whatever, while an efficient cause is that which produces something distinct from itself and dependent upon it for its very being (*esse*). A "principle" is not an absolute thing; it is strictly a relative concept of a reality entirely unintelligible except in terms of what proceeds from it, the *principiatum.* For Aristotle, "nature" (φύσις) is properly a principle,

---

[18] A. Maier, *An der Grenze von Scholastik und Naturwissenschaft,* 2. Auflage (Roma, 1952), pp. 147–49.

a source, the ultimate root of all the natural characteristics we observe. Thus, natural characteristics of motion and rest are the *principiatum* observable to the senses and intelligible to the intellect used to give meaning to the "principle" behind the phenomena, *from which* (*a quo*) flow necessarily the natural manifestations observed to occur always or for the most part. The principle called "nature" is not an absolute term like a "thing" or *res* or *id quod est* that could be understood in its own right; rather it is a relative term signifying a source, a root from which (*a quo*) spring definite observable characteristics in such a way that whatever is intelligible in the *principiatum* is projected back to the *principium* as to its inevitable source. From this source observed characteristics flow necessarily and always in the same way or at least for the most part (*ut in pluribus*). Thus a "principle" does not move itself to produce these manifestations; rather they emanate necessarily, or flow spontaneously and inevitably from the source once that source exists, provided there is no impediment. Just as size, texture, place, and the like follow necessarily upon specific natures, so do motions toward that size, texture, and place. In other words, just as static characteristics manifest specific nature, so do all its natural activities and movements, as well as its passivities, as we shall see.

An efficient cause, on the other hand, is an absolute thing in its own right, and, in a certain sense, *per se* intelligible. It is always really distinct from the effect it produces in exercising causality on something really distinct from itself. Moreover there is always the real dependence of the distinct effect upon its cause for coming into being. It just so happens that some natures are also efficient causes of certain limited effects. This efficient causality is found in only two kinds of phenomena. First, there is the case of natural bodies producing an effect in another kind of body. Second, there is the case of animals which move themselves from place to place; self-movement requires the distinction of parts whereby the animal moves one part and through it another until the particular type of motion is accomplished. These self-motions are limited to such activities as walking, crawling, swimming, running, flying, and the like. These two kinds of phenomena are similar in that they both require a real distinction between bodies or parts of bodies. Thus the power to be an efficient cause is not itself efficiently produced; it is found naturally and necessarily in certain natures. But if it exists, it can effectively move other bodies in the production of an effect, and animals which have it can move themselves from place to place. It must be clear that an animal's self-motion is greatly limited in the range of possibilities. For example, self-motion is not said to include growing, aging, digesting, perspiring, or the beating of the heart. All of these motions are just as natural and inevitable in an animal as its size, color, weight, or shape and vastly different from the limited phenomenon of self-motion. Among activities manifested by animals, only self-motion from place to place through parts is an example of efficient causality; all others come about by nature as from a "principle" and not a "cause." The failure to understand this distinction, an important distinction, has been the cause of incalculable errors among commentators on Aristotle.

The word "nature," however, is used in two different senses by Aristotle, as is clear from Book II of the *Physics.* Just as all bodies are composed of "matter" and "form," so "nature" when applied to them is used in a passive and an active sense. "Nature" in reference to matter is a passive and potential principle. Thus it belongs to "nature" *as matter* to be passive, to be acted upon, to receive from another. But "nature" in reference to form is an active and formal principle. Thus it belongs to "nature" *as form* to be what it is and to act spontaneously in accord with its nature. The term "nature" is used principally and primarily of nature as a formal principle and only secondarily and potentially of nature as matter.[19] Whatever belongs to "nature" as form follows automatically, necessarily, and immediately from the form of the species as from a positive, active "principle," as we have described above. Therefore characteristic motions and rest derive from "nature" as from an active principle just as spontaneously, immediately, and necessarily as do all of its inert characteristics, such as size, weight, shape, color, texture, and the like. It is proper to all species to flourish and thrive in a suitable place, called "natural." Heavy bodies *de facto* fall down and rest in a stable place; therefore downward movement must be just as "natural" as being down. Only an obstacle can prevent the heavy body from falling; once this is removed, the body automatically falls by its own power.

What we have been saying can be conveniently summarized in terms of the twofold distinction of "act" to which Anneliese Maier alludes.[20] First act (*actus primus*) is the first actualization of pure potentiality by substantial form, or act; it is brought into existence by the efficient causality of a *generans.* Second act (*actus secundus*) is the exercise or realization of an act already fully constituted *in virtute;* it is the external realization of the whole power already in the first act and "intended" by nature as form. To explain the actual falling of a heavy

[19] Arist., *Phys.* II, 1, 193b7.
[20] A. Maier, *op. cit.,* pp. 149–50.

body in existence, Aristotle uses the example of the geometer actually exercising the powers of his science already possessed. Just as the geometer already has everything he needs to geometrize in the science actually possessed, so too the heavy body has everything it needs to fall down in its first act of being a heavy body. No further efficient causality is needed, except the removal of an impediment, if there be one. Thus only in the case of *actus primus* is there need to look for an efficient cause, except the removal of any impediment. For Aristotle, this efficient cause, called the *generans,* must be in contact with the matter in order to produce the substantial form. But once this form is in existence, it immediately and spontaneously does what comes naturally and it already has the full power to do so. For this reason Aristotle says that the word "potentially" is used in two different senses as the term is applied to the two different uses of "act," first or second. It is clear that the manifestations of "nature" are many and different, depending on whether they are found in inanimate bodies, living plants, or self-moving animals. But even in plants and animals there are many different activities that arise spontaneously from "nature" as from an active, formal principle. In plants there are not only the movements and alterations proper to inanimate substances but also the movements of growing, fading, being nourished, and bearing seeds. In animals there are not only similar movements but also the heartbeat and other vital signs, as well as self-movement motivated by desire. Only in the case of self-movement initiated by appetite is it proper to speak of efficient causality; all other movements come about immediately and spontaneously from "nature" as from a principle. It is clear that for Aristotle no further efficient cause need be looked for after the substantial nature is in existence in order to explain its further actualization to *actus secundus.*

In all motions it is the goal of the movement that exercises another kind of causality, called "final." But final cause is said to "move" the body to act only metaphorically. That is to say, a final cause does not move the agent in the same way as an efficient cause moves the effect, and so the final cause is said to "move" metaphorically, since it moves not by efficiency but by being desired. Thus natural place is a final cause of motion inasmuch as it is "intended" and "desired" by nature as a formal and active principle. It is the goal to which that nature is ordained intrinsically. Later theories of quasi-attraction attributed to natural place, such as the one suggested by Roger Bacon, try to reduce the Aristotelian final causality of place to some kind of efficient cause; and these have no place in Aristotle's own explanation of natural local motion. In his explanation of movement of heavy bodies,

downward movement arises naturally and necessarily from the "nature" of heavy bodies seeking their own natural end, as a final resting
place in which they are conserved.

It can be said that the substantial form or "nature" has the ability of
itself (*in virtute*) to move immediately (*statim*) to the goal intended by
nature without the intervention of any other efficient cause, except a
removens prohibens, should that be necessary. This *removens prohibens*,
however, is the *per se* cause, as we have said, not of the actual falling
but only of the removal of the obstacle. Thus there is no need to look
for any other moving cause to explain the actual falling of the heavy
or the rising of the light. There is no *motor coniunctus* needed in
Aristotle to explain the continued movement of the heavy body downward once it has been generated from a light body. Aristotle explicitly
says, "The light body is generated from a heavy one, e.g., air from
water (for water is the first thing that is potentially light), and air is
actually light, and will *at once* realize its proper activity as such unless
something prevents it."[21] The heavy body moves downward without
the movement of any other body causing it to do so; there is no
"mover" conjoined to the body to make it move downward. Aristotle's
proof that there can be no "mover" rests on the infinite divisibility of
the continuum. Since an inanimate body is a homogeneous continuum, lacking all organs or parts, it is infinitely divisible, meaning
that there is no "first part" less than which there is no other. Therefore, in such a continuum, if any minimal part is at rest, the whole will
be at rest; and if any minimal part is in motion, the whole will be in
motion. "Consequently, everything that is moved must be moved by
something else; for that which is in motion will always be divisible, and
if a part of it is not in motion the whole must be at rest."[22]

In this context the meaning of the Aristotelian axiom *Omne quod
movetur ab alio movetur* is that an efficient cause or "mover" is required
to reduce radical potentiality to first substantial act; this "mover" must
be distinct from the effect and in actual contact with it in its production. It is not applicable to the movement from first act to second act.
That is to say, it has nothing to do with the continuation of natural
motion once the formal "nature" exists. Consequently it is erroneous
to translate *Omne quod movetur* as "everything that is in motion" or as
"everything that moves." It applies only to the generation of a natural
form when understood of the free fall of heavy bodies and the rising
of light or of other natural motions.

---

[21] Arist., *Phys.* VIII, 4, 255b9–11.
[22] Arist., *Phys.* VII, 1, 242a14–16.

To summarize: Aristotle introduces an efficient cause or "mover" to explain the generation of substantial natures, all violent motions, and the self-motion of animals in place. In these cases a "mover" in actual contact with the effect is necessary. Once "nature" as a formal, active principle exists in a body there is no further mover (*motor*) needed to explain the *actus secundus* of that nature. It immediately (*statim*) and spontaneously moves to second act by its own formal power (*virtus*), already implanted in the *actus primus*. No further efficient cause is needed to explain the continued movement of the nature once it has left the womb of the generator (*generans*). In other words, for all natural motions of whatever kind there is no *motor coniunctus* invoked by Aristotle to explain the *actus secundus*, or the realization of that *virtus*. It just comes into being by its own formal power (*virtus*) without ever moving itself (*a seipso*) into act, for this would be to make every "nature" as a formal "principle" into an efficient cause, which it cannot be. It means that all living things naturally and spontaneously take in nourishment, grow, and even throb with a rhythmical heartbeat *by nature* as from a formal "principle." To say that animals and plants "move themselves" (*a seipsis*) to grow, to digest, or to beat the heart is to use words improperly and fail to understand the causalities involved. It is also to introduce the specter of a *motor coniunctus* into Aristotelian physics. Such a specter is nothing more than a ghost, a myth, which has no basis in the actual text of Aristotle.

2. ALBERTUS MAGNUS AND THOMAS AQUINAS

The teaching of Albertus Magnus and Thomas Aquinas is no different from that of Aristotle himself, as Anneliese Maier has noted.[23] Albert the Great recognized only two efficient causes of natural motion: the *generans* as the *per se* cause, and the *removens prohibens* as the *per accidens* cause.[24] He does not recognize the substantial form or "nature" of an inanimate body as a *motor coniunctus*. For him the nature once generated has all it needs to do what comes naturally. In Book VIII of the *Physics* Albert paraphrases Aristotle exactly when he discusses the axiom *Omne quod movetur ab alio movetur* (tr. 2, c. 4). He clearly distinguishes natural motion from violent and says that, in the latter case, the cause of the motion is obviously extrinsic. But in natural motion, even of fire upward and of earth downward—the extreme elements whose motions are obvious—the cause of that motion is not so obvious. The solution to the difficulty lies in the two different kinds

---

[23] A. Maier, *op. cit.*, pp. 158–59.
[24] Albertus Magnus, *De caelo* IV, tr. 2, c. 3, ed. Borgnet, IV, 304a–305a.

of potentiality: the coming into being from pure potentiality, which has only an *inchoatio formae,* and the exercise of a form already in act but not yet in its ultimate perfection. Using the example of the knower given by Aristotle, Albert notes that the *per se* cause of *sciens in habitu* becoming *sciens in actu* is the teacher who taught the doctrine in the first place: "Docens ipsum movet eum per se ad considerandum; quia dat ei formam, ad quam necessario consequitur considerare si non impediatur."

But one may object to this straightforward answer that the knower really moves himself to know by his act of will. Albert replies that this is to move oneself *per accidens,* just as the physician who cures himself of a malady is said to "cure himself" *per accidens.*[25] Therefore, Albert insists, the true cause of the actual consideration of a scientific truth is the teacher of that truth in the first place, because the one who taught that truth "dat ei omne quod sequitur ad scientiam." Thus the teacher is the *per se* mover toward both motions, that of coming into being and that of attaining all that necessarily follows upon that being. Just as fire causes the wood to become hot and then to burn, so too the cause of a heavy body becoming heavy is the cause of its falling. Therefore both the proper place and the motion toward that place are caused *per se* by the generator of that body. And, for Albert, it is not correct to say that the body "moves itself" (*a seipso*) to that place. "Ideo locus et motus datur a generante sicut forma, sed forma datur principaliter, et locus et motus dantur per consequens, sicut ea quae propria accidentia sunt formae datae per generationem."[26]

Albert ascribes to Plato the quandary of what moves the heavy body down and the light body up in the absence of any observable mover internal or external. Albert insistently answers that there is *no other* cause but the form received from the generator which is of itself apt to be moved naturally and be in a final condition proper to it. It is interesting to note that Albert always refers to this motion in the passive voice of "sursum moveri" and "deorsum moveri" for light and heavy bodies, because the body does not move itself and is therefore rather moved than moves. The active voice of "move" would imply efficient causality on itself or on another. Therefore the Latin always uses the passive voice to signify natural motions.

It is evident therefore, Albert concludes, that none of the simple inanimate bodies move themselves, as Plato thought in antiquity, and after him Galen, and in the course of time Seneca. "All such bodies have within themselves a principle of their motion, not indeed of

[25] Albertus Magnus, *Physica* VIII, tr. 2, c. 4, ed. Borgnet, III, 571b.
[26] *Ibid.,* ed. Borgnet III, 572a–b.

moving themselves actively, but of receiving these motions from the one generating them and giving them the form to which belong motion and place to which they are moved."[27] Albert in this passage could not be more explicit in his rejection of any other efficient cause to explain natural motions.

What Albert has said of natural local motion, he applies to all other natural motions, such as that toward *quale* and *quantum:* once the form is generated from a suitable potentiality, it immediately moves toward those sensible qualities and that size it ought to have by nature.

For Albert the axiom is valid for all bodies that do not move themselves but *are moved* either naturally or violently; both must be moved by another. In the case of violent motion this fact is evident and it is clear that one cannot proceed *ad infinitum* in the search for a first mover. If there were no first, there would be no violent motion in the present, since all moved things move only insofar as they are moved: if there is no first, there can be no last. Likewise in the case of natural motion. All such motions here and now must be accounted for by the generator of the form and "nature" in the first instance. If there were nothing to account for the coming into being of the "nature," there would be no explanation of why natural *motion* takes place at all. The immediate explanation is to be found in a form that is generated by another for the sake of having certain characteristics fulfilled, such as being in a natural place and functioning in a certain way.

In the immediate analysis the first *per se* cause of many natural generations is the sun, which by its heat and light causes water to evaporate, earth to coalesce, and fire to burn. The sun is clearly an equivocal cause outside the series of univocal causes producing particular generations of specific forms. For Aristotle, the sun too *is moved* by the intelligence which animates it; for Albert, the sun *is moved* by the separated intelligence which moves it solely by efficient causality. In either case, the sun too is moved by another, and so on to the very first unmoved mover of the universe. Albert never tires of repeating that all motion takes place by the efficient causality of an *unmoved mover;* without some unmoved mover somewhere in the animal body or in the universe there can be no motion whatever. Thus the first unmoved mover is the initiator of all motion. Since the animal soul must itself be generated, it cannot be the absolutely first but can only be first relative to animal motions.

The doctrine of St. Thomas Aquinas is identical to that of Albert in

---

[27] "Sed omnia talia sui motus in se habent principium, non quidem movendi se active et faciendi et recipiendi hoc a generante ipsa, et dante eis formam cuius est motus et locus ad quem moventur." Albert, *ibid.*, ed. Borgnet, III, 573a.

this matter, but he is more explicit in his exposition of the text. First Thomas explains how certain beings come about *by nature* and others by other causes, such as by art or chance.[28] Among those things that come about by nature are all animals and their parts, as well as plants, and simple bodies such as the four elements. These differ from non-natural things in that they have a "principle" of motion and rest intrinsic to them. Some of these move naturally as to place, such as heavy and light bodies; others move naturally as to increase and decrease, such as plants and animals; others again move naturally as to alteration, such as the simple bodies with their contrary qualities.

Bodies that do not originate in nature, such as a couch or clothing, as such do not *do* anything, not having within themselves any intrinsic "principle" of motion, except insofar as they are made of natural elements and fibres. A knife, for example, falls down, not because it is an instrument, but because it is made of metal.

The only objection Thomas levels against this point is that many natural things seem to be moved extrinsically, as water is heated by fire, or air is ignited by heat. For this reason, Thomas says, some of the ancients thought that privation must be an imperfect active "principle" within matter initiating the change.[29] But, Thomas replies, this privation can be nothing more than an aptitude for form, which at the time is lacking; therefore, it cannot be an active principle of change but can only be a condition for change. Privation can be no more than an absence within matter, which itself is a passivity for change, a passive principle proper to "nature" *as matter.*

Thomas's basis for determining how motions belong to "nature" is that such "principles" are determined by the kind of motion belonging to it: if it belongs to natures to move (*movere*), then they have an active principle proper to form; if it belongs to natures to be moved (*moveri*), then they have a passive principle proper to matter. Thomas then shows that even celestial motions can be called "natural" inasmuch as they have a natural passivity to being moved by intelligences. Heavy and light bodies, on the other hand, have within themselves a *formal principle* of their motion, "because just as other accidents are consequent upon the substantial form, so also is place and consequently motion to place, not however such that the natural form is the mover [*motor*], but the *motor* is the *generans* which gave such a form on which such a motion follows."[30]

---

[28] Thomas Aquinas, *In II Phys.*, lect. 1, n. 2.
[29] *Ibid.*, n. 3.
[30] "In corporibus vero gravibus et levibus est principium formale sui motus; quia sicut alia accidentia consequuntur formam substantialem, ita et locus, et per consequens

This brings Thomas to Aristotle's definition of "nature," which he is careful to classify as a pure "principle." For Thomas, Aristotle's definition of nature is "principium motus et quietis in eo in quo est primo et per se et non secundum accidens."[31] The word *principium* is placed in the definition as a quasi genus, and not as something absolute, "because the word 'nature' implies a relationship of 'principle.'" The word *principium* is a relative noun and does not signify an absolute entity like *vis insita rebus* or some such figment. In Aristotle's own definition the word *causa* is also found, but Thomas explains this to mean that "nature" is not a principle of all motions in the same way; of some motions, as the self-movement of an animal, it is also the efficient cause by means of parts. Further on Thomas explains that "in natural things the generator is said to move heavy and light bodies insofar as it gives the form by which [*per quam*] those bodies are moved."[32]

In Book VIII of the *Physics,* St. Thomas explains the causes of free-fall of heavy bodies and the rising of light bodies.[33] A body that is only potentially heavy must first *be moved* to being a heavy body; for this an extrinsic generator is needed. Once it is generated, then immediately (*statim*) it moves downward without any other cause, not even resistance. The only other efficient cause that enters the picture is whoever removes any obstacle to the natural accomplishment of the motion. "This motion it has from the one who first generated the body which gave it a form on which follows such an inclination. Thus the generator is the *per se* mover of heavy and light bodies, but whoever removes the obstacle is the *per accidens mover.*"[34] From this Thomas concludes that "none of these bodies move themselves [*movet seipsum*], namely, heavy and light bodies; nevertheless their motion is natural, because they have a 'principle' of motion within themselves, not indeed a motivating and active principle, but a passive principle, which is a potency for such an act." Thomas explicitly says that once the substantial nature is generated, "it is not necessary that it be reduced to secondary act by some agent; it immediately [*statim*] of itself [*per seipsum*] operates, unless there is something to prevent it."[35] This is true not only of the geometer who already has the science of geometry but also of the heavy body which already exists; it im-

---

moveri ad locum; non tamen ita quod forma naturalis sit motor, sed motor est generans, quod dat talem formam, ad quam talis motus consequitur." Thomas, *ibid.,* n. 4.
   [31] *Ibid.,* n. 5.
   [32] Thomas, *In II Phys.,* lect. 5, n. 5.
   [33] Thomas, *In VIII Phys.,* lect. 8, nn. 5–7.
   [34] *Ibid.,* n. 7.
   [35] *Ibid.,* n. 3.

mediately falls. In Latin, however, this is always expressed in the passive voice of *movetur*, because "nature" is ultimately a passive principle to be moved rather than to move other things. But Thomas is explicit that once a substantial nature is generated, no *per se* cause other than the generator need be sought to explain its natural motions toward place, qualities, or quantity.

Contrary to Averroes, Thomas holds that natural motions of light and heavy bodies do not need resistance against which to move. Therefore a heavy body will move in a void in a natural period of time without any resisting medium.[36] Likewise Siger of Brabant disagreed with the Commentator on this point, as did the author of the *Physics* commentary in Clm 9559. The substantial nature is in a body that occupies dimensions; therefore it requires time to move. This natural time over a given distance toward a natural place is sufficient to determine the natural velocity of a body even in a void.

3. AVICENNA, AVERROES, AND *MOTOR CONIUNCTUS*

Avicenna in his *Sufficientia*[37] and Algazel's paraphrase *Maqâcid el-falâcifa*,[38] both of which were translated in the twelfth century, propound the influential theory that in natural movement the "form" is the *mover* of the body which it informs. That is, Avicenna, followed in a fuller way by Averroes, thought that the form is the mover (*motor coniunctus*) accompanying the body which it moves, actually moving it as an efficient cause. The origin of Avicenna's view was his conception of "form" as an active thing (*res*) and "matter" as a passive thing (*res*), each complete in its own right. Such a dichotomy, no doubt, was due to his neo-Platonic view of matter and form as autonomous *things* in nature, rather than as two "principles" of a unique thing.[39] The big innovation in Avicenna's philosophy of nature is clearly his *dator formarum*, an entirely un-Aristotelian notion, introduced primarily to explain how natural bodies can produce substantial changes. For Avicenna[40] natural agents do nothing more than dispose a substance up

---

[36] See Chapter VI below.
[37] See H. A. Wolfson, *Crescas' Critique of Aristotle* (Cambridge, Mass., 1929), pp. 672–75; also B. Carra de Vaux, *Avicenne* (Paris, 1900), pp. 184–85. The late fourteenth-century Jewish philosopher Crescas also followed this Arabic tradition; see *Critique* (*Or Adonai*), ed. Wolfson, prop. XVII, pp. 296–99.
[38] *Algazel's Metaphysics*, ed. J. T. Muckle (Toronto, 1933), pp. 30–31, 99–102. Concerning the nature of the *Maqâcid*, see D. Salman, "Algazel et les Latins," *Arch. d'hist. doctr. et litt. du M. A.* 10 (1935), 103–27.
[39] See St. Thomas, *Sum. theol.* I, q. 110, a. 2; *Sum. cont. gent.* III, c. 68.
[40] Avicenna, *Metaphysica*, tr. IX, c. 5, in *Opera omnia*, ed. Venice 1508, fol. 105va–b. Cf. St. Thomas, *Sum. cont. gent.* II, c. 76; III, c. 65 and c. 103.

to a certain point, at which point the *dator formarum* implants the new substantial form into the "effect." Avicenna invoked the "giver of forms" not only to explain new intellectual knowledge in the learning process but, more importantly for natural philosophy, to explain efficient causality between bodies. Thus Avicenna claimed that natural agents can induce only certain dispositions for a "form" that is actually induced from outside the body, from the *dator formarum*.[41]

It is ironical that Avicenna could grant that substantial "form" in inanimate bodies is the true efficient cause of self-motion upward and downward and at the same time deny true efficient causality to it in the production of new effects in other things.[42] Avicenna was one of the first to conceive a natural form as a *motor coniunctus* to explain the continuation of motion in a body once begotten. It is a point that Averroes developed in much greater detail.

Averroes followed Aristotle in identifying the *generans* as "illud quod dat corpori simplici generato formam suam et omnia accidentia formae, quorum unum est motus in loco."[43] But he was un-Aristotelian in trying to find a *motor coniunctus* to explain the downward movement of heavy bodies even after the heavy body had been generated. Against Avicenna, he realized that the "form" could not be the *per se* mover of inanimate bodies, for this is characteristic of living things. Therefore in Book IV of the *Physics* Averroes insisted on the absolute necessity of resistance for all natural local motion. Thus for Averroes the "form" *per se* moves the resisting medium, which then *per se* moves the body, much like a rower moving himself in a boat by moving against the water.[44] This is to make the "form" in heavy bodies a *per accidens* cause of self-motion by means of the resisting medium. For this reason Averroes insisted that all motion must take place against some positive resistance, so that motion in a void is absolutely impossible.[45] Averroes, then, allowed the form to be a *motor coniunctus* to explain how bodies once generated could move naturally in the absence of the *generans*. E. J. Dijksterhuis explains the Averroist view by attributing to the medium the functions of a *motor coniunctus* in the downward movement of a heavy body.[46] But it would be truer to say that Averroes saw the "form" itself as the *motor coniunctus* acting by means of the medium in moving downward. In any case, Averroes did

---

[41] *Ibid.*, fol. 103vb.
[42] See J. A. Weisheipl, "Aristotle's Concept of Nature: Avicenna and Aquinas," in *Approaches to Nature in the Middle Ages*, ed. L. D. Roberts (Binghamton, 1982), pp. 137–60.
[43] Averroes, *Physica* VIII, comm. 32.
[44] Averroes, *Physica* IV, comm. 71.
[45] See Chapter VI below.
[46] E. J. Dijksterhuis, *op. cit.*, p. 177.

try to preserve some distinction between animate and inanimate natures by saying that animate natures move themselves *per se* from place to place, while inanimate natures move themselves *per accidens* by means of the medium. Nevertheless the influence of Avicenna and Averroes was so great in the Middle Ages that the specter of the *motor coniunctus* remained in the mind of many scholastic writers.

The example most frequently used to illustrate the *motor coniunctus* in late medieval physics is the impetus given to the projectile to explain its continued movement. In the original theory proposed by the Franciscan Francis de Marchia in the early fourteenth century, *impetus* or *vis impressa* given to the projectile was presented as an example of instrumental causality whereby the initiator of the motion continued his effect in the separated projectile. Thus Francis de Marchia saw the theory as a way to explain the sacraments instituted by Christ as separated "instruments" of Christ's continued causality in the soul. For him it was not a case where *impetus* needed to be a new "mover" or efficient cause of a new effect but rather a continuation of Christ's original causality now in the sacramental sign.

John Buridan and Albert of Saxony, however, continued to see the substantial form of heavy bodies as the *agens principale,* the *agens principalissimum* and the *causa prima* of downward motion,[47] *gravitas* acting as an instrument of substantial form. From this it was easy to conceive the *impetus* given to the projectile as the *motor* and *causa efficiens* of violent motion. Speaking of the impetus theory E. J. Dijksterhuis comments, "It was assumed that the *projiciens* imparted this power to the *mobile,* for which it formed the *motor conjunctus.*"[48] Again he notes, "It may further be noted that according to the terminist conception, the impetus was regarded as the cause of a motion, the *motor conjunctus* urging the *projectum separatum* forward."[49] In strict instrumental causality, however, the *virtus impressa* given to the instrument is conceived in no way as a *motor* but solely as a borrowed and alien "principle" by which the agent moves the instrument, even when separated. In this case there is no need for an additional "motor" to move the instrument; the principal agent is sufficient.

4. DUNS SCOTUS AND DENIAL OF THE AXIOM

The traditional Aristotelian view of natural motion was entirely replaced by Duns Scotus with a doctrine of universal self-motion.

---

[47] See A. Maier, *op. cit.,* pp. 168–70.
[48] E. J. Dijksterhuis, *op. cit.,* p. 179.
[49] *Ibid.,* p. 183.

With this doctrine Scotus rejected the Aristotelian axiom of *Omne quod movetur ab alio movetur.* Scotus's new doctrine consisted in thinking that all natural motions are self-motions (*a seipsis*) and so do not require to be moved by another.[50] Scotus saw that all "coeval" and proper accidents flow immediately from a substantial form once generated in substantial change. But he preferred to call this self-motion and deny the need of any further mover.[51] Thus if all natural bodies move themselves to their proper accidents, it was inevitable that the downward motion of heavy bodies be seen as a case of self-motion. Similarly water that has been heated by fire will immediately "reduce itself to coldness when the heating agent has been removed" ("sicut patet de aqua summe calefacta, quae subtracto reducit se ad frigiditatem").[52] In the case of hot water becoming cool, Scotus argues that the whole water moves itself to the state of being cool in the absence of any outside mover. Therefore this must be self-motion: "tota aqua agit, et tota patitur."[53]

It is, however, in the sphere of spiritual activity, as in intellection and volition, that Scotus gives the strongest defense of self-motion and the rejection of the principle *Omne quod movetur ab alio movetur.* Even though Aristotle and the older tradition considered intellection and volition to be examples not of true physical motion but of immanent activity, Scotus nevertheless considered them clear examples of self-motion. If the intellect moves itself to think and the will moves itself to willing, there is no need of an outside "mover" to account for this. Therefore not everything that moves is moved by another. In effect it was a rejection of Avicenna's *motor coniunctus* which demanded a real distinction between mover and moved. For Scotus, since the whole moves the whole and the whole at the same time suffers motion, there is no distinction between mover and moved. If it is not moved by another (*ab alio*), it must be considered a case of self-motion.

All cases of natural motion in traditional Aristotelian physics, such as the falling of heavy bodies, the rising of light, growth and nutrition in living things, as well as all natural alterations, were interpreted by Scotus as examples of self-motion. To these Scotus added the strong cases of intellection and volition, even though Thomas and Albert interpreted these immanent activities in a different light. For Scotus it was sufficient that the "whole" be the mover and the "whole" the

---

[50] See R. Effler, *op. cit. per totum.*
[51] *Ibid.,* pp. 98–103.
[52] Scotus, *Opus oxon.,* II, dist. 25, q. un., ed. Wadding, XIII, 209.
[53] *Ibid.,* XIII, 210.

moved to constitute self-motion. Therefore not everything that moves is moved by another. Scotus replaced the Aristotelian axiom, as traditionally understood, with his doctrine of universal self-motion of all things.

The obvious objection an Aristotelian of the older tradition would raise against Scotus would be that this view eliminates the distinction between living and nonliving things, the same objection Aristotle himself raises in *Physics* VIII, 4. To this objection Scotus replied that the difference between animals and nonliving things is that animals have cognition of the end they desire, whereas nonliving things have no knowledge. But this is a distinction based not on motion but on knowledge. Surely there is a difference in the motion of animals and non-animals that do not move from place to place. In order to move from place to place animals must have knowledge and desire; this is manifested in their manner of moving.

In all natural motions for Scotus "mover" and "moved" are not really distinct but only two aspects of the same body. For him they are modally distinct and not really distinct, since the "whole" is mover and the "whole" is moved. For this reason Effler says, "In the sphere of inorganic substances, such as light and heavy bodies and spiritual substances, the distinction between mover and moved has no place" for Duns Scotus.[54] That is to say, Scotus rejected the Avicennian and Averroist concept of *motor coniunctus* in his view that all natural motions are self-motions. For this reason Scotus rejected the Aristotelian axiom *Omne quod movetur ab alio movetur,* claiming it to be no principle at all, not even a tenth one: "Non credo quod Aristoteles posuisset aliquod complexum esse principium non solum primum, sed nec decimum, ex quo in multis singularibus evidentia absurda sequerentur."[55]

The only real difficulty with Scotus's solution to the problem of natural motion is that he makes the natural body the *efficient cause* of the motion as a real self-mover. But in every case of true efficient causality there must be a real distinction between "cause" and "effect," for the cause must already have the actuality which the effect does not yet have. Scotus's modal distinction between "whole" and "whole" is not sufficient for real efficient causality or real self-motion. Roy Effler sees no difficulty in calling the substantial form of inanimate bodies the "efficient cause" of motion and rest. Thus he says, "The active efficient principle of free fall is intrinsic to the body,"[56] "The heavy

---

[54] R. Effler, *op. cit.,* p. 125.
[55] Scotus, *Metaph.* IX, q. 14, ed. Wadding, VII, 600.
[56] Effler, *op. cit.,* p. 110.

thing is the efficient cause of its rest,"[57] and so on. This stems from a basic inability to distinguish a true formal "principle" that spontaneously brings forth proper accidents from an "efficient cause" that moves the body by parts from one position to another. For Aristotle only a body with distinct parts can be the true efficient cause of physical motion in place. This is because the distinction between "mover" and "moved" must be real. St. Thomas sometimes speaks of the intellect moving itself from principles to conclusions and the will moving itself from end to means. These, however, are presented as examples not of physical motion but of intensely immanent activity in which there is no movement of "parts."

Scotus elaborated a vast theory of universal self-motion in material and spiritual things to show that not everything that is moved or is moving must be moved by another. He thought that for this it was sufficient to show that the "whole" moves the "whole" and, therefore, there is no need for a *motor coniunctus*. In this he failed to see the precise nature of an "efficient cause" and failed to distinguish it from a formal "principle." If Scotus had known of the theory of impetus, he would not have made *impetus* an efficient "cause" but would have said that the "whole" moves the "whole" in his universal doctrine of self-motion. This is another example of a small error in the beginning, the error being the failure to distinguish "principle" from "cause."

CONCLUSION

It is commonly said that the scholastic axiom *Omne quod movetur ab alio movetur* had to be rejected before modern classical physics could begin with its principle of inertia. In the first place this is taken to mean a rejection of the *motor coniunctus* to explain the continuation of motion once the body has left the projector or the generator. As we have seen, in Aristotelian physics there never was any need for a *motor coniunctus* to explain the natural motion of bodies once generated. The substantial form itself was the active formal "principle" of all that comes naturally to the body, including motions and rest. Among natural motions that come immediately and spontaneously on the constitution of a body are local motions, nutrition, growth, production of seed, and even the heartbeat. The only efficient cause acknowledged in all these motions was the *generator* of that body. Once the body exists, it immediately manifests all its natural characteristics, including

[57] *Ibid.*, p. 111.

local motion to a natural place. Whoever removed an impediment to the natural motion was also considered an efficient "cause" of that motion, but only *per accidens* in that an obstacle was removed to the immediate actuality of motion. In Aristotelian physics there is no need to look for any other efficient cause. This substantial form in no way was considered the efficient cause of the motion or of the proper accidents. It is only an active, formal "principle" of all that comes from it immediately and spontaneously, no obstacle being present.

A grave error is committed by those who see the substantial form or "nature" of a thing as a true efficient "cause" of natural activity. This comes from thinking of substantial form as a thing, a *res* in its own right, and the "body" as a distinct thing upon which it acts. Avicenna and Averroes both saw the form as a "mover" of the body and the efficient cause of natural motions, at least *per accidens.* For them, the form could be said to be a *motor coniunctus* to explain continued motion after the body was generated. Both Albert and Thomas rejected this notion and returned to the truer Aristotelian view that form as "nature" is an active principle of all natural motions. Only in the case of animals that move themselves is the body a true efficient cause of self-motion. But the animal is able to move itself from place to place only because it has really distinct parts. A homogeneous body, being infinitely divisible, has no really distinct parts, and no first "part" that could be a mover. The animal, however, is the efficient cause only of those limited motions in which it moves itself from place to place, not of all those other motions it has naturally, such as growth, nutrition, production of seed, circulation of the blood, and the like.

In the cases of natural motion the axiom *Omne quod movetur ab alio movetur* applies directly to the generation of the body in the first place; all subsequent natural motions, as the falling of heavy bodies, are due to the original generator and to no other *per se* cause. In Aristotle's physics the substantial form is not the *motor coniunctus* to explain the production of motion after the body has been generated. There is no need of any *motor coniunctus,* except to explain violent motion where the "cause" is clearly outside the "nature."

Duns Scotus introduced an entirely new concept when he called all natural motions "self-motion." For him that meant that the "whole" body moves itself to a natural goal. In this he eliminated any real distinction between "mover" and "moved." In his doctrine of universal self-motion there is no need of any *motor coniunctus.* But that hardly means that he anticipated the modern doctrine of inertia. In the classical principle of inertia the body does not move itself but moves with the force impressed upon it at the beginning. The principle of inertia is not so much a denial of *Omne quod movetur ab alio movetur* as it is a denial of a real distinction between natural and violent motions. Scotus kept that distinction but saw all nature as self-moving. For Scotus there was no need of a real distinction between "mover" and "moved," since the "whole" moved itself wholly; the same body was both agent and patient. In this, Scotus's doctrine of natural motion is as un-Aristotelian as the myth of a *motor coniunctus.*

Only by preserving the distinction between "principle" and "cause" as well as between "mover" and "moved" can the authentic doctrine of Aristotle be understood. Modern historians who present Aristotle as requiring a *motor coniunctus* to explain the continuation of natural motion grossly misunderstand the elements of Aristotle's natural philosophy.

VI

MOTION IN A VOID:
AQUINAS AND AVERROES

The concept of the void has attracted the attention of philosophers and scientists since pre-Socratic times. There are, however, a number of aspects of the void that should be distinguished before discussing the particular one we are concerned with in this paper. One generic category for the concept of the void is some kind of space or "place in which there is nothing."[1] On the Aristotelian hypothesis that every body is either heavy or light, one might concretize the definition of the void in the phrase "that in which there is nothing heavy or light."[2] Aristotle has very little to say about space, but he devotes five chapters to the nature of "place" and four to the concept of the "void." The notion of place is a very complex one, involving both the innermost boundary of the containing body and the formal immobility of the containing body itself, so that bodies can be said to move in and out of places. It can be defined as "the innermost (immovable) boundary of the container."[3] Place thus involves a qualitative environmental container that is somehow immobile relative to the system of the universe. While the qualitative environmental container is sufficient to explain the natural movement of bodies for Aristotle, the quantitative immobility of the container need not be taken as something absolute, as I have tried to show elsewhere.[4] For Aristotle the whole universe is a plenum. Therefore a void would be some kind of place devoid of every body. A *locus sine corpore locato* is not a contradiction in terms, as E. J. Dijksterhuis would have us believe,[5] but an attempt to define and circumscribe the notion of void.

---

[1] Arist., *Phys.* IV, 7, 213b32–33.
[2] *Ibid.*, 214a4–5.
[3] *Phys.* IV, 4, 212a20–21.
[4] *Nature and Gravitation* (River Forest, Ill., 1955), pp. 74–76.
[5] *The Mechanization of the World Picture* (Oxford, 1961), p. 39.

P. H. Wicksteed and F. M. Cornford are undoubtedly correct when they say that κενόν (void) comes nearer to our "space" than τόπος (place).[6] Space, as such, denotes essentially some kind of dimensionality. This dimensionality can be real and physical, as when we give the extension between two bodies and there is real quantity belonging to another body between them. This is one common usage in all measurements. These dimensions are quantities belonging to the intervening body, but for practical purposes they can be temporarily disregarded. In other words, the intervening dimensions or quantity are not relevant to the case. We simply want to know the space available or the distance to be covered. Even if there were no intervening body with its proper dimensions, we would still speak of dimensions. Thus dimensionality, as such, abstracts from the question whether or not there is a real accident of quantity belonging to any body. Further, there is mathematical space, which is nothing more than a geometrical description of a situation in reference to determined coordinates. In Euclidean geometry there is nothing between a point, line, or figure and the coordinates. While we do not speak of mathematical space as a void, because there is no advantage in doing so, it can nevertheless suggest the nature of emptiness, nonbeing, the void. Finally, there is imaginative space, a kind of mental framework, within which objects of imagination are placed. Immanuel Kant was so struck by the natural inevitability of some spatial dimensionality that he thought it must be an *a priori* condition of the human mind, a condition which makes experience possible. This framework or screen is a kind of absolute space, much like Plato's "matter" or "winnowing basket" within which, or against which, we project images, including mathematical points, lines, and figures. When we speak of "space" beyond the universe, whether this be the Aristotelian universe or our present collection of galaxies, the kind of space that is required by human philosophy is nothing more than a *quid imaginativum*.[7]

By "void" in this paper we mean an empty space existing outside the mind, a space that has absolutely nothing in it. Even the term "nothing" is to be taken strictly as meaning no objective reality whatever, neither being nor force nor resistance. When we ask the more sophisticated question whether there could be a motion of a real body through a void, we grant the existence of such a void as a hypothesis. We wish to know whether there would be movement of a natural body through such a void if one did exist.

[6]*Aristotle, The Physics*, Loeb ed. (London, 1963), I, 271.
[7]St. Thomas, *In III Phys.*, lect. 7, n. 6; see J. A. Weisheipl, "Space and Gravitation," *The New Scholasticism* 29 (1955), 175–223.

The question was a serious one in Greek antiquity and it aroused considerable discussion in the Middle Ages, as we shall see. The question is also of interest to modern historians of science, who see in the medieval position on this question one of the fundamental obstacles to the rise of the new physics of the seventeenth century. Anneliese Maier in particular maintains that the universal teaching on the question of motion in a void involved a major obstacle to the rise of modern science. In her paper of 1960[8] she noted that two basic medieval hypotheses may be singled out as the most significant and the most fatal for the birth of classical physics.

The first of these[9] is the theorem that qualities, as such, are independent factors with their own laws in natural processes, quite distinct from quantitative factors. That is, as "intensive magnitudes" they are only parallel to extensive and quantitative magnitudes, and although presumed by some to be susceptible to mathematical treatment, they are not. This aspect of Anneliese Maier's hypothesis will not be considered in this paper.

The second is much more important and relevant to the problem with which we are concerned.[10] Since "omne quod movetur ab alio movetur," according to A. Maier every movement requires a particular mover bound to it and generating motion directly. Moreover, every normal movement of a successive nature requires, over and above the mover, a resistance that opposes the moving force and is overcome by that force, for without resistance there would be no motion (*motus*), but change (*mutatio*), that is, an instantaneous change of place.[11]

This second theorem of the so-called scholastics is highly complex. Each part must be considered before the implications of the whole can be fully understood. The first part is "Omne quod movetur ab aliquo movetur": every movement requires a particular mover bound to it and generating motion directly. I have presented my views on this point in *Isis* some years ago.[12] Briefly, I argued that practically all

[8] "'Ergebnisse' der spätscholastischen Naturphilosophie," *Scholastik* 35 (1960), 161–87.

[9] *Ibid.*, 169–70.

[10] *Ibid.*, 170.

[11] "Dans andere Prinzip ist der Satz 'Omne quod movetur ab aliquo movetur': jede Bewegung erfordert einen partikulären, mit ihr verbundenen und sie unmittelbar erzeugenden Beweger; und jede normal, sukzessiv sich vollziehende Bewegung erfordert überdies einen Widerstand, der sich der vis motrix entgegensetzt und von ihr überwunden wird; denn ohne Widerstand würde sich kein *motus*, sondern eine *mutatio*, d.h. eine in instanti erfolgende Ortsveränderung ergeben." *Loc. cit.*

[12] "The Principle *Omne quod movetur ab alio movetur* in Medieval Physics," *Isis* 56 (1965), 26–45; reprinted as Chapter IV above.

historians, and many philosophers interested in medieval thought, have mistranslated and misunderstood the Latin phrase. It does not mean, and never did mean, that everything here and now moving needs a mover; for Aristotle this is true only of violent motion. This principle was formulated in antiquity, particularly by Aristotle, as applicable to passive principles of motion. Today it is largely a question of bad grammar, turning the Greek middle or passive voice and the Latin passive into a vernacular active. Even Averroes was misled by the Arabic rendering of the Aristotelian principle, and it was upon this that he built his own natural philosophy. Whatever is to be said of the Arabic formulation, it is not the meaning in Latin or for the Latin scholastics. St. Thomas Aquinas, Albertus Magnus, and even Siger of Brabant, an ardent Averroist, saw the predicament this would lead to and opposed the Averroist view, but they had few followers in a detail such as this. Ockham also dismissed the necessity of the scholastic principle, but for very different reasons. We must remember that in the fourteenth century there were at least five different philosophical schools: the Averroists, the Thomists, the Scotists, the nominalists, and a variety of eclectics defending Platonic and Augustinian elements. Therefore care must be taken when speaking of "scholastic physics" in the Middle Ages. We must be especially careful not to fall into the Averroist error of thinking that Aristotle was god and that Averroes was his prophet.

In this paper I should like to consider the other elements in Anneliese Maier's "most important and most fatal" hypothesis of the scholastics: (1) that all motion properly so-called requires a resistance which opposes the moving force, (2) that without resistance there would be no motion (*motus*), strictly so-called, but only change (*mutatio*), and (3) that without resistance, such as in a void, there could be only instantaneous change, that is, change without time. Miss Maier goes on to say that "these principles hold for every local motion, inertial movement as it was called later, as well as others that flow from local motion . . . and which one and all stand in contradiction to classical physics."[13] For A. Maier, as for Averroes before her, motion in a void would be motion without resistance, and therefore it cannot possibly exist. The crucial point for Maier and for Averroes is that resistance is essential to the possibility of motion; without resistance, as would be the case of motion in a void, there cannot be any motion (*motus*, $\varkappa\acute{\iota}\nu\eta\sigma\iota\varsigma$) at all.

The problem of motion in a void and, indeed, of the existence of a

[13] *Loc. cit.*

void itself, goes back to the dilemma raised by Parmenides, who insisted that only what *is* can be real; whatever does not exist cannot be real.[14] However, a void seems to exist between bodies of whatever kind and between numbers; therefore it would seem that the void is real. But by definition a void is "that which does not exist"; therefore bodies cannot be separated by a void, since a void is nonbeing and cannot exist. Separation, for Parmenides, is only an illusion. Moreover, local motion also seems to require a void, for bodies can move only into places devoid of bodies. However, since the void is nonbeing and cannot exist, neither can local motion exist. More important, there cannot be γένεσις or coming-into-being, for every "coming into being" must come from something or nothing. If it comes from something, then it already exists; if it comes from nothing, then it can never begin, for nothing does not exist. Latin philosophers and historians pose the dilemma of Parmenides very simply: a being cannot come into being from nothing, for *ex nihilo nihil fit;* and it cannot come from something already existing, for *quod est, non fit.* Consequently all motion and change is logically impossible; what appears to be multiplicity and movement is only an illusion. They belong to the way of "seeming," or "opinion." The way of "truth" declares that all being exists as one and immobile.[15]

The first serious response to the dilemma of Parmenides came from the atomists Leucippus and Democritus. They conceded that real being, ultimate being, namely, the atoms, could not be generated or annihilated. However, by making one simple alteration in the philosophy of Parmenides, the appearance of change and motion—even the multiplicity of being—could be preserved. That one simple alteration was the admission that nonbeing, the void, was just as real as being itself. If this were granted, there could be a multiplicity of atoms, constructs from atoms, and numbers. More important, the possibility of motion—at least local motion—could be preserved.[16] But as for the atoms themselves, they were as ungenerable and indestructible as the single Being of Parmenides.

Even the demonstration by Anaxagoras that air is a body did not deter the atomists, because even air had to be considered a body insufficient to constitute a void. The atomists could explain all kinds of motion without admitting the generability of atoms. In other words, atoms themselves could not be generated or corrupted. The

---

[14]*Die Fragmente der Vorsokratiker,* ed. H. Diels (7th ed. with additions by W. Kranz), frags. 7–8.
[15]See Kirk and Raven, *The Presocratic Philosophers* (Cambridge, 1957), pp. 277–82.
[16]*Ibid.,* pp. 404–9.

void within bodies could explain condensation and rarefaction, while a void outside bodies could explain local motion, growth, alteration, birth and death. This solution was an alluring one to physicists and to metaphysicians. Even Aristotle commended Democritus for his method and for having brought the study of physics back to respectability.[17] We must remember that for the atomists the void was not only a condition of motion but the very cause of motion. It is not a question of whether some vacua exist in the universe, or whether man can produce a vacuum. It is a question of whether the movements we see in the universe are to be explained in terms of bodies and the void. It is not even a question of "nature abhorring a vacuum," or whether the void outside the entire universe is real or not. For Leucippus and Democritus it was simply whether the movements evident in the universe must be explained by postulating a void. "In the acceptance of void [Leucippus] was consciously correcting an Eleatic axiom."[18] "At the same time Leucippus remained faithful to the principles of his probably Ionian background."[19]

Aristotle took the view of the atomists seriously, even though he deals specifically with the void in only four chapters of his *Physics*, Book IV, cc. 6–9. His arguments are not always demonstrative. Dealing with the void, he arrives at different conclusions; many are simply arguments contradicting the hypothesis of a void. Because of the complexity of these chapters, many readers of Aristotle have been misled by the apparent variety of conclusions. While Aristotle was aware of the atomists throughout his works, notably the *Physics* and *De generatione*, we are concerned only with the difficult chapters of Book IV, cc. 6–9.

After discussing the nature of place (τόπος) in Book IV of the *Physics*, Aristotle turns to the void (κενόν) and says, "The investigation of similar questions about the void, also, must be held to belong to the physicist—namely whether it exists or not, and how it exists or what it is—just as about place" (213a11–13). The entire four chapters, 6 to 9, are a kind of disputation in which arguments are given for and against the existence of a void, and in which is finally established the limited sense in which it can be said to exist. In the sixth chapter he lists the three previous arguments from the atomists and two additional arguments from the Pythagoreans, namely, that there must be a void in the heavens to separate the stars, and that there must be a void between numbers to keep them distinct. In the seventh chapter,

---

[17] Arist., *Gen. corr.* I, 2, 315a34–315b32; cf. 316a14–15; 324b35–325a2.
[18] Kirk and Raven, *op. cit.*, p. 406.
[19] *Ibid.*

where he tries to determine the exact meaning of the void, he shows that there is often a confusion between place and void, "void" often serving the function of "space" and "place." In essence, a void is a place devoid of any body whatever (213b30–214a6).

In a lengthy chapter 8, Aristotle refutes the notion of the void as existing separate from body, using six different arguments leading to different immediate conclusions, but all leading up to the general conclusion that there can be no motion in a void. The first argument (214b13–35) considers the vacuum as undifferentiated space. If a natural body were placed in it, the body could not move, for there are no directions. Second (215a1–13), if there is no natural motion there can be no unnatural or violent motion. Third (215a13–18), if there is no medium, as is required for violent motion, there can be no violent motion. Fourth (215a19–23), the void is completely undifferentiated; there is no "up" or "down," and therefore there cannot be motion, but there can only be eternal rest, or, if a body were put into motion, it would continue *ad infinitum* until stopped by a weightier body. Fifth (215a23–24), the void is postulated because it yields to bodies, but this quality is equally present in every direction; therefore it would have to move in all directions at once, and consequently it would not move at all. Finally (215a24–216a8), between any two movements there must be a ratio, as there is between any two times as long as both are finite; but there is no ratio of void to full. In other words there is no ratio between zero and any number. Therefore motion would be instantaneous, and hence impossible. Concluding this section, Aristotle says, "These are the consequences that result from a difference in media" (216a12).

It is relatively clear what might happen according to Aristotle if the motion of bodies had to be explained by a void instead of by natural place. A variety of things might happen, but it would not be the motion we know bodies to have in the world we live in. First, there could be no natural motion of certain bodies "up" and other bodies "down," for in a void there are no preferential environments towards which different bodies are wont to move. Second, there could be no "violent" or compulsory motion, for this presupposes that it is "natural" for light bodies to move up and heavy bodies to move down. Third, in Aristotle's view and in that of Plato, all violent or non-natural motion must be explained in terms of some "medium" as the extrinsic instrumental cause of continued motion.[20] Fourth, a body might be eternally at rest unless moved by something already in mo-

---

[20] For a fuller explanation of this, see Chapter II above.

tion, or a body in motion might go on *ad infinitum* in a straight line unless a more powerful body stopped or deflected it. Fifth, there might be no motion at all, or motion in every direction at once, for the void is equally susceptible to motion in all directions. Sixth, there might be instantaneous motion, which is not true motion at all because there is no medium to be divided, and between zero and any number there must be a ratio such that $S = 1/0$, where S is the speed and the divisor is zero, as in the absence of any medium. For Aristotle, all of these arguments, or perhaps any one of them, is sufficient to show that natural motions in the universe cannot be explained by postulating a void distinct from bodies, as the atomists contend.

In chapter 9, Aristotle considers briefly the interstices in bodies as voids, e.g., when one body absorbs another and when one body expands and occupies more room. If there were no vacuum within bodies, the atomists say, there could be no contraction and expansion. But if there were no contraction and expansion, either there would be no movement of this kind, such as we see taking place, or the universe would bulge, as Xuthus, the Pythagorean of Croton, said, or air and water must always change into equal amounts. For example, if air has been made out of a cupful of water, then conversely out of an equal amount of air a cupful of water must have been made—or there must be a void within bodies. There is no other way—so the argument of the atomists goes—for compression and expansion to take place. There are four possibilities, and three of them are absurd; therefore compression and expansion must be explained in terms of a void existing within bodies.

Aristotle answers this briefly. The atomists want to place little void spaces within the interstices of bodies. But if nothing moves in a void separate from bodies, neither can anything move in the interstices. Aristotle goes on to state his own doctrine of condensation and rarefaction, based on the doctrine of potency and act, which was not considered by the atomists. "Our statement is based on the assumption that there is a single matter for contraries, hot and cold and other natural contrarieties, and that what exists actually is produced from a potential existent [ἐκ δυνάμει ὄντος ἐνεργείᾳ ὂν γίγνεται], and that matter is not separable from the contraries but its being is different, and that a single matter may serve for color and heat and cold" (217a22–26). This is Aristotle's own doctrine of alteration, one type of which is condensation and rarefaction, or compression and expansion. Therefore, there is no void outside of bodies or within them, unless one wishes to call the *potential* a void. In this case, the matter of the heavy body is "void" with respect to the natural place downward, just as the matter of light bodies is "void" with respect to their natural place upward. Thus, in locomotion the void is the potential element in the body that needs to be fulfilled. Alteration, on the other hand, has to do with passivity and impassivity, which permit or resist change (217b23–27). In this case passivity could be called a void. Aristotle concludes, "So much, then, for the discussion of the void, and of the sense in which it exists and the sense in which it does not exist" (217b27–28). Since neither the atomists nor anyone else uses the term "void" to designate the potential principle in moving bodies, it must be said that Aristotle denies the need for postulating a void to explain motion.

Are we to say, then, that Aristotle denies the possibility of motion in a void outside the context of the arguments presented?

The most devastating argument of the atomists, and the one Aristotle spends most time on, is the sixth one presented above. He seems to argue from the necessity of some resisting medium not only to show that differentiation of speed arises from differentiation of the medium but also to the absolute necessity of some resisting medium for the possibility of motion at all. His stated principle is that between any two movements there must be a ratio of times (216a9); in the absence of a medium "there is no ratio of void to full" (216a11). Therefore, the commentators concluded, in a void motion would be instantaneous, for the body would have to be in position A and in position B at the same time, *in instanti*. Aristotle does not say explicitly that motion in a void would be instantaneous, but it is the only conclusion one can draw from his premises.

Most commentators have taken this to be Aristotle's personal position, forgetting that he is arguing from the premises of the atomists. Thus David Ross says, "[Aristotle] has been misled by thinking of velocity as essentially the overcoming of resistance and not as the traversing of a certain distance in a certain time."[21] E. J. Dijksterhuis also understands this to be Aristotle's personal opinion: "In a void there would be no resistance to motion, and thus, in view of the inverse proportion between the velocity and the density of the medium, the fall would have to proceed instantaneously, i.e., the falling body would have to reach the end-point at the same moment at which the fall starts."[22] For Dijksterhuis, this and the other arguments are "emotional rather than logical in character, an expression of self-assertion rather than a refutation."[23] A. C. Crombie states that "Aris-

[21] *Aristotle's Physics* (Oxford, 1936), p. 61.
[22] *The Mechanization of the World Picture* (Oxford, 1961), p. 40.
[23] *Ibid.*

totle's 'law' (that $V = P/R$) expressed his belief that any increase in velocity in a given medium could be produced only by an increase in motive power. It also followed from the 'law' that in a void bodies would fall with instantaneous velocity; as he regarded this conclusion as absurd, he used it as an argument against the possibility of a void."[24] In like manner all the modern exegetes of Aristotle's arguments against the void presume that the content of each argument, particularly the sixth, is an expression of Aristotle's own doctrine. The number of medieval and modern exegetes who interpret Aristotle in this way is too numerous to list here. They credit Aristotle with the formula $V = F/R$, maintaining that resistance is essential for all motion in such a way that if $R = 0$, then motion must be instantaneous.

More attentive exegetes are careful to point out that in the passage on the void Aristotle argues from the position of the atomists to intrinsic absurdities. Thus, for the atomists, the void is postulated as the sole source of motion, while for Aristotle the *natural body itself* is the principle of motion and rest; all that is needed is a place to go, namely, natural place. After discussing the sixth argument at great length, St. Thomas says, "And so it is better and simpler to say that the argument induced by Aristotle is an argument to contradict a position taken [*ratio ad contradicendum positioni*], and not a demonstrative argument strictly speaking [*simpliciter*]."[25] Those who postulate a void do so so that motion would be possible, and so according to them the cause of motion arises on the part of the medium that permits motion. Consequently Aristotle argues against them "as though the whole cause of swiftness and slowness were on the part of the medium."[26] But if "nature" is the cause of velocity, as Aristotle firmly believes, then there is no need to postulate the void. However, Aristotle makes no mention of his own doctrine in this argument, as he does in the first, second, and third—namely, the distinction between "natural" and "violent" motion. All that he is saying in the sixth argument is that, if the void is the whole cause of motion and its velocity, then in a void there would be no way to account for obviously different ratios of velocity through it; with the reason for slowness gone, there could be only instantaneous velocity, which is not *motus*. In other words, Aristotle would not admit that the void or the medium is the whole cause of motion. Rather, the cause of motion is the nature of the body itself moving through some medium that must be divided over some

---

[24] *Medieval and Early Modern Science* (New York, 1959), II, 48–49. For Crombie, V stands for velocity, P for motive power, and R for the resistance of the medium.
[25] *In IV Phys.*, lect. 12, n. 10.
[26] *Ibid.*

distance in a given time. This is the only interpretation consistent with Aristotle's teaching throughout the *Physics*. For him, all natural bodies contain within themselves the principle of motion and rest, i.e., φύσις; the medium can only resist or assist in the traversal of distance in a given time. Since in the sixth argument Aristotle makes no mention of the nature in bodies as the cause of motion, it must be taken not as an expression of his own doctrine but only as an argument "to contradict the position" of his adversaries.

In late antiquity John Philoponus (fl. 480–547) objected to Aristotle's sixth argument precisely on the grounds that speed is proportional to the weight of the body, and that the function of a resisting medium is only to retard the body's motion, thereby allowing the possibility of motion in a void.[27] While Philoponus considers this to be contrary to Aristotle's position, it is in fact a principle of Aristotle's own doctrine that he is defending.

In a relatively long comment on text 71 (= 215a25–b20) of *Physics*, Book IV, devoted to this matter, the Spanish Moslem Averroes (1126–1198) preserves an objection of Ibn Badja (d. 1138), another Spanish Moslem, known to the Christians as Avempace. Ibn Badja's contention that Aristotle's argument is "false" is based on time and the divisibility of all motion: Aristotelian notions used show that the sixth argument will not hold good on Aristotelian grounds.[28]

Avempace contends that every motion has a determined natural velocity by virtue of a proportion between the body itself and the cause that generated it. By removing all additional resistances, such as that produced by the medium and friction, there is still left a natural body capable of moving in a natural time. In Book VII of his *Physics* commentary, according to Averroes (*Phys.* IV, comm. 71), Avempace proves this by a visible example and by a rational argument: (1) we see every day that the celestial bodies, whose motion is in no way impeded by resistance, move with a definite velocity according to a definite time; (2) the distance over which all bodies must traverse is divided by

---

[27] See relevant section in M. R. Cohen and I. Drabkin, *A Source Book in Greek Science* (Cambridge, 1958), pp. 217–21; Edward Grant, "Motion in a Void and the Principle of Inertia in the Middle Ages," *Isis* 55 (1964), 266.

[28] The text of Averroes used in this paper is that of the *editio princeps*, Padua 1472, containing the medieval translation of both Aristotle and Averroes. However, this edition has no foliation. For recent discussion of the opposition between Averroes and Avempace, see Pierre Duhem, "Le vide et le mouvement dans le vide," in *Le Système du Monde*, 10 vols. (Paris 1913–59), 8, 7–120; Avempace is discussed on pp. 10–16. E. A. Moody, "Galileo and Avempace," *Journal of the History of Ideas* 12 (1951), 163–93, 375–422; abbreviated in *Roots of Scientific Thought*, ed. P. P. Wiener and A. Noland (New York, 1957), pp. 176–206. Edward Grant, "Motion in a Void and the Principle of Inertia in the Middle Ages," 265–92.

prius and *posterius,* before and after, from which it follows that motion takes place not in an instant but in a determined time. It is true, Avempace says, that one can subtract "accidental impediments" such as a medium. But it does not thereby follow that the proportion between speeds of motion is like the proportion of one impediment to another, so that if there were no resisting medium, the motion would be without time; rather it is like the proportion of one slowness (or velocity) to the slowness of the other. In other words, there would still be a proportion between the velocity of one body with an "accidental impediment" to another body with no accidental impediment, because their times are proportionate. Thus, for Avempace, all impediments are to be subtracted from the natural velocity of the body; and when all are subtracted, as in a void, there is still left a body moving with natural velocity. Moody expresses this in the modern formula: $V = P - M$.[29] Hence a resisting medium is not at all necessary for motion. At this point we come into conflict with Averroes' entire doctrine of motion and his opposition to Ibn Badja.

Basic to Averroes' concept of motion is the medium. According to Averroes, for all free-fall of heavy bodies there must be not only the natural mover (*movens,* or *motor*) attached to the body and generating motion but also a resisting medium to help the movement downward. The same holds true of light motion upward; there must be a mover moving the body upward and a resisting medium to help it climb. In other words, every body moving must have a mover conjoined to the body, a *motor coniunctus,* here and now moving it. But Averroes knew perfectly well that he could not say that the "form," or mover, *per se* moves the body, for this would be to describe a living body. Living things move themselves *per se* by parts, the living soul being the efficient cause of these parts moving one another. Averroes' ingenious explanation was that the "form," or mover, in inanimate things *per se* moves the resisting medium, which in turn moves the matter. Thus, for Averroes, the substantial form of the body moves the matter only *per accidens* by means of the resisting medium.[30] By allowing form to act in its own right on the resisting medium, instead of acting directly on the matter, Averroes preserves the important distinction between living and nonliving movement.

Basically Averroes' doctrine of motion rests on a complete dichotomy between matter and form, body and soul, moved and mover, in a given composite. He believes that form in inanimate

[29] *Op. cit.,* 186.
[30] Averroes, *De caelo* III, comm. 28; cf. St. Thomas, *In III De caelo et mundo,* lect. 7, nn. 8–9; Chapter IV above.

bodies can act as a true *efficient* cause of its own motion, instead of being simply an active principle of natural motions.[31] "Motor est forma et res mota est materia."[32] Such a dichotomy between matter and form is much more than Aristotle would allow between two intrinsic principles of a natural substance that is an *unum per se*. Nevertheless, for Averroes the resistance to motion is an absolutely essential element in every motion. Without resistance there can be no motion.

Averroes gives a lengthy answer to Avempace's argument in favor of natural velocity even in a void. For Averroes, resistance can arise from three sources. First, it can arise from the *position* of the mobile body which is to be moved to another place; in this case resistance arises from the body to be moved. Second, it can arise from the *nature* of the body moved, as in violent motion where nature overcomes the imposed force. Third, it can arise from the *medium* through which the body moves. In celestial bodies there is only resistance arising from position. In living things there is a resistance to the mover both from the body and from the medium. According to Averroes, Avempace's objection applies only to the third kind of resistance, namely, the medium. In this case, if the medium were subtracted from the movement of animals, there would still remain the proportion of times to times. But in heavy and light bodies there is no increase in velocity unless this is done by decreasing the resistance. Thus, if all increase of velocity arises solely from the medium, then removing all resistance, such as in a void, the speed would be infinite. Averroes rejects the idea of "subtracting" or adding velocities by adding or subtracting media, for when motion is slower every part of that motion is decreased, while by increasing a line not every part of that line is made greater. Therefore, the speed of motion can be increased not only by subtracting the medium but by increasing or decreasing the proportion between mover and body moved. And if the moving force is divided by zero, the velocity can only be instantaneous.[33] The cause of Avempace's error, according to Averroes, is that he thinks that slowness and swiftness are motions to be added or taken away from natural motion, just like a line added to a line. In other words, Averroes claims that velocity arises from the proportion between the moving force and the body moved; for him there must always be some proportion between a moving force and the resistance. If no resistance arises from the body itself, or from the medium, or from the nature of the body,

---

[31] See Chapter I above.
[32] Averroes, *Phys.* IV, comm. 71.
[33] "In naturalibus vero diversitas aut equalitas est propter diversitatem aut equalitatem proportionis motoris ad rem motam." Averroes, *Phys.* IV, comm. 71.

there can be no proportion between the velocities of the two motions compared one to the other. If there is no resistance (that is, zero resistance), the body will move instantaneously, that is, without time and without divisibility of that motion.

Averroes answers Avempace's argument about celestial motions by saying that there is indeed resistance between body and the moving force, both of which are *in act*, whereas in natural motions there is no resistance between the form and matter, which is only *potential*. Therefore in natural free-fall of bodies motion can arise only from the resistance of the medium.

Thomas Aquinas, in his commentary on the *Physics*, Book IV, lect. 12, rejects Averroes' arguments as *omnino frivola*. He goes on to explain:

Although the quantity of slowness is not like a continuous quantity, so that motion is added to motion, but rather like an intensive quantity, as one whiteness is more white than another, nevertheless the quantity of time, from which Aristotle argues, is like a continuous quantity, so that time can be made longer by adding time to time. Hence by subtracting all the time that is added by the resistance, there would still be a natural time for natural speed.

For St. Thomas, what is added and subtracted is not the medium but time. Even when all resistance is taken away together with the additional time taken because of it, there still remains natural velocity in the time necessary to traverse a distance: "Unde subtracto tempore quod additur ex impediente, remanet tempus naturalis velocitatis."[34]

Applying this view to natural motions upward and downward, St. Thomas says,

If the form, which the generator gave, were removed, there would theoretically remain a quantified body [*corpus quantum*]; by the very fact that it has a natural inertia to being moved, it has a resistance to the mover. There is no other way of conceiving resistance in celestial bodies to their movers. Hence not even in heavy and light bodies would the argument of Aristotle follow, according to what he says.[35]

A natural body with its form needs nothing else to move in a void. This should not be taken to imply that, for St. Thomas, the form is in any way the mover, the efficient cause, the *motor* of natural motion downward or upward.[36] The form is nothing more than the active principle of natural motion and rest. Therefore all that is needed is a natural body with an active principle of movement and the term

---

[34] St. Thomas, *In IV Phys.*, lect. 12, n. 10.
[35] *Ibid.*
[36] See Chapter IV above.

toward which the motion is destined. The resisting medium in itself contributes nothing to the possibility or impossibility of motion unless it is greater than the moving power, in which case there is no motion at all.

To recapitulate the discussion up to this point, it can be said that the sixth argument of Aristotle against the atomists is not Aristotle's own doctrine. He takes a position contrary to his own and argues from it to a patent absurdity. On the other hand, Averroes accepts the sixth argument as part of Aristotle's teaching, and he makes it a cornerstone of his own doctrine of motion. St. Thomas is fully aware of the difference between Avempace, who claims that Aristotle's argument is false, and Averroes, who insists on its absolute validity. St. Thomas insists that Aristotle's argument is only *ad contradicendum positioni,* and that according to Aristotle's own principles motion in a void is possible.

Aquinas was about 45 when he wrote his commentary on the *Physics* and about 47 when he wrote his unfinished commentary on *De caelo et mundo* in 1272. After a clear and precise recognition of the errors of Averroes, he says,

... the motion of heavy and light bodies does not come into being from the generator by means of any other moving principle; it is not even necessary [*neque oportet*] to look for any other resistance in this motion than that which exists between the generator and the body generated. And so it follows that air is not required for natural motion out of necessity, as in violent motion, because that which moves naturally has within itself an innate power [*sibi inditam virtutem*], which is the principle of motion.[37]

In this passage St. Thomas does not discuss the void but simply rejects Averroes' position demanding a resisting medium both for natural free-fall of bodies and for violent motion of heavy bodies upward. In other words, St. Thomas does not recognize any resistance necessary for motion other than that exerted by a body being generated in the first place. Once a body is generated, it needs no resistance for it to move upward or downward or any other natural way. This is diametrically contrary to the foundation of Averroes' principles of natural science.

It is interesting to note that when Aquinas was only a young man of about 30, he was already aware of Averroes' rejection of Avempace in text 71. In Book IV of the *Sentences,* dist. 44, q. 2, a. 3, ql. 3 ad 2, which was written in 1256, he raises various questions about the resurrected body, among them the possibility of its moving from one place to

---

[37] *In III De caelo,* lect. 8, n. 9.

another instantaneously. In the second objection favoring the instantaneous transportation of glorified bodies from place to place, the objector quotes the Philosopher in text 71.[38]

He argues that . . . if there is motion in a void, [the body] would have to move in an instant, i.e., without time, because a void does not resist a body at all, while a plenum does. Thus there would be no proportion between motion which takes place in a vacuum and one which takes place in a resisting medium. For two motions to take place in time, there must be proportional velocities, since every time is proportional to time. But no plenum can resist a glorified body, which can coexist with another body in the same place, however this may take place. Therefore, if [a glorified body] moves, it moves in an instant.

This is the objection. Although the reply is rather long, I shall quote a substantial part of it, since the passage is rarely, if ever, referred to in contemporary literature, and never translated.[39]

To understand the proof of the Philosopher, as the Commentator expounds it in the same place [comm. 71], it must be noted that one must take the whole as a unit, namely, resistance of the body to the moving power, and resistance of the medium through which it moves, and any other resisting force whatever, so that one talks about the *quantitas tarditatis* of the whole motion according to the proportion of resistance of moving power to the body resisting in any way whatever, either *ex se* or *ex alio extrinseco*. For it is necessary that the moving body always resists the mover in some way, because the moving power and the body moved, the agent and the patient, inasmuch as they are such, are contraries. (1) Sometimes the body resists the mover *ex seipso* or because it has the power inclining it to move in the opposite direction, as is evident in violent motions, or at least, because it has a place contrary to the place intended by the mover; this kind of resistance is found in celestial bodies with respect to their movers. (2) Sometimes, however, the body resists the moving force *ex alio tantum* and not *ex seipso*, as is evident in the natural motion of heavy and light bodies, since by their very form they are inclined to such motion, for it is a form impressed by the generator which is the *per se* mover of heavy and light bodies. On the part of matter there is no resistance or power inclining to a contrary motion or to a contrary place, because "place" does not pertain to matter unless it is quantified by dimensions brought about by natural form. Hence there cannot be any resistance except on the part of the medium, which resistance is connatural to their motions. (3) Sometimes resistance arises from both sources, as is evident in the movement of animals. When, therefore, there is no resistance to motion except on the part of the body, as happens in celestial bodies, then the time of motion is measured by the proportion of mover to body. In cases such as these, the argument of Aristotle does not apply, because if all media are removed, there would still remain motion in time.

[38] The Vives edition of 1874 gives the erroneous source, text 75, and the Parma edition of 1858 refers to text 73. The correct reference is text and comm. 71.
[39] The text used for this translation is the Paris, Vives edition of 1874, 11, 332.

But in those motions where there is resistance only on the part of the medium, one takes the measure of time arising from the impediment of the medium solely. Hence, if one were to subtract the medium altogether, there would remain no impediment. In this case either it would move in an instant or it would move in an equal time through both an empty space and a plenum.[40] It is possible, however, to imagine another body with the same proportions more subtle than the body by which the space was full; and if another equal space were filled by that body, then the mobile body would move through that plenum in the same short time as formerly it did in a vacuum, because the more one adds to subtlety, by that much one subtracts from the quantity of time [*quantitate temporis*]; and the more subtle the medium, the less it resists. But in other motions in which there is resistance from the mobile body and from the medium, the quantity of time is computed from the proportion of the moving force to the resistance of the body and from the medium together. Hence, granted that the medium is totally subtracted or does not impede, it follows, not that motion would be in an instant, but that the time of motion would be measured only by the resistance of the body. Nothing absurd follows if a body were to move at the same rate of time in a plenum as in a void, if we imagine an extremely subtle body, because the greater the determined subtlety of the medium, the greater is its tendency to diminish the slowness in motion. Hence one can imagine a subtlety so great that it would tend to make less slowness than that slowness which the resistance of the body would have. And so the resistance of the medium would add no slowness to the motion.

It is, therefore, evident that although the medium does not resist glorified bodies inasmuch as it does not prevent two bodies from being in the same place, in no way whatever would their motions be instantaneous, because the very body itself offers resistance to the moving power by the fact that it has a determined position [in place], just as has been said of celestial bodies.

The basic position St. Thomas takes throughout the entire discussion in the *Sentences* is that if all media and all additional forces were taken away, there would still be movement in a void. St. Thomas recognizes only three kinds of resistance: (1) *ex seipso*, (a) that coming from the body itself in coming into being, i.e., the resistance between the body being generated and the generator, (b) the force of the natural inclination resisting a contrary motion, as in violent motions, and (c) the internal inertia of bodies being moved in place, as in celestial bodies; (2) *ex alio extrinseco*, that coming from the resisting medium through which the body must pass, as in free-fall of bodies; and (3) a combination of internal and external resistance, as in the case of animals moving themselves. Once a body has been generated, like water from air, there may or may not be a resisting medium to hinder its natural motion. If there is a medium, the heavier the body

---

[40] All the printed editions consulted have "per vacuum" in this place; but this fails to make sense. However, the fragment preserved by Capreolus (*Defensiones theologiae* II, dist. 6, q. 1 ad 7, ed. Tours 1902, 3, 419) reads "per plenum," which is correct.

is, the slower it moves; if there is no medium, the body moves with natural velocity because of the distance to be traversed in a natural time. The basic reason for this is that all bodies and all distances are divisible. Granting this divisibility of the continuum, there follows that time itself is divisible. Therefore a body would move in a void more swiftly than it would in a plenum. But in either case these motions would take time, and time is proportional to time as long as both are finite. Therefore $T_1 : T_2 :: V_1 : V_2$. For St. Thomas, at least in the commentary on the *Sentences*, it is possible for a body to move in a void with the same time as a body moving in a very subtle medium. In this case the medium would make little or no difference; there is always the natural velocity of a given body, whether there is a medium or not. Thus, unlike Averroes, who demands a medium for the very possibility of motion, St. Thomas holds that the medium is irrelevant to the possibility of motion, and may even be absent altogether, as in a void.

It is important to note that for St. Thomas, as for Aristotle and perhaps for Averroes, the motion under discussion is not only local motion but also alteration and augmentation. These too can take place in a void, and these too encounter analogously the same kind of resistance.

The position taken by St. Thomas was adopted and maintained by his followers throughout the centuries. Philosophers and theologians, such as John Capreolus,[41] Domingo de Soto,[42] John of St. Thomas,[43] Cosmo Alamanno,[44] and many others strongly defended the position of St. Thomas against Averroes. Domingo de Soto, for example, is well aware that he is arguing against "an extremely common opinion that is being proposed as Aristotle's, which some think can be gotten out of chapter 8, text 71 and the following" ("vulgatissima illa sententia, quae circumfertur tanquam Aristotelis, quam elici putant ex c. 8, text 71 et infra"). There can be no doubt that the opinion of Averroes, demanding resistance for every motion, and the correlative notion that in a void a body would move instantaneously, were common in late medieval physics. Domingo de Soto refers to Paul of Venice (*In II Sent.*) and Gregory of Rimini (*In II Sent.*, dist. 6, q. 3, a. 2), "whom

[41] *Defensiones theologiae* II, dist. 6, q. 1 ad 7, ed. C. Paban and T. Pègues (Tours, 1902), 3, 418–22.
[42] *Super octo libros Physicorum Arist. quaestiones* IV, q. 3, a. 2 (Salamanca, 1555), fol. 66v–67v. I am grateful to Rev. W. A. Wallace for the use of the text and his translation of the question.
[43] *Cursus philosophicus:* Phil. nat. I, q. 17, a. 2, ed. B. Reiser (Turin, 1933), pp. 365–69.
[44] *Summa philosophiae:* Physica, q. 20, aa. 3–4, ed. F. Ehrle (Paris, 1885), pp. 197–202.

practically all of the nominalists follow."[45] It was a prevalent opinion when Galileo was a student and professor at Pisa.

In his early work *De Motu* (ca. 1590), c. 10, Galileo goes to great lengths[46] to demonstrate, in opposition to Aristotle, that if there were a void, motion in it would take place not instantaneously but in time. His arguments are not so much against Aristotle as against the Averroist interpretation of Aristotle. Galileo begins by saying:

Aristotle, in Book 4 of the *Physics,* in his attempt to deny the existence of a void, adduces many arguments. Those that are found beginning with [text 64][47] are drawn from a consideration of motion. For since he assumes that motion cannot take place instantaneously, he tries to show that if a void existed, motion in it would take place instantaneously; and, since that is impossible, he concludes necessarily that a void is also impossible. But, since we are dealing with motion, we have decided to inquire whether it is true that, if a void existed, motion in it would take place instantaneously. And since our conclusion will be that motion in a void takes place in time, we shall first examine the contrary view and Aristotle's arguments.[48]

It should now be clear that Galileo was not the first to refute the Averroist interpretation of Aristotle. There was a long tradition on this subject reaching back to St. Thomas, Avempace, and Philoponus. Galileo was certainly aware of this, for in defending motion in a void, he explicitly cites "Scotus, Saint Thomas, Philoponus, and others."[49]

By way of conclusion it would be well to summarize the views explained above. Although the problem is very difficult, and the scholastic terms are unfamiliar to many, this is an important subject in high and late scholastic thought. In this paper we have discussed the opinions of four major figures on the question of motion in a void: Aristotle, Avempace (Ibn Badja), Averroes, and St. Thomas Aquinas. Aristotle dealt with the void in Book IV of his *Physics.* Having discussed the problems of place, he felt it also necessary to discuss the void. The void was a vital problem in pre-Socratic philosophy, because the atomists, notably Leucippus and Democritus, tried to explain the possibility of motion in face of the paradox of Parmenides and his disciples. The atomists postulated the void and indivisible atoms as

---

[45] *Op. cit.,* fol. 66vb.

[46] *De Motu,* trans. and annotated by I. E. Drabkin (Madison, 1960), p. 41f.

[47] I. E. Drabkin translates this as "section," but he mistakenly identifies the Bekker numbers; the reference should be to 214b11ff.

[48] *Ibid.,* p. 41.

[49] *Ibid.,* p. 49.

the only possible explanation of movement witnessed in the real world. Aristotle tried to revive the concept of φύσις or "nature" to explain motion, and therefore he postulated natural place and natural motion. In order to maintain his overall philosophy of nature, he had to face the real problem of motion in a void. He presented six difficulties about motion in a void in order to deny the need of a void in nature. Some of the arguments against the void postulated by the atomists presuppose a distinction between "natural" and "violent" motions. But the sixth and last argument tried to show that if the void were postulated as the cause of motion, then it would follow that motion in a void would be instantaneous, that is, without time, for force divided by zero resistance would be instantaneous.

A great number of commentators thought this expressed Aristotle's personal view of dynamics, which can be stated in the formula: $V = F/R$, where V is the velocity, F the moving force, and R the resistance of a medium. The implication of interpreting Aristotle in this way is that all motion needs *resistance* in order for bodies to move at all. In the Latin West, the first to oppose this notion was Avempace, or Ibn Badja. He claimed that even if all media were removed, as in a void, there would still be the natural resistance of the body coming into existence, that is, between mover and moved, and the natural body would still move in time over a given distance. Avempace argued that if there were no resistance, such as a medium, the measure of motion would be the subtraction of all resistance from the natural force of the body, as in free-fall of bodies. His position has been interpreted to mean $V = F - R$. The crux of the problem discussed is not so much the instantaneous or temporal nature of motion but the need for resistance in all motion. This brief passage from Avempace's argument in Book VII of the *Physics* was reported by Averroes in Book IV, commentary on text 71.

Averroes, the ardent defender of the very words of Aristotle on all occasions, opposed Avempace, insisting that all movement, natural or violent, required a medium. The natural fall of free bodies required a medium, so that the form could move the matter of the body downward; for Averroes, "form" was the *per se* mover of the medium and the *per accidens* cause of the body's movement. Averroes, like Aristotle, had no problem in showing that violent motion needed a medium, for in their view the medium carried "the power to move." Thus both natural and violent motion needed a resisting medium, though in different ways. Without a medium there could be no movement at all under any circumstances. Therefore, Averroes concluded that movement without a medium would have to take place in an instant (*in instanti*), and this is not motion (*motus*) at all but the simultaneous occupation of two places at once. If the resistance is zero in the formula $V = F/R$, then motion will be instantaneous.

St. Thomas Aquinas rejected Averroes' arguments as "frivolous," contending that whenever one removes a hindrance, like a resisting medium, the body will move naturally in a given time over a given distance with "natural velocity." This "natural velocity" depends upon the distance to be covered, a magnitude that can be divided, and the time taken to cover that distance, a derived magnitude that can also be divided. Therefore, without resistance, the force of the φύσις itself would move over a given distance in a given time. In other words, St. Thomas denied that motion in a void would be instantaneous. More important, he denied the need for resistance derived from the medium. From this it follows that St. Thomas denied in principle that the formula $V = F/R$ expresses Aristotle's dynamics except for violent or mechanical motion. Although many modern historians of Aristotelian physics accept this formula as authentically Aristotelian, St. Thomas and his followers would not consider it to be an expression of authentic free-fall of bodies. For them, once a body is generated it has an innate force to do what comes naturally; it does not move the medium or the "matter" but just moves faster in a void than in a plenum.

What we have tried to show is that the sixth argument in chapter 8 against the void does not represent Aristotle's own view but is only an argument *ad contradicendum positioni*. The formula $V = F/R$ cannot be derived from Book IV, c. 8, for it neglects the essential element in the whole of Aristotelian physics, namely, that φύσις is the principle of motion and rest, and therefore the body moves spontaneously downward if it is a heavy body, and upward if it is a light body. The formula $V = F/R$ is also found by modern historians of science to be implicit in Book VIII, c. 5, of Aristotle's *Physics*. We have not discussed this problem, for it is a different one altogether. In that passage Aristotle gives the example of the "shiphaulers," but there Aristotle is clearly discussing a problem of mechanics, which is not "natural" motion.[50] In this paper we have been concerned not with mechanical motion but only with the free-fall of bodies in a void. We have argued that such motion does not need resistance or a medium according to Aristotle and St. Thomas, whereas it does need resistance according to Averroes and his followers.

[50] See Edward Grant, "Aristotle's 'Shiphaulers' and Medieval Criticisms of His Law of Motion," in *Acts of the Ithaca Congress of the History of Science* (Paris, 1962), 587–90.

At the beginning of this paper we noted the view of Anneliese Maier regarding the obstacles in medieval physics that prevented the growth of modern classical physics. She pointed to two basic hypotheses as the most important and the most fatal for the birth of modern classical physics. The more significant of the two was the hypothesis that every movement requires a particular mover bound to it and generating it directly and that every normal movement of a successive nature requires, besides, a resistance which opposes the moving force and which is overcome by that force, for without resistance there could be no motion (*motus*), but only change (*mutatio*), i.e., an instantaneous change of place.[51]

The first part of this "fatal" hypothesis was discussed in my paper on "Omne quod movetur ab alio movetur," already cited. In that paper we showed that the view proposed by Maier is Averroist and not universally held in the Middle Ages. The second part of the "fatal" hypothesis was discussed in this paper. We have pointed out that this opinion was also Averroist, and not universally held in medieval physics. There can be no doubt that it was commonly held by Averroists and nominalists; Domingo de Soto even called it *sententia vulgatissima*. Nevertheless, the notion that "every motion requires a resistance which opposes the moving force and which is overcome by that force," and that without this force, as in a void, all motion would take place instantaneously, was rejected by the whole Thomistic and probably the whole Scotistic tradition. Galileo rejected the Averroist hypothesis, and he was well aware that he had precursors in this rejection, namely, "Scotus, Saint Thomas, Philoponus, and some others." When there is a strong vital tradition for the opposing view, it is misleading to present the Averroist position as the common "scholastic teaching."

The teaching of St. Thomas, rejecting both a conjoined mover (*motor coniunctus*) and the need for resistance in all natural motion, is much more compatible with the views of modern classical physics than the Averroist teaching on both points. By this we do not mean that Thomistic natural philosophy prepared the way for classical physics. This would be to claim too much. But it is clear that a specifically Averroist physics did exist in medieval philosophy and that it was vigorously opposed by St. Thomas and others. Only when the Averroist physics was rejected could modern classical physics begin.

[51] A. Maier, *loc. cit.*

VII

THE CELESTIAL MOVERS IN MEDIEVAL PHYSICS

In the spring of 1271 John of Vercelli, master general of the Order of Preachers, sent a list of forty-three questions to three Dominican masters in theology for their consideration. Independently of each other, the three theologians were to consider each question carefully and reply promptly keeping in mind the directive of the master general: (i) Do accepted authorities, the *Sancti*, maintain the doctrine or opinion contained in the articles listed? (ii) Apart from the weight of authorities, does the consultor maintain the aforesaid doctrine or opinion? (iii) Apart from the consultor's personal views, could the aforesaid doctrine or opinion be tolerated without prejudice to the faith?[1] Clearly the purpose of this questionnaire was to safeguard the truths of faith, even where the question raised was one of philosophical opinion or strictly natural science.

St. Thomas Aquinas had previously given his decision on most of these questions in two private communiques to the lector of Venice, Bassiano of Lodi.[2] The official questionnaire of the master general contained nothing of importance which had not already been considered by St. Thomas in his two private replies. The questions are for the most part idle curiosities and useless fantasies, as the consultors themselves realized. However, the official questionnaire was sent to three outstanding masters in the order, and not all the questions are without interest to the modern reader. St. Thomas's reply to the official questionnaire has always been known to Thomists, even though little studied. The reply of the second consultor, Robert Kilwardby, later archbishop of Canterbury, was discovered and pub-

---

[1] St. Thomas, *Responsio ad fr. Joannem Vercellensem de articulis XLII*, prooem., ed. R. A. Verardo, O.P., *Opuscula Theologica* (Turin, 1954), I, p. 211. In this list the original q. 8 is missing.

[2] *Responsio ad Lectorem Venetum de articulis XXX* and *Responsio ad eundem de articulis XXXVI*, ed. R. A. Verardo in *Opuscula Theologica*, pp. 193–208.

lished by Fr. M.-D. Chenu, O.P., about fifty years ago.[3] Now with the discovery and publication of the reply of the third consultor, the great St. Albert himself,[4] we are in a position to compare the views of the three Dominican masters point by point.

Among the relatively few interesting questions in the list of forty-three, the first five stand out as particularly important for the historian and philosopher of science. They have to do with the cause or causes of celestial motion. In the order of appearance they are as follows:

1. Does God move any physical body immediately?
2. Are all things which are moved naturally, moved under the angels' ministry moving the celestial bodies?
3. Are angels the movers of celestial bodies?
4. Is it infallibly demonstrated according to anyone that angels are the movers of celestial bodies?
5. Assuming that God is not the immediate mover of those bodies, is it infallibly demonstrated that angels are the movers of celestial bodies?

To the casual reader these questions, too, might appear to be useless in this age of scientific progress. Angels, it is frequently thought, have no place in a discussion of scientific questions. Some Catholic scientists, and even some Thomistic philosophers, feel considerable embarrassment at the mention of angels; they would rather not mention them at all, or at least not mention them as having anything to do with the real world in which we live. In medieval literature the problem of celestial movers was not created by theologians, nor did it take its origin in any point of Catholic faith, although St. Thomas was keenly aware of the guiding role of faith in this matter. The problem of celestial movers was entirely a scientific one having many ramifications. But here, as in other problems of medieval science, it is not sufficient to know what a particular author maintained. It is far more important to understand the scientific problem in its philosophical context and to evaluate the arguments leading to the solution proposed. After all, the best of medieval science is not to be found in the lapidaries, herbals, or bestiaries of the Middle Ages; least of all is it to be found in pious legends, sermons, or morality plays. Rather it is to

[3] M.-D. Chenu, O.P., "Les Réponses de s. Thomas et de Kilwardby à la consultation de Jean de Verceil (1271)," in *Mélanges Mandonnet,* Bibl. Thomiste, XIII (Paris, 1930), I, 191–222.

[4] James A. Weisheipl, O.P., "The *Problemata Determinata XLIII* Ascribed to Albertus Magnus (1271)," *Mediaeval Studies* 22 (1960), 303–54.

be found in the speculative commentaries, treatises, and disputations of the schoolmen. These writings, emanating largely from various faculties of the university, are not readily intelligible to modern readers, as anyone who has tried to read them can testify. To understand the writings of medieval authors one needs a considerable background in the sources, a speculative competence to follow the argumentation, and a familiarity with medieval practice. Neither the questionnaire of the master general nor the replies of Albertus Magnus, Thomas Aquinas, or Robert Kilwardby can be evaluated correctly without reference to the sources, the argumentation, and medieval practice.

In a review of Chenu's edition of Kilwardby's reply to the questionnaire, Fr. Mandonnet noted the similarity between the view of Robert Kilwardby and that of John Buridan, the fourteenth-century proponent of "impetus" to explain violent motion. Inspired by the thesis of Duhem's *Études sur Léonard de Vinci* (3me série), Mandonnet was quick to point out the modernity of Kilwardby's universal mechanics.[5] This suggestion was developed at some length by Fr. Chenu in a special study devoted to the origins of "modern science."[6] Whatever may be said of the validity of Duhem's well-known thesis, one may perhaps doubt the utility of isolating a particular medieval thesis—in this case one of dubious modernity—to extol the modernity of medieval science. Even if there should happen to be considerable similarity between some aspect of medieval science and a current scientific view, this would be no more than an interesting curiosity, unless we come to grip with an objective philosophical problem and analyze the issues historically and scientifically.

A short paper such as this cannot sketch even in broad outlines a picture of medieval astronomy or the history of its development.[7] All that can be attempted here is an examination of the problem as seen by each of the three Dominican masters consulted by the master general, and an explanation of the views proposed, especially in their response to the official questionnaire. Since our purpose here is to understand the medieval view, we need be concerned not about the true historical intent of ancient sources but only about how the medieval schoolmen interpreted them. That is to say, it is not essential here to understand what Plato, Aristotle, Ptolemy, or Al-Biṭrûjî really meant; it is essential only that we understand what St. Albert, St.

---

[5] P. Mandonnet, O.P., *Bulletin Thomiste* 3 (1930), 137–39.

[6] M.-D. Chenu, O.P., "Aux origines de la 'science moderne,'" in *Revue des Sc. Phil. et Théol.* 29 (1940), 206–17.

[7] An outline can be found in P. Duhem, *Le Système du Monde* (Paris, 1954), vol. III.

Thomas, and Kilwardby thought them to mean. There is always the possibility that these great schoolmen misunderstood or misinterpreted their sources, but this makes little, if any, difference to the medieval view of the scientific problem.

PRELIMINARY OBSERVATIONS

In the traditional division of the speculative sciences derived from Plato and Aristotle, astronomy occupied a peculiar position. By astronomy we do not mean the elementary calculation of movable feast days, the epact, or the golden number; nor do we mean identification of the signs of the zodiac or prognostications from conjunctions. By astronomy is meant the theoretical science which attempts to make celestial phenomena intelligible by means of mathematical principles. The peculiar position of this theoretical science can be recognized clearly in the writings of the three consultors.

In the first place, astronomy was classified with optics, mechanics, harmonics, and other *scientiae mediae* between the sciences of pure mathematics and natural science.[8] As a science intermediate between mathematics and physics, astronomy was considered from three points of view. First, it was considered in relation to the higher science of mathematics, to which it is subalternated and on which it depends for its scientific validity. Astronomy, it was said, accepts as established all the conclusions of geometry and applies them to the known measurements of celestial phenomena. In this consideration, astronomy and the other *scientiae mediae* "have a closer affinity to mathematics, because what is physical in their consideration functions as something material, while what is mathematical functions as something formal."[9] Intelligibility in every science was taken as derived from the principles, the formal element, as contrasted to the material element which is the conclusion, or fact now understood scientifically.[10] We know that mathematical astronomy did not begin until Eudoxus of Cnidos accepted the challenge from Plato "to find out what are the uniform and ordered movements by the assumption of which the phenomena in relation to the movements of the planets can be saved."[11] The obviously irregular motions in the heavens, tabulated for centuries before Plato, could not be made intelligible except by reducing them, at least

---

[8] St. Thomas, *In I Post. Anal.*, lect. 1, n. 3; *In II Phys.*, lect. 3, n. 8; *In Boeth. de Trin.*, q. 5, a. 3 ad 5–7; *Sum. theol.* I-II, q. 35, a. 8; II-II, q. 9, a. 2 ad 3.
[9] *In Boeth. de Trin.*, q. 5, a. 3 ad 6; *Sum. theol.* II-II, q. 9, a. 2 ad 3.
[10] *In I Post. Anal.*, lect. 41, n. 11; *Sum. theol.* II-II, q. 1, a. 1; q. 9, a. 2 ad 3.
[11] Simplicius, *De caelo*, ed. Heiberg, Comm. in Arist. Graeca, VII, p. 488, 18–24.

in theory, to perfectly regular movements of geometric spheres. In other words, astronomy was taken formally to be a mathematical type of knowledge, extending to measurable quantities of celestial phenomena, such as size, distance, shape, position, and velocity.

Considered in its own right, astronomy was presented as a true speculative science, demonstrative within its own limits. Unless there be some true demonstrations in astronomy, true causal dependencies between principle and conclusion, this knowledge would not deserve the name of science. The mathematical principles of astronomy are themselves demonstrated in one of the purely mathematical sciences. Moreover, in theory "mathematical principles can be applied to motion,"[12] and sometimes the application is clear. But very often geometrical figures and principles must be assumed as applicable to the celestial phenomenon under consideration, as in the case of Eudoxus's four spheres to explain the motions of Jupiter, Callippus's seven spheres, and Ptolemy's epicycle. Nevertheless, the relationship between the principles assumed, even assumed as applicable, and the celestial phenomenon to be saved can be one of necessity. This connection of necessary dependency of the conclusion on the assumed principles is sufficient to establish astronomy as a demonstrative science. It was in this sense that St. Thomas and St. Albert interpreted Aristotle's statement that "it is the business of the empirical observers to know the fact, of the mathematicians to know the reasoned fact."[13] Between the mathematical principle and the quantified aspect of the fact, there may well be a *propter quid* relationship, that is, the immediate, proper, and convertible middle term of the measured facts of the conclusion may be the mathematical principle invoked. To this extent astronomy should be called, and was called, a true science subalternated to mathematics. To be sure, astronomical science fell far short of the ideal of scientific knowledge described by Aristotle in the *Posterior Analytics*. It did not demonstrate through the immediate, physical cause of celestial phenomena; at best, it demonstrated through a kind of extrinsic formal cause (*secundum causam formalem remotam*) of the natural phenomena.[14] Even this, as has already been suggested, is most often in a tentative, dialectical, and hypothetical manner.

Considered in relation to the physically real celestial bodies and their movements, astronomy was recognized fully as hypothetical.

---

[12] St. Thomas, *In Boeth. de Trin.*, q. 5, a. 3 ad 5.
[13] *An. post.* I, 13, 79a2–3. St. Thomas, *In I Post. Anal.*, lect. 25, n. 4; St. Albert, *Lib. I Post. Anal.*, tr. III, c. 7.
[14] St. Thomas, *In I Post. Anal.*, lect. 25, nn. 4 and 6.

The true causes of celestial motion are extremely difficult for any science to discover. "These matters into which we inquire are difficult since we are able to perceive little of their causes, and the properties of these bodies are more remote from our understanding than the bodies themselves are spatially distant from our eyes."[15] Simplicius, and possibly Plato before him, was aware that the aim of astronomy is to give some rational account of celestial phenomena, saving all the known facts (σώζειν τὰ φαινόμενα).[16] But as it turns out, all the known facts of astronomy can be explained by a variety of hypotheses. Of course, when a new fact is discovered which cannot be accommodated by the existing hypothesis, then some new hypothesis must be devised to account for the new fact. St. Thomas, commenting on the homocentric spheres of Plato and Eudoxus, observes:

The hypotheses which they devised [adinvenerunt] are not necessarily true, for although the appearances are saved on the assumption of those hypotheses, one does not have to say that they are true, because the phenomena of celestial bodies may perhaps be saved in some other way not yet known to man.[17]

An astronomical hypothesis which accounts for all the known facts is indeed worthy of provisional credence. But every astronomical hypothesis by its very nature was considered by St. Thomas to be provisional and indemonstrative. Speaking of this type of reasoning, St. Thomas notes:

Reasoning is employed in another way, not as furnishing an adequate proof of a principle, but as showing how the existing facts are in harmony with a principle already posited; as in astronomy the theory of eccentrics and epicycles is considered as established, because thereby the sensible appearances of celestial movements can be explained; it is not, however, as if this proof were [demonstratively] adequate, since some other theory might explain them.[18]

The tentative and hypothetical character of astronomical theories was commonly recognized from the thirteenth century onward, that is, after the acceptance of both Aristotle and Ptolemy in Latin translation. The homocentric hypotheses of Eudoxus and Callippus were taught in the faculty of arts together with the Ptolemaic hypotheses of

---

[15] St. Thomas, In II De caelo, lect. 17, n. 8.
[16] Cf. P. Duhem, "Σώζειν τὰ Φαινόμενα: Essai sur la notion de théorie physique de Platon à Galilée," Annales de philosophie chrétienne (Paris), 4 série, 6 (1908), 113ff., 277ff., 352ff., 482ff., 561ff.
[17] St. Thomas, In II De caelo, lect. 17, n. 2.
[18] St. Thomas, Sum. theol. I, q. 32, a. 1 ad 2.

epicycles and eccentrics. The schoolmen frequently discussed the preferability of one over the other in their commentaries on Aristotle. This brings us to the second peculiar characteristic of astronomy recognized in the Middle Ages, namely, that mathematical astronomy was ordained to the discovery of true physical causes in nature. The mathematical character of astronomy was clearly evident to the schoolmen. But as mathematical, it abstracted from all questions of efficient, final, and material causality; its concern was with the quantitative formalities of celestial phenomena related functionally to assumed mathematical principles. "[Astronomi] non considerant motum caelestium secundum principia motus, sed potius secundum numerum et mensuram quantitatis suae."[19] This being the case, one might have expected such an abstract science to be an end in itself, a purely speculative science sought for its own sake. In actual fact, however, this was not the view of Albertus Magnus, Thomas Aquinas, or Robert Kilwardby. These three men, it is true, did not consider the functional use of astronomy in the same way, but they did consider astronomy to have a functional use in discovering real physical causes beyond quantity.

In Book II of the *Physics* Aristotle had raised the problem concerning the relation between the mathematical sciences and natural science.[20] Taking the case of astronomy, Aristotle posed the dialectic: astronomy is obviously a part of mathematics, but it is also a part of natural science since it considers the sun, moon, and stars; therefore mathematics also is a part of natural science. In reply Aristotle distinguished purely mathematical definitions from those of natural science; this is sufficient to establish the sciences as distinct. In confirmation Aristotle pointed to the *quasi*-physical character of optics, harmonics, and astronomy, which he called τὰ φυσικώτερα τῶν μαθημάτων (*Phys.* II, 2, 194a7). Modern translators give the more probable rendering of this phrase as "the more physical of the branches of mathematics." It was in this sense that Averroes (text. comm. 20) and St. Albert (*ibidem*) had understood the text. William of Moerbeke, however, rendered this phrase with equal grammatical correctness as *magis physica quam mathematica*. This translation presented St. Thomas with the opportunity of explaining how astronomy, harmonics, and optics pertain, in a certain sense, rather to natural science than to mathematics:

[19] St. Albert, *Lib. XI Metaph.*, tr. II, cap. 10, ed. Borgnet (Paris, 1890–99), VI, 628a.
[20] Arist., *Phys.* II, 2, 193b22–194a12.

Sciences of this kind, although they are intermediate between natural science and mathematics, are here described by the Philosopher as more natural than mathematical, because each thing is denominated and specified by its ultimate term; hence since investigation in these sciences terminates in natural matter, though by means of mathematical principles, they are more natural than mathematical. . . . Hence astronomy is more natural than mathematical.[21]

Both St. Albert and St. Thomas recognized two types of astronomy: mathematical astronomy, such as was studied by Eudoxus, Ptolemy, and others, and physical astronomy, such as Aristotle discussed in the *Physics* and *De caelo et mundo*. This latter astronomy was considered an integral part of natural philosophy. Unlike mathematical astronomy, physical astronomy attempts to discover all the physical causes of celestial phenomena, the ultimate efficient and final cause as well as the material and intrinsic formal cause. For Albert and Thomas physical astronomy alone indicates the real system of the universe. The difficulties involved in discovering the real system of the universe, the moving causes of celestial motion, their number and order, are obvious. Consequently this part of natural philosophy abounds with tentative views and arguments, having need of mathematical astronomy to suggest possibilities. Discussing the number of celestial movements, Aristotle himself realized the need of "that one of the mathematical sciences which is most akin to philosophy, namely, of astronomy."[22] He was unable to determine the exact number of distinct celestial motions, but he tentatively adopted the astronomical hypotheses of Callippus minus eight uncertain motions, taking the number of spheres to be forty-seven. From this he argued that "the unmovable substances and principles also may probably be taken as just so many; the assertion of *necessity* must be left to more powerful thinkers."[23] That there must be many movements and movers was accepted by St. Albert and St. Thomas as certain, but their exact number was hypothetical and not essential to the argument pursued.[24]

In other words, for St. Albert and St. Thomas mathematical astronomy and the other physical parts of mathematics are considered as ordained to the discovery of physical causes in natural philosophy. The mathematical sciences are, as it were, the dialectical preparation for the real demonstrations in natural philosophy. Since all mathematics, even the more physical parts of mathematics, prescind from

[21] *In II Phys.*, lect. 3, nn. 8–9. See also *Sum. theol.* II-II, q. 9, a. 2 ad 3.
[22] *Metaph.* XII, 8, 1073b4–5.
[23] *Ibid.*, 1074a15–17.
[24] St. Albert, *Lib. XI Metaph.*, tr. II, c. 17 and c. 27; St. Thomas, *In XII Metaph.*, lect. 9, n. 2565; lect. 10, n. 2586.

motion and sensible matter,[25] they are that much removed from reality and need to be evaluated by that science which studies nature as it really exists, *in motu et inabstracta.* That is to say, the mathematical sciences are subordinated to and ordained to the philosophy of nature. Consequently, "if there were no substance other than those which are formed by nature, natural science would be the first science."[26]

Robert Kilwardby, on the other hand, represents a different tradition in medieval thought.[27] His is the Platonic tradition of Robert Grosseteste, Pseudo-Grosseteste, and Roger Bacon, which considered natural science ordained to the mathematical, and mathematics ordained to metaphysics. The Platonic hierarchy of the sciences was seen to correspond to a real priority of forms in nature, not, of course, existing apart from sensible reality, but within physical bodies. Thus motion and sensible qualities, the object of natural science, are radicated in the prior forms of pure quantity, the object of mathematics; the forms of quantity, in turn, are radicated in the prior form of nude substance, the concern of metaphysics. Kilwardby, discussing the four mathematical sciences, sees a perfect hierarchy of priority and dignity among the mathematical forms. The lowest of all the mathematical sciences is astronomy, for it considers celestial motion through the principles of geometry; hence astronomy is prior to and more abstract than natural science.[28] Since discrete quantity is simpler than and prior to extension, all the sciences which deal with number are prior to geometry. Among these the lower is the ideal harmony of numerical proportions; the science of numerical harmony, therefore, is prior to geometry.[29] The highest and most abstract of all the mathematical sciences is arithmetic, or algebra, "quia ipsa ut sic, nulla aliarum indiget."[30] Thus arithmetic, the science of pure number, is "quasi mater aliarum [scientiarum]."[31] But as Kilwardby failed to distinguish the numerical "unity" discussed in mathematics from the entitative "unity" convertible with being, he said that it belongs to the metaphysician to explain the cause of plurality in mathematics.[32]

---

[25] Boethius, *De Trinitate,* c. 2.
[26] *Metaph.* VI, 1, 1026a28–29, and XI, 7, 1064b9–10.
[27] See my "Albertus Magnus and the Oxford Platonists," *Proceedings Am. Cath. Phil. Assoc.* 32 (1958), 124–39.
[28] Kilwardby, *De ortu scientiarum,* cap. 16 ad 1. Merton College, Oxford, MS 261, fol. 25v.
[29] *Ibid.,* cap. 24 ad 4, fol. 32ra.
[30] *Ibid.,* cap. 19, fol. 27va.
[31] *Ibid.,* cap. 22, fol. 28vb.
[32] *Ibid.,* cap. 24 ad 1, fol. 29rb; also cap. 14 ad 2, fol. 24vb.

It may perhaps be a fair interpretation of Kilwardby's mind to say that if there were no metaphysics, arithmetic would be the supreme universal science. This contrast, however, with the view of St. Albert and St. Thomas is not perfectly symmetrical, since Kilwardby did not consider metaphysics to rest on the real existence of "substance other than those which are formed by nature." Nevertheless a clear contrast can be seen between the Platonic orientation upward from nature to mathematics and the Aristotelian orientation subordinating mathematics to natural philosophy. St. Albert and St. Thomas both defended the autonomy of natural science within the limits of its own *principia propria illuminantia,* distinct from metaphysics and superior to mathematics.[33]

The third peculiar characteristic of astronomy recognized in the Middle Ages was the special role it had in the discovery of God's existence. This characteristic was not entirely new. In pagan mythology the celestial bodies were themselves considered gods or at least the inhabitation of the gods. Pagan philosophers such as Plato and Aristotle did not hesitate to call celestial bodies divine. Ptolemy himself saw in astronomy the only secure path to theology:

For that special mathematical theory would most readily prepare the way to the theological, since it alone could take good aim at that unchangeable and separate act [God], so close to that act are the properties having to do with translations and arrangements of movements, belonging to those heavenly beings which are sensible and both moving and moved, but eternal and impassible.[34]

Al-Biṭrûjî, St. Albert frequently points out, had this advantage over the complicated system of Ptolemy that he considered all celestial motions to be derived from a single first mover, who is God.[35] For Kilwardby the path to God rose more tortuously from nature through astronomy, geometry, harmonics, arithmetic to the One of metaphysics; for him the proper subject of metaphysics is God precisely as the first cause of all plurality, material and immaterial.[36]

St. Albert's view of the matter is most interesting. Throughout the *Metaphysics* and *Liber de causis* St. Albert repeatedly rejected the "Pla-

---

[33] Cf. J. A. Weisheipl, "Albertus Magnus and the Oxford Platonists," pp. 136–39.

[34] Ptolemy, *Almagest,* Bk. I, chap. 1, trans. by R. C. Taliaferro, Great Books of the Western World, 16 (Chicago, 1952), p. 6.

[35] Al-Biṭrûjî, *De motibus celorum* III, 10–14, trans. by Michael Scot, ed. Francis J. Carmody (Berkeley, 1952), pp. 79–80; St. Albert, *Problemata determinata,* q. 1, *ed. cit.,* p. 321; *Liber de causis* I, tr. IV, c. 7, ed. Borgnet X, 426b–427b; Lib. II, tr. II, c. 1, ed. Borgnet X, 479b–480a *et alibi.*

[36] Cf. Kilwardby, *De ortu scientiarum,* cap. 26, fol. 32rb–va.

tonic view" which would admit into philosophy certain separated substances totally unrelated to celestial movement. "The statement of certain Platonists that there exist separated substances not related to movable bodies is entirely outside the realm of philosophical discourse, since this cannot be proved by reason."[37] The separated substances called angels by Avicenna, Algazel, Isaac, and Moses Maimonides have nothing to do with celestial movement or with celestial bodies; they are independent intermediaries between God and man. For Albert the only demonstrative way to separated substances and to God is through the study of celestial motions. Consequently not only are angels, as revealed in Sacred Scripture, outside philosophical discussion, but the *intellectus universaliter agens* of celestial motions can be none other than God. That is to say, the first cause of the *primum mobile* and its diurnal motion is God, and not an intermediary. That God is "the immediate natural mover" of the universe in its diurnal motion is taken by St. Albert as true and demonstrated among those who know anything about philosophy.[38]

Whatever modern Thomists may have to say about the famous *quinque viae* of St. Thomas, it cannot be denied that for Thomas all the proofs progress from terrestrial phenomena through celestial phenomena eventually to God. The question of angels in St. Thomas's philosophy will be considered later. For the present it is important to establish only that in St. Thomas's proofs celestial phenomena do have an important part to play. This is not to say that the validity of those proofs depends upon the antiquated astronomy of the Middle Ages. The principle of each proof has universal validity, and the line of argumentation transcends all astronomy, ancient, medieval, and modern. Nevertheless to see the proofs as St. Thomas saw them, it is necessary to accept, at least historically, the system of the universe as he understood it.

There can scarcely be any doubt that St. Thomas's first proof is derived historically from Aristotle's *Physics* and *Metaphysics*. This is clearly evident in the detailed analysis presented in *Summa contra gentiles* I, c. 13, where Aristotle is explicitly cited as intending to prove the existence of God *ex parte motus duabus viis*. The first way is a paraphrase of *Phys.* VII, c. 1, to VIII, c. 5, text. 35; the second corresponds to *Phys.* VIII, c. 5, text. 36, to the end. The first starts with the example of solar movement and ends disjunctively with Plato's self-mover

---

[37] St. Albert, *Liber XI Metaph.*, tr. II, c. 17, ed. Borgnet VI, 638a; cf. *Problemata determinata*, q. 2, *ed. cit.*, pp. 323–27.
[38] St. Albert, *Problemata determinata*, q. 5, *ed. cit.*, p. 328.

of the first sphere or Aristotle's separated mover of the whole. The second starts with various types of self-movents, showing how all must be reduced to some *primum movens se quod sit sempiternum,* and ends with God as a self-movent. "But since God is not a part of any self-movent, Aristotle in his *Metaphysics* further discovers from this mover which is a part of a self-movent another mover entirely distinct, who is God." Two objections to the Aristotelian argument are easily handled. The first, that it assumes the eternity of motion contrary to the Catholic faith, is shown to be irrelevant, for it makes no difference whether or not motion is eternal; there is still need of an adequate mover. The second, that Aristotle assumes the animation of celestial bodies contrary to the view of many, is likewise shown to be irrelevant, for even if the celestial bodies are animated, one must still conclude according to Aristotle's principles to an unmoved mover entirely separated from bodies. A simplified form of this *manifestior via* is the only one presented by St. Thomas in his *Compendium theologiae* for Brother Reginald of Piperno.

The involvement of celestial bodies in the other proofs for God's existence is not so patent in the text of St. Thomas. However, it ought to be obvious that the argument from efficient causality includes the universal agency of celestial bodies operating in elementary bodies and in animal reproduction:

Even among naturalists it is admitted that above those contrary agencies in nature there is a single first agent, namely, the heaven, which is the cause of the diverse motions in those lower bodies. But since in the very heaven there is observed a diversity of position to which the contrariety of lower bodies is reduced as to a cause, [this diversity] must further be reduced to a first mover who is moved neither *per se* nor *per accidens.*[39]

Similarly the argument from possible and necessary beings includes not only terrestrial necessities and contingencies but also the sempiternal celestial bodies and spiritual substances, which are radically necessary beings. Their necessity for being can, indeed, be seen as derived; therefore beyond them there must exist an absolutely necessary being whose necessity is in no way derived.[40] The Platonic, or more specifically, the Avicennian,[41] argument concerning perfections clearly includes the immutable celestial bodies in the participated inequality of being and goodness, an inequality which needs to be derived from a single source which is essentially being, goodness, and supreme perfection. The fifth argument likewise includes the in-

[39] St. Thomas, *De pot.,* q. 3, a. 6.
[40] St. Thomas, *De pot.,* q. 5, a. 3.
[41] *De pot.,* q. 3, a. 5.

fluence of celestial bodies and separated intelligences on natural operations.[42] Natural terrestrial operations, influenced by celestial
motions, the light and heat of the sun, are apparently purposeful
operations of nature; all such operations of nature require the direction of intelligence ("opus naturae est opus intelligentiae").

Historically, then, the five proofs of St. Thomas for the existence of
God involve celestial bodies and their movement as he understood
them. Therefore a careful consideration of celestial phenomena in
the physics of St. Thomas is not without value to the modern Thomist, however much the modern Thomist may wish to adapt the traditional arguments.

To understand the problem of celestial movers in medieval physics,
it is necessary to present the views of Albertus Magnus and then those
of Robert Kilwardby before examining the crucial problem in the
doctrine of St. Thomas.

ST. ALBERT THE GREAT

For St. Albert both physics and metaphysics attain the existence of
God, but under different formalities and in different ways. Physics,
although it demonstrates through all the real causes in nature, is
primarily concerned with the efficient and material cause: "if we have
said anything about the form or about the end [in physics], this was
only of form insofar as it is mobile and of end only insofar as it is the
termination of the motion of a mover."[43] But metaphysics deals with
substantial being and its causes; therefore in metaphysics "we directly
show that the first efficient cause is the universal end, that from him
flow all mobile substances, and that he is like a leader of an army with
respect to the universe."[44] This task is proper to metaphysics, and in
this respect nothing is borrowed from natural science. It is true that
natural science proved by way of motion the absolute immobility of
the first mover, but it did not reveal him "prout ipsum est causa
universi esse et forma et finis." This is proper to metaphysics. Hence,
Albert concludes, it is evident that metaphysics is a loftier contemplation by far than physics.

The task of physics is to explain all changes in nature, both terrestrial and celestial. Terrestrial movements, alteration, generation, and
corruption can be explained in large measure by the celestial bodies,
but since these celestial bodies themselves are moved, the ultimate

---

[42] *De verit.*, q. 5, a. 2; *Sum. cont. gent.* I, cap. 13. Cf. Averroes, *In II Phys.*, comm. 75.
[43] St. Albert, *Lib. XI Metaph.*, tr. I, c. 3, *ed. cit.*, VI, 584b.
[44] *Ibid.*

source of this movement must itself be immovable. This ultimate unmoved mover, proved in the *Physics,* is considered by St. Albert to be God, the Christian God. But the approach is different in metaphysics. Since the term of terrestrial movement and alteration is *per se* the generation of a substantial being,[45] and since the substantial being of the very heavens must be produced, beyond the physical universe there must exist a *principium universi esse,* who is the efficient source of being, the formal principle of all being, and the universal end of all things.[46] Hence it belongs to both physics and metaphysics to consider celestial phenomena and God, but physics considers these through the principles of motion (*secundum principia motus*), while metaphysics considers these through the principles of being (*essendi*). In other words, the natural philosopher arrives at the existence of God as the first mover, but the metaphysician arrives at His existence as the efficient cause, the formal principle, and the ultimate end of all being.

This does not mean, Albert points out, that the metaphysician gives the *propter quid* reason for changeable substance, and the physicist the *quia,* as some would have it. "For if the physicist borrowed from the metaphysician, it would follow that physics is subalternated to first philosophy, which from the opening pages of this science we have shown to be false."[47] Thus physics and metaphysics are each autonomous sciences with special principles of investigation proper to each. However, unless it is first demonstrated in physics that there exists some real separated substance, there is no need for the subsequent investigation called metaphysics. The Platonists, Albert repeatedly points out, postulated ideas and mathematical entities separate from matter in order to explain sensible being; but these cannot exist apart from matter, and if they did, they could not be responsible for motion in the universe.[48] Therefore if some separated substance exists to be studied in metaphysics, this substance can be demonstrated only as the cause of motion, specifically as the cause of celestial motion.

St. Albert accepted the order of celestial spheres commonly taught by the Arabian astronomers. The spheres were considered generically to be ten in number: the *primum mobile* causing diurnal movement of the whole universe, the sphere of fixed stars, the spheres of Saturn, Jupiter, Mars, the Sun, Venus, Mercury, the Moon, and the terrestrial

---

[45] St. Albert, *Lib. VIII Phys.,* tr. II, c. 4, *ed. cit.,* III, 572a.
[46] St. Albert, *Lib. XI Metaph.,* tr. I, c. 3, *ed. cit.,* VI, 584b–585a.
[47] *Ibid.*
[48] St. Albert, *Lib. XI Metaph.,* tr. I, cc. 4 and 8; Lib. I, tr. V, cc. 8, 12, and 14; Lib. VII, tr. II, c. 3, *et alibi.*

sphere of active and passive elements.[49] It was well understood by all that each so-called sphere was subject to many distinct motions, each of which required some kind of mover. But it was simpler to talk in terms of the clearly visible planets, the fixed stars, and the unseen cause of diurnal motion than in terms of the precise number of celestial motions postulated to save the appearances of each planet. Similarly, it was understood among the better-informed that the notion of "sphere" was postulated to regularize the errant motions of the planets and to give intelligibility to their complicated movements. Those spheres were no more "solid," contrary to some modern interpretations, than the familiar sphere of terrestrial change.

In the view of Avicenna each sphere was moved and ruled by a separated substance, whatever may have been the number of distinct movements required for each planet. It is within this context that St. Albert discusses the problem of celestial movers. But Avicenna further identified those intelligences and the proximate mover (*anima nobilis*) with angels.[50] St. Albert, as has already been noted, was unwilling to identify the separated substances of the philosophers with the angels of Sacred Scripture. Further, the tenth intelligence for Avicenna was the *intellectus agens hominum*, which ruled the terrestrial realm of mutable substances by infusing forms from without. This *dator formarum* was invoked by Avicenna to explain the apparent generation of new substances in the world of nature. St. Albert repeatedly rejected the Avicennian innovation with sound Aristotelian arguments, which need not concern us here.

The real problem for St. Albert was the obvious difference between terrestrial changes arising from nature and celestial motions which could not arise from nature. The term "nature" is a technical one and it designates that "principle of motion and rest in those things to which it belongs properly (*per se*) and not as a concomitant attribute (*per accidens*)."[51] Technically it was contrasted with soul (*anima, ψυχή*) and with intelligence (*intelligentia, νοῦς*), particularly in Platonic and neo-Platonic writings; and it was also contrasted with art (*ars, τέχνη*) and with chance (*casus, αὐτόματον*) by Aristotle. Nature as an intrinsic principle always acts in a determined manner for a predetermined end.[52] This nature must always be efficiently produced by some

---

[49] St. Albert, *Problemata determinata*, q. 2, *ed. cit.*, p. 324; see *ibid.*, note 9.
[50] An excellent discussion of this has been given by Henry Corbin in his *Avicenna and the Visionary Recital*, trans. by W. R. Trask, Bollingen Series, LXVI (New York, 1960), pp. 46–122.
[51] Arist., *Phys.* II, 1, 192b21–23. Cf. Chapter I above.
[52] Cf. Albert, *Lib. VIII Phys.*, tr. II, c. 4, *et passim*.

generator of the form. Once this natural form has been generated by an efficient cause, that nature spontaneously moves toward the unique end proportioned to it and rests in the possession of the end. "Hence place and motion are given by the generator just as the form is, but the form is given principally, while place and motion are given *per consequens,* just as proper accidents are given to the form by generation."[53] Moreover, strictly speaking, "nature" designates the internal power of inanimate substances ("natura non est nisi virtus inanimatae substantiae").[54] Finally, nature is a source of individual attainment, and not of transient activity. Hence "locomotion is never derived [efficiently] from nature as 'the principle of motion and rest in those things to which it belongs properly and not concomitantly,' as defined by Aristotle in *Physics* II; for which reason, as we have said, locomotion must be derived either from a generator or from one removing an impediment or from a soul."[55] In other words, since celestial motions do not attain any end, these motions cannot arise spontaneously from the nature of celestial bodies. For St. Albert, as for Plato and Aristotle before him, celestial motions must be derived immediately from some kind of *soul,* or self-mover.

Comparing the views of Plato and Aristotle,[56] Albert notes that both agree on three points: (i) that all natural motions must be reduced to some self-movement; (ii) that a celestial body cannot move itself but must be moved by a spiritual substance which is either a soul or an intellect; (iii) that the spiritual mover of the body must itself be indivisible, without magnitude, possessing adequate power to move the celestial body. However, Albert notes, Plato and Aristotle differ on two essential points: (i) Plato considered the conjoined mover to be the ultimate mover, while Aristotle considered this soul to be the instrument of a higher intellect entirely separated from all matter; (ii) Plato considered the celestial soul to be perpetual and descendent from the stars, while Aristotle conceived the conjoined mover to be produced by the separated intellect and moved by it. In other words, Aristotle, according to St. Albert's understanding, admitted a conjoined mover for each celestial motion, a mover which was somewhat similar to a spiritual, intellectual soul, but without sense faculties. This conjoined mover explained how a celestial body like the *primum caelum* could be moved perpetually without attaining any end or finality intrinsic to itself. However, the conjoined mover itself was moved by

[53] *Ibid., ed. cit.,* III, 572a–b.
[54] St. Albert, *Lib. XI Metaph.,* tr. I, c. 13, *ed. cit.,* VI, 604.
[55] St. Albert, *Problemata determinata,* q. 2, *ed. cit.,* p. 325.
[56] St. Albert, *Lib. VIII Phys.,* tr. II, c. 8.

reason of the celestial body; that is, the *anima caeli* moved concomitantly (*per accidens*) with the celestial body, much as the human soul is moved by the movement of the body. Therefore, the *anima caeli* is a moved mover, needing to be moved by another, a substance entirely separated from matter not only in definition, but also in existence. The spiritual *anima caeli* can be moved only by intellection and desire. The initial intellectual light emanating from the subsisting acting intellect, giving the soul the idea and the desire to move, is the true immediate mover of the universe.

As St. Albert understands it, when Aristotle speaks of the heavens or the celestial bodies, he usually means the composite of soul and body, mover and moved; the heavens are for Aristotle animated substances (*substantiae animatae*). While it is easier to talk of the sun as though it were a simple substance, the movement of the sun is complex and due to many animated substances. For Aristotle at least the diurnal, longitudinal, and latitudinal motions are distinct; each of these is caused by an animated celestial body. Ultimately these motions of the sun and all other planetary motions are due to the diurnal motion of the entire universe, the *primum caelum*, the first animated cause of the universe.

Now the animated substance is the cause not only of inanimate substances, but also of their order and motion. According to the teaching of the Peripatetics, this animated substance is the *corpus caeli*. Moreover, it was shown in Book VIII of the *Physics* that the first mover, which is a composite of mover and moved, or pushed, is the first heaven [*primum caelum*]. In this manner it was therefore shown that the animate precedes the inanimate. We have likewise shown in that same place at the end of Book VIII of the *Physics*, first that the first mover is absolutely simple, and that this, since it is related to the first body as its mover, unquestionably will have the character of soul, and not nature [*pro certo habebit rationem animae et non naturae*], because nature never moves that body whose nature it is according to local motion.[57]

Plato, according to St. Albert, stopped here with the *anima mundi* as God, but Aristotle realized that each soul, since it is moved along with the body, must be moved by the desire for some absolutely separated intelligence. Thus for Aristotle the separated intelligence known and desired by the first animated mover is the actual source of all physical movement and the ultimate end of every celestial motion. There is, in other words, a hierarchy of intelligences proportioned to the various orders of animated substances. There is, for example, at least one illuminating intellect for all the animated movers of Venus, another for Jupiter, and so forth. The highest separated intelligence is the

---

[57] St. Albert, *Lib. XI Metaph.*, tr. I, c. 13, *ed. cit.*, VI, 604b.

true immediate mover of the entire universe, the *primum caelum*. The mind and will of God are obediently accepted and executed by the animated substances, who consequently move as moved movers.

When discussing this matter on his own terms, St. Albert prefers to keep three elements distinct: the celestial body, the soul-like mover, and the separated intelligence. The reason for this is that Albert could not accept Aristotle's concept of celestial "souls" as the substantial form of the body. For Albert these "souls" could not be the substantial form of an inorganic, insensitive body, such as the moon and sun; this kind of body would be entirely useless for intellectual processes. Consequently these "souls" move the body only as an efficient cause, not as a formal cause.[58] In his early work, the *Summa Parisiensis*, Albert was willing to reconcile Aristotle's "souls" with the Catholic doctrine of angels.[59] Later, however, Albert became most insistent that the angels of revelation should not be identified with celestial souls or intelligences. According to Giles of Lessines, a disciple of St. Albert, "Haec est positio multorum magnorum et praecise domini Alberti quondam Ratisponensis episcopi, ob cuius reverentiam rationes praedictam positionem confirmantes addidimus."[60] Albert's strong views distinguishing angels from intelligences and souls were shared by Theodoric of Freiberg, another disciple of his.[61] The reason for Albert's view is clearly stated in the reply to John of Vercelli's questionnaire: the separated intelligence known to philosophers is entirely immobile locally, "nec mittitur nec venit nec recedit."[62] This is entirely contrary to what we know of Gabriel, Raphael, and Michael according to the Scriptures. Further, the separated intelligence is known to philosophers solely as the cause of celestial motion and of inferior

---

[58] "Nos cum Sanctis confitemur caelos non habere animas, nec esse animalia, si anima secundum propriam rationem sumatur. . . . Operatur autem ad corpus ut nauta ad navem, hoc est, secundum rationem movendi ipsum et regendi." *Summa de creaturis*, tr. III, q. 16, a. 2, ed. Borgnet XXXIV, 443a. In this edition "natura" is erroneously printed for "nauta."

[59] "Ita non est contrarium fidei quosdam angelos iuvare naturam in movendo et gubernando sphaeras caelorum, quos Angelos moventes sive intelligentias Philosophi dicunt *animas*." *Ibid.*, ad 6, p. 445b.

[60] Giles de Lessines, *De unitate formae*, P. II, c. 5, ed. M. de Wulf in Les Philosophes Belges, I (Louvain, 1902), p. 38.

[61] "Est autem et hoc circa iam dicta tenendum, quod dicti philosophi, loquentes de intelligentiis, non loquebantur de angelis, de quibus scriptura sacra loquitur, quae loquitur mysteria abscondita a sapientibus et prudentibus et revelat ea parvulis." Theodoric of Freiberg, *De intellectu et intelligibili*, P. I, cap. 12, ed. E. Krebs in *Beiträge z. Gesch. d. Phil. d. MA.*, Bd. V, H. 5–6 (Münster, 1906), pp. 132*–133*. Cf. *ibid.*, P. II, cap. 34, pp. 164–165*. I am grateful to Fr. William A. Wallace, O.P., for allowing me to utilize his transcription of Theodoric's *De intelligenciis et motoribus celorum* and *De corporibus celestibus quoad naturam eorum corporalem* from MS Vat. lat. 2183.

[62] St. Albert, *Problemata determinata*, q. 2, *ed. cit.*, p. 323.

forms, while the angels of Scripture are the messengers of God, a function which cannot be proved by natural reason.[63]

To understand St. Albert better, we must consider celestial motion itself and its three distinct causes, namely, the body, the soul-like mover, and the separated intelligence.

St. Albert clearly insists throughout all his writings that celestial motion cannot be accounted for by the nature of the celestial body. That is to say, perpetual motion of the spheres cannot originate spontaneously from "nature" as from a formal principle. Scholastic philosophy, following Aristotle, distinguished two uses of the technical term "nature."[64] The primary and principal use of the term was to designate an intrinsic active source of regular, teleological activity and attainment; nature in this sense was called a formal principle, since form is the ultimate source of these activities. In a secondary and analogical sense the innate, passive receptivity for the form could also be called "nature," since potency is a true principle of change; nature in this sense was called a material or passive principle. For St. Albert none of the characteristics of nature as a formal principle could be verified in celestial motions. Nature as a formal principle always moves toward a determined end and, when it has attained it, rests in that attainment. "The reason for this is that nature does not cause local motion except *per consequens*, for in moving toward the form it consequently moves to the place which belongs to its form." In the celestial motions there is never any attainment and possession. "The mover of the heaven never moves to any position, but to move out of it again. But to move into a position and to move out of it again is not from nature, but from soul."[65] For this reason Albert frequently insisted that celestial motions are not from nature, but from intelligence ("caeli motus non dicitur naturae motus, sed intelligentiae").[66] Albert undoubtedly would have admitted that celestial motions are "natural" in the sense of coming from a passive principle, the celestial body. But invariably he prefers to deny the natural character of celestial motions, insisting always that they are not from nature, but from soul or intelligence. Precisely because the body itself is not the source of its

---

[63] *Ibid.*, q. 5, *ed. cit.*, p. 328.

[64] Cf. Chapter I above.

[65] "Adhuc autem natura non movet nisi ad unum, et cum pervenerit, quiescit in illo. Cuius causa est, quia natura non est causa motus localis nisi per consequens: movendo enim ad formam, per consequens movet ad locum qui est illius formae. Motor autem caeli non movet unquam ad aliquem situm, nisi moveat etiam ex illo. In aliquid igitur movere et ex illo non est naturae, sed animae." St. Albert, *Lib. XI Metaph.*, tr. I, c. 13, *ed. cit.*, p. 605b.

[66] St. Albert, *Lib. II Phys.*, tr. I, c. 2, *ed. cit.*, p. 95b.

perpetual movement, it is said *to be moved.* "Everything which *is moved*
has a mover conjoined to itself, as was proved in the Seventh Book of
the *Physics.*"[67]

The nature of the conjoined mover is difficult to determine in the
writings of St. Albert, largely, no doubt, because Albert retained the
Aristotelian terminology while denying the substantial union of the
two "parts" of the sphere. The conjoined mover is clearly a spiritual
substance, indivisible, and separated from all matter, at least in
definition.[68] It moves the body by its knowledge and desire of something higher.[69] "Since every motion of the heaven is according to the
form which is in the intellect, as the artistic idea is in the mind of the
artist, so in the intellect of the mover there is the image to be effected
by its motion; otherwise its motion would be unintentional, a chance
result and an accident."[70] At times St. Albert does call this conjoined
mover a "soul," particularly the *anima nobilis* of the *Liber de causis*
(prop. 3). But more frequently he conceives the mover as a luminous
form of intelligence and desire, produced by the separated intelligence. "Since the intelligence by its light produces every form in its
sphere and order, and since those forms are its light [*lumen*] and this
light desires to produce beings in existence [*lumen desiderans ad esse
deducere*], the proximate mover of the orb moves the orb and by moving produces forms in existence."[71] The conjoined mover, therefore, is
an intelligent form but not the "soul" of the sphere. "Thus it is evident
that the intelligence is not an angel; and if it were, it would still not be
the proximate mover of any celestial sphere."[72]

It is important to note that for St. Albert the luminous forms, the
conjoined movers of celestial bodies, are the true causes of everything
which is produced within that sphere. That is to say, the luminous
form, obedient to a higher intelligence, is the active principle of such
mysterious phenomena as animal reproduction and the spontaneous
generation of living things from inanimate matter.[73] "Every lower motion which is in the matter of generable things is reduced to the
motion of the heavens, which is the cause and measure of lower
motion by means of (i) the form of the moving intelligence, (ii) the

[67] St. Albert, *Lib. XI Metaph.*, tr. II, c. 3, *ed. cit.*, p. 614a; see *Lib. VII Phys.*, text et comm.
10.
[68] St. Albert, *Lib. XI Metaph.*, tr. II, cc. 12–13.
[69] *Ibid.*, c. 13, *ed. cit.*, p. 605a.
[70] *Ibid.*
[71] St. Albert, *Problemata determinata*, q. 2, *ed. cit.*, p. 327.
[72] *Ibid.*
[73] St. Albert, *Lib. XI Metaph.*, tr. I, cc. 6 and 8.

form of the celestial orb, and (iii) stellar rays."[74] The active powers of light, heat, conjunctions of the planets and stars are, for St. Albert, instrumental causes of the celestial forms whereby the natural powers of the elements can be productive of higher forms. One can say that these higher forms produced preexist in the elements *virtually* insofar as these elements are instruments of celestial movers. Of course, the celestial mover is itself a voluntary, intellectual instrument of the absolutely first intelligence, which is God. Similarly the male sperm virtually and actively contains the living and sentient souls of the embryo, but only as the instrument of celestial forces and intelligences. In other words, the natural heat, density, mobility, and structure of the male sperm are used instrumentally by celestial agents to produce an effect higher than their own active powers.[75] It was in this way that St. Albert understood and explained the famous Aristotelian phrase "Homo ex materia generat hominem et sol" (*Phys.* II, 2, 194b13).[76] The only qualification which Albert, the philosopher and theologian, makes to this phrase is the direct creation of the human soul.[77]

Finally, for Albert, the separated movers of celestial bodies are the active intelligences (*intellectus agens*). Each intelligence is like a practical intellect of an artist who conceives the image to be produced and implants this in his instruments as he uses them. The instruments of the active intelligence are threefold, namely, the conjoined spiritual mover, the celestial body itself, and the inherent powers of terrestrial nature. Consequently the ultimate mover of each celestial body is, in fact, the separated active intelligence proportioned to the spheres. Since, however, all celestial spheres depend upon the diurnal motion of the first heaven, the absolutely first mover of all the celestial bodies is the separated, active intelligence commanding the *primum caelum*. This absolutely first mover is the *primum principium universi esse*, not only the cause of all motion but also the absolute efficient cause, formal principle, and ultimate end of all being. Not only does he produce the hierarchy of conjoined celestial movers, their bodies and motion, but he is also the first efficient cause, formal principle, and

---

[74] *Ibid.*, c. 8, *ed. cit.*, p. 594a; cf. *Problemata determinata*, qq. 7–15 and qq. 34–36.

[75] St. Albert, *Problemata determinata*, q. 34; *De animalibus* XVI, tr. I, cc. 11–13.

[76] "Quod enim impressiones separatorum a materia generabilium sint in materia patet per hoc quod ex materia hominis homo generat hominem, et sol et motor solis; et ideo oportet considerare separata in quantum impressiones earum per motum caelestium sunt in generabilibus et corruptibilibus." St. Albert, *Lib. II Phys.*, tr. I, c. 11, *ed. cit.*, pp. 113–14. See Averroes, *ibid.*, comm. 26.

[77] *Problemata determinata*, q. 33; *De nat. et orig. animae*, tr. I, c. 5; *De animalibus*, Lib. XVI, tr. I, cc. 11–12; *Summa de creaturis*, P. II, q. 5, a. 4.

final end of each intelligence. The first principle of universal being is commonly designated by St. Albert as the *intellectus universaliter agens*, who, as has already been noted, is God Himself. As first mover of the heavens He is attained in natural science; as first cause of being He is attained in metaphysics.

Once Albert has established in his reply to the master general that angels are not the same as intelligences discovered by the philosophers, he can easily dismiss the first five questions as fatuous. The existence of angels, the messengers of God, cannot be proved in philosophy; they have nothing to do with problems of natural science; and even if God were not the first mover of the heavens—which He really is—the existence of angels would still not be demonstrated. God, for St. Albert, is the first cause of celestial motions, not as a form conjoined to the universe, but as a separated active intelligence commanding the motions of all, "since Aristotle says that the first cause moves the first heaven, to the motion of which all motions of celestial bodies are referred, as all movements of organic members are referred to the movement of the heart."[78] The only body which God moves immediately as conjoined to Himself is the body of Christ, joined hypostatically to the Word.

ROBERT KILWARDBY

The approach of Kilwardby is very different from that of St. Albert. Kilwardby, in fact, reflects much more the schools of Oxford than those of Paris, despite his own regency in arts at Paris (ca. 1237–ca. 1245). He had been a master in theology of Oxford about fifteen years when he was asked to reply to the questionnaire of John of Vercelli. We cannot be certain that Kilwardby always maintained the views presented in the reply of 1271, but we can be certain of his views at that date.

Replying to the first question, Kilwardby explicitly denies that God is the immediate mover of the heavens moving either eternally or temporally in place: "certissime tenendum est et asserendum quod Deus non movet primum caelum nec aliquod corpus immediate motu locali."[79] He admits that Aristotle seems to consider God as the first mover of the eternal spheres, "but the truth is that God does not move any body immediately" by continual locomotion. If God did move any

---

[78] *Problemata determinata*, q. 1, ed. cit., p. 321; cf. Aristotle, *De caelo et mundo* II, 2, 284b6–286a2.

[79] Kilwardby, *Responsio*, q. 1, ed. Chenu, loc. cit., p. 194.

body in this way, He would be either the substantial act of that body and a part of the whole or a simple mover like a man on a horse. The first alternative is obviously erroneous. The second is awkward and unreasonable for it implies that the first heaven is moved by violence: "secundo modo caelum primum videretur moveri violenter." Kilwardby, however, does admit that God can and does move bodies immediately by a certain supernatural change, as in creation, the production of light, the formation of Eve, and similar events. In such events God operates without the assistance of nature or angels. Concluding his reply to the first query, Kilwardby categorically states:

From these considerations, therefore, the reply to the question must be that God moves no body immediately by continuous motion, but only by His word when a body is changed instantaneously so that something supernaturally begins to exist.

The second question has to do with natural motions and their dependence on angelic movers of the celestial bodies. Kilwardby first distinguishes between natural and violent motions. Nature is an intrinsic principle of motion; only bodies which have such a principle *per se* are said to move naturally. Motions are called violent when their moving force is extraneous, the subject contributing nothing to the motion ("quando principium motivum est extraneum, passo non conferente"). Among natural motions Kilwardby enumerates continuous movement of bodies, instantaneous transmission of light, the irascible and concupiscible emotions of spiritual beings, and intellectual activity. Clearly, intellectual and appetitive activities of spiritual beings are not affected by celestial movement; rather, such spiritual activities are productive of celestial motion.

There are for Kilwardby two types of celestial motion. The first emanates from celestial bodies in the form of energy and light rays affecting all the active and passive powers of terrestrial bodies, both elementary and composite. This cosmic influence is produced by the celestial bodies, but the influence is subjectively located in terrestrial bodies. "And perhaps if this influence of light and energy were withdrawn from elements and composites, all active and passive powers of bodies would cease to act or react; hence this influence seems to be the *per se* cause of natural activity and movement in the elements."[80] There is, however, another motion located in the celestial body itself; this is the continual rotation of the sphere. Kilwardby does not con-

---

[80] *Ibid.*, q. 2, *ed. cit.*, p. 196.

sider this rotational movement of the spheres to have any direct or proper bearing on natural terrestrial motion. Such motions do provide variations of temperature, humidity, and the like, but this is secondary to the direct cosmic influence affecting natural changes.

Finally Kilwardby proceeds to discuss the crucial question of celestial movers. He notes that there are three opinions concerning the motion of celestial bodies. The first is that of Aristotle and certain other philosophers. Kilwardby's interpretation of Aristotle's view is essentially that of St. Albert: "celestial bodies are animated, having animal life and intelligence by which they perceive the will of the first cause, and motion in place by which they fulfill the known will of God; by this motion of theirs they conserve things and preserve generation and the limited being of generable natures."[81] In this view celestial bodies are moved by spirits which are their "souls" just as man is moved by his spirit, or soul. It is interesting to note in passing that the author of *Errores philosophorum* attributes animation of the heavens not to Aristotle or Averroes but exclusively to Avicenna:

Again [Avicenna] erred on the subject of the animation of the heavens. For he held that the heavens were animated. He said that the soul of the heavens is not only a suitable moving power, as the Philosopher and the Commentator were intent upon saying, but that a single being is produced by the union of the soul of the heavens with the heavens, just as by the union of our soul and our body.[82]

Concerning this presumed view of Aristotle, Kilwardby notes that it is philosophically sound and supported by reason: "since those bodies seem to be more noble than living bodies, they ought to have a higher form of life." Nevertheless in 1277 the bishop of Paris condemned the proposition "that celestial bodies are moved by an intrinsic principle, which is a soul."[83] And St. Albert, as we have seen, clearly rejected celestial animation as alien to the Catholic faith.

The second opinion listed by Kilwardby is in reality that of St. Thomas: "others hold that those bodies are moved by angelic spirits who govern and move them in such a way that they are not their act, or form." Kilwardby dismisses this view as unphilosophical, and he remarks, "Nor do I recall it being approved by any of the *Sancti* as

---

[81] *Responsio*, q. 2, § *De tertio*. For this part of the reply we rely on the emended edition published by Chenu in *Revue des Sc. Phil. et Théol.* 29 (1940), 211.

[82] Giles of Rome, *Errores philosophorum* VI: Avicenna, 10, ed. Josef Koch, trans. by J. O. Riedl (Milwaukee, 1944), p. 31.

[83] *Chartularium Univ. Paris.*, ed. H. Denifle, O.P., I, n. 473, p. 548, prop. 92; see also prop. 213. Cf. E. Krebs, *Meister Dietrich*, in *Beiträge z. Gesch. d. Phil. d. MA.*, Bd. V, H. 5–6 (Münster, 1906), pp. 75–76.

true and certain." However, Kilwardby does admit in passing that it could be held *absque errore* by Catholics.[84]

Kilwardby's own view of celestial motion is presented succinctly as the third opinion:

Just as heavy and light bodies are moved to a place in which they rest by their own inclinations and tendencies, so celestial bodies are moved circularly in place by their own natural inclinations similar to weight [*quasi ponderibus*] in order to conserve corruptible things lest they suddenly perish and fail.

Some spheres rotate naturally from west to east, others from east to west, and still others move naturally as epicycles, and others on the eccentric. To each planet and orb God gave an innate natural inclination to move in a particular way in rotational motion; to each He accorded an innate order, regularity, and direction without the need of a distinct agency like a soul, an angel, or Himself here and now producing the motion. "Just as the forces [*pondera*] of heavy and light move bodies consistently, not permitting them to stray outside a determined path, so it is with the forces of each and every celestial body." Consequently rotational motion is as natural to celestial bodies as gravitational motion is to heavy bodies. Both arise spontaneously from *nature* as an intrinsic active principle, *instinctu propriorum ponderum* (q. 3). It was commonly recognized among the schoolmen that heavy bodies need nothing more than their own generated nature to account for gravitational motion; heavy bodies need no conjoined mover to account for the continued downward fall.[85] Kilwardby wished to explain celestial motions by a similar intrinsic formal principle. Terrestrial bodies are unattached and hence move rectilinearly to a place of relative rest. But for Kilwardby the heavens are spherical; stars and planets are attached to their proper orbs within a sphere. Consequently the only "natural" motion the heavens have is rotational, a continual rotation of each orb on its axis. The combination of various rotations on suitable axes together with the required uniform velocity of each rotation produced the apparent motion of the planet. Kilwardby thus dispenses with the need of any conjoined or separated mover, whether that mover be called a soul, an angel, intelligence, or God. It is clear from this that Kilwardby could not prove the existence of God through physical motion. He cannot even prove the existence of a separated substance.

---

[84] Cf. J. A. Weisheipl, "The *Problemata Determinata* Ascribed to Albertus Magnus," p. 304, note 8.

[85] Cf. J. A. Weisheipl, *Nature and Gravitation* (River Forest, Ill., 1955), pp. 19–21, 25–28, and Chapter I above.

Because of the great diversity of opinion concerning celestial movers, Kilwardby maintained that it is impossible to prove that angels
move the spheres (q. 4). Philosophers think that they have infallibly
demonstrated the existence of spiritual movers for the heavens, but
these are certainly not the angels discussed by Catholics. Even assuming that God is not the immediate mover of the heavens—which according to Kilwardby He is not—it is in no way proved that angels
have to be celestial movers (q. 5). Unlike St. Albert, Kilwardby conceives the physical universe as perfectly self-contained, perfectly
"natural," having no need of immaterial agencies directing and moving the heavens. His is the closed world created by God in the beginning with sufficient innate tendencies to move rectilinearly and
rotationally.

This view was not original with Robert Kilwardby. Fr. Daniel A.
Callus has pointed out that this idea can be traced to the earliest days
of Aristotelianism in Oxford. Some sixty years before Kilwardby's
reply, John Blund gave as his considered opinion that the heavenly
bodies are not moved by souls, nor by intelligences, but by their own
active nature moving *orbiculariter*.[86] As is commonly known, this opinion found favor among many in the fourteenth and fifteenth centuries.

Fr. Chenu saw in Kilwardby's view an anticipation of John Buridan's
famous suggestion about celestial motions, that an impetus (given by
God) is also found in the celestial spheres, but one which cannot be
diminished by resistance, since celestial matter offers no resistance.[87]
In all terrestrial projectiles impetus is diminished and overcome by
nature resisting the violent force. But in Aristotelian theory celestial
bodies could offer no resistance, since they had no weight or gravity;
they were considered completely passive, having "nature" only as a
passive principle of motion. Consequently Buridan's suggestion of an
initial impetus for celestial motion was a perfectly obvious one; it
presupposes Aristotle's doctrine of the pure passivity of those bodies.
In other words, it is precisely because such bodies have no active
"nature" that they can, in the scheme of Buridan, receive a perpetual
impetus for continued motion. This is quite different from Kilwardby's conception of celestial spheres actively inclined to circular motion, for here the "nature" of celestial bodies is an active principle.
The final result of both views may be similar or even identical, but the

---

[86] "Dicimus quod firmamentum movetur a natura, non ab anima, et alia superceles-
tia." The full passage is published by Daniel A. Callus, O.P., "The Treatise of John
Blund On the Soul," in *Autour d'Aristote* (Louvain, 1955), pp. 487–89.
[87] Cf. Pierre Duhem, *Études sur Léonard de Vinci*, III (Paris, 1955), p. 42.

theoretical foundation of Buridan's theory of impetus for the heavens is profoundly dissimilar to the views of Kilwardby.

Kilwardby's view, however, was common enough in later centuries. It was favored particularly by Platonists and semi-Platonists. Notably Nicholas of Cusa attempted to explain the circular motion of the heavens by an appeal to their orbicular shape; their matter, being different from terrestrial matter, naturally tended to move orbicularly, that is, by rotating.[88] Copernicus himself explained the circular motion of the heavenly bodies by their spherical nature:

Now we note that the motion of the heavenly bodies is circular. Rotation is natural to a sphere and by that very act is its shape expressed. For here we deal with the simplest kind of body, wherein neither beginning nor end may be discerned, nor, if it rotates ever in the same place, may the one be distinguished from the other.[89]

For Copernicus, as for Kilwardby before him, the substantial form of a spherical body naturally tends to move spherically. Surprisingly, for Copernicus the outermost sphere of the fixed stars, though spherical by nature, was said to be at rest.[90] It must be admitted, however, that Copernicus was not concerned with explaining the physical causes of celestial motion, as this is beyond the scope of mathematical astronomy.

We may seriously doubt that Kilwardby's reply influenced later writers; it certainly did not influence John Buridan. Nevertheless it does represent an important medieval view concerning celestial motion.

ST. THOMAS AQUINAS

The reply of St. Thomas is the shortest and most succinct of the three. He adheres strictly to the *forma* expected, appealing to the *Sancti* (Scripture, Augustine, Pseudo-Dionysius, Gregory, Jerome) and evaluating all questions in the light of Catholic faith. "It seems to me safer," he says in the prooemium, "that doctrines commonly held by philosophers which are not contrary to the faith be neither asserted as dogmas of faith (although they may sometimes be introduced as philosophical arguments) nor denied as contrary to the faith, lest occasion be offered to men learned in human wisdom to ridicule the doctrine of faith."

---

[88] Nicholas of Cusa, *De ludo globi*, Lib. I (Basel, 1565), pp. 210–14.

[89] N. Copernicus, *De Revolutionibus Orbium Caelestium*, Lib. I, c. 4 (Thorn, 1873), p. 14; also c. 8, pp. 21–24.

[90] *Ibid.*, c. 10, pp. 28–29.

In his important theological treatise, *De substantiis separatis*, St. Thomas considers the relative merits of Plato and Aristotle on the question of angels.[91] Plato—really Proclus—is understood by St. Thomas to have postulated various orders of spiritual substances between the human soul and God. Under God, the supreme unity and goodness, there is the order of secondary gods who are the Forms or Ideas eternally radiant. Inferior to these is the order of separated intellects, "which participate in the above-mentioned Forms in order to have actual understanding." Next come the various orders of soul, each one inhabiting a certain kind of body. Celestial souls animate celestial bodies and move them, in such a manner that "the highest of the bodies, namely the first heaven, which is moved by its own motion, receives motion from the highest soul, and so on to the very lowest of the heavenly bodies." Below celestial souls are the demons who inhabit unearthly bodies. The lowest intellectual soul is man, who, although he inhabits a visible body "as a sailor in a ship," also has another nobler body belonging to the soul, incorruptible and everlasting, even as the soul itself is incorruptible. Souls below man, such as plant and animal souls, lack intelligence and immortality. If all these views of Plato were true, notes St. Thomas, then all orders between God and man would be called "angels" by Catholics.

The fundamental weakness of Plato's position, as St. Thomas sees it, is that it is without proof, for his separated intelligences are merely postulated, not demonstrated. "That is why Aristotle proceeded by a more manifest and surer way, namely, by way of motion, to investigate substances that are separate from matter." St. Thomas's interpretation of Aristotle is substantially that of St. Albert and Kilwardby. Since all generable and celestial bodies are moved, they must be moved ultimately by a substance which is not material. The immaterial soul conjoined to celestial bodies is moved concomitantly with the body, therefore it is moved by knowledge and desire of absolutely separated intelligences. "Therefore each of the heavenly bodies is animated by its own soul and each has its own separate appetible object which is the proper end of its motion." For Aristotle, then, there are as many intelligences as there are celestial souls, and as many celestial souls as there are motions. It was Avicenna, according to St. Thomas, who erroneously limited the number of separated intelligences to ten, thinking that the multiple motions of a planet could be "ordered to the motion of one star." In any case, according to the position of Aristotle, between man and God "there exists only a two-fold order of

[91] Cap. 1–4. For the treatise *De substantiis separatis* we rely on the excellent English version of Fr. Francis J. Lescoe (West Hartford, 1959).

intellectual substances, namely the separated substances which are the ends of the heavenly motions, and the souls of the spheres, which move through appetite and desire."[92] Aristotle and Plato both agree that all immaterial substances have their entire being from God, that they are entirely immaterial, and that they are ruled by divine providence. They differ, however, with respect to the number and precise character of separated substances as well as to their relevance to the physical order.

For St. Thomas the theologian, Aristotle made three serious errors concerning angels. First, he erroneously limited their number to what could be ascertained by celestial motion; there is no demonstrative reason why they cannot be more numerous, as Catholic theology teaches.[93] Second, he erred by considering some to be substantially united to celestial bodies as their soul; such a union is unreasonable and contrary to Catholic teaching.[94] Finally, Aristotle erred in considering angels and the universe to have existed from all eternity; such eternity cannot be demonstrated by reason.[95] St. Thomas himself never doubted that Plato and Aristotle admitted another mode of "coming-into-being" besides physical generation for immaterial substances and the universe. "Over and above the mode of becoming by which something comes to be through change or motion, there must be a mode of becoming or origin of things, without any mutation or motion through the influx of being [*per influentiam essendi*]."[96] St. Thomas goes on to say that, although Plato and Aristotle did posit that immaterial substances and even heavenly bodies always existed, "we must not suppose on that account that they denied to them a cause of their being."[97] On this point they did not depart from the position of the Catholic faith.

We can now return to St. Thomas's reply to the official questionnaire. His reply to the first three questions simply states that God normally rules His creation through intermediaries, the lower and

[92] *Ibid.*, c. 2, n. 10; cf. *In II De caelo*, lect. 18, n. 16.

[93] *Ibid.*, c. 2, nn. 12–13; cf. *Sum. cont. gent.* II, c. 92.

[94] *Ibid.*, c. 18, nn. 100–101; cf. *De spirit. creat.*, a. 5; *Sum. cont. gent.* II, c. 91; *Sum. theol.* I, q. 51, a. 1; *De pot.*, q. 6, a. 6.

[95] *Ibid.*, c. 2, n. 14; cf. *Sum. theol.* I, q. 46, a. 1; *Sum. cont. gent.* II, cc. 31–38; *De pot.*, q. 3, a. 17; *De aeternitate mundi*.

[96] *Ibid.*, c. 9, n. 49.

[97] *Ibid.*, n. 52. For this reason St. Thomas frequently insists that those who interpret Aristotle's God as a mere physical mover or a mere final cause are in complete error. For St. Thomas Aristotle's God is a *causa essendi ipsi mundo*, a *causa quantum ad suum esse*, a *factor caelestium corporum*. "Ex hoc autem apparet manifeste falsitas opinionis illorum, qui posuerunt Aristotelem sensisse, quod Deus non sit causa substantiae caeli, sed solum motus eius." *In VI Metaph.*, lect. 1, n. 1164. Also *In VIII Phys.*, lect. 3, n. 6; *In I De caelo*, lect. 8, n. 14; *In II Metaph.*, lect. 2, n. 295.

more gross bodies being ruled by the higher and more subtle. The divine power, however, is in no way limited to the order it has established. Assuming that angels are the celestial movers, then no learned man can doubt that all natural motions of lower bodies are caused by the motion of celestial bodies (q. 3). Dionysius himself notes that the sun's rays induce the generation of sensible bodies, generate life itself, nurture, strengthen, and perfect it. All of this is within the power of angels.

For some reason St. Thomas omitted to answer the fourth question directly. It asks whether it is infallibly demonstrated according to anyone that angels are the movers of celestial bodies. In two earlier replies to the lector of Venice, St. Thomas answered this very question in clear terms:

The books of the philosophers abound with proofs for this, proofs, which they consider demonstrations. It seems to me therefore that it can be demonstrated that celestial bodies are moved by some intellect, either by God immediately or by means of angels moving them.[98]

Consequently his reply to the fifth question comes as no surprise. He categorically insists that if God does not move those bodies immediately, then some other spiritual substance is demonstrated as mover, either a celestial soul or a separated angel. The fundamental reason for this assertion is stated clearly: "Quod autem corpora caelestia a sola natura sua moveantur, sicut gravia et levia, est omnino impossibile."[99] In other words, for St. Thomas it is absolutely impossible that circular motion be explained by nature as an active (formal) principle within celestial bodies. This view is directly opposed to the position represented by Kilwardby.

Throughout all his writings St. Thomas insisted on the essential difference between rectilinear motion and rotational motion. Rectilinear motions, such as those of heavy and light bodies, arise spontaneously from within bodies, from nature as an active (formal) principle. Nature in this sense is predetermined to a certain end and to the means of attaining it. The end, therefore, is already within the intentionality of nature as form. Once nature has attained the end, it must rest in its acquisition, since it is its *good*. Physically there is no need for any "conjoined mover" to account for this motion downward or upward. Nature itself spontaneously moves toward the end which is its goal. "There is in heavy and light bodies a formal principle of its motion, because, just as other accidents proceed from the substantial

---

[98] St. Thomas, *Resp. de art. XXXVI*, a. 2; also *Resp. de art. XXX*, ad 4.
[99] St. Thomas, *Resp. ad Joan. Vercel.*, q. 5; cf. *Sum. cont. gent.* III, c. 23 *per totum*.

form, so does place and, consequently, movement toward place; not however that the natural form is a mover [*motor*], but the mover is the generator which begot such a form upon which this motion follows."[100] Therefore nature as an active principle is always ordained to rest in the possession of some good proper to itself.

For St. Thomas the profound difference between celestial and terrestrial phenomena lay in the motions. The heavens move continuously in time, aiming at no rest or possession of a goal. Whether the heavens are eternal or created in time is not relevant to the question. Likewise it makes no difference whether the celestial bodies in motion are real spheres or independent planets; in either case the motion is always ordered to further motion. Clearly these motions cannot be striving for a rest as yet unattained, since such a rest would be disastrous for the celestial body and no nature can desire its own destruction as a good. Nor can it be said that the purpose of such motion is motion itself. Motion by its very nature is a tending, a continual otherness; it has within its very nature a deformity which is incapable of being the final cause of any natural agent. "Therefore it is impossible that nature intend motion for the sake of motion."[101] Now for St. Thomas, if there is no intrinsic end attainable by a body in motion, then that motion cannot have sprung spontaneously from nature as form. Like the matter in generable substances, the celestial body must be moved by another, by one in continual contact with it. Consequently celestial bodies have "nature" only in the sense of a passive (material) principle, which means the natural aptitude to be moved by another. Hence "the motion of a celestial body, as far as its active principle is concerned, is not natural but voluntary and intellectual; however, in relation to its passive principle, the motion is natural, for a celestial body has a natural aptitude for such motion."[102] In this matter, notes St. Thomas, it makes no difference whether we conceive the celestial bodies to be moved by intellectual substances conjoined to the body after the manner of a soul or by one entirely distinct like an angel. "Non autem esset via solvendi, si moverentur per solum naturae impetum, sicut corpora gravia et levia."[103]

[100] St. Thomas, *In II Phys.*, lect. 1, n. 4. Also *In I De caelo*, lect. 18, n. 1; II, lect. 2, n. 6; III, lect. 7, nn. 5–9; *In II Phys.*, lect. 5, n. 5; IV, lect. 12, n. 9; VIII, lect. 8, nn. 5–7; *Sum. cont. gent.* III, cc. 82, 84; *De pot.*, q. 5, a. 5.

[101] "Impossibile est igitur quod natura intendat motum propter seipsum." *Sum. cont. gent.* III, c. 23, §6. Also *De pot.*, q. 5, a. 5: "impossibile est quod aliqua natura inclinet ad motum secundum se ipsum."

[102] *Sum. cont. gent.* III, c. 23, §8. Also *In II Phys.*, lect. 1, n. 4; *In II De caelo*, lect. 3, n. 2, and lect. 18, n. 1; *De pot.*, q. 5, a. 5 ad 12.

[103] St. Thomas, *In II De caelo*, lect. 18, n. 1.

It is true that for St. Thomas celestial bodies can have only a passive nature, whether the mover be a conjoined soul, as Aristotle wished, or a separated angel, as he himself believed. Nevertheless in establishing the existence of God along Aristotle's lines, whether the mover is a soul or an angel does make a difference. St. Thomas, as St. Albert before him, was well aware that the First Mover of the *Physics* was for Aristotle identical with the First Being of *Metaphysics* XII. That is to say, St. Thomas knew St. Albert's interpretation to be correct. However, there is a serious difficulty. If the celestial movers are not souls but angels, as St. Thomas himself held with the *Sancti*, then Aristotle's argument is not conclusive. A soul conjoined to the sphere is necessarily moved *per accidens*, that is, concomitantly with the sphere. Since this kind of mover is insufficient to account for the primary source of physical motion, one can validly conclude to the existence of an intelligence which is entirely separated from matter. And if one erroneously limits the number of spiritual substances to the number of celestial movements, then the separated intelligence moving the first animated sphere (*primum caelum*) must be God. On the other hand, if the immediate mover of the celestial bodies is not a soul, then it is in no way moved *per accidens*. This immediate mover could be God Himself or an angel. And if the number of angels is greater than Aristotle conceded, then it is impossible to demonstrate that God is the immediate mover of the heavens. This is precisely the difficulty envisaged in St. Thomas's reply to the fifth question: assuming that God is not the immediate mover, then it is indeed demonstrated that an angel is the mover. This assumption, however, cannot be made on philosophical, much less on physical, grounds. This is not to say that Aristotle failed to prove the existence of God in *Metaphysics* XII. Quite the contrary. St. Thomas was convinced that Aristotle perceived that other mode of becoming *per influentiam essendi*, whereby every spiritual substance is necessarily dependent on the first cause of being. It is this other mode of "being moved" that St. Thomas sees in Aristotle's conception of the conjoined mover of the first heaven.[104] It is the totality of movers which are in some true sense *moved* that validates the Aristotelian argument for St. Thomas. "Hence, unless the celestial bodies are moved immediately by God, they must either be animated and moved by their proper souls or be moved by angels, *quod melius dicitur.*"

Concluding his reply to the fifth question, St. Thomas notes that there are some philosophers who would have God move the first heaven by means of its *anima propria*, and the other heavens by means

---

[104] For example, *In XII Metaph.*, lect. 7, nn. 2519–22; lect. 8, nn. 2539–43; *In II De caelo*, lect. 18, n. 6.

of intelligences and souls. St. Thomas's own view is that God directs the universe through a hierarchy of angels, only the lower of which directly move the celestial bodies.

The view of St. Thomas is openly defended in the anonymous *Quaestio de motoribus corporum caelestium*, a work formerly attributed to St. Thomas and still published among his works.[105] Strangely, there is no known manuscript of this work extant, but it seems to be of English origin, written, as Grabmann has pointed out, some time after June 1271.[106] In it the author rejects at length the tradition represented by Robert Kilwardby as well as the animation theory presented by Simplicius. The author defends vigorously the Thomistic view that celestial movers are twofold: the passive nature of the celestial body and the active power of angels ministering to the will of God.

The medieval views of celestial movers which we have outlined in this paper are rarely considered today. Yet they are important for an understanding of St. Thomas, and they do have serious implications which deserve the attention of modern Thomists, implications of interest to theologians as well as to philosophers of nature.

---

[105] *Opera Omnia* (Parma, 1869), XXIV, pp. 217a–219b. This treatise was first published by Thomas Boninsegnio, O.P., in his edition of the *Summa* with Cajetan's commentary (Venice) in 1588. The first folio announced: "Quaestiones duae S. Thomae de Aquino nuper repertae ac in lucem editae, una de principio individuationis, altera vero de motoribus coelestium corporum, quae nuper repertae fuerunt Florentiae in bibliotheca S. Marci." This new manuscript was copied for San Marco by order of Cosmo de Medici and notarized on June 5, 1587; this document is published on fol. 2r of the edition. Boninsegnio rests his argument for the authenticity of the treatise (fol. 2vff.) on the Thomistic character of the doctrine and on the credibility of the manuscript, which also contained St. Thomas's *De potentia*. The same scribe had written the two new questions on folios 287–90 of the original manuscript, which is now lost.

[106] M. Grabmann, *Die Werke des hl. Thomas von Aquin*, 3d ed., *Beiträge z. Gesch. d. Phil. u. Theol. d. MA.*, Bd. XXII, H. 1–2 (Münster, 1949), p. 415.

VIII

THE COMMENTARY OF ST. THOMAS ON THE *DE CAELO* OF ARISTOTLE

The "commentary" or *Sententia de caelo et mundo* of St. Thomas is a work of great maturity and profundity. It is one of Thomas's last writings, and it reveals a breadth of scholarship and achievement wanting, for the most part, in his earlier Aristotelian commentaries, such as those on the *Ethics, Physics, De anima,* and early parts of the *Metaphysics*; but it comes to grips with profound problems of Aristotelian philosophy inherent in the conflicting views of Greek and Arab commentators. I. T. Eschmann rightly noted that "it represents the high water-mark of St. Thomas's expository skill."[1] In long, subtle digressions, Thomas discusses and evaluates the views of other commentators reported by Simplicius, as well as the views of Simplicius himself, who is a primary source in this commentary. As in earlier commentaries, Thomas was also concerned with the teaching of Averroes, which deeply influenced the masters in arts at Paris in the late 1260s and throughout the 1270s. The excessive adoption of Averroes by masters in arts resulted in the condemnation of thirteen Averroist theses on December 10, 1270, by the bishop of Paris, Etienne Tempier, and in the more sweeping condemnation by the same bishop on March 7, 1277. Simplicius and Averroes are in fact the two basic sources for Thomas's commentary on *De caelo*.

Thomas did not comment on *De caelo* until he had the full text in hand, together with the commentary of Simplicius. Although there were a number of translations of Aristotle's *De caelo* available from the Arabic, Thomas insisted on having a good translation from the Greek corrected by his friend and confrère William of Moerbeke. Wherever translations existed from the Greek, Moerbeke did not translate anew but rather revised specific readings of words and phrases according to

---

[1] "A catalogue of St. Thomas's Works: Bibliographical Notes," in E. Gilson, *The Christian Philosophy of St. Thomas Aquinas* (New York, 1956), item 31, p. 402.

a Greek exemplar. The first translation of *De caelo* from the Greek was made by Robert Grosseteste, the bishop of Lincoln, between 1247 and 1253, the date of his death. Grosseteste's translation went only as far as Book III, c. 1, 299a11; but he also translated the corresponding commentary of Simplicius. We do not know how much influence this translation had, for it has not yet been found intact in any manuscript. Moerbeke, it would seem, used the Grosseteste translation for his own revision of Books I and II, before proceeding with an original translation of Books III and IV, together with the full commentary of Simplicius. Moerbeke completed his revision and translation on June 15, 1271, at Viterbo, where the papal court of Pope Gregory X resided. Within a relatively short time, Moerbeke's translation of *De caelo* became the "common," or "vulgate," text used in the schools as part of the *Corpus recentior* of Aristotle's writings.

Moerbeke's translation was not the only one available to Latin scholastics. In fact, they had five versions in whole or in part from which to study the thought of Aristotle's *De caelo*:

1. A *summary* in sixteen chapters by Avicenna as the "second book" of the *libri naturales,* translated from the Arabic, probably by Dominic Gundissalinus and John Avendehut around 1150.
   Incipit: "Collectiones exposicionum ab antiquis Graecis in libro Aristotilis qui dicitur liber celi et mundi. . . . Differentia inter corpus et quamlibet aliam magnitudinem hec est . . ."
   Remarks: Undoubtedly this summary was included in the general condemnation of Aristotle's works in 1210 ("nec commenta") and in 1215 ("nec summe de eisdem") because it taught the eternity of the world. It exists in several MSS, and a much-emended text was published at Venice in 1508.

2. *De caelo veteris translationis,* translated from the Arabic by Gerard of Cremona (d. 1187).
   Incipit: "Summa cognicionis nature et scientie ipsam demonstrantis . . ."
   Remarks: This version was the common one used in the schools before being replaced by the new version of Moerbeke. Without doubt this version is the one intended by the statutes of the arts faculty in Paris, March 19, 1255 (*Chart. U. P.,* I, 277–79, n. 246). Albertus Magnus used this version for his own commentary, and it is printed in the new edition of Albert's works, *Opera Omnia,* V (Cologne, 1971).

3. *De caelo cum commentario magno Averrois,* translated from Arabic
   by Michael Scot, ca. 1231–35.
   Incipit: "Maxima cognicio nature et scientia demonstrans ip-
       sam. . ."
   Remarks: This version was frequently published with the commentary of Averroes, e.g., the italic type in the Venice edition of
   1574. Michael Scot dedicated this work to Stephen de Pruvino,
   who with two other masters was commissioned by Pope
   Gregory IX in 1231 to examine Aristotle's writings on natural
   philosophy and to report on their contents (*Chart. U. P.,* I, 143–
   44, n. 87; see note 2 by Denifle, *ibid.,* p. 144).

4. *De caelo translationis Lincolniensis,* incomplete, covers Books I–
   III, 1, 299a11 ("huc usque d. R." MS Vat. lat. 2088), translated
   from the Greek together with the corresponding commentary of
   Simplicius by Robert Grosseteste in England between 1247 and
   1253. Cf. *Aristoteles Latinus,* I, 53.
   Incipit: uncertain because "no complete MS of Grosseteste's
       translation has yet been identified" (S. H. Thomson, *The
       Writings of Robert Grosseteste* [Cambridge, 1940], p. 66).
   Remarks: D. J. Allan has shown that Book II of this version is to
   be found in full in Oxford, Balliol Coll. MS 99; see "Mediaeval
   Versions of Aristotle, *De caelo,* and of the Com. of Simplicius,"
   Mediaeval and Renaissance Studies 2 (1950), 82–120. D. A. Callus
   remarks that "the *De caelo,* left incomplete, was his [Grosseteste's]
   last work" (*Robert Grosseteste* [Oxford, 1955], p. 67).

5. *De caelo novae translationis,* I–II revised, III–IV translated from
   the Greek by William Moerbeke with the commentary of Simplicius, completed in Viterbo, June 15, 1271.
   Incipit: "De natura scientia ferre plurima videtur circa corpora
       et magnitudines et horum existens passiones et
       motus. . ."
   Remarks: This new version, the common text used in the schools
   in the late thirteenth century, replacing the translation of Gerard
   of Cremona, was the base text used by St. Thomas for his commentary on *De caelo;* the commentary of Simplicius was thoroughly exploited in Thomas's work on the heavens, and he had
   partially used it earlier, without sufficient comprehension, in his
   commentary on the *Metaphysics,* Book XII (Lambda). A contaminated form of this version is generally printed with the
   works of Thomas; it was also published at Venice in bold Roman
   type with the commentary of Averroes (*De caelo,* 1574). The

Moerbeke version of Aristotle's *De caelo,* with the full commentary of Simplicius, was published in Venice by Heronymus Scotus in 1548.

Aristotle's treatise *De caelo* was written in four books after completion of the *Physics,* as is proved by the numerous cross-references Aristotle himself makes to the *Physics* (e.g., *De caelo* 270a18; 273a13; 275b18; 305a21; 311a13, etc.). All Arab and Latin commentators refer to *De caelo* as the "second book" of natural philosophy, and Thomas notes that it is the first treatise after the *Physics.*[2] In the first two books, Aristotle discusses the constitution and simple movements of the universe as a whole; in the third and fourth books, he discusses the simple motions of the sublunar elements. In Thomas's view, the first two books discuss "bodies which move with circular motion," whereas the last two discuss "bodies which move with rectilinear motion."[3]

Thomas did not comment on all four books, but stopped abruptly at III, 3, 302b9 (III, lect. 8, n. 9), as all of Thomas's bibliographers acknowledge. The so-called official catalogue drawn up by Reginald of Piperno for the canonization process lists the work as "super libros de Caelo tres."[4] Nicholas Trevet lists it as "caeli et mundi, primum, secundum et tertium."[5] Tolomeo of Lucca simply notes that the commentary is not complete: "De caelo et De generatione, sed non complevit."[6] Bernard Gui lists the work as "super tres libros de caelo et mundo."[7] The second Prague catalogue lists it as "glosas super 3 libros celi et mundi."[8] After Tolomeo of Lucca noted that *De caelo* and *De generatione* were left incomplete, he stated that "these books were completed by master Peter of Alvernia [Auvergne], his most faithful disciple, master in theology and a great philosopher, later bishop of Clermont." Grabmann notes that at least two MSS (Paris, Bibl. Mazarine 3484 and Oxford, Balliol College 321) explicitly state at the end of the composite commentary: "In hoc completur expositio magistri Petri de Alvenia in tertium et quartum Caeli et Mundi Aristotelis, ubi praeventus morte venerabilis vir frater Thomas de Aquino

---

[2] Thomas, *In I De caelo,* prooem., n. 3.
[3] Thomas, *In III De caelo,* lect. 1, n. 1.
[4] P. Mandonnet, *Des Écrits Authentiques de S. Thomas D'Aquin,* ed. 2 revue et corrigée (Fribourg, 1910), p. 31.
[5] *Ibid.,* p. 49
[6] *Ibid.,* p. 61.
[7] *Ibid.,* p. 69.
[8] M. Grabmann, *Die Werke des hl. Thomas von Aquin,* 3d ed. (Münster Westf., 1949), p. 97.

omisit."[9] At the commentary on III, 3, 302b9, in Vatican MS Vat. lat. 2181, fol. 111v, the scribe wrote: "Usque huc frater Thomas. Incipit magister Petrus de Alvenia usque in finem quarti celi et mundi." There can be no doubt that the authentic commentary of Thomas breaks off in chapter 3 at the words "Itaque palam et quod sunt elementa, et propter quid sunt" (302b) in the version of Moerbeke.

One basic question is, why did Thomas not finish his commentary? All the traditional sources say that he was prevented by death. I. T. Eschmann, however, claims that the commentary is not "unfinished": "Whether it is an unfinished work, as is commonly asserted, seems doubtful."[10] He gives no arguments in support of this view, but he says, "The beginning of Aquinas's exposition of *De generatione et corruptione* gives us to understand that he [Thomas] knew no more Aristotelian text of *De caelo* than [that] which he explained." A study of the text, however, renders such a view most implausible.

Thomas certainly knew two versions of the complete text translated from the Arabic; in earlier works, such as *Summa theologiae* I, Thomas knew and referred to all four books in these versions. The question is whether Thomas had more text of the Moerbeke version than that which he commented upon. Moerbeke, as we know, translated Books III and IV directly from the Greek, and Thomas obviously knew this translation, for he commented on III, 1–3, well beyond the version of Robert Grosseteste, and well into the versions from the Arabic. Therefore Thomas had at least chapters 1–3 in the version of Moerbeke. The force of this argument will become clear when the Latin versions of *De caelo* are published in the *Aristoteles Latinus*.

Further, in the commentary itself, Thomas indicates that he knew the existence of the part not commented upon by him: e.g., at III, lect. 2, n. 1: "in quarto libro ibi *De gravi autem et levi*" (= IV, 1, 307b29); and at III, lect. 3, n. 2: "Partim autem inferius in hoc eodem libro" (= III, 5). These references seem to indicate the portion of the Moerbeke text not commented upon by Thomas.

Also, the opening passage of *De generatione* does not sustain Eschmann's argument. The passage reads:

First he [Aristotle] expresses what he principally intends; and this continues to the end of the book *De caelo*, where he says: *De gravi quidem igitur et levi determinandum sit hoc modo*. And there then follows: *De generatione autem et corruptione natura generatorum et corruptorum*, that is, of those things which naturally are generated and corrupted.

[9] Grabmann, *ibid.*, p. 276.
[10] Eschmann, "Catalogue," item 31, p. 402.

In this passage, the first lemma is the concluding sentence of *De caelo*, and the second lemma is the opening sentence of *De generatione*. Without further study, it is difficult to say what version of *De generatione* Thomas had in mind, but it was probably that of Moerbeke. The important point is that Thomas had at hand the concluding sentence of Book IV of *De caelo*, and there is no reason why Thomas could not have completed his commentary on *De caelo* had he lived. The traditional view that Thomas's commentary on *De caelo* is "unfinished" must stand. He was undoubtedly unable to finish the work when he was unexpectedly afflicted by a stroke or breakdown on December 6, 1273. Scribes, unaware of what happened to Thomas on December 6, would naturally think that he was prevented by death—"praeventus morte."

From what has been said, it is clear that Thomas's *Sententia de caelo et mundo* must be dated late in his life. It was composed after Moerbeke finished his translation of the text and of the commentary by Simplicius on June 15, 1271. Thomas obtained this translation while he was still in Paris (January 1269 to spring 1272), as is confirmed by the letter of the Parisian faculty of arts sent to the general chapter of the Order of Preachers meeting in Lyons in 1274 after the death of Thomas. In the letter, dated May 3, the faculty of arts asked for four favors, the third of which was a request for the books that Thomas himself had promised to send them:

And permit us also to mention the commentary of Simplicius on the *De caelo et mundo*, and an exposition of Plato's *Timaeus*, and a work entitled *De aquarum conductibus et ingeniis erigendis;* for these books in particular he himself promised would be sent to us.[11]

Moerbeke's translation arrived in Paris while Thomas was commenting on Book Lambda (XII) of the *Metaphysics* in 1271, for in certain passages Thomas made use of Simplicius's commentary. Whether or not Thomas's commentary on *De caelo* was begun in Paris and continued in Naples cannot yet be determined. The masters in arts of Paris in their second petition asked the Dominican chapter to send them "some writings of a philosophical nature, begun by him [Thomas] at Paris, left unfinished at his departure, but completed, we have reason to think, in the place to which he was transferred."[12] Thomas could have begun his commentary on *De caelo* at Paris after June 1271 and continued it in Naples, where he was assigned in

---

[11] A. Birkenmajer, "Vermischte Untersuchungen," *Beiträge z. Gesch. d. Phil. d. MA.*, Bd. XX, H. 5, pp. 6ff.

[12] *Ibid.*

September 1272; or he could have begun it in Naples. What is certain is that Thomas took Moerbeke's text with him to Naples.

At Naples, William of Tocco saw Thomas writing his commentary on Aristotle's *De generatione et corruptione,* which he believed to have been Thomas's "last work in philosophy."[13] It is unfinished, ending abruptly in I, 5, 322a33 (I, lect. 17), and exists in only four manuscripts; it was unknown to the Parisian stationers even as late as 1304. When Thomas wrote his commentary on *De generatione* I, lect. 7, n. 1, he used the phrase "as we have made clear [*manifestavimus*] in VIII *Physic.* and in I *De caelo,*" thus signifying that at least the first book of *De caelo* was completed before *De generatione* I, lect. 7, which was written in Naples. Therefore Thomas must have written his commentary on *De caelo* between June 1271 (Paris) and December 6, 1273 (Naples). It is accordingly one of Thomas's last works in philosophy, and one of considerable maturity and reflection. The influence of Simplicius is clear on almost every page; it seems to have aroused Thomas's critical acumen to the utmost. It can be considered the profoundest of all his commentaries on Aristotle. It has no equal. Even Albert's scholarly commentary on the *De caelo* fades in comparison with Thomas's. For this we have to thank the genius of Thomas and the stimulus of Simplicius, the celebrated sixth-century Greek commentator on Aristotle.

In this brief study it is impossible to do justice to Thomas's commentary. But perhaps certain highlights can be pointed out for further study.

THE SUBJECT MATTER OF *DE CAELO*

Every scholastic introduction to a new book to be discussed examines first the location of this book in the ensemble of the whole science, and its unique and proper subject matter distinct from other treatises. All of Aristotle's *libri naturales* were universally thought to belong to the unique science of the philosophy of nature. The unique character of natural science, or the philosophy of nature, is derived from the manner of defining concepts in that science, as Thomas shows in his *In Boethium De Trinitate,* q. 5, aa. 1–2. Every concept in the philosophy of nature, no matter how analogous it may be, is defined in terms of sensate matter, *materia sensibilis.* These definitions leave out of consideration, or abstract from, individual matter. That is to say,

---

[13] "Processus Canonizationis S. Thomae Aquinatis, Neapoli," n. 58, *S. Thomae Aquinatis Vitae Fontes Praecipuae,* ed. A. Ferrua (Alba, 1968), p. 287.

the natural philosopher is primarily concerned not with individual instances of his encounter with nature but rather with the species, or common nature, as such. In reality, the species (or common nature) does not exist as such outside the mind; there are only individual instances. But those species and common natures do exist as individuals. Individuals, as such, come into being and pass away, and there can be no speculative science of such individuals, except history. Therefore the philosopher who wishes to study nature must abstract the universal elements of his concern from the individual instances of his experience and experimentation. This kind of abstraction was called "total abstraction" (*abstractio totalis*) by the scholastics, for it temporarily leaves out of consideration the "parts" or existent individuals of which the species, or common nature, can be predicated. Without individual instances existing in nature, the natural philosopher could never comprehend the universal whole; but the truth he seeks must be formulated in terms of universal definitions, statements, laws, and hypotheses. Whatever is retained necessarily involves *materia sensibilis*, i.e., definitions formulated in terms of what can be sensed by touch, sight, sound, taste, and smell, as well as magnitude and number. All such tangible characteristics are needed to define concepts and laws in natural philosophy. Thus if the natural philosopher wants to talk about gravitation, he does not limit his concern to the free-fall of this particular body at this particular instant of history but formulates statements and laws about all heavy bodies in various circumstances that are of universal validity.

The kind of abstraction used in natural science can be grasped more easily by comparing its subject to that of the mathematical sciences. Mathematics, to get anywhere, must leave out of consideration all aspects that are properly sensible, like apples and pears, and consider only the quantitative "form," namely, number and magnitude, which are "common sensibles." Every degree of mathematical abstraction retains a quantitative "form"; this abstraction is called, in scholastic language inherited from the Arabs, *abstractio formalis*, or *abstractio partis*, because a part of reality, namely, sensible matter, is left out of consideration. This kind of abstracting a formal part from the whole is legitimate, as Aristotle says, and does not result in any falsity,[14] because the mathematician does not assert that such a separation really exists in nature. If the mathematician asserted that "surfaces and volumes, lines and points" exist in nature as separated from

[14] Aristotle, *Phys.* II, 2, 193b34.

sensible matter, he would be in error.[15] Nevertheless, a certain kind of matter is still retained in mathematical abstraction; it is called *materia intelligibilis*, because mathematical entities can be imagined distinctly by the mind, so that we can speak of parallel lines, variously plotted points, different kinds of circles, and the like. Intelligible matter allows for infinite multiplicity in mathematical reasoning. Like individual matter in sensible objects, intelligible matter is the principle of individuality in mathematics. On a more superficial level, one must also admit that the mathematician leaves out of consideration the individual instances of an imagined quantity; for this reason, some of the later scholastics maintained that total abstraction is common to all the speculative sciences. This is no more than a consequence of intellectual behavior, which cannot know the individual as such but must deal with the intelligible, which is universal.

Consequently, all the concepts and statements in natural philosophy are in terms of sensible matter in general, so that an animal is defined in terms of "blood and bone," and not "this blood and these bones."

In a science as vast as natural philosophy, there must be an orderly procedure whereby one progresses from the most general to the particular. The general principle of all human study is that the mind must proceed from the more common and general aspects, better known to us, to the more special and particular aspects, less known to us but better knowable in themselves. Consequently, the study of natural science should progress from the general aspects considered in the *Physics* to the more detailed considerations of the other *libri naturales*. The eight books of the *Physics* are an overall consideration of problems basic to the study of nature itself, that is, of the concept of nature as the principle of motion and rest in all natural things, and include a consideration of all the physical aspects of motion, such as causality, place, time, space, kinds of motion, continuity, and the necessity of a first mover of the universe. After such general considerations of nature and motion, required for an understanding of the whole of natural science, the philosopher should progress to a consideration of the particular species of motions and natures. This scientific progression is explained simply by St. Thomas when he says:

Scientific knowledge which is possessed of things only in general is not a complete science in its ultimate actuality but stands midway between pure potentiality and ultimate fulfillment. . . . Hence it is clear that the fullness of scientific knowledge requires that it not remain simply in generalities but proceed even to its species.[16]

---

[15] *Ibid.*, 193b24. [16] Thomas, *In I Meteorol.*, lect. 1, n. 1.

In his commentary on the *Physics,* one of Thomas's earliest commentaries on Aristotle, he describes the contents of the *libri naturales* subsequent to the *Physics.*[17] *De caelo* analyzes natural bodies as mobile according to local motion, "which is the first species of motion." *De generatione* analyzes motion toward form and the basic changes in elementary bodies precisely as mutable in general. The *Meteororum* discusses specific types of transmutation in nature. The pseudo-Aristotelian book *De mineralibus* discusses inanimate mobile bodies whose motions are composite, while the motion of composite animate bodies is discussed in the book *De anima* and in books subsequent to it.

In the prooemium to *De caelo,* therefore, Thomas again follows the general pedagogical method of proceeding from the general to the particular.[18] Aspects common to all of nature are seen as treated in the *Physics.* Thus "what remains in the other books of natural science is to apply these common aspects to their proper subjects." In this application, the more simple and general are discussed before the complex and specific. In this view, Book I of *De caelo* considers the entire corporeal universe prior to considering its parts; Book II considers simple bodies prior to the mixed; and Books III and IV consider elemental bodies prior to the complex and compound bodies. Since one aspect common to all the books of *De caelo* is body, "the first topic of discussion in the very beginning of this book is body, to which must be applied all that was set forth about motion in the *Physics.*"

Aristotle's *De caelo* is a complicated treatise in four books, and it is difficult to find the unifying thread. But commentators and scholastics had a penchant for discovering unity before proceeding to dissect it. Even though the *De caelo* discusses "bodies" throughout, this fact does not sufficiently identify the precise subject matter of the four books. Even though "the first topic of discussion in the very beginning of this book is body, to which must be applied all that was set forth about motion in the *Physics,*" this topic does not sufficiently unify the treatise, since there are many kinds of bodies in the heavens and on the earth.

The title, *De caelo,* can be understood in three senses. It can refer to (1) the outermost sphere that moves with diurnal motion; (2) all the heavenly bodies that move circularly; or (3) the entire universe. According to Simplicius in his prooemium, Alexander of Aphrodisias "believed that the subject primarily treated therein is the universe." Alexander assumed that Aristotle restricted himself to discussing gen-

---

[17] Thomas, *In I Phys.,* lect. 1, n. 4.
[18] Thomas, *In I De caelo,* lect. 1, n. 3.

eral characteristics of the heaven and the earth—its eternity, finiteness, uniqueness, and the like. However, Iamblichus and Syrianus, according to Simplicius, thought the term "heaven" to apply to the heavenly bodies that move circularly. Iamblichus maintained that other bodies in the universe are discussed in *De caelo* "consequentially, insofar as they are contained by the heavens and influenced by them," whereas Syrianus held that other bodies are discussed "incidentally [*per accidens*] insofar as a knowledge of other bodies is assumed in order to explain what is being said of the heavens." But one might object that the consideration of elementary bodies and their motions cannot be called "incidental," or *per accidens*. The heavens and the four elements are simple bodies; and after Aristotle discusses the heavenly bodies in Book II, he proceeds to discuss the four terrestrial elements of earth, water, fire, and air as a principal consideration in Books III and IV. "The Philosopher is not wont to assign a principal part in some science to things that are brought up only incidentally."[19]

Therefore Simplicius argued that the subject matter of *De caelo* has to be "simple bodies," and since among all simple bodies the heavens predominate, it is reasonable to entitle the whole book *De caelo.*[20] If Aristotle had in fact intended to talk about the universe as such, Aristotle would have had to discuss all the parts of the world, even plants and animals, as Plato does in the *Timaeus.*

But Thomas argues against Simplicius, saying that if Aristotle were talking only about simple bodies, he would have had to discuss everything pertaining to simple bodies. In fact, Aristotle discusses only one aspect, that of their being light and heavy, leaving out of discussion their qualitative aspects, such as their being cold or hot, reserving this for the subsequent book *De generatione.*

Thomas prefers to follow the view of Alexander in saying that the subject of this book is the universe itself, and that simple bodies are discussed insofar as they are parts of the universe. Parts of the universe constitute the whole insofar as they have a determined position (*situs*) in the whole. That is, the heavenly bodies and the four terrestrial elements primarily and *per se* have a determined position by reason of their basic motions, which are simple. Since it is a question of position, Aristotle discusses the terrestrial elements not in terms of hot and cold, dry and moist, and so forth, but only in terms of their lightness and heaviness, which determine their position in the whole. For this reason, continues St. Thomas, there is no need to discuss

[19] Thomas, *In I De caelo*, prooem., n. 4.
[20] Simplicius, *op. cit.*, prooem., fol. 2rb.

other parts of the universe, such as stones, plants, and animals, according to their proper natures, but only insofar as their movements are dominated by heavy and light elements, which constitute them in their being. This proper, or specific, consideration of such compound bodies belongs to other books of the *libri naturales.*

Thomas goes on to conclude that this view agrees with what is usually said among the Latins, that "this book discusses mobile body with respect to position, or place, which motion indeed is common to all parts of the universe."[21] Among the "Latins" Thomas certainly included himself and Albertus Magnus. In his earlier work on the *Physics,* Thomas specifies the subject matter of *De caelo* as being "mobile [body] according to local motion, which is the first species of motion."[22] In his paraphrase of *De caelo,* Albert, writing around 1251, says, "There is a single science about those mobile bodies, not because here we discuss them precisely as moved by different natures, but rather precisely as they have a singular potentiality in general and a singular act, which is local motion."[23]

Later Thomists, with only partial justification, classified the *libri naturales* according to their generic motions. Thus the books of the *Physics* were said to discuss motion in general, while *De caelo* considers bodies in simple local motion, *De generatione* considers alterations leading to substantial changes, and *De anima* and its subsequent books consider augmentation of animals. Such mental gymnastics are oversimplifications of the contents of the Aristotelian books as understood by Albert and Thomas. It is true enough, however, that *De caelo* is concerned with simple bodies that move with local motion. It is not concerned with the local motion of animals precisely as living beings who are the cause of their own voluntary motions, for this subject is discussed in *De motibus animalium;* rather it is concerned with their rectilinear motion resulting from the predominance of certain elements, as when an animal loses balance and falls to the ground or when a bird in flight is shot down.

Thus, in Thomas's view, *De caelo et mundo* is concerned with the universe and the place of simple bodies in it. The place of these bodies in the universe is determined by their local motion, namely, the motion of celestial bodies circularly and the motion of the elements upward and downward, depending on their natural heaviness and lightness. Whatever is scientifically determined in *De caelo* is to be applied to other books in the *libri naturales.*

---

[21] Thomas, *In I De caelo,* prooem., n. 5.
[22] Thomas, *In I Phys.,* lect. 1, n. 4.
[23] Albert, *I De caelo,* tr. 1, c. 1, *ed. cit.,* 1, 60–63.

CELESTIAL MOTIONS

For Thomas, there are two basically distinct sciences that study the movements of the heavenly bodies: natural science, meaning the philosophy of nature, and astronomy. Both of these sciences have a common subject matter, the motions of the heavens. But the principles used in studying these motions are formally different. That is, natural philosophy uses the principles of nature outlined in the eight books of the *Physics,* with "nature" (φύσις) regarded as an active or passive principle of specific activity. Nature as an active principle is the innate form of the body that spontaneously and dynamically determines both the motion and the goal, unless some other body impedes its natural activity. Nature as a passive principle is the innate receptivity of the matter for actions performed on it by natural agencies. These principles will be discussed again shortly. For the present it is sufficient to see that natural philosophy discusses the physical and natural motions of the heavens from the viewpoint of "nature" (φύσις). It is also concerned with natural magnitudes, distances, velocity, and natural causes of those movements seen in the heavens in terms of nature, sensible matter, and motion.

Astronomy, on the other hand, is a science radically dependent on mathematical principles, such as those proved in geometry and in the highest branches of mathematics. Since both natural science and astronomy deal with the same celestial phenomena, they are said to share in the same material object (*obiectum materiale*). But since they differ profoundly and radically in their medium of demonstration, they constitute two separate and distinct sciences, each having its own identity and validity by reason of its formal object, its *ratio formalis obiecti.*[24]

The distinction between natural science and astronomy does not mean that they are mutually exclusive. On the contrary, they are of mutual interest and concern. The conclusions of the one can provoke the other to further inquiry and possible corroboration, as in the earth's sphericity, center of movement, the meaning of time, and so forth. Both approaches are useful and even necessary. Both construct hypotheses to account for the phenomena perceived by sense. However, the hypotheses postulated by the naturalist involve natural causes and natural mathematical devices to account for the phenomena, even if those devices cannot be verified in nature.

The basic problem faced by early astronomers was the obvious irregularity of planetary motion. These planets, or "wandering stars,"

[24] Thomas, *Sum. theol.* II-II, q. 1, a. 1.

sometimes seem to move faster, sometimes slower; sometimes they
seem to be stationary, and at other times they seem to move backward
with a retrograde motion.[25] Not only is such irregularity unbecoming
in celestial motions, thought to be the domain of the gods, but it is
impossible to study these motions scientifically without some reference to rational regularity. According to Simplicius:

> Eudoxus of Cnidos was the first Greek to concern himself with hypotheses of
> this sort, Plato having, as Sosigenes says, set it as a problem to all earnest
> students of this subject to find what are the uniform and ordered movements
> by the assumption of which the phenomena in relation to the movements of
> the planets can be saved.[26]

Eudoxus started with the assumption that all planetary movements
must be regular and homocentric, i.e., having the same center around
which to revolve, namely, the center of the earth. For Eudoxus the
phenomena of celestial movements could be saved by postulating a
number of regular spheres for each planet, each rotating around
different axes at different speeds. For him each of the planets, including the sun and moon, has three basic motions: first, in respect to the
sphere of the fixed stars moving from east to west; second, in respect
to the middle of the zodiac through which the planets move; and
third, in respect to the breadth or longitude of the zodiac.[27] All told,
Eudoxus postulated twenty-seven spheres and motions to account for
the phenomena rationally.[28]

Callippus, a younger contemporary of Eudoxus, postulated a far
greater number of spheres, amounting to fifty-five in all (or forty-
seven, if one did not postulate the additional eight for the rotation of
the sun and moon).[29] Aristotle himself could not decide on the exact
number of spheres (and consequently movers) needed "to save the
appearances." In fact, Aristotle was not particularly concerned about
the exact number of movers and decided to leave this question open
"to more powerful thinkers."[30] For Aristotle the important issue was
that celestial bodies cannot move themselves but must be moved by
something else that is not physical.

Aristotle and the astronomers of his day assumed that all celestial
motion had to be regular, circular, and homocentric. Pedestrian observation indicates that the earth and its center are the stationary point

---

[25] Thomas, *In II De caelo,* lect. 17, n. 2.
[26] Simplicius, *In II De caelo,* 12, comm. 43, fol. 74r–v.
[27] Arist., *Metaph.* XII, 8, 1073b18–31.
[28] Cf. T. L. Heath, *Aristarchus of Samos* (Oxford, 1913), pp. 195–96.
[29] Arist., *Metaph.* XII, 8, 1073b31–1074a14.
[30] *Ibid.,* 1074a16.

around which all the celestial bodies rotate. But this simplistic explanation involves many difficulties and does not account for all the
phenomena. Because of these difficulties, "Hipparchus and Ptolemy
hit upon eccentric and epicyclic motions to save what appears to the
senses concerning celestial motions."[31] It is impossible, as all scholastics realized, that Aristotle and Ptolemy should be both right in the
domain of a single science. While Aristotle's natural philosophy made
sense, it did not account for all the data accumulated by astronomers.
And while Ptolemy's astronomy accounted for all the phenomena, it
assumed such mathematical devices as eccentrics and epicycles that
could not be physically true. For Thomas, such an escape is not a
demonstration but a kind of supposition, that is, a hypothesis.[32] But
even if Ptolemy's supposition were true in nature, continues Thomas,
"nevertheless all the celestial bodies would be moved around the center of the earth in its diurnal motion, which is the motion of the
outermost sphere rotating the whole [universe] and all things within
it."[33]

The status of astronomical hypotheses, such as epicycles and eccentrics, was of particular interest to Thomas, because they could not be
verified physically; but their assumption in astronomy did account for
the known motion of the planets within the sphere of the fixed stars.
Thomas's views are clear:

It is not necessary that the various suppositions (i.e., hypotheses) which they
[the astronomers] hit upon be true. For although these suppositions save the
appearances, we are nevertheless not forced to say that these suppositions are
true, because perhaps there is some other way men have not yet discovered by
which the appearance of things may be saved concerning the stars.[34]

This same view was also expressed by Thomas some six years earlier
in his *Summa theologiae:*

There are two kinds of argument put forward to prove something. The first
goes to the root of the matter and fully demonstrates some point; for instance, in natural philosophy there is a conclusive argument to prove that
celestial movements are of constant speed. The other kind does not prove a
point conclusively but shows that its acceptance fits in with the observed
effects; for instance, an astronomical argument about eccentric and epicyclic
motions is put forward on the ground that by this hypothesis one can show
how celestial movements appear as they do to observation. Such an argument
is not fully conclusive, since an explanation might be possible even on another
hypothesis.[35]

---

[31] Thomas, *In I De caelo,* lect. 3, n. 7.   [32] *Ibid.*
[33] *Ibid.*   [34] Thomas, *In II De caelo,* lect. 17, n. 2.
[35] Thomas, *Sum. theol.* I, q. 32, a. 1, ad 2.

In other words, the hypotheses of astronomy are significant in that they may account for all the phenomena without forcing the mind to acknowledge their physical certainty. As in the case of the movement of the earth, the appearances could be saved by holding either that the earth is stationary and the heavens are moving about it, or that the heavens are stationary and the earth is moving within the heavens, or that both the earth and the heavens are moving.[36]

In the first part of Aristotle's *De caelo* there are two main issues: the nature of celestial bodies, and the nature of celestial motion. From the nature of the motion, one can argue to the nature of the body—but not vice versa. The celestial body is said to be incorruptible, different from terrestrial bodies, eternal, and perfect, and its motion is said to be uniform, regular, and circular. The celestial body was said to be incorruptible because no corruption or even alteration had been seen to occur in the heavens despite long centuries of observation by astronomers. Had Aristotle noted the sunspots observed by Galileo, he undoubtedly would have acknowledged corruption, or at least alteration, in the sun. But the fact was that neither Aristotle nor any of the ancient astronomers ever observed any change in celestial bodies. From this it follows that the matter in celestial bodies must be different from terrestrial matter, for on earth, matter is the root of corruptibility. Hence celestial matter was designated as the "fifth element," different from the prime matter of earth and having no "privation" for change. Further, if there is no "privation" in celestial matter, it must be "perfect," since in it there is nothing wanting. Furthermore, it follows that celestial bodies and the whole universe must be eternal, for there can be no "before" before time and motion, as Aristotle proved in the *Physics* and assumed in *De caelo*. Thomas knew perfectly well that Aristotle maintained the eternity of the universe. But on this point, Thomas argued that there is no conclusive argument one way or the other with regard to the eternity or temporality of the universe. The only basic issue for Thomas was that the universe had to be created by God either in time or in eternity.[37]

Similarly, the only kind of motion observed in the heavens is local motion that is perpetual, never tending to rest but ever flowing. While observation shows that planetary motion is irregular, this irregularity cannot be understood except in terms of regularity that is thought not to be. In other words, all irregularity must be defined in terms of regularity. The same is true of uniformity in velocity, for there can be

---

[36] Thomas, *In II De caelo,* lect. 11, n. 2.
[37] Thomas, *In II De caelo,* lect. 1, nn. 2–3; I, lect. 22, n. 1; *Sum. theol.* I, q. 46, a. 1; *De aeternitate mundi.*

no difform motion except in relation to that which is uniform. That is to say, there can be no denial of uniformity and regularity except in terms of uniformity and regularity. But the only local motion that can be uniform and regular is circular motion. All motions on earth (1) come to rest in some finality achieved and (2) tend to accelerate as they approach the term of motion. Celestial motions are not like that, for it needs be that they continue forever in a state of uniform velocity. Consequently, the task of the ancient astronomer was to determine the exact number of uniform circular motions needed to account for the irregularity of planetary motion.

The important issue for Thomas, as for Aristotle, was the cause of celestial motion, i.e., the efficient cause responsible for all the motions needed in the heavens to account for the phenomena. There were many observers in antiquity and in the Middle Ages who maintained that it is the very nature of a spherical body to rotate with uniform circular motion. This was the view of Plato and Copernicus; but others, including Aristotle and Thomas, insisted on the radical difference between celestial and terrestrial motions. Terrestrial motions are of two kinds: natural and violent. All natural motion comes about from some internal principle that determines the body to act in a certain kind of way, while violent motion must be explained by some external force acting upon the body, the body itself contributing nothing to it.[38] Violence, like chance, happens only rarely and unpredictably, and it cannot be said that the regularity of the heavens is due to violence or chance. While violent action can be seen on earth, Aristotle totally excludes it from celestial motions. Natural motions, on the other hand, are of two kinds: animate and inanimate. Animate motions are those produced by living bodies, whose "soul" is the efficient cause of movement through its various parts. Inanimate motions are those emanating from an internal active or passive principle, but not through efficient causality. That is to say, the soul of living things is the efficient cause, the *motor*, of animate motions, whereas the "nature" of inanimate things moves spontaneously and dynamically toward a specific kind of motion and finality by the active principle within the inanimate body, provided that these motions are not impeded by some obstacle. The formal nature of a nonliving body is not a *motor*; it is not an efficient cause of its own motion. The true efficient cause of such spontaneous natural activity is the "generator" of the body in the first place; it is the generator who produced the natural form. Once the form is generated by a distinct agency, the body im-

---

[38] Arist., *Eth. Nic.* III, 1, 1110a1–3.

mediately, spontaneously, and dynamically (*subito* and *statim*) manifests all its natural accidents, motions, and finality.[39] Once the natural body is generated, there is no need to look for another *motor* or efficient cause to account for its natural motions.

Celestial motions, for Aristotle, cannot be explained by the nature of the physical sphere, as Plato would have it. For Aristotle, the celestial body has no intrinsic formal principle causing it to move spontaneously in circular rotation. Nevertheless, these regular, uniform, and eternal motions are "natural" and partake of the divine. Therefore, for Aristotle, celestial bodies are animated by a soul, which is the *motor,* the efficient cause of celestial movement.[40] Thus for Aristotle, each sphere was animated by a special soul, which was the formal cause, as well as the efficient cause, of celestial motion. The number of souls (or divinities) depended on the number of motions required to explain celestial motions. Aristotle, adopting the view of Callippus, postulated fifty-two or forty-seven. Each soul of the sphere was itself a substance separate from matter, and hence these souls were called separate substances. For Thomas it did not make much difference (*nec multum refert*) whether the sphere was moved by a soul inherent in the body or by a distinct substance, separate from matter, moving the sphere through its efficient causality.[41] What was clear to him was that a heavenly body had to be moved by something distinct from itself, and that this mover had to be a substance separate from matter. One could, therefore, conclude that each celestial sphere moves itself by reason of its animate form, so that the ultimate soul of the first sphere was the first mover of the universe. Thomas, of course, preferred to think of these separate substances not as souls animating celestial bodies but as separate efficient causes, like an "angel" moving the body.[42]

Since, for Aristotle, there can be only one universe, the mover of the outermost sphere has to be unique and supreme, for all other motions depend upon it. This ultimate mover, it would seem, was the unmoved mover. At least this is the view many recent historians take in explaining the views of Aristotle. It would seem from Aristotle's discussion in *Metaphysics* XII, however, that the ultimate unmoved mover is a separate substance for whose sake the first mover acts, a substance which is subsistent thinking thought.[43] Already in Thomas's day there were some who maintained that God was (according to

---

[39] Thomas, *In III De caelo*, lect. 7, nn. 5–8; Chapter I above.
[40] See Chapter VII above.   [41] Thomas, *In II De caelo*, lect. 3, n. 3.
[42] *Ibid.*   [43] Arist., *Metaph.* XII, 7, 1072b25–29.

Aristotle) only the final cause of all; there were also others who maintained that Aristotle's God is only a *causa movendi* and not a *causa essendi*. Rejecting these views, Thomas says, "It should be noted that Aristotle here [*De caelo* I, 4, 271b33] posits God to be maker [i.e., the efficient cause] of the celestial bodies, and not just a cause after the manner of an end, as some have said."[44] In other words, each celestial sphere has a separate substance, either animating it or pushing it, but beyond the first "soul," the *anima mundi*, there is the creator and final cause of all, whom Aristotle, according to Thomas, calls God, who creates as well as moves the entire universe. "And so it is evident that although Aristotle postulated the eternity of the world, he did not for this reason deny that God is the *causa essendi* of the universe, as some would have it, claiming that God is only a *causa movendi*."[45]

THE EARTH AND TERRESTRIAL MOTIONS

Apparently in antiquity there were some who thought that the earth is flat. Aristotle mentions Anaximenes, Anaxagoras, and Democritus as giving "the flatness of the earth as the cause of its immobility."[46] To those who thought the earth flat, one might add the Jews, for whom the firmament was like an inverted bowl or upper hemisphere. No one in the age of Columbus had reason to think that the earth is flat or that if one came to the "edge" of it, one would fall off. This might have been the popular opinion of some unlearned men, but it was never the view of philosophers and scientists. Even those who postulated a cosmic fire, the sun, as the center of the universe, like the Pythagoreans, maintained that the earth is a sphere or globe which moves with uniform motion around the sun. The sphericity of the earth is most readily seen in an eclipse of the moon, when the earth comes between the sun, the source of light, and the moon, upon which the shadow of the earth is cast. Aristotle frequently referred to the free-fall of heavy bodies as proof of the earth's sphericity: no matter how distant the points of experiment are, heavy bodies always fall perpendicular to the earth as its center, and not parallel to each other. One could also argue, as many ancients did, from the experience of watching ships come into port: at first only the uppermost part of the mast is visible before the whole ship is seen.

[44] Thomas, *In I De caelo*, lect. 8, n. 14; cf. *In VI Metaph.*, lect. 1, n. 1164; *In VIII Phys.*, lect. 3, n. 6.
[45] Thomas, *In VIII Phys.*, lect. 3, n. 6.
[46] Arist., *De caelo* II, 13, 294b14–15.

The real problem in antiquity, and in the Middle Ages too, was in determining the center of the universe; or, to put the question in another way: Is the earth at rest or in motion? Heraclitus, Aristarchus of Samos, and the Pythagoreans maintained that the earth revolves around the sun, or cosmic fire, which is the center of the universe. Aristotle and the great majority of thinkers opted for the experience of sense, in which the earth is stable and the heavens revolve. If the universe is finite and revolving, then its center, whatever it may be, must be immobile. The center of any revolving sphere is immobile. As far as calculations are concerned, it makes little difference whether the earth is mobile or immobile, but it makes a great deal of difference to the natural philosopher, who wants to know what things really are in their nature. In antiquity, Anaximander, Anaxagoras, Democritus, Empedocles, Platonists, and Aristotelians opted for a stable earth around which all the heavens revolve.[47] If the center of the universe is taken to be the center of the spherical earth, then it necessarily follows that the center of the earth is immobile. If that be granted, it also follows that "up" and "down" are absolute terms, so that if a piece of terrestrial earth were to be put where the moon now is, that earth would tend to move toward the center where the earth now is. Aristotle defines the terms "up" and "down" in terms of the local motion of bodies toward the center of the universe (earth) or away from it. Thus bodies are called "heavy" if they tend toward the center of the earth, and "light" if they tend away from the center and toward the celestial bodies.

Both Aristotle and Thomas considered the earth to be a "sphere of no great size."[48] Relying on the mathematicians of his day, Aristotle gave the earth's circumference as 400,000 Greek stades. Thomas calculated this as 50,000 Roman miles, since for him a Greek stade is one-eighth of a Roman mile. Hence the universe, Aristotle contends, is "of no great size." Thomas, however, notes that

according to the more careful measurements of present-day astronomers, the earth's circumference is much less, i.e., 20,400 miles as Al-Fragani says; or 180,000 stades as Simplicius says, which is roughly the same, since 20,000 is one-eighth of 160,000.[49]

In explaining what Aristotle meant by "no great size," Thomas notes that astronomers of his day hold that the sun is 170 times greater in

[47] Thomas, *In II De caelo*, lect. 20, n. 3.
[48] Thomas, *In II De caelo*, lect. 28, n. 3; Arist., *De caelo* II, 14, 298a7–8.
[49] Thomas, *In II De caelo*, lect. 28, n. 4.

size than the earth. Today we hold that the sun's radius is 109 times greater than the earth's equatorial radius.

The method used by Thomas's sources, which he carefully explained, is based on the terrestrial length compared to one degree of difference in the heavens:

> Astronomers were able to calculate this [distance] by considering how much space of earth makes for a difference of one degree in the heavens; and they found that it was 500 stades according to Simplicius, or 56 and ⅔ miles according to Al-Fragani. Hence, multiplying this number by 360, which is the number of degrees in the heavens, they found the size of the earth's circumference.[50]

According to the calculations of modern scientists, Aristotle's estimate is twice too large, and Simplicius's and Thomas's figure not large enough; for Aristotle's measurements came to approximately 46,000 miles, and Al-Fragani's and Simplicius's come to about 20,500, whereas a rough modern calculation is 24,900 miles at the equatorial circumference. It would seem that Thomas learned the method of calculating the size of the earth from Simplicius or from Albert the Great, who claims to be following Alcemenon (whoever he was) and Ptolemy.[51] Albert's commentary was written some twenty years earlier than Thomas's.

In Books III and IV, Aristotle considers the position of heavy and light bodies, but Thomas commented only as far as III, c. 3, 302b9 (lect. 8). In this brief space there are two important points to consider.

First, Thomas carefully identifies the first mover of the universe in the order of natural movers. This first mover, being made up of "soul" and "heavenly body," moves itself and in its motion moves everything in the heavens. This first mover is comparable to Plato's mover who first initiates the movement of elements into a structured universe. Such a "first mover," which moves itself in the perpetual movement of the first sphere, "should not be understood as the absolutely first, because this latter is absolutely immobile [*omnino immobile*], as proved in Phys. VIII and in Metaph. XII." Rather, such a mover is "the *primum movens* in the category of natural movers, which moves itself, as composed of a *motor* and a *motum*, as proved in Phys. VIII, 5 (lect. 10)."[52] In this passage, Thomas admits that the first physical mover could, if one wished to hold it, be considered a self-mover, i.e.,

---

[50] See Simplicius, *Comm. in libros De caelo* II, comm. 67.
[51] Albert, *De caelo,* Lib. 2, tr. 4, cap. 11, ed. Cologne 1971, V/1, p. 201, lines 26–63.
[52] Thomas, *In III De caelo,* lect. 6, n. 2.

a composite of a celestial body and an immaterial, immortal soul, as Aristotle seems to suggest. But Thomas insists both here and elsewhere that beyond such a self-mover there is another reality, whom we call God. It would seem that this passage in the commentary on *De caelo*, written at the height of his intellectual powers, agrees satisfactorily with the position advanced when Thomas was a young master in theology composing the first book of the *Summa contra gentiles*, in which he discussed various proofs for the existence of God.[53] In the earlier *Summa*, Thomas had argued to the existence of a first mover who is not moved by anything outside itself. But, he suggests, since such a mover is not necessarily totally unmoved, Aristotle argues further, saying that this idea can be understood in one of two ways: either totally unmoved, in which case it is God, or self-moved, in which case there must be a first mover beyond, who is in no way moved, not even *per accidens*, and this mover we call God. For Thomas, movers of the spheres were not souls but angels who move the bodies in the order of efficient causality. Beyond the highest angel who moves the outermost sphere, there is another reality who is the efficient and final cause of all. This reality he calls God, the Christian God. Never once did Thomas doubt that Aristotle had demonstrated the existence of the one, true God.

The second point Thomas discusses at some length in his commentary on the third book of *De caelo* pertains to gravitational motion. For Aristotle, natural bodies have a natural motion which belongs *per se* to that body. Bodies which naturally move with rectilinear motion have "gravity" and "levity," the latter being a term awkward to translate. Nature, as defined by Aristotle, is a principle (ἀρχή) of motion and rest in those things in which it resides *per se*.[54] Bodies, therefore, are called "natural" which have such a nature and such a natural motion. But all natural rectilinear motion is either up or down, i.e., either heavy or light. Therefore all natural bodies on earth have a natural rectilinear motion. But all rectilinear motion is either up or down. Therefore all natural bodies on earth move either up or down.[55] Among the four simple bodies on earth, namely, earth, water, air, and fire, only two can be said to move absolutely up or absolutely down, namely, earth and fire. Earth is said to move down absolutely because it always tends to fall below water, while fire always tends to move beyond air. Water and air are said to be *relatively* heavy or light because water moves downward in relation to air, but upward in relation

[53] *Sum. cont. gent.* I, c. 13.
[54] Arist., *Phys.* II, 1, 192b21–23.
[55] Thomas, *In III De caelo*, lect. 7, n. 2.

to earth, while air moves up in relation to water, but down in relation to fire. Statements such as these are to be understood only in a broad and relative sense, for nature often shows mountains to be higher than lakes, and air higher than fire. Whatever small validity Aristotle's theory of the elements has today, the natural movement of all simple bodies must be seen strictly in a relative context, as I have tried to show elsewhere.[56]

The important point is that a heavy body, for example, has within it a formal, active, dynamic principle whereby it moves downward *secundum principium activum sive formale.* This principle is "nature" as *form.* But all bodies have "nature" also as *matter,* which is an intrinsic passive principle for being acted upon by other natural bodies; this is "nature" *secundum principium passivum, receptivum sive materiale.* This concept of "nature" (φύσις) as an intrinsic active or passive principle is essential to all of Aristotle's philosophy; without an understanding of it, nothing can be correctly understood in any branch of his teaching, least of all in natural philosophy.

The concept of "nature" as an intrinsic principle, both active and passive, distinguishes natural motion from violent ones. Violent motion is one forced upon the body from without; that is, the source of that motion lies in another body, and the body being forced reacts contrary to its nature. "An unnatural movement presupposes a natural movement which it contravenes."[57] Thus violence presupposes nature, as the motion of a heavy body upward presupposes its natural tendency downward. Following Aristotle, Thomas explains the movement of projectiles after they have left the hand of a thrower in terms of the medium which has the means of carrying the projectile against its nature.[58] Thus the Aristotelian explanation of violent motion requires that there be a medium, such as water or air, to allow the possibility of violent motion; in this case, the medium is a necessity, not just a convenience *ad bene esse.*[59]

But Averroes claimed that the medium is absolutely necessary not only for violent motion but for natural motion as well.[60] As Thomas points out, Averroes gives two basic arguments for the need of resistance in natural motion.[61] The first argument is drawn from the need for an efficient cause of all natural movement. The *motor separatus,* or

[56] J. A. Weisheipl, "Space and gravitation," *The New Scholasticism* 29 (1955), 175–223.
[57] Arist., *De caelo* III, 2, 300a24–25.
[58] Thomas, *In III De caelo,* lect. 7, nn. 5–6.
[59] *Ibid.,* n. 6.
[60] Averroes, *De caelo* III, comm. 28.
[61] Thomas, *In III De caelo,* lect. 7, n. 8.

efficient cause, of all heavy and light bodies is the generator, which, in giving the form, gives as a consequence all the natural motions that derive from that form, just as it gives all natural accidents which flow from that form; and so the generator causes natural motion by means of that form. Natural motion, however, ought to follow immediately from its *motor*, its efficient cause. But since natural motion follows immediately not from its efficient cause (the generator) but from the substantial form, it would seem that the substantial form is the proper *motor coniunctus*, the immediate cause of natural motion. And so it would seem, according to Averroes, that heavy and light bodies—in a certain sense—move themselves: of course, not *per se*, for things that move themselves properly (*per se*) have to be divided into "mover" and "moved," which division cannot be properly found in heavy and light bodies, which are divided only into form and matter, the latter of which is not, strictly speaking, "moved." Hence it remains that a heavy or light body moves itself *per accidens*, i.e., much as a sailor moves a ship through whose movement he himself is moved. Similarly, both the light and the heavy body, through their substantial forms, move the air, upon whose motion the heavy and the light body are moved. Hence, Averroes concludes that air is indispensable for natural motion.

The second argument Averroes gives is in his commentary on *Phys.* IV, text. comm. 71, where he says that there must be some kind of resistance between the mover and the moved. But there is no resistance between the matter of a heavy or a light body and their substantial form, which is the principle of their motion. Therefore it is necessary that there be resistance from the medium, which is air or water. Therefore Averroes concludes that air is indispensable for natural motion.

Thomas notes that both of these arguments are based on the same error.[62] Averroes believed that the substantial form of the heavy or light body is an active principle of motion after the manner of a *motor*, or efficient cause of motion, in such a way that there would have to be some resistance to the form's inclination, and also that the motion does not immediately proceed from the generator who produced the form in the first place. Thomas insists that this assumption is altogether false: *hoc est omnino falsum.* For Thomas, the substantial form of heavy and light bodies is a principle of motion not as an agent, a *motor coniunctus*, but as a principle, or source, *by which* (*quo*) the mover causes motion; it is like color, which is the principle by which we see.

[62] *Ibid.*, n. 9.

In all natural inanimate motion the substantial form is no more than an instrument *by which* the agent acts.

Thomas explicitly says that "the motion of heavy and light bodies does not derive from the generator by means of any other moving source." That is, there is no need to look for any resistance beyond what already obtained between generator and generated, agent and patient. Consequently, natural motions do not need a medium in which to move, whereas violent motions do. Whatever moves naturally already has everything it needs to move; it has an innate source, or power, of moving. In short, it has "nature" as an active formal principle, which is not an efficient cause. So there is absolutely no need to look for any other efficient cause to impel such bodies when they move naturally; there is no need to postulate a *motor coniunctus*; there is no need to look for any other efficient cause of motion distinct from the generator which produced the natural form in a given body. The case of violent motion is different, for in violent motions the source of movement is always outside the body being moved, impelling the projectile along. Thomas is explicit here and elsewhere: natural motion is possible even in a void, or vacuum; natural motions do not need the resistance of a medium.[63]

The commentary on Aristotle's *De caelo* by St. Thomas Aquinas is a valuable source for his mature thought on the basic principles of natural philosophy. There is no evidence of a change of teaching, but there is ample evidence to show that we have here a deeper understanding of the basic elements of his philosophy of nature.

[63] Cf. Chapter VI above.

IX

CLASSIFICATION OF THE SCIENCES
IN MEDIEVAL THOUGHT

In modern usage the word "science" has connotations and implications notably different from those of medieval usage. The English word "science" is derived from the Latin verb *scire*, to know, by way of the French substantive, *science*. The Latin root, it would seem, came from an early Greek form of the verb χεάζω (the radical form χείω for σχείω) meaning to split, to cleave. In early Latin usage the verb simply meant to discern, or to penetrate to the bottom in the sense of cutting a situation to its very roots. Thus in Latin the term *scientia* was used to designate a discerning, penetrating, intellectual grasp of a situation or of a given subject. Technically it was employed of knowledge that explained the situation fully and accurately through all or any of its true causes. This causal knowledge was considered possible in speculative research and in practical affairs, in theological analysis and in philosophical investigations. Generally scientific knowledge was contrasted with the arts and technical skills, on the one hand, and with mere probability, on the other. In other words, in medieval usage the term "science" was given to every field of intellectual endeavor in which true causal explanations could be discovered.

The medieval views of scientific knowledge and the classification of the sciences reached full development in the thirteenth century. Three distinct sources must be noted in order to clarify the thirteenth-century discussions concerning the sciences. First, there was the Greco-Roman heritage of a liberal arts education, which always remained the foundation of learning in the Middle Ages; second, the profound influence of Manlius Boethius, who before his tragic death bequeathed to the Middle Ages a schema and a few gems of Greek philosophy; third, the twelfth- and thirteenth-century translations from the Greek and Arabic which helped to make this schema intelligible to the Latins.

When Rome came under the influence of Greek culture she im-
plicitly surrendered to a higher civilization. Rome under the republic
tried to assimilate and oftentimes to imitate the best ancient Greece
had to offer. Roman education under the empire was modeled on the
Greek system, but with important differences. Philosophy and
medicine, for example, never really became part of a Latin education;
these specialized studies could be pursued in Greek. The basic education in the arts, however, was modeled on the Greek liberal tradition,
and even before the reign of Augustus boys of the Roman aristocracy
learned the liberal arts in both Latin and Greek.[1]

The earliest Latin classification and exposition of the liberal arts
seems to have been incorporated in the now-lost work of Terence
Varro (116–27 B.C.) entitled *Disciplinarum libri IX*. Varro's compendium of disciplinary or encyclical studies embraced successively:
(1) grammar, fragments of which are extant,[2] (2) dialectics,
(3) rhetoric, (4) geometry, (5) arithmetic, (6) astrology, (7) music,
(8) medicine, (9) architecture. Medicine and architecture were understandably dropped from later discussions of the liberal arts, and there
remained the well-known classification later to be designated as the
trivium and *quadrivium*. Varro personally had a high reputation as a
teacher of grammar, dialectics, and rhetoric in the schools of Italy, but
his four books on the *quadrivium*, it would seem, were little more than
insignificant summaries of Greek sources.[3] Varro's classification of the
seven liberal arts became the foundation of later Roman manuals and
summaries of the *artes*. Cicero, Varro's contemporary, listed geometry,
letters, physical sciences, moral and political philosophy among the
artes liberales preparing one for the supreme art of oratory,[4] but this
was never the actual practice or theory of Roman education. In the
Roman theory of education the seven liberal arts were a preparation
for one of the specialized branches of learning: philosophy, medicine,
or law.

After obtaining an elementary training from a tutor or school master the Roman youth was sent to the nearest grammar school, con-

[1] On the study and use of Latin and Greek in the Roman world see H. I. Marrou,
History of Education in Antiquity (New York, 1956), pp. 255–64, and A. Gwynn, *Roman
Education from Cicero to Quintillian* (Oxford, 1926).

[2] H. Funaioili, *Grammatica et Romana Fragmenta* (Leipzig, 1907), I, 205–6.

[3] R. M. Martin, "Arts libéraux (Sept)," in *Dict. d'hist. et de géog. ecclés.*, IV, 830; see the
collection of studies edited by Josef Koch, *Artes Liberales von der antiken Bildung zur
Wissenschaft des Mittelalters*, Studien u. Texte, V (Leiden, 1959); on the Greek origin of
the quadrivium see P. Merlan, *From Platonism to Neo-platonism* (The Hague, 1953),
pp. 78–85.

[4] Cicero, *De oratore* I, 72–73; III, 27.

ducted by a *grammaticus;* normally the boy would have different masters for Latin and Greek grammar. The primary duty of the *grammaticus* was, of course, to teach grammar and literature, but it seems that he also taught the rudiments of arithmetic, geometry, music, and astronomy.[5] From the grammar school the youth might proceed to higher studies, which consisted in attending the school of a *rhetoricus,* from whom he learned not only composition and declamation but also dialectics, or logic.[6] Thus in practice the Roman schools assigned grammar and a rudimentary *quadrivium* to the secondary school master, the grammarian, while it reserved rhetoric and dialectics for the more advanced teacher, the rhetor. This distribution of the arts course through grammar school and the school of rhetoric is reflected in the *Institutio oratoria libri XII* of Quintilian (ca. 35–95 A.D.), which, although primarily a discussion of rhetoric and dialectics, indicates the subjects assumed to have been taught in the grammar school. It is clear that in practice the entire curriculum of both schools embraced the seven *artes liberales;* these arts were the indispensable foundation for any respectable specialization. While the Romans never regarded philosophy or medicine as special subjects to be acquired in Latin, they did consider the study of Roman law to be strictly a Latin specialization to be studied by Latins and Greeks only after completing a liberal education in the arts.[7]

Thus the general plan of Roman education reflected its Greek prototype, just as the general plan of all medieval education revealed its Roman inheritance. Clement of Alexandria, writing around the year 200, was thoroughly traditional in his outlook when he insisted that after the elementary training a youth should study all the liberal or ἐγκύκλια disciplines as a foundation for the higher study of philosophy, and not grow old in the exclusive study of music, geometry, grammar, or rhetoric, as so many do.[8] For, Clement observes, the liberal arts are a preparation for philosophy, just as philosophy itself is a preparation for true Christian wisdom. For St. Augustine the seven liberal arts embrace grammar, dialectics, rhetoric, music, geometry, astronomy, and philosophy,[9] but he too considered the arts a preparation for Christian doctrine and an aid to its interpretation.[10] The Fathers of the Church found no difficulty in adapting Greek and

---

[5] See R. M. Martin, *op. cit.,* cols. 830–31.
[6] *Ibid.,* col. 831.
[7] See H. I. Marrou, *op. cit.,* pp. 289–91.
[8] Clem. Al., *Strom.* I, 5 (PG 8, 721B); see also *Strom.* I, 7.
[9] August., *De ordine* II, 12–16 (PL 32, 1011–16); *Retract.* I, 6.
[10] August., *De doctr. Chr.* II, 27–39.

Roman culture to the needs of Christianity. Even after the barbarians put an end to the Roman Empire and its numerous educational institutions scattered throughout the West, the basic conception of the seven liberal arts as the indispensable foundation for philosophy (and beyond philosophy for theology, medicine, and law) remained in the Christian schools of the Middle Ages.

A. THE EARLY MIDDLE AGES

The Latin Middle Ages inherited not only the general plan of education, but important textbooks as well. Cicero served as an invaluable source for the philosophical ideas of antiquity; his latinity was a model, though rarely imitated, and his *De inventione* was taken as a textbook of rhetoric in the Middle Ages. Aelius Donatus, a rhetor of Rome around the middle of the fourth century and tutor of St. Jerome, wrote a highly popular, though unoriginal, textbook known as the *Ars grammatica*. In the Middle Ages the elementary part of this treatise dealing with the parts of speech was known as the *Ars minor;* the more detailed consideration of grammar distributed into three books was known as the *Ars maior.* Early in 387 St. Augustine started to write an encyclopedia of the seven liberal arts, his *Disciplinarum libri,*[11] but only the grammar, six books on music, and a beginning of "the other five disciplines, namely, concerning dialectics, rhetoric, geometry, arithmetic, and philosophy" seem to have been written by him. The popular and curious *Satyricon,* or *De nuptiis Philologiae et Mercurii et de septem artibus liberalibus libri novem* by Martianus Capella (early fifth century) was of no doctrinal value, but it was instrumental in establishing the accepted enumeration of the seven liberal arts in the Middle Ages, namely grammar, dialectics, rhetoric, geometry, arithmetic, astrology, and music. Around the year 500 A.D. Priscian, about whom practically nothing is known, composed his very influential *Institutiones grammaticae* in eighteen books. During the Middle Ages the first sixteen books were taught as *Priscianus maior;* the last two books were commonly called *Priscianus minor,* or *De constructionibus.* The Latin Middle Ages did indeed inherit many other important works from Roman authors, and not the least were the translations and commentaries on Plato's *Timaeus,* but none were more influential on the medieval conception of the sciences than the bequest of Manlius Severinus Boethius.

---

[11] August., *Retract.* I, 6. This is the reading printed in the Vienna edition (CSEL 36, 28); one might have expected "astronomica" in place of "arithmetica" (line 6) to give a closer parallel to *De ordine* II, 15.

i. Boethius and the Division of the Sciences

Boethius (ca. 475–524) was a man of extraordinary learning and versatility, well acquainted with the best of ancient Latin and Greek thought.[12] He has justly been called "the last Roman and the first scholastic,"[13] because he preserved the ideal of the classical Roman tradition when the Roman world was crumbling and he established the foundation of Latin scholasticism both in theology and in philosophy. He was, as P. Mandonnet observed, "le véritable introducteur d'Aristote en Occident."[14] His translations of almost the whole of Aristotle's *Organon* established the foundation of the scholastic method and offered the only direct contact with Aristotle's thought before the twelfth century. Philosophically Boethius was a convinced Platonist, as were many others of his day, but he was fully aware of the importance of Aristotelian logic. While a Roman consul, Boethius undertook the impossible task of translating, interpreting, and harmonizing all the works of Aristotle and the *Dialogues* of Plato.[15] Boethius, however, was unjustly put to death by Theodoric, a former friend and patron, before this dream could be realized.

Besides his translations of Aristotle's logical works Boethius supplied textbooks for the other liberal arts, thus enabling students of the next six hundred years to acquire a liberal education. Earlier Romans had provided sufficient textbooks for grammar and rhetoric; Boethius added abundant works for logic, and elementary adaptations from the Greek for music, arithmetic, and geometry. Theodoric also mentions translations of Ptolemy's *Astronomy* and Archimedes' *Mechanics* as coming from his pen,[16] but nothing is known of these translations or summaries today.

It was particularly through the short theological treatises that Boethius laid the foundation for the scholastic method of the early Middle Ages. He showed the utility of grammar and logic in the

---

[12] See R. Bonnaud, "L'Education Scientifique de Boèce," *Speculum* 4 (1929), 198–206.
[13] M. Grabmann, *Gesch. d. schol. Methode*, I, 148–77.
[14] P. Mandonnet, *Siger de Brabant* (Louvain, 1911), I, p. 7.
[15] ". . . ego omne Aristotelis opus, quodcumque in manus venerit, in Romanum stilum vertens eorum omnium commenta Latina oratione perscribam, ut si quid ex logicae artis subtilitate, ex moralis gravitate peritae, ex naturalis acumine veritatis ab Aristotele conscriptum sit, id omne ordinatum transferam atque etiam quodam lumine commentationis inlustrum omnesque Platonis dialogos vertendo vel etiam commentando in latinam redigam formam. His peractis non equidem contempserim Aristotelis Platonisque sententias in unam quodammodo revocare concordiam eosque non ut plerique dissentire in omnibus, sed in plerisque et his in philosophia maximis consentire demonstrem." *Comm. in lib. Arist.* ΠΕΡΙ ΕΡΜΗΝΕΙΑΣ, ed. 2a, II, c. 3 (Leipzig, 1880), pp. 79–80.
[16] Letter of King Theodoric to Boethius in Cassiodorus, *Lib. var.* I, ep. 45, PL 69, 539.

discussion of difficult theological doctrines and the importance of definition and division in harmonizing apparently contradictory authorities. The method of arriving at a satisfactory solution through a tangle of apparently "sic et non" views was greatly developed during the twelfth century. This always remained the foundation of the scholastic method, but it was not until the *Posterior Analytics* of Aristotle was fully understood in the thirteenth century that theology could be developed as a scientific discipline. But to understand the Aristotelian scientific method presented in the *Posterior Analytics* the schoolmen needed to see its application in physics, metaphysics, and ethics. These works of Aristotle, however, were not known to medieval scholars before the middle of the twelfth century, at the earliest. Nevertheless, through Boethius and other authors the early Middle Ages knew that these parts of philosophy did exist. The early schoolmen, however, since they did not have the actual works of antiquity, could do little more than repeat what Boethius had said.

In his first commentary on Porphyry, an early work (ca. 509),[17] Boethius discussed the nature of philosophy as the love and study of wisdom. Following Ammonius's commentary on the same work, Boethius divides philosophy into two species, theoretical and practical, that is, speculative and active. "There are, however, as many parts of speculative philosophy as there are things which can suitably be considered speculatively." For Boethius as for Ammonius before him, there are three kinds of things which fulfill this requirement, hence there are three kinds of speculative philosophy: "est enim una theoretica pars de intellectibilibus, alia de intelligibilibus, alia de naturalibus."[18] Boethius claimed that he coined the word *intellectibilia* to express the Greek νοητά, that is, the object of νόησις, or intuition. This corresponds to Plato's supreme wisdom of dialectics, which contemplates eternal forms. The lowest type of speculative philosophy is natural science, "which explains the natures and properties of bodies." Intermediate between the highest and lowest species of speculative philosophy lies the consideration of *intelligibilia,* a term already coined by Marius Victorinus. Although Boethius gives no name to this branch of philosophy, it seems to be the study of celestial movers.[19] Ammonius had listed mathematics in this position, and

---

[17] S. Brant, *Boethii In Isagogen Porphyrii Commenta*, CSEL 48, xxvii.

[18] Boethius, *In Isagogen Porphyrii Comm.*, ed. prima, Lib. I, c. 3, CSEL 48, 8. Ammonius not only places mathematics in the middle position between natural science and divine science in the hierarchy of speculative disciplines but insists that mathematics is divided into no more and no less than four parts: geometry, astronomy, music, and arithmetic. *Explanatio in Quinque Voces Porphyrii*, prol.

[19] E. Gilson, *History of Christian Phil.* (New York, 1955), p. 97, suggests that the name

Boethius himself later replaced this intermediate science with mathematics, thus returning to the classical tripartite classification of speculative philosophy.

Boethius likewise divided practical philosophy into three branches: the study of personal morality, political morality, and domestic morality. Later these practical sciences are reordered and simply called ethics, domestics, and politics. The position of logic, or rational discipline, is also discussed briefly: some consider logic to be a part of philosophy, others do not, thus showing that there is reasonableness in both positions. In his second commentary on Porphyry Boethius judiciously remarks of logic that it is "not a part of philosophy but rather an instrument" of philosophy.[20]

In his mature treatise *De Trinitate* (ca. 520) Boethius gave the Middle Ages the standard tripartite classification of speculative philosophy.[21] The first part of speculative science is called *naturalis*, or physics; it considers forms which are not abstract or separable, i.e., ἀνυπεξαρετοσί, because this science is concerned with forms which cannot exist or be considered apart from matter and motion. The second part of speculative science is called *mathematica;* it considers forms which are actually "inabstracta" as though they were without matter and motion. Since mathematical forms are really the forms of bodies, they can never exist "separate" from matter. The third part is *theologica*, which considers forms which are actually abstract and separable from matter and motion, "for the divine substance is without either matter or motion." To each of these parts of speculative philosophy there is an appropriate method which ought to be used. The method of natural science is the process of reasoning scientifically (*rationabiliter*); the method of mathematics is disciplinary (*disciplinaliter*); and that of theology is intuitive or intellectual (*intellectualiter*) in the sense that theology must not be diverted by imagination but must contemplate that form which is pure *esse* and not a mere image.

The terminology used by Boethius to designate the methodological procedures of the various parts of philosophy is indeed strange, and it

"psychology" could be given to this intermediate science, since it is the science that deals with souls. But Boethius, it would seem, is here describing the blessed condition of intellectual substances when they understand the "first intellectible," an understanding which could be mathematics. Hence, G. Fraile, *Historia de la Filosofía*, I (Madrid, 1956), p. 785, prefers to identify this unnamed science with "mathematics" as described in *De arithmetica* and *De musica.*

[20] Lib. I, c. 3, *ed. cit.*, p. 142.

[21] The pioneer efforts of Joseph Mariétan, *Problème de la Classification des Sciences d'Aristote à s. Thomas* (thesis, Paris, 1901), to trace the influence of this division need to be supplemented by further research.

was variously interpreted by medieval commentators. The method of theology, viz., *intellectualiter,* undoubtedly refers to noetic intuition or direct contemplation as explained by Boethius in his first commentary on Porphyry. This was the type of knowledge Plato had reserved for the supreme wisdom of dialectics. *Disciplinaliter* as the method of mathematics means nothing more than "mathematical" procedure, which for Plato was hypothetical in the sense that mathematics must assume certain axioms without investigating their ontological foundation. Plato identified the method of mathematics with reasoning and science (ἐπιστήμη) as distinct from intuition and wisdom. But Aristotle had insisted on the scientific status of physics, which studies universal and necessary natures existing individually in sensible matter. Hence by *rationabiliter* Boethius undoubtedly intended to signify the scientific, or demonstrative, procedure which Aristotle had extended to natural science.

The Boethian division and designation of the philosophical sciences is clearly a fusion of Platonic and Aristotelian views. The division between speculative and practical, the scientific status of physics, and the rejection of sensible forms subsisting apart from matter are all Aristotelian. The tripartite hierarchy of forms suitable for speculative consideration, the position and division of mathematics are purely Platonic and Pythagorean. Describing the mathematical disciplines, to which he gives the name *quadrivium,* Boethius insists that these constitute the "four-lane road to wisdom," that is, to theology, and whoever spurns this road to wisdom will never know how to philosophize.[22] "Constat igitur quisquis haec praetermiserit, omnem philosophiae perdidisse doctrinam." Among the quadrivial disciplines there are determined grades of priority and posteriority. In the order of nature number and the science of number, arithmetic, are prior in the sense that without number there can be nothing subsequent, while when the subsequent figures, etc., are removed, number remains. Subsequent to number and the science of arithmetic is harmony, or music. Then come figures and the science of geometry; and finally the study of geometrical solids in motion, the science of astronomy. Astronomy, therefore, is the most physical of the mathematical sciences and the closest to natural science.

It is difficult to determine how Boethius conceived the study of nature and where he would place it in the curriculum of studies.

---

[22] "Quibus quatuor partibus si careat inquisitor, verum invenire non possit, ac sine hac quidem speculatione veritatis nulli recte sapiendum est. . . . Quod haec qui spernit, id est, has semitas sapientiae, ei denuntio non recte philosophandum." Boethius, *De arithmetica* I, 1, PL 63, 1081C.

Clearly the ascending hierarchy of the mathematical sciences, astronomy, geometry, music, and arithmetic, was meant to lead to the supreme wisdom designated simply as theology. It is also clear that for Boethius the study of nature inevitably leads to the mathematical sciences, but it is not clear whether or not a student was expected to study nature before studying the mathematical sciences of the *quadrivium*. This problem never arose in the early Middle Ages simply because the early schoolmen had at hand textbooks for the liberal arts, while they had nothing of the "three philosophies": physics, metaphysics, and ethics.

ii. The Arts and the Three Philosophies

The *Institutiones* of M. Aurelius Cassiodorus, a junior contemporary of Boethius, was written as a manual of divine and secular literature for the monks of Vivarium about the year 544–45. The first book is a compendium of Sacred Scripture, exegesis, hagiography, and religious discipline; the second book is a summary of the seven liberal arts: grammar, rhetoric, dialectic, arithmetic, music, geometry, and astronomy. This second book, which became exceedingly popular in later centuries, is drawn largely from Boethius, Cicero, Donatus, Quintilian, Varro, and St. Augustine. At the beginning of his summary of dialectics (lib. II, c. 3) Cassiodorus discussed the definition and division of philosophy, a procedure which was frequently followed throughout the Middle Ages. The schematic classification of philosophy given by Cassiodorus is simply that of Boethius, but in one popular recension, probably of the eighth century, this classification is attributed to Aristotle:[23]

Philosophy	theoretical, or *inspectiva*	divine	
		doctrinal	arithmetical, musical, geometrical, astronomical
		natural	
	practical, or *actualis*	moral	
		dispensative, or domestic	
		civil	

Natural philosophy discusses the nature of each thing which is produced naturally; doctrinal philosophy is the science which considers abstract quantity, i.e., quantity which has been mentally separated

---

[23] This is recension III, signified by Δ in the edition of R. A. B. Mynors (Oxford, 1937), p. 110.

from matter or from the other accidents; philosophy is called "divine" when it considers the ineffable nature of God or when it discusses spiritual creatures. Cassiodorus briefly defined each of the doctrinal, or mathematical, sciences as well as the practical. The rest of the second book is devoted to the seven liberal arts. In the early Middle Ages the second book of Cassiodorus's work seems to have been copied separately and expanded by scholars desiring a fuller compendium of the arts.

The encyclopedic *Etymologiae libri XX* of St. Isidore of Seville was composed early in the seventh century and enjoyed great popularity as a reference work throughout the Middle Ages. A summary of the seven liberal arts was given in the first three books: I, grammar; II, rhetoric and dialectics; III, arithmetic, geometry, music, and astronomy. Following Cassiodorus and Boethius, Isidore discusses the definition and division of philosophy at the beginning of his compendium of dialectics (lib. II, c. 3), but he gives two divisions of philosophy.[24] The first is the familiar Stoic classification, which St. Augustine attributed to Plato, namely, the division of philosophy into physics, ethics, and logic. According to Isidore, Plato divided physics, or natural philosophy, into arithmetic, geometry, music, and astronomy. The division of logic into dialectics and rhetoric is also attributed to Plato, while the division of ethics according to the four cardinal virtues is said to have originated with Socrates, who first established moral science. St. Isidore's version of this classification can be represented briefly as follows:

	physics	arithmetic geometry music astronomy
Philosophy	ethics	prudence justice fortitude temperance
	logic	rhetoric dialectics

For Isidore the whole of theological teaching can also be adapted to this classification, for it discusses nature (Genesis and Ecclesiastes) and

[24] Isidore, *Etymologicarum libri XX*, ed. W. M. Lindsay (Oxford, 1957), Lib. II, xxiv.

ethics (Proverbs and other books), as well as logic (Canticle of Canticles and the Gospels). The second division of philosophy given by Isidore is taken directly from Cassiodorus without alteration.[25]

St. Augustine, Boethius, Cassiodorus, and St. Isidore served as the principal sources for all later discussion of the seven liberal arts and the tripartite division of philosophy. As the early Middle Ages were unaware of the numerous Greek works on natural science, metaphysics, and ethics, repetition of the Boethian and Stoic classification of the sciences had little significance and no practical value for teachers of the arts. Misunderstanding of the original divisions and confusions of the issues involved were the inevitable result of not having the Aristotelian corpus. This confusion can be seen in writers from the ninth through the twelfth century. Alcuin of York selected the Stoic division from Isidore as the point of departure for his *De dialectica*,[26] presumably because it included the mention of dialectics, while the Boethian division did not. Rhabanus Maurus likewise took the Stoic division, but he included under physics seven arts: arithmetic, astronomy, astrology, mechanics, medicine, geometry, and music.[27] Scotus Erigena combined the Boethian and Stoic classifications when he divided philosophy into (i) *activa* or ethics; (ii) physics, or natural science, subdivided into the quadrivial arts; (iii) theology, which discusses God; (iv) logic, or rational philosophy, which shows the rules by which the other "parts of wisdom" are to proceed.[28]

In the twelfth century a more thorough synthesis of the two ancient classifications was presented in the various *Didascalia*, or general introductions to the *artes*. These summary treatises follow the general pattern of the traditional *Disciplinarum libri*, discussing the nature and classification of learning and briefly explaining the nature of each art. The best known of these is the *Didascalion* of Hugh of St. Victor (1096–1141). In this remarkable treatise seven mechanical arts are introduced as parts of philosophy in order to balance the seven liberal arts; all seven liberal arts, including grammar, find a place in this classification; and it is a successful combination of the Boethian and Stoic divisions of science. "Philosophy is divided into theoretical, prac-

---

[25] "Alii definierunt Philosophiae rationem in duabus consistere partibus, quarum prima inspectiva est, secunda actualis. Inspectiva dividitur in tribus modis, id est prima in naturalem; secunda in doctrinalem; tertia in divinam. Doctrinalis dividitur in quattuor, id est, prima in Arithmeticam, secunda Musicam, tertia Geometriam, quarta Astronomiam. Actualis dividitur in tribus, id est, prima in moralem, secunda dispensativam, tertia civilem." *Ibid.*

[26] Alcuin, *Didascalia*, Opusc. IV (*De dialectica*), cap. 1. PL 101, 952.

[27] Rhabanus Maurus, *De universo*, Lib. V, c. 1. PL 111, 413–14.

[28] Scotus Erigena, *De div. nat.*, Lib. III, 29. PL 122, 705; see also col. 778–79.

tical, mechanical, and logical; these four branches embrace all
scientific knowledge."[29] Except for the mechanical arts, the basic division of scientific knowledge is that of the Stoics.[30] In this case "physics"
is taken to be equivalent to "theoretical" and coextensive with Boethius's tripartite classification of speculative philosophy:

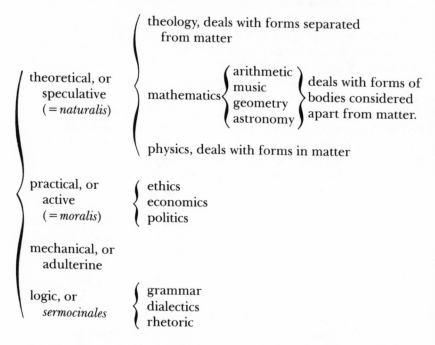

theoretical, or speculative (= *naturalis*)
- theology, deals with forms separated from matter
- mathematics
  - arithmetic
  - music
  - geometry
  - astronomy
  - deals with forms of bodies considered apart from matter.
- physics, deals with forms in matter

practical, or active (= *moralis*)
- ethics
- economics
- politics

mechanical, or adulterine

logic, or *sermocinales*
- grammar
- dialectics
- rhetoric

Hugh of St. Victor's classification of scientific knowledge was taken
over by Clarenbaud of Arras around the middle of the twelfth century,[31] and it enjoyed continuous circulation from the time it was
written.[32] But in practice it did not affect the actual teaching of arts at
Chartres, Paris, or elsewhere. Gilbert of la Porrée,[33] Thierry of

[29] Hugh of S. Victor, *Didascalion*, Lib. II, c. 1, ed. C. H. Buttimer (Washington, 1939),
p. 24.
[30] "Physica aliquando large accipitur aequipollens theoreticae, secundum quam ac-
ceptionem philosophiam in tres partes dividunt, i.e. *physicam, ethicam, logicam*, in qua
divisione mechanica non continetur, sed restringitur philosophia circa physicam,
ethicam, logicam." Lib. II, c. 16, *ed. cit.*, p. 35.
[31] *Der Kommentar des Clarenbaldus von Arras zu Boethius De Trinitate*, ed. W. Jansen
(Breslau, 1926), pp. 26*–27*.
[32] R. W. Hunt, "The Introduction to the *Artes*," in *Studia Mediaevalia* in honorem R. J.
Martin, O.P. (Bruges, 1948), p. 99.
[33] Gilbert de la Porrée, *Commentaria in lib. de Trin.*, c. 2. PL 64, 1265.

Chartres,[34] and others could continue to include theology, physics, and ethics in the classification of scientific knowledge, but without the works of Aristotle such branches could not but remain meaningless. In actual practice the schools of the twelfth century, that is, monastic schools, cathedral schools, and some court schools, taught only the seven liberal arts. By the term "philosophy" or "science" was understood the seven liberal arts already known to them. In the prologue to the *Heptateucon* Thierry of Chartres (fl. 1124–1149) points out that there are two instruments (*organa*) of philosophy, the spirit and its expression. The spirit is illuminated by the *quadrivium;* its expression, congruous, reasonable, and ornate, is provided by the *trivium.*[35] William of Conches (ca. 1080–ca.1154) expresses the same attitude when he proposes the order of studying the arts.[36] One should first acquire the various parts of eloquence, first grammar, then dialectics, and after this rhetoric. Being instructed and well-armed in the *trivium*, one ought then to approach the study of philosophy ("ad studium philosophiae debemus accedere"). Here the order of study is first the *quadrivium*, proceeding from arithmetic to music to geometry and finally to astronomy; only after this can one approach the study of the *divina pagina.*

Concerning the early medieval classifications of the sciences three points ought to be noted before discussing the new views of the thirteenth century. First, the distinction between grammar on the one hand and the combination of dialectics and rhetoric on the other hand in all the classifications before Hugh of St. Victor may help to illuminate the antagonism between "grammarians" and "dialecticians" during the eleventh and twelfth centuries. Peter Abelard, the dialectician *par excellence,* felt justified in dismissing grammar from the realm of philosophical disciplines; for him dialectics and arithmetic are the principal disciplines of philosophy.[37] Second, it might be noted that the identification of "physics" with the *quadrivium* was not at all

[34] Thierry of Chartres, *Glossa super lib. Boeth. de Trin.,* c. 2, 24–28, ed. N. Haring, *Arch. d'hist. doctr. et litt. du M. A.* 23 (1956), 285–87.
[35] A French translation of this passage is given in H. Clerval, *Les Écoles de Chartres au Moyen Âge* (Chartres, 1895), p. 221.
[36] "Ordo vero discendi talis est ut, quia per eloquentiam omnis sit doctrina, prius instruatur in eloquentia. Cuius sunt tres partes, recte scribere et recte pronuntiare scripta, quod confert *grammatica;* probare quod probandum est, quod docet *dialectica;* ornare verba et sententias, quod tradit *rhetorica.* Initiandi ergo summus in grammatica, deinde in dialectica, postea in rhetorica; quibus instructi et ut armis muniti, ad studium *philosophiae* debemus accedere. Cuius hic ordo est, ut prius in *quadrivio,* id est in ipsa prius *arithmetica,* secundus in *musica,* tertius in *geometria,* quartus in *astronomia.* Deinde in divina pagina." William of Conches, *De phil. mundi,* Lib. IV, c. 41. PL 172, 100.
[37] Abelard, *Introd. ad theol.,* Lib. II, c. 2. PL 178, 1040ff.

inconsistent with the general Platonism of the early Middle Ages. This identification may have been strengthened by familiarity with the two Latin versions of Plato's *Timaeus*. It is also possible that this traditional identification of physics and the *quadrivium* exerted some influence on the thought of the thirteenth and early fourteenth centuries. Third, it is clear that the early masters of arts did not teach anything which might be called "ethics" or "natural theology" (metaphysics); these "parts of philosophy" were studied in sacred doctrine, which was taught by a bishop or master of sacred theology. Hence the emphasis on logic and physics in the arts faculty of the later Middle Ages, and the apparent neglect of metaphysics and ethics, ought not to be considered novel or in itself clear proof of decadence in scholastic thought. The mainstays of the faculty of arts at Oxford in the early fourteenth century were in fact logic and physics.

When the "new" Aristotle was finally admitted to the curriculum of studies in the first half of the thirteenth century, "philosophy" was added to the existing curriculum of the liberal arts. The *trivium* and *quadrivium* remained the basic curriculum, at least in theory, preparatory for the study of philosophy. Arabian philosophers had considered logic and mathematics to be propaedeutic disciplines required for the study of philosophy.[38] The medieval faculty of arts already taught these "propaedeutic" disciplines. Thus all that needed to be added were the Aristotelian *libri naturales*, metaphysics, and moral philosophy. In the Oxford statutes these new sciences introduced into the curriculum of arts are commonly referred to as "the three philosophies."

B. THE THIRTEENTH CENTURY

With the introduction of the "new" Aristotle into the West there came new treatises concerning the classification of the sciences, shedding light on the Aristotelian books and not infrequently casting a Platonic shadow over their interpretation. Alfarabi's *De scientiis*[39] and *De ortu scientiarum*[40] were translated by Dominic Gundissalinus from

---

[38] For example Alfarabi, *De scientiis;* Averroes, *Phys.*, prooem.; II *Phys.*, comm. 35; VI *Metaph.*, comm. 1; on this point and the classification of the sciences see L. Gauthier, *Ibn Rochd (Averroès)* (Paris, 1948), pp. 47–51.

[39] The most recent edition of this translation is that of M. A. Alonso, *Domingo Gundisalvo, De Scientiis* (Madrid, 1954); Gerard of Cremona's translation was edited by A. Palencia, *Alfarabi, Catalogo de las Ciencias* (Madrid, 1932).

[40] Edited by C. Bäumker, *Alfarabi, Über den Ursprung der Wissenschaften, Beiträge z. Gesch. d. Phil. u. Theol. d. MA.*, Bd. XIX, H. 3 (Münster, 1916).

the Arabic around 1150 at Toledo. Dominic's own *De divisione scientiarum* is a lengthy and detailed analysis of the individual sciences compiled from Arabic and earlier Latin sources.[41] In the thirteenth century Gerard of Cremona produced a new version of Alfarabi's *De scientiis* around 1230, and Michael Scot is said to have composed a treatise, *Divisio philosophiae*, about the same time based on Gundissalinus.[42] There are clear indications that these treatises from the Arabic or dependent on Arabic sources influenced later medieval interpretations of the Boethian classification of the sciences.

For Alfarabi (d. 950) the study of the various sciences ought to follow the natural order in which they originated. Substance, in his view, is the basic reality, and it was first of all divided into many; this gave rise to the science of arithmetic. Each substance was then given a particular figure and disposition of parts; this gave rise to geometry. But since substance is naturally moved with different velocities, fast, slow, or regular, there arose the science of comparative velocities in celestial motions, namely, the science of astronomy. From these velocities there followed various sounds (*accidit ei sonus*), and the science which studies tonal proportionalities is called music. But since these substances sometimes alter in quality, change, act and are acted upon, there arose the study of their natures, *quae est scientia de actione et passione*.[43] In the course of studying these natures four primary qualities were discovered, hot, cold, humid, and dry; from these four natural qualities and the four mathematical disciplines there arose the science of terrestrial physics.[44] Alfarabi lists eight branches of terrestrial physics: practical astronomy (*de iudiciis*), medicine, natural necromancy, iconography (*de imaginibus*), agriculture, navigation, alchemy, and perspective (*de speculis*). The natural sciences are the most extensive of the sciences and they should be cultivated only after the mathematical disciplines have been acquired; practical astronomy and medicine in particular should not be studied until one is well versed in the disciplinary branches. Finally one is ready to study the nature of the higher substance (*massa substantiae superioris*), the study of which will lead to a knowledge of God. By "higher substance" Alfarabi here means the eternal, celestial sphere which is moved by the power and

---

[41] See the edition and detailed study by L. Baur, *Dominicus Gundissalinus, De divisione philosophiae, Beiträge z. Gesch. d. Phil. d. MA.*, Bd. IV, H. 2–3.

[42] *Ibid.*, pp. 364–67; fragments of this work have been collected from Vincent of Beauvais by Baur, pp. 398–400. For the probable date of Michael Scot's treatise see C. Haskins, *Studies*, 279.

[43] Alfarabi, *De ortu scientiarum*, cap. 1, 5, *ed. cit.*, 20.

[44] "Et ex his quatuor radicibus cum primis quatuor, quae sunt quatuor scientiae disciplinales, emersit scientia quae cadit sub circulo lunae." *Ibid.*, lines 20–22.

wisdom of God.[45] Almost as an afterthought Alfarabi adds that before one begins mathematics, he should learn languages, grammar, logic, and poetry as a first step toward learning. In the *De scientiis* Alfarabi presents a more detailed schema of the sciences, other branches of learning are included, logic and natural science are divided according to the Aristotelian books, but the fundamental order of the sciences is retained.

The *De divisione philosophiae* of Dominic Gundissalinus was composed some time after his translation of Alfarabi's two treatises, perhaps shortly after 1150. L. Baur in his detailed analysis of the work has admirably shown that it is "a cleverly fabricated collection of materials from Arabic (Al-Kindi, Al-Farabi, Avicenna, An-Nairizi, Al-Gazel, and other, unknown authors) and Latin (Boethius, Isidore, Bede) sources."[46] Baur, however, maintained that the treatise as a whole is "based on an entirely Aristotelian foundation."[47] To the extent that Gundissalinus recognized the tripartite classification of both speculative and practical knowledge, and to the extent that he mentioned all the currently accepted Aristotelian books, the treatise might be said to have an "Aristotelian foundation." However, Gundissalinus's conception of this classification and his interpretation of the various sciences are far from Aristotelian.

Gundissalinus recognizes, as did all his predecessors, that grammar is a mere instrument of philosophy and that it should be studied first. Poetry, then rhetoric, should follow in the curriculum, even though these arts are taken as parts of "logic" in the wide sense.[48] These should be followed by the full course in logic, including the study of demonstration, dialectics in the sense of probable argumentation, and fallacies. After these preparatory studies one is ready to study the three parts of philosophy: physics, mathematics, and theology (metaphysics). But first one should study physics, because forms existing in matter and in motion are better known to us. Gundissalinus takes from Alfarabi the eight special parts of physics and the enumeration of the Aristotelian *libri naturales*. Gundissalinus, however, adds that physics utilizes the "dialectical syllogism," which argues from true and probable principles; this interpretation is given to

[45] "Nolo autem intelligere substantiam superiorem nisi sphaeram circumvolubilem et mobilem motu naturali deservientem constitutioni huius mundi secundum potentiam dei et sapientiam et voluntatem eius." *Ibid.*, p. 21, lines 7–10.
[46] L. Baur, *op. cit.*, p. 314; see the detailed study of the text, pp. 164–314.
[47] *Ibid.*, p. 314.
[48] The classification of poetry and rhetoric under logic or dialectics in the wide sense is derived from Alfarabi's *De scientiis*, cap. 2, ed. Alonso, pp. 72, 78–79; ed. Palencia, pp. 137, 142.

Boethius's *rationabiliter.*[49] He also adds that physics should be studied after logic, because logic teaches the art of composing the dialectical syllogism, which is used in physics.[50] The mathematical sciences ought to be studied after this, because after the study of forms in matter should come the study of forms abstracted from matter in order to prepare the mind for those pure forms existing separate from matter.[51] Following Avicenna, Gundissalinus identifies the mathematical sciences with the abstractive knowledge proper to the intellect and adds that this is acquired by the "demonstrative syllogism." Mathematics, however, is a wide term embracing seven particular arts: arithmetic, music, geometry, optics, astrology, statics (*de ponderibus*), and engineering (*de ingeniis*). Gundissalinus recognized, as did all the Arabian philosophers, a theoretical and a practical aspect to these mathematical sciences. Among the theoretical disciplines priority, both ontological and pedagogical, is given to arithmetic, for number is prior to all other considerations.[52] After arithmetic comes music, which is the science of number related to harmony.[53] But since magnitude necessarily follows upon multitude, sciences of continuous quantity should next be studied.[54] The order of study envisaged by Gundissalinus follows a descending order of concreteness: geometry, optics, astronomy (*astrologia*), statics, and engineering. The last science to be studied in the curriculum is the highest of all, the divine science called theology or metaphysics. This supreme wisdom is concerned with realities which are "separate from matter and motion" both in fact and in our understanding of them, namely, being, separate substances, and God. This science also employs the "demonstrative syllogism,"[55] and its principal function is "to prove the principles of all the other sciences."[56] In order to acquire this science astronomy is indispensable, and this presupposes arithmetic and geometry; "but music, the other particular disciplines of mathematics, as well as ethics

[49] "Instrumentum autem huius artis est sillogismus dialecticus, qui constat ex veris et probabilibus. Unde Boecius: in naturalibus racionabiliter versari oportet." *De div. phil.,* ed. Baur, p. 27, lines 9–11.

[50] *Ibid.,* lines 18–21.

[51] "Post naturalem autem legenda est quia, qui per naturalem scienciam formam simul cum materia iam considerat, profecto quantum ad profectum sciencie pertinet dignum est, ut formam sine materia considerare discat, quatenus assuefactus in hiis ad speculandas formas, que nullius materie sunt, proficiendo perveniat." *Ibid.,* p. 35, lines 3–8.

[52] *Ibid.,* p. 94.

[53] *Ibid.,* p. 102.

[54] *Ibid.,* p. 111.

[55] *Ibid.,* p. 38.

[56] *Ibid.,* p. 92, line 12.

and political science are useful, although not necessary, for the acquisition of wisdom."[57]

Clearly Gundissalinus conceived the Boethian classification of the speculative sciences as a carefully ordered hierarchy of realities descending from God through mathematical being to various sensible expressions. The acquisition of philosophy follows the reverse order: ascending from physics, about which we can have only probable knowledge, through mathematics to supreme wisdom. Far from being fundamentally Aristotelian, this conception is clearly neo-Platonic in foundation. It is the well-known doctrine of emanation adapted to the Boethian classification of the sciences.

The use of Arabian sources to explain the new Aristotelian books can be seen throughout the thirteenth century, particularly at Oxford.

i. Oxford Platonism

Apart from possible early influences from the school of Chartres, the one who most influenced Oxford Platonism in the thirteenth century was the secular master Robert Grosseteste (ca. 1168–1253), first teacher of the Oxford Franciscans and first chancellor of the university. Grosseteste's "metaphysics of light" has been sufficiently discussed by L. Baur,[58] P. Duhem,[59] C. K. McKeon,[60] and A. C. Crombie[61] so as not to need further elaboration here. Briefly, Grosseteste conceived all creatures, material and spiritual, to be composed of common matter and the first form of "light." This universal hylemorphic composition of creatures has been traced to the Jewish philosopher Ibn Gebirol, but Grosseteste clearly believed this to be the doctrine of the Stagirite, as can be seen from his gloss, or marginal notes, on the first book of the *Physics*.[62] The first general form of light which actuates the common matter of both material and immaterial substances is itself an indivisible point of light. The form, however, of material substances diffuses itself in an infinite number of ways into three directions, thus generating the first *forma corporeitatis*.[63] Subsequent

---

[57] *Ibid.*, p. 39, lines 10–14.

[58] *Die Philosophie des Robert Grosseteste, Beiträge z. Gesch. d. Phil. d. MA.*, Bd. XVIII, H. 4–6 (Münster, 1917), esp. pp. 76–93.

[59] *Le Système du Monde*, V, 356–74.

[60] *A Study of the 'Summa philosophiae' of the Pseudo-Grosseteste* (New York, 1948), pp. 156–66.

[61] *Robert Grosseteste and the Origins of Experimental Science* (Oxford, 1953), pp. 128–34.

[62] MS Oxford, Bodley, Digby 220, fol. 84r–88r. See the passages and discussion by R. C. Dales, "Robert Grosseteste's Commentarius in octo libros Physicorum Aristotelis," *Medievalia et Humanistica* 11 (1957), 15–21.

[63] Grosseteste, *De luce*, ed. L. Baur, *Die philosophischen Werke, Beiträge z. Gesch. d. Phil. d. MA.*, Bd. IX (Münster, 1912), pp. 51–9

self-multiplication of this luminous form, which accounts for dimensionality, begets the variety of material things in the universe. But the rays of light which are produced in every such self-multiplication follow determined laws of mathematical proportionality and are derived from God, the *lux prima*.[64] Hence for Grosseteste the key to understanding physical nature lies in geometrical optics.[65] But geometrical optics itself, for Grosseteste, is only a concrete example of that higher mathematical proportionality which could explain the generation of immaterial light rays from the first light.

In his remarkable commentary on the *Posterior Analytics*, which was probably written before 1210,[66] Grosseteste gave much consideration to the application of mathematics to physical phenomena, particularly in those sciences "subalternated" to geometry, namely, optics and astronomy. Exemplifying Aristotle's discussion of optics (I, text. 42), Grosseteste compares a simple geometric proof of the equality of two triangles (Theorem I of Euclid's *Catoptrica*) and a dependent optical conclusion that "every two angles, of which the ray incident with the mirror makes one and the reflected ray the other, are two equal radiant angles."[67] The syllogism of the higher science is properly geometrical, demonstrating *propter quid* the equality of the two geometrical triangles. The syllogism, however, of the lower science unites the subject and predicate of optics by means of a middle term taken from geometry. This syllogism of the lower science, Grosseteste observes, is different from that of the higher science and is properly called *quia*, "for the cause of the equality of the two angles made on a mirror . . . is not the middle term taken from geometry but the nature of the radiant energy generating itself according to rectilinear progress."[68] This is explained later in the commentary. Paraphrasing Aristotle's distinction of *quia* and *propter quid* knowledge according to different sciences (I, c. 12, text. 67), Grosseteste concludes that in subalternated sciences, the superior science (*subalternans*) provides the reason (*propter quid*) for that predicate of which the inferior science (*subalternata*)

[64] Grosseteste, *Commentaria in lib. Post. Arist.*, Lib. I, c. 7 (ed. Venetiis, 1552), fol. 8rb–va; *De luce, loc. cit.; De veritate*, ed. Baur, p. 137.

[65] See A. C. Crombie, *Robert Grosseteste*, p. 131; L. Baur, *Die Philosophie des Robert Grosseteste*, pp. 93–109.

[66] D. A. Callus, "The Oxford Career of Robert Grosseteste," *Oxoniensia* 10 (1945), 45, and "Robert Grosseteste as Scholar," in *Robert Grosseteste* (Oxford, 1955), pp. 12, 251.

[67] Grosseteste, *Comm. in lib. Post. Arist.*, Lib. I, c. 8, *ed. cit.*, fol. 9rb.

[68] "Causa namque equalitatis duorum angulorum . . . non est medium sumptum ex geometria, sed eius causa est natura radiositatis sese generantis. . . ." *Comm. in Post.* I, 8, *ed. cit.*, fol. 9va. A. C. Crombie translates *namque* as "yet" (*op. cit.*, p. 95); this alters considerably the sense of the passage (cf. *ibid.*, p. 96).

provides the fact (*quia*). "But it must be noted that a lower science always has an added condition through which the subject and predicates of the higher science are appropriated to itself, and they are in the conclusion of the subalternated science like two natures, namely, the nature which it received from the higher and the additional nature proper to itself; and so the higher science says nothing about the causes of this additional nature; sometimes the lower science indicates its causes [*quia*] and sometimes not. The higher science, however, does declare the causes of that nature which the lower science took from the higher."[69]

The distinction perceived by Grosseteste in the composite nature of the subject of all such subalternate sciences as astronomy, optics, harmonics, and the like was acknowledged by all later schoolmen. But not all the schoolmen agreed with Grosseteste's conclusion. For Grosseteste, explanations derived from the nature of the subject of subordinated sciences, that is, those derived from that part of the subject which is proper to it, cannot be explanations *propter quid*. Not even his theory of the nature of light provided him with a *propter quid* explanation in optics. This ability is accorded only to mathematics. Grosseteste, however, went further and extended the importance of mathematics to the whole of natural philosophy. "It is impossible," he says, "to know natural philosophy without considering the geometry of lines, angles, and figures."[70] "All causes of natural effects have to be expressed by means of lines, angles, and figures, for otherwise it is impossible to have *propter quid* knowledge concerning them."[71] In *De natura locorum* Grosseteste shows how the principles of geometry can be used to explain not only the general aspects of nature but also all particular natural effects.[72] Explanations offered by natural philosophy, Grosseteste had declared in his commentary on the *Posterior Analytics*, are "probable rather than strictly scientific. . . . Only in

---

[69] Commenting on Aristotle's statement that in subalternate sciences the higher science knows *propter quid* and the lower science knows *quia* (text. 67: "Hic enim ipsum quia, sensibilium est; propter quid autem, mathematicorum") Grosseteste observes: "Sciendum autem quod scientia inferior semper addit conditionem per quam appropriat sibi subiectum et passiones superioris scientiae, et sunt in conclusione scientiae subalternatae sicut naturae duae, natura scilicet quam accipit a superiori, et natura propria quam superaddit proprii; itaque superadiecti causas non dicit scientia superior, et quandoque dicit eas causas scientia inferior et quandoque non. Illius vero quod accipit scientia inferior a superiori, causas dicit scientia superior." *Comm. in lib. Post.* I, 12, fol. 15vb. Also *Glossa in lib. Phys.* II, MS Oxford, Digby 220, fol. 88v, cited in part by R. C. Dales, *loc. cit.*, 19–20.

[70] *De lineis, angulis et figuris*, ed. L. Baur, pp. 59–60.

[71] *Ibid.*, p. 60.

[72] See *De natura locorum*, ed. L. Baur, pp. 65–66.

mathematics is there science and demonstration in the most proper sense."[73] Here one may detect the Platonic influence of Alfarabi.

The influence of Arabic neo-Platonism can be seen in greater detail in the *De ortu scientiarum* of Robert Kilwardby. This is a monumental treatise on the nature, division, and relation of the speculative and practical sciences, composed not earlier than 1246–47, probably about 1250, while Kilwardby was a Dominican student of theology at Oxford.[74]

Kilwardby's important treatise contains 67 chapters.[75] After a brief discussion of the nature and division of scientific knowledge in general (chaps. 1–4), he discusses the speculative sciences (chaps. 5–33): natural science, the four mathematical sciences, and metaphysics. Under the practical sciences he considers the three moral sciences, the seven mechanical arts, and the three *sciencie sermocinales*, namely, grammar, logic, and rhetoric. In chapter 25 Kilwardby raises four questions, the responses to which clearly show his view of the classification and study of the sciences. First, he asks, how can abstracted knowledge be true? Second, why is the term "abstraction" applied especially to the mathematical sciences? Third, what is the difference and the order of abstraction in the three speculative sciences? Fourth, what is the difference and the order of abstraction in the four mathematical sciences?

Answering the first question, Kilwardby says that the veracity of abstractions is based on the priority and posteriority of different forms in nature. What is prior in nature can be conceived by the intellect without that which is posterior. There is no error in such conceptions, for when the intellect conceives the prior without the latter, it does not affirm that the prior actually exists in nature without the latter addition.[76] In nature one finds this priority of forms between substance and accident, number and magnitude, quantity and

[73] "Versatur in his rationabiliter magis et probabiliter quam scientifice. . . . In solis enim mathematicis est scientia et demonstratio maxime et principaliter dicta." *Comm. in lib. Post.* I, 11, fol. 13ra.

[74] D. A. Callus, "The 'Tabulae super Originalia Patrum' of Robert Kilwardby, O.P.," in *Studia Mediaevalia* in honorem R. J. Martin, O.P. (Bruges, 1948), pp. 247–49.

[75] I am indebted to Father Bernard Delany, O.P., for allowing me to use his text of Kilwardby's *De ortu scientiarum*, prepared from four MSS. Certain obvious corrections have been made, however, without noting the variants, and references given below are to Merton College MS 261, fol. 19r–66r.

[76] "Quod enim est prius per naturam potest ab intellectu concipi per se sine posteriori. Quando ergo illud prius ab intellectu concipitur cum suis proprietatibus preter posterius et eius proprietates, non est in hoc conceptu nec in hac consideracione falsitas, quia intellectus non dicit quod illud prius est in re per se sine omni posteriori ei concreto. . . ." *Ibid.*, cap. 25 ad 1, *MS cit.*, fol. 31rb.

sensible qualities; it is also found between every form *absolute con-siderata* and any form here and now existing in *materia signata*.[77]

In his answer to the second question Kilwardby admits that mathematics is more abstract than natural science, and that metaphysics is more abstract than mathematics.[78] However, it is mathematics which most deserves the designation of being abstract, "because everything which the mathematician considers is *per abstractionem*." Almost all the objects considered in mathematics are concretely realized in sensible reality. Kilwardby insisted on the word "almost," because, regardless of what philosophers may think, one can legitimately speak of the "number" of angels, although this is not the concern of the mathematician.[79] Since, on the other hand, metaphysics discusses not only material substances in as much as they are substances but also substances which are really separated from matter, metaphysics is said to be *de separatis* rather than *de abstractis*.[80]

In his reply to the third question Kilwardby presents a clear and direct picture of three ascending "grades of abstraction." The first and lowest grade of abstraction is from concrete matter (*a sensibili signato*), and this belongs to the physicist. The second and higher grade abstracts from qualitative motion and changeable matter, and this belongs to the mathematician. Kilwardby excludes qualitative motion in this grade of abstraction but retains change of place in order to account for astronomy and the other mathematical sciences which deal with locomotion. The third and last grade abstracts from all accidents and considers substance in all its purity, and this belongs to the metaphysician.[81] Thus abstraction is a process of removing men-

---

[77] "Eodem modo se habent ad inuicem substancia et accidens, similiter numerus et magnitudo, ut patet, et quantitas ad qualitates actiuas et passiuas, et omnino forma absolute considerata preter materiam signatam ad formam in materia signata hic et nunc, que forte eadem est per essenciam solo esse differens." *Ibid.*, fol. 31va.

[78] Also cap. 24 ad 1, fol. 29rb.

[79] Cap. 25, fol. 32ra; also cap. 24 ad 1, fol. 29rb.

[80] "Ad secundum dicendum quod uerum est quod phisica et omnis sciencia abstrahit, et metaphisica plus quam mathematica. Et tamen mathematica pocius dicitur esse de abstractis quam phisica, quia maioris abstraccionis est quam illa, sicut dicit Aristoteles in 2° *Phisicorum* quod minus abstrahunt phisica mathematica. Item pociusquam metaphisica: quia omnia que mathematica considerat per abstraccionem considerat, quia aut omnino omnia aut fere sunt concreta cum rebus phisicis. Et dixi fere propter numerum qui in spiritibus separatis est, quicquid super hoc sentirent philosophi. Uerumtamen de numeris illorum non est cura arismetico secundum quod talis est. Set metaphisica non solum considerat substanciam que est in rebus phisicis abstrahendo ipsam ut in se consideret secundum quod substancia est, set substancias omnino separatus a motu et a materia secundum esse; et quia illa est potissima pars metaphisice que huiusmodi substancias considerat, ideo magis dicitur esse de separatis quam de abstractis." Cap. 25 ad 2, fol. 31va–b.

[81] "Ad tercium dicendum quod omnis sciencia abstrahit, et maxime speculatiua. Et

tally the succession of natural forms which Kilwardby believed necessary for the constitution of every creature. To clarify his position Kilwardby further notes that whatever there is of substance in the metaphysician's consideration is also in mathematics and physics, and whatever quantity there is in the mathematician's consideration is also in physics.[82]

According to Kilwardby natural science considers *materia transmutabilis* and motion, and for this a knowledge of all four causes is necessary. Mathematics considers quantity which is "antecedent to natural forms" and qualities, and for this consideration efficient and final cause are not needed.[83] Finally metaphysics considers the unity and plurality of pure substance. Therefore Kilwardby said that it also belongs to the metaphysician to explain the cause of plurality in mathematics.[84] It was because of Kilwardby's inability to distinguish between the meaning of "number" in mathematics and its meaning in metaphysics that he found difficulty in expressing the difference between mathematics and metaphysics.[85] To the extent that all sciences use number and proportionality, they are subordinated to arithmetic, which is "quasi mater aliarum [scientiarum]."[86] But it is the task of metaphysics to explain the source of multiplicity in mathematical being, for when mathematical being is divested of quantity there is nothing left but substance in undisguised plurality. Through consideration of this plurality the metaphysician perceives God, "substancia eterna que est causa omnis substancie et accidentis in triplice genere cause."[87]

In his response to the fourth question Kilwardby summarized his view of the four mathematical sciences. The lowest of all the mathematical sciences is astronomy, for it considers celestial motion through

---

primus et minimus gradus abstraccionis est a sensibili signato, et iste competit phisico. Secundus et ulterior gradus est omnino a motu alteratiuo et materia transmutabili, non tamen omnino a motu et omnino a materia, et iste competit mathematico. Tercius et ultimus est omnino ab accidente, ut consideretur substancia in sua puritate, et iste competit metaphisico. Tertio, tolle dimensiones quantitatiuas et restat nuda substancia, et hec est ultima abstraccio et pertinet ad metaphisicum." Cap. 25 ad 3, fol. 31vb; see also cap. 24 ad 1, fol. 29ra.

[82] *Ibid.*, fol. 31vb–32ra; also cap. 24 ad 1.

[83] Cap. 14 ad 2, fol. 24v.

[84] "Tolle igitur has differencias que pertinent ad naturalem et dimitte eas ei, et superest corpus scil. substancia corporea, que quia substancia est composita unitatem habet, que multiplicata numerum facit; et hoc uidetur per hoc quod unitas et numerus uniuoce sunt in spiritibus, et ideo unicam causam habent utrimque." Cap. 24 ad 1, fol. 29rb; also cap. 14 ad 2, fol. 24vb.

[85] This is apparent throughout chapters 29 to 31, fol. 33vb–38ra.

[86] Cap. 22, fol. 28vb; see whole of cap. 22.

[87] Cap. 26, fol. 32rb–va.

the principles of geometry. Hence astronomy is prior to and more abstract than natural science.[88] Since discrete quantity is simpler and prior to extension, all the sciences which deal with number are prior to geometry. Among these the lowest is the science of harmony, by which Kilwardby meant not the audible harmony of music but the pure harmony of numerical proportion.[89] The highest and most abstract of all the mathematical sciences is arithmetic, or algebra, "quia ipsa ut sic, nulla aliarum indiget."[90]

Thus for Kilwardby the three stages of abstraction together with the subdivision of mathematical abstraction correspond to real forms which are prior and posterior in nature. Clearly Kilwardby never held the pure Platonic doctrine of universal natures, figures, and numbers existing apart from material things or apart from the mind of God. However, the reality of these forms in created substances and the reality of the divine exemplars are fundamental to Kilwardby's whole philosophical doctrine. The acceptance of universal hylemorphism and divine exemplarism was by no means confined to Kilwardby, but he did express perhaps more clearly than others the classification of the speculative sciences according to three ascending "grades of abstraction." Underlying his discussion of the speculative sciences is the conviction that the science of numerical proportions is the key to understanding all the other sciences, even metaphysics, because numerical proportions are, as it were, the intrinsic principle of created multiplicity. This typically neo-Platonic conviction was undoubtedly due rather to the influence of Arabic sources than to any predilection for mathematics on the part of Kilwardby. A true predilection for mathematics, however, is conspicuous in the writings of Roger Bacon, a junior contemporary of Kilwardby.

Roger Bacon (d. 1292), it would seem, became a master in arts at Paris by about 1237 and continued to lecture there until about 1247.[91] We do not know under whom Bacon studied at Paris, but it is probable that he had Kilwardby for a master, at least at some period of his studies. Bacon tells us that he heard many masters and that he taught arts at Paris for many years: "audivi diligenter plures, et legi plus quam alius."[92] Unfortunately many of his writings and lecture notes

[88]Cap. 16 ad 1, fol. 25v.
[89]"Deinde armonica adhuc naturaliter precedere uidetur geometriam, quia numerus armonicus de quo considerat prior uidetur esse magnitudine, et est secundum ueritatem." Cap. 24 ad 4, fol. 32ra. In chapter 18 Kilwardby divides music or harmony into "mundannam, humanam et instrumentalem" (fol. 27rb).
[90]Cap. 19, fol. 27va.
[91]A. B. Emden, *Biog. Reg.*, I, p. 88a.
[92]*Compendium studii phil.*, c. 8, ed. Brewer, p. 468.

from this period have not been identified, among them his commentary on the *Metaphysics*.[93] The three well-known *Opera* were all written after 1265, by which date Bacon was already a dissatisfied Franciscan friar living in Oxford. Hence we do not know in detail what Bacon taught concerning the classification of the sciences. However, his repeated insistence that "without mathematics no science can be had"[94] clearly shows that for Bacon the principles of natural science are to be found in mathematics.

Bacon, like Kilwardby, conceived the three speculative sciences (natural science, mathematics, and metaphysics) as corresponding to a real hierarchy of forms in nature. But unlike Kilwardby, he did not emphasize the supreme role of metaphysics in human knowledge. Rather, he followed Grosseteste in according mathematics the power of opening all doors. This view is clearly implied in the *Opus maius* where Bacon states, "Without mathematics neither what is antecedent nor what is consequent to it can be known."[95] The natural sciences are antecedent to mathematics in the hierarchy of knowledge, and metaphysics is consequent. Clarifying the function of the mathematical sciences, Bacon continues, "They perfect and regulate that which precedes and dispose and prepare the way for that which succeeds." Mathematics perfects natural sciences by giving a true explanation of natural phenomena and regulates them by determining the utility and validity of experimentation in each branch of natural science. Because mathematics alone could perfect and regulate the natural sciences, Roger Bacon was convinced that "it is impossible to know the things of this world [*huius mundi*] unless one knows mathematics."[96] In confirmation of this view, Bacon, like Grosseteste and Kilwardby before him, could point to the role of mathematics in astronomy and optics.[97]

Perhaps the most detailed and erudite elaboration of the "metaphysics of light" in the various sciences is to be found in the

---

[93] In the *Communia mathematica* Roger Bacon frequently refers to his own commentary on the *Metaphysics*, e.g.: "et hoc manifesti in *Metaphysica* mea"; "hec in metaphysicis ostendi certitudinaliter"; "declaravi quidem in Metaphysica, quod mathematica dicitur dupliciter" (*Op. Hac. Ined.*, XVI, p. 2). This work, as far as I know, has not yet been identified. Cf. *Roger Bacon, Commemoration Essays*, ed. A. G. Little (Oxford, 1914), pp. 377, 406–7, and P. Glorieux, *Répertoire*, II, 56–76.
[94] *Opus tertium*, ed. Brewer, pp. 35, 64, 57 and in many other passages.
[95] *Opus maius* IV, 1, ed. Bridges, I, 97.
[96] *Opus maius* IV, 2, ed. Bridges, I, 109.
[97] Concerning the influence of Grosseteste on Bacon's theory of science see L. Baur, "Der Einfluss des Robert Grosseteste auf die wissenschaftliche Richtung des Roger Bacon," in *Roger Bacon*, ed. A. G. Little, pp. 33–54; P. Duhem, *Le Système*, III, 411–13; A. C. Crombie, *Robert Grosseteste*, pp. 139–62.

anonymous *Summa philosophiae*, which before the studies of L. Baur was generally ascribed to Grosseteste. The treatise was undoubtedly written, probably around 1263 or 1264, by an Englishman who was strongly adverse to the innovations which had been produced by Albertus Magnus on the Continent. The undeniable influence of Roger Bacon upon this treatise led P. Duhem to believe that the author of the *Summa philosophiae* was a disciple of Bacon.[98] Whoever the author may have been, he elaborately explains the procession of translucent light from its primordial source through the hierarchy of forms generated by self-multiplication down to the specific composition of natures in the visible world. Problems of astronomy, psychology, biology, and alchemy are discussed with the aid of elementary geometry and some principles of optics. Although the author was little concerned with preserving the distinction of sciences, either philosophical or theological, the approach to all these problems is patently neo-Platonic, pseudo-mathematical, and at times mystical.

The depreciation of purely natural science, the appeal to mathematics for an explanation of natural phenomena, and the approach to metaphysics through mathematics—all of which express one aspect of the Platonic view of scientific knowledge—was by no means confined to Oxford or to masters associated with Oxford. Nor were these authors consciously Platonic in the sense that they rejected the Aristotelian books recently introduced into the university curriculum of arts. It is well known that the new Aristotelian books were eagerly expounded at Oxford,[99] Paris,[100] and Toulouse[101] in the first half of the thirteenth century, and that by the middle of the century the "three philosophies" were a recognized part of the curriculum in arts. However, it would be a mistake to think that these early masters understood fully the Aristotelian texts they expounded in the schools. Unconsciously and inevitably these masters expounded the text in the light of the traditional, living Platonism, derived from St. Augustine and confirmed by twelfth-century translations of Arabian philosophers. Historians who presume that all masters who expounded the text of Aristotle were necessarily Aristotelian fail to consider the ob-

---

[98] Duhem, *Le Système*, III, 461ff.; this suggestion was made earlier by Baur, p. 137*. However, it is doubtful whether one who was never a master in theology could be called "in theologia perfectissimus," even if one were to grant that Bacon had been "vitaque et religione sanctissimus." Tr. XV, cap. 31, ed. Baur, p. 589, lines 15–16.

[99] See D. A. Callus, "Introduction of Aristotelian Learning to Oxford," *Proc. Brit. Acad.* 29 (1943), 229ff.

[100] See M. Grabmann, *I divieti ecclesiastici di Aristotele sotto Innocenzo III e Gregorio IX*, Miscel. Hist. Pont., V (Rome, 1941).

[101] *Chart. Univ. P.*, I, 131 n. 72.

scurity of Aristotle's text and the normal laws of human psychology. Each commentary on Aristotle must be considered on its own merits and in the light of its sources. Perhaps it would not be extravagant to say that at least a whole generation of masters and the aid of Averroes were required to bring out the Aristotelianism of the Aristotelian books.

ii. A New Aristotelianism at Paris

The real innovation in Western philosophical thought came from the pen of Albertus Magnus,[102] who, although he was himself a theologian, introduced an Aristotelianism which appeared strange to many of his contemporaries. The theological implications of Albert's Aristotelianism became disturbingly clear in the writings of his disciple, St. Thomas Aquinas. These disturbing elements together with the exaggerated Aristotelianism of Siger of Brabant and his followers eventually evoked episcopal censure at Paris and Oxford, as is well known to all. This aspect of the new Aristotelianism, however, is of no concern to us here. We are interested only in their view of scientific knowledge in the classification of the sciences.

In the new Aristotelianism of Albertus Magnus and Thomas Aquinas what place did mathematics occupy in the classification of the sciences? What kind of assistance could mathematics give to the solution of physical problems? What kind of scientific "explanation" did they think mathematics could offer for natural phenomena? The view of Albertus Magnus and Aquinas can be said to be essentially that of Aristotle, but greatly refined and more precise, particularly with regard to the *scientiae mediae*. Scientific knowledge had developed considerably since the days of Aristotle: Euclid had systematized geometry, Archimedes had discovered important laws in hydrostatics, Ptolemy had devised a highly satisfactory system of astronomy and had contributed greatly to the development of optics among the Arabs. These developments encouraged and apparently confirmed the Platonic view of scientific knowledge in the twelfth and thirteenth centuries. The new Aristotelianism of Albert and Aquinas, however, took issue with the Platonic view of mathematics as affording the only scientific explanation of natural phenomena.

At the very beginning of his paraphrase of the *Metaphysics*, probably composed between 1265 and 1270, Albertus Magnus directed his

---

[102] This interpretation of Albert's position in medieval thought was originally proposed in my "Albertus Magnus and the Oxford Platonists," *Proc. Am. Cath. Phil. Assoc.* 33 (1958), 124–39, and in *The Development of Physical Theory in the Middle Ages,* Newman Phil. of Sc. Series, 4 (London, 1959).

attack on "the error of Plato, who said that natural things are founded on mathematical, and mathematical being founded on divine, just as the third cause is dependent on the second, and the second on the first; and so [Plato] said that the principles of natural being are mathematical, which is completely false."[103] The basis of this error, Albert explains, is that Plato had seen a certain ascending order from natural bodies to mathematical to divine being, but he had misunderstood the explanation of this order. Perceiving that all changeable beings are continuous, and that all continuous beings are simple, Plato had thought that the principles of natural science are mathematical, and that the principles of mathematics are metaphysical, or divine. "And this is the error which we have rejected in the Books of the *Physics*, and which we shall again reject in the following Books of this science [of metaphysics]."[104] Actually in his commentary on the *Physics* Albert rejected this Platonic error only in passing, discussing it infrequently and very briefly. But in the *Metaphysics* it is a central theme running throughout the whole of his paraphrase. Albert, it would seem, had in mind not only the historical Plato, but also the *amici Platonis*, who were Albert's own contemporaries.

As Albert understands the information given by Aristotle (*Metaph.* I, 6), Plato postulated immutable ideas of natural species separated from the ever-changing reflections seen in the world of sense. These exemplars were to account for the stability of natural species, which belong to the study of natural philosophy.[105] But antecedent to the subsistent ideas are their formal generative principles, namely abstract figure and its generative number (*numerus principians entia*).[106] Just as antecedent to every physical body there is abstract tridimensionality, so antecedent to every figure there is an abstract generative number. These subsisting figures and numbers are the proper subject of geometry and arithmetic respectively.[107] The principle of all number, however, is unity, which is the eternally subsistent God from Whom all being flows; hence for Plato this separated unity, namely, God, is the proper subject of metaphysics, the divine science.[108] Thus

[103] "Cavendus est autem hic error Platonis, qui dixit naturalia fundari in mathematicis, et mathematica in divinis, sicut causa tertia fundatur in secunda, et secunda in prima, et ideo dixit esse principia naturalium mathematica, quod omnino falsum est." *Lib. I Metaph.*, tr. I, c. 1, ed. Borgnet, VI, p. 2b.

[104] "Et hoc est error quem in libris physicis reprobavimus, et iterum in consequentibus huius scientiae reprobabimus eundem." *Ibid.*

[105] *Lib. I Metaph.*, tr. V, cc. 5–15; *Lib. VII Metaph.*, tr. II, cc. 1–9.

[106] *Lib. I Metaph.*, tr. IV, c. 2, ed. cit., p. 63b; see also *Lib. I*, tr. V, c. 10, pp. 102b–103a; *Lib. III*, tr. II, c. 11, pp. 162a–164b; *Lib. VII*, tr. III, c. 10, pp. 463a–464b.

[107] *Lib. I. Metaph.*, tr. I, c. 1, p. 3b.

[108] *Ibid.*, tr. I, c. 2, pp. 4b–5b.

for Plato and the Platonists there are three ascending grades of separated being, and there are three corresponding grades of scientific knowledge. And just as the lower grade of being depends upon the higher for its very existence, so the lower grade of scientific knowledge depends upon the higher for its very intelligibility.

The *error Platonis,* as seen by Albertus Magnus, is not a simple error; it is a complex view of scientific knowledge and of reality. Every element of that complex view, however, is vigorously rejected by Albertus Magnus. In fact, in his commentary on the *Metaphysics* Albert is more vehement in his repeated rejection of the *error Platonis* than he is in his explicit rejection of the Averroist doctrine of one intellect for all mankind.

The view of Albertus Magnus concerning scientific knowledge, a view which was thoroughly Aristotelian, may be stated briefly under the following five points:

(1) The proper principles of natural science are not mathematical, "for dimensions are not principles of bodies according to any *esse*; rather they are consequent upon the fact that they are concrete physical bodies having proper principles like matter and form, and that the form giving existence is in this matter."[109] Physical dimensions are consequent upon the natural constitution of bodies; abstract, or mathematical, dimensions are consequent upon a mental abstraction. "That a natural body should be constituted by the dimensions of quantity, and that mathematical measures should be the principles of physics, are both absurd for all who know anything about the astuteness of the Peripatetics."[110] For Albertus Magnus natural science, including its numerous branches, is an autonomous science having its own principles of research, its own *principia propria illuminantia.*[111]

(2) The object of the mathematical sciences is not an antecedent

---

[109]"Dimensiones enim non sunt principia corporum secundum esse aliquod sed potius consequentia esse eius quod est corpus, et sua principia secundum esse ratum quod habet sicut forma et materia et illius materiae subiectae inesse quod dat forma." *Lib. I Metaph.,* tr. I, c. 1, pp. 2b–3a.

[110]"et secundum hoc corpus naturale constitueretur dimensionibus quantitatum, et mathematica secundum esse accepta erunt principia physicorum, quae ambo sunt absurda apud omnes qui aliquid noverunt de peritia Peripateticorum." *Ibid.,* tr. IV, c. 8, p. 75a. "Mathematica ergo principia naturalis corporis esse non possunt; et quia multa talia in *prima philosophia* a nobis contra Stoicos dicta sunt, haec quantum ad dictam opinionem dicta sufficiant." *Lib. I de causis et processu universitatis,* tr. I, c. 4, ed. Borgnet, X, p. 369a.

[111]*Lib. I Post. Anal.,* tr. V, c. 6, ed. Borgnet, II, p. 140a–b; *Lib. I Phys.,* tr. I, c. 5, ed. Borgnet, III, pp. 10b–11b.

form, but "abstracted measures and number."[112] Not only is physical quantity subsequent to physical natures, but mathematical quantity is further subsequent to physical quantity and requires the mental act of "abstracting" one special aspect of bodies, while disregarding the natural constitution of bodies, their change, proper activities, and causes. Figures and numbers, therefore, can be studied mathematically only inasmuch as they are "abstracted from sensible matter and motion," as Boethius had declared.

(3) The subject of *scientiae mediae,* such as optics and mechanics, has a twofold condition: one mathematical, the other physical.[113] To the extent that the lower science is subalternated to mathematics, the higher science of mathematics can give *propter quid* explanations of strictly quantitative properties. But there are other properties which are caused by the particular physical subject considered, and for these the lower science itself can give the proper explanation. "Si autem passiones aliquae sunt, quae causantur ab hoc vel illo secundum quod hoc vel illud, in illis non dicit propter quid scientia superior, sed inferior."[114] Albert thus accepts Grosseteste's distinction of the two aspects in such sciences, but he insists that the physical properties of the subject can be explained by the subalternated science. "It is not under this aspect, if one considers it carefully, that perspective is subalternate to geometry; moreover a science is supposed to consider the properties of its own subject."[115]

(4) The subject of metaphysics is not God. "In accordance with all the Peripatetics speaking the truth," Albert says, "being is the subject insofar as it is being, and not insofar as it is this kind of being."[116] This common notion of being as such is reached once the mind realizes that there exists something which is not physical.[117] Following Aristotle, Albert insists that if there were no immaterial substance existing in reality, natural science would necessarily be the supreme wisdom.[118]

---

[112] *Lib. XII Metaph.,* tr. I, c. 3, *ed. cit.,* pp. 696b–697a.

[113] *Lib. I Post. Anal.,* tr. III, c. 7, *ed. cit.,* p. 85b.

[114] *Ibid.,* pp. 85b–86a.

[115] *Ibid.,* p. 86a.

[116] *Lib. I Metaph.,* tr. I, c. 2, pp. 4b–5b. "Ideo cum omnibus Peripateticis vera dicentibus dicendum videtur, quod ens est subiectum inquantum ens est, et ea quae sequuntur ens inquantum est ens (et non inquantum hoc ens) sunt passiones eius, sicut est causa tantum substantiva et accidens, separatum et non separatum, potentia et actus, et huiusmodi." *Ibid.,* p. 5b.

[117] *Lib. IV Metaph.,* tr. I, c. 3, pp. 206a–207a; tr. I, c. 6, pp. 211b–212a.

[118] "Si enim non est aliqua substantia diversa existens a physicis . . . tunc oporteret quod physica esset scientia prima et universalis." *Lib. VI Metaph.,* tr. I, c. 3, p. 387a–b.

The proper subject of metaphysics, however, is not this separated, immaterial substance, nor is it God, for then there would be nothing to look for in metaphysics. *Deus autem et divina separata quaeruntur in ista scientia.*[119]

(5) Metaphysics is the last science to be studied, and hence it presupposes all the other sciences and arts. The particular sciences and arts, however, are in no way rendered superfluous by metaphysics. The transcendental and universal truths of metaphysics cannot explain things in their *propria natura*; this explanation can be had only in the particular sciences and arts, which are never rendered superfluous.[120] Albert considered the natural order of learning to be (1) logic, (2) mathematics, (3) natural science, (4) moral philosophy (a practical science), and finally (5) metaphysics.[121] Thus for Albertus Magnus each science and art is autonomous in its own sphere of inquiry, and natural science has no need of mathematics in order to solve its own problems.

From this summary it is clear that although Albertus Magnus utilized the traditional tripartite classification of the speculative sciences,[122] his own understanding of the division was vastly different from that of Alfarabi, Gundissalinus, Grosseteste, Kilwardby, Bacon, and pseudo-Grosseteste. For Albert the traditional division preserved

[119]*Lib. I Metaph.*, tr. I, c. 2, p. 5b. See also *Lib. I Phys.*, tr. III, c. 18, *ed. cit.*, p. 91b, where Albert defends this doctrine of Avicenna against the objection of Averroes: "nescio quare reprehendit Averroes, cum ipsum sit necessarium quod dicit Avicenna. Scimus enim quoniam ens est subiectum primae philosophiae, et divisiones et passiones entis esse, quae in prima philosophia tractantur, scil. per se et per accidens, et per potentiam et actum, et unum et multa, et separatum et non separatum. Et cum separatum sit differentia et passio entis, non potest esse subiectum. Et cum dicitur quod metaphysicus est de separatis, non intelligitur hoc modo de separatis sicut intelligentiae sunt separatae, sed intelligitur de his quae separata sunt per diffinitionem et esse."
[120]"Nec aliae scientiae superfluunt eo quod causae omnium et principia stabiliuntur in ista, quia primo a transcendentibus scitis, non propter hoc scitur scientia vel ars particularis. . . . Et ideo ad sciendas res in propria natura, summe requiruntur scientiae particulares." *Lib. I Metaph.*, tr. I, c. 2, p. 6a–b.
[121]See *Lib. VI Ethic.*, tr. II, c. 25, ed. Borgnet, VII, pp. 442–44; *Lib. I Metaph.*, tr. I, c. 1, pp. 2–4a. Robert Kilwardby also considered this to be the natural order of learning, except that he, following Alfarabi (*De scientiis*, c. 5), places moral philosophy after metaphysics (*De ortu scientiarum*, cc. 63–64, Merton College MS 261, fol. 62rb–64vb); Roger Bacon also places moral philosophy after metaphysics in the order of learning (*Communium naturalium*, ed. R. Steele, *Op. Hac. Ined.*, II, pp. 1–3; *Moralis philosophia*, P. I, proem., ed. Delorme-Massa [Zürich, 1953], 4–7).
[122]See for example, *Lib. I Phys.*, tr. I, c. 1; *Lib. I Metaph.*, tr. I, c. 1; *Lib. VI Metaph.*, tr. I, c. 2. In the *Philosophia pauperum* or *Summa naturalium*, attributed to Albertus Magnus by some historians, philosophy is divided into logic, ethics, and physics (ed. Borgnet, V, 445).

by Boethius does not represent an ascending hierarchy of forms; nor does it represent an ascending hierarchy of scientific knowledge. Albert clearly conceives the mathematical sciences to be speculatively inferior to natural science and a preparation for the science of nature, physics. For him applied mathematics (*scientiae mediae*) can be useful in the study of physical reality, but not a substitute for it. Finally, Albert insists on the autonomy of natural science, which needs neither mathematics nor metaphysics in order to solve its problems. Natural science may indeed lead the mind to a higher and more sublime study, once the existence of some immaterial substance is recognized, but in the investigation of physical problems the natural sciences have no need of metaphysics.

A study of the writings of Albertus Magnus on Aristotle shows that they are not mere paraphrases of the Stagirite, or even mere encyclopedias of medieval science. Albert in fact rewrote almost the whole of philosophy, following the order of Aristotle and other authorities, adding new sciences and correcting wherever he thought necessary.[123] Throughout his philosophical writings Albert strove to render the true doctrine of the Peripatetics "intelligible to the Latins." Thus Roger Bacon could complain that many people thought, although mistakenly, that "philosophia iam data sit Latinis, et completa, et composita in lingua Latina."[124] The rewritten Aristotelianism of Albertus Magnus was the point of departure for the theological synthesis of Thomas Aquinas, who produced critical analyses of the Aristotelian text only when the right to use Aristotle was challenged by the Averroist threat to Christian orthodoxy.

In an early work, *In Boethium De Trinitate*, which was written between 1252 and 1259, Thomas Aquinas revealed his opposition to classifying the speculative sciences according to ascending degrees of abstraction. L. B. Geiger's study of the first and second versions shows that Aquinas deliberately restricted the term "abstractio" to the consideration of things separated not in fact but only in thought.[125] For Aquinas the natural sciences "abstract" only in the sense that they are directly concerned with the universal nature and not with singulars as such. This *abstractio totius*, however, is the condition of all intellectual knowledge. Of the three traditional speculative sciences only mathe-

[123] *Lib. I Phys.*, tr. I, c. 1, pp. 1b–2a.
[124] Bacon, *Opus tertium*, c. 9, ed. Brewer, p. 30.
[125] L.-B. Geiger, "Abstraction et séparation d'après s. Thomas," *Revue des Sciences Phil. et Théol.* 31 (1947), 3–40. Words and phrases in the autograph which were changed or deleted by Aquinas have been published by B. Decker in the appendix to his edition, *Expositio super librum Boethii De Trinitate* (Leiden, 1955).

matics properly "abstracts" by considering only a part of reality, idealized extension and number; this consideration is called *abstractio formae*, because it disregards the "material" part of existing bodies. But since number and extension are conceived in mathematics not as pure accidents but rather after the manner of things, that which is imagined to be a line, point, circle, or any given number is said to have *materia intelligibilis*, a condition for all mathematical thought. Metaphysics, unlike the other sciences, presupposes that there exists in reality at least one substance which is not physical, not material, but "separated" from matter. Although this separated substance is not the subject of metaphysics for Aquinas, the science of metaphysics rests on the proven judgment that such a separated being exists in reality.[126] Unlike mathematics, the science of metaphysics leaves nothing out of consideration; it considers all things, even individual things, matter and motion, *secundum communem rationem entis*, that is, according to that which is common to material and immaterial substances.[127]

The view of Thomas Aquinas, therefore, is essentially that of Albertus Magnus. Mathematics for Aquinas does not present a deeper explanation of natural phenomena, nor does it offer to natural science the true principles of scientific demonstration. On the contrary, mathematics looks to natural science for its justification. Mathematical principles for Aquinas can be applied to motion and time as well as to physical dimensions, but such an application in the mixed sciences (*scientiae mediae*) touches only the quantitative aspects of physical phenomena, and not the sensible, or natural, aspects.[128] In his analysis of *scientiae mediae* Aquinas went further than Albert or any of his predecessors. After discussing subalternation of the sciences and Aristotle's use of the terms *quia* and *propter quid* with regard to science, Aquinas notes that both terms when used of sciences are to be included in the previous explanation of *demonstratio quia*, "scilicet quando fit demonstratio per causam remotam."[129] Thus in sciences subalternated to geometry "the geometer explains *propter quid* in those

---

[126]*Expos. Boeth. De Trin.*, q. 5, a. 3; see also *In I Metaph.*, lect. 12 (ed. Cathala), n. 181; *In IV Metaph.*, lect. 5, n. 593; *In VI Metaph.*, lect. 1, n. 1170.

[127]*Expos. Boeth. De Trin.*, q. 5, a. 4 ad 6; also *In VII Metaph.*, lect. 11, n. 1526; *In XII Metaph.*, lect. 2, n. 2427.

[128]*Expos. Boeth. De Trin.*, q. 5, a. 3 ad 5–8; *In II Phys.*, lect. 3 (ed. Leon.), nn. 8–9.

[129]"Sciendum autem est quod illa differentia *quia* et *propter quid*, quae est secundum diversas scientias, continetur sub altero praedictorum modorum, scilicet quando fit demonstratio per causam remotam." *In I Post. Anal.*, lect. 25 (ed. Leon.), n. 6. Cardinal Thomas de Vio Cajetan went to great lengths to determine the exact meaning of this sentence in his own *Commentaria in libros Posteriorum Analyticorum*, Lib. I, cap. 13, *Quomodo in diversis* (ed. Venetiis, 1599), pp. 131a–133a.

sciences according to the formal cause,"[130] but this quantitative formality is a remote cause as far as the natural phenomenon is concerned. In other words, the mathematical principles used in astronomy, optics, and mechanics can indeed demonstrate the quantitative characteristics measured, but they can only describe, and not demonstrate *propter quid*, the production of natural effects. Since every science is determined by the type of probative principles employed, the formal structure of these *scientiae mediae* is more mathematical than physical.[131] Some scientific truths—for example, the sphericity of the earth—can be demonstrated by both astronomy and physics, if the attribute to be demonstrated is a physical quantity. The principles employed in the two demonstrations are different. But since astronomy, like all the mathematical sciences, abstracts from natural matter, motion, efficient and final causes, it cannot demonstrate *propter quid*, or *why* any of these effects occur in nature. From this it follows that the aim and method of such *scientiae mediae* are essentially different from the aim and method of natural science. Nevertheless Aquinas conceived all the mathematical sciences as preparatory for the more valuable science of nature.

The ideal order of learning indicated by Aquinas is identical to that of Albertus Magnus.[132] First boys should be instructed in logic, because logic gives the common method of all the sciences. Second, they are to be instructed in the mathematic sciences, which neither demand experience nor transcend the imagination. Third, they should study the natural sciences, which, although not exceeding sense and imagination, require experience. Fourth, they should be instructed in the moral sciences, which require experience and a mind not perturbed by emotions. Finally, they may study divine things, which transcend the imagination and require a sturdy intellect. Of course, in the medieval faculty of arts this ideal order of learning was never followed; it would have been impractical, no doubt, to impose such an order on youths.

---

[130] "Unde patet quod geometra dicit *propter quid* in istis scientiis secundum causam formalem." *Ibid.*, n. 4 fin.

[131] *Expos. Boeth. De Trin.*, q. 5, a. 3 ad 6; see also *In II Phys.*, lect. 3, nn. 6–9; *Sum. theol.* I-II, q. 35, a. 8; II-II, q. 9, a. 2 ad 3.

[132] "Erit ergo congruus ordo addiscendi, ut *primo* quidem pueri logicalibus instruantur, quia logica docet modum totius philosophiae. *Secundo* autem instruendi sunt in mathematicis quae nec experientia indigent, nec imaginationem transcendunt. *Tertio* autem in naturalibus, quae etsi non excedunt sensum et imaginationem, requirunt tamen experientiam. *Quarto* in moralibus, quae requirunt experientiam et animum a passionibus liberum, ut in primo habitum est. *Quinto* autem in sapientibus et divinis, quae transcendunt imaginationem et requirunt validum intellectum." *In VI Ethic.*, lect. 7, n. 1211; also *In librum de causis*, prooem., ed. H. D. Saffrey, p. 2.

In the view of Albertus Magnus and Thomas Aquinas each science is granted autonomy within its own field of inquiry; particular sciences are not absorbed into more universal sciences, such as metaphysics; and all the mathematical sciences are considered subordinate to natural philosophy, which is the point of departure for metaphysics. This view may be considered authentically Aristotelian. According to the other view which was predominant in the thirteenth century the classification of the sciences corresponds to the hierarchy of forms in nature: natural science is subalternated to the four mathematical sciences, and mathematics is subalternated to metaphysics. Each science is resolved into a higher and more universal science, and mathematics is the key which unlocks both nature and metaphysics. This view, although contaminated with the doctrine of universal hylemorphism, may be considered representatively Platonic.

The writings of the fourteenth century which have been preserved reveal very little concern about the classification of the sciences or the polemic of the thirteenth century. Nevertheless, the writings of Avicenna, Averroes, Grosseteste, Albertus Magnus, and Thomas Aquinas were well known in the fourteenth century; they were accepted together with earlier authors as *auctoritates* in the schools and they comprised the scientific "tradition" upon which later masters could build. Each generation, however, must learn for itself truths discovered with great labor by earlier generations. The *auctoritates* recognized in the schools were those authors who could guide students in the acquisition of those truths. But students were expected to become masters who were not only equipped with ancient learning but also capable of raising new problems in new fields of inquiry.

Scientific learning at Oxford in the early fourteenth century was concerned with new problems in the fields of logic and physics, a physics which was to become kinematics and dynamics, and eventually a new science of classical mechanics.

X

THE EVOLUTION OF
SCIENTIFIC METHOD

To the best of my knowledge the history of scientific method has not
yet been written. While there are many histories of science and many
excellent studies of method for particular periods and individuals, no
full history of scientific method has yet been attempted.[1] One major
obstacle to such a history, no doubt, is the vagueness, or perhaps
confusion, which exists concerning the very concept of scientific
method itself. It is by no means uncommon to find the scientific
method defined in such vague terms as "observation" and "experimentation." The closest Henri Poincaré came to defining the expression in his famous *Science et méthode* (1909) was in his opening line:
"The scientific method consists in observing and experimenting; if
the scientist had at his disposal infinite time, it would only be necessary to say to him, 'Look and notice well.'"[2] But such a declaration
fails to define either "scientific" or "method."

More commonly in current studies the scientific method is defined
as "the exact measurement of physical properties and the formulation
of hypotheses in equations which permit the mathematical manipula-
tion of these quantitative results." But this definition unreasonably
restricts the concept of scientific method to the field of modern phys-

---

[1] Besides the classical works of William Whewell, Ernst Mach, Pierre Duhem and
Karl Pearson, a number of studies of particular methods can contribute to an eventual
history of scientific method. Special mention should be made of the following:
R. McKeon, "Aristotle's Conception of the Development and the Nature of Scientific
Method," *J. Hist. Ideas* 8 (1947), 3–44; Emile Simard, *La Nature et la Portée de la Méthode
Scientifique* (Québec, 1956); Herbert M. Evans (ed.), *Men and Moments in the History of
Science* (Seattle, 1959); R. M. Blake, C. J. Ducasse, E. H. Madden (eds.), *Theories of
Scientific Method: The Renaissance through the Nineteenth Century* (Seattle, 1960); Neal W.
Gilbert, *Renaissance Concepts of Method* (New York, 1960); Robert McRae, *The Problem of
the Unity of the Sciences: Bacon to Kant* (Toronto, 1961).
[2] H. Poincaré, *Science and Method*, in *The Foundations of Science* (Lancaster, Pa., 1946),
p. 359.

ics, thereby excluding vast areas of modern science from having a method which is truly "scientific." The life sciences for the most part are not amenable to the method of mathematics, and we have not yet succeeded in reducing substantial parts of chemistry, paleontology, geology, mineralogy, and climatology to useful equations and mathematical hypotheses.

Since the seventeenth century, theoreticians of science have assumed that there must be only one method which is truly "scientific." In other words, it is assumed that the concept of scientific method is a *univocal* one. No attempt is made today to justify such an assumption. Descartes, at least, argued that his method had worked for analytic geometry, and that therefore it should work for all knowledge. Descartes' argument, of course, is logically unsound. Apparently, however, it has been universally accepted as a necessary postulate in modern methodology. In order to obtain this univocal concept, philosophers and historians of scientific method have had to select one particular aspect of scientific procedure: observation of facts, induction, experimentation, measurement and mathematical deduction, hypothetical postulation, predictability, or possibly verification and falsification. The attempt to form a univocal concept necessarily entails the exclusion of other recognizably essential elements. The real tragedy of this univocation is not so much the exclusion of some particular characteristic, however, for the excluded element is usually rescued by some other author. The real tragedy is rather the loss of the concept of method itself.

Consequently, before examining the three stages of evolution which I have selected, it would be well for us to determine what we mean by method, and specifically what we mean by scientific method.

I. THE CONCEPT OF SCIENTIFIC METHOD

Our English word "method" comes directly from the postclassical Latin transliteration of the Greek μέθοδος, which does not even occur in Aristotle's great methodological work, the *Posterior Analytics*, although it does occur elsewhere in Aristotle.[3] Derived from μετά, meaning "after" or "according to," and ὁδός, meaning a "way," the Greek compound originally was taken to mean the "way," "order," or "logic" of rational inquiry (*ratio inquirendi*). In this sense it signified the rules, or norms, according to which logical inquiry was to be conducted. In this first sense logic itself was said to be a method. The

[3] See H. Bonitz, *Index Aristotelicus* (Berlin, 1870), pp. 449–50.

word was then transferred to signify the actual discussion or inquiry conducted according to a logical plan. In this second sense we speak of the Socratic "method." Finally, the word was taken to mean any doctrine or science obtained as a result of this logical inquiry. In this last sense there would be as many "methods" (μέθοδοι) as there are sciences or even schools of doctrine. We find this last sense of the term used frequently by Galen and by early ecclesiastical writers when they refer to Platonic, Peripatetic, Epicurean, and Stoic philosophies as so many different "methods."

The classical Latin term for the concept of method, and one which St. Thomas Aquinas invariably uses, is *modus*. It was not until the sixteenth century that *methodus* came into common Latin usage under the egis of humanist learning.[4] By that time the subtleties of *modus* had been lost. The Latin *modus* originally meant a "measure" or "norm" according to which something is measured, for example, its size, circumference, quantity, or bulk; in this first sense a mode was a standard of measurement for qualities as well as for quantities.[5] Soon, however, the term was taken passively to mean the determination within a thing because of an extrinsic measure; thus a mode was taken as a limit, a restriction imposed by some standard, as when we speak of a mode or manner of life, and of *mode*ration in activity. It was in this second sense that St. Augustine said, "Mensura modum praefigit."[6] Invariably it was this sense of the term that St. Thomas used whenever he defined *modus*.[7] In other words, there are two uses of the Latin term *modus* corresponding to the first two uses of the Greek μέθοδος. Strictly speaking, the Latins did not use *modus* in the third sense employed by the Greeks; instead, they used such terms as *doctrina, scientia*, and the like.

Considering both the Greek and the Latin uses of the term, we must distinguish two fundamental senses of "method" or "mode," namely, the objective and the subjective uses of the term corresponding to its first two meanings in classical usage.

---

[4] N. W. Gilbert, *op. cit.*, p. 69, note 4. In this otherwise excellent study Gilbert completely neglects the more common Latin term *modus* used by Cicero and the schoolmen. Ironically, the author blames Cicero for not transliterating the Greek μέθοδος: "Evidently Cicero did not consider the concept worth baptizing with a new Latin word. . . . The result of Cicero's omission was that the specific Greek concepts of method were lost in the vagueness of circumlocution in Latin philosophy, only to be regained when writers using Latin once more had access to Greek works" (*ibid.*, p. 49).

[5] See A. Ernout and A. Meillet, *Dictionnaire étymologique de la langue Latine*, 4th ed. rev. (Paris, 1960), pp. 408–9.

[6] St. Aug., *De Gen. ad lit.* IV, 3. PL 34, 299.

[7] *Sum. theol.* I, 5, 5; I-II, 49, 2. For a more detailed listing of this usage in St. Thomas, see the *Tabula aurea* of Peter of Bergamo (Rome, 1960), *s.v.* "Modus."

"Method" or "mode" can be taken as the objective measure or norm to be followed in any procedure or endeavor. In rational inquiry this objective guide is none other than logic, the art of right reasoning. Both the Greeks and the Latins recognized Aristotle's *Organon* as the general method of all scientific knowledge, "quia logica tradit communem modum procedendi in omnibus aliis scientiis." St. Thomas goes on to say, "It is absurd for a man to seek simultaneously science and the methodology belonging to science; for this reason he should learn logic before learning the other sciences."[8]

More commonly, however, *modus* is taken in the subjective sense of a modification, a determination, a modality within a subject because of the objective norm. This corresponds to the second usage in Greek and Latin. In English we have many expressions reflecting this sense of the word: one's manner or mode of life, musical modes, modes (or moods) of speech, different ways or manners of viewing, and moderation as a characteristic of virtue. Philosophy even speaks of various "modes" of being. The Latin word *modus* is rendered in many different ways in English, but fundamentally they all express the same sense of the term. We could render it as "method"—but then there are as many methods or moods as there are, let us say, virtues.

Even a casual consideration of the virtues in general shows that the method of one virtue differs greatly from that of every other virtue. The method of prudence, for example, differs considerably from the method of speculative knowledge. Prudence aims at determining the means suitable for a composite end to be attained; for this reason the ancients called its method "synthetic" or "compositive" (*modus compositivus*). Speculation, on the other hand, even in practical sciences, starts with a complex problem and attempts to resolve it into its simple principles, causes, and elements; for this reason the ancients called the speculative method "analytic" or "resolutive" (*modus resolutivus*).[9] There should be no need here to point out that "wisdom" has a unique method proper to itself, and that the method of sacred theology is radically different from the method of all the philosophical sciences. The great differences in *modus* are seen even more conspicuously in the moral virtues as discussed by St. Thomas. All the virtues belonging to justice derive their mode from *ius*, which is a *medium rei*, while the virtues belonging to fortitude and temperance derive their mode from a *medium rationis*.

[8] St. Thomas, *In II Meta.*, lect. 5, n. 335 (ed. Cathala).
[9] "Necessarium est enim in qualibet scientia operativa, ut procedatur *modo composito*. E converso autem in scientia speculativa, necesse est ut procedatur *modo resolutorio*, resolvendo composita in principia simplicia." St. Thomas, *In I Ethic.*, lect. 3, n. 35 (ed.

In this paper we are concerned specifically with methods of scientific knowledge, and the first point to be established is that each science has its own modality or method. The problem here has nothing to do with general logic, for it has already been established that logic proposes the general method of all scientific inquiry. The present question has to do with the special methodology of individual sciences. The discussion of this methodology does not even belong to general logic but belongs rather to the individual sciences themselves. St. Thomas notes that "the method proper to the individual sciences ought to be discussed at the beginning of each science."[10]

St. Thomas, following Aristotle, frequently points out that one cannot expect to use the same method in all the sciences, nor can he expect to find the same certitude.[11] Commenting on Aristotle's statement that "the mathematical method is not that of natural science,"[12] St. Thomas explains that the clarity and precision of mathematics ought not to be expected in all areas of research but only in those areas which are treated abstractly and quantitatively. Consequently, the mathematical necessity found in mathematical definitions and demonstrations cannot be found in natural phenomena, which regularly occur "ut in pluribus." St. Thomas goes on to say:

Since that most certain method of argumentation [found in mathematics] does not befit natural science, one must first examine carefully what is nature [*quid sit natura*] in order to discover the proper method of natural science. It will be obvious then what sort of reality natural science is concerned with. Further, one ought to consider whether the investigation of all causes and principles belongs to it or to different sciences. In this way one can know the method of demonstrating proper to natural sciences. Aristotle himself discusses this method in the second book of the *Physics*, as is evident to the perceptive reader [*ut patet diligenter intuenti*].[13]

Thus it is clear that Aristotle and St. Thomas, at least, recognized

---

Pirotta). Also *Sum. theol.* I-II, 14, 5. However, even practical sciences, sciences like ethics, economics, and politics, use the speculative method (*modo speculativo*) when they search for definitions, divisions, and arguments in their theoretical part. This use of composition and resolution should not be confused with the convertibility of demonstrations "*quia*" *per effectum convertibilem* (resolution) and *propter quid* (composition) discussed by Aristotle in *An. post.* I, 13, 78a30–40. On the various senses of *compositio* and *resolutio* in St. Thomas, see L.-M. Régis, O.P., "Analyse et synthése dans l'oeuvre de s. Thomas," in *Studia Mediaevalia* in honorem R. J. Martin, O.P. (Bruges, 1948), pp. 303–30, and S. E. Dolan, F.S.C., "Resolution and Composition in Speculative and Practical Discourse," *Laval Théologique et Philosophique* 6 (1950), 9–62.

[10] "Modus autem proprius singularium scientiarum in scientiis singulis circa principium tradi debet." *In II Meta.*, lect. 5, n. 335.

[11] *In Boeth. De Trin.*, expos. c. 2, ed. B. Decker (Leiden, 1955), pp. 158–60.

[12] Arist., *Metaph.* II, 3, 995a16–17; St. Thomas, *In II Meta.*, lect. 5, n. 336.

[13] *Ibid.*, n. 337.

different kinds of scientific method. It is not so easy, however, to understand what they meant by a "method" proper to each science. Defining *modus* in general, St. Thomas simply states that it is a "determinatio sive commensuratio principiorum, seu materialium, seu efficientium ipsam [formam]."[14] In this definition there are three factors to notice: (1) it is an intrinsic determination or configuration imposed by some objective norm: "mensura modum praefigit"; (2) it is both the material and the efficient principles which are thus modified; and (3) this radical molding is responsible for the type of reality (*species*) under discussion, and hence it is prior to the form.

The reality or *species* under discussion is scientific knowledge, and scientific knowledge is an intellectual habit of perceiving causal connections between true "reasons" and true facts. For this reason Aristotle defined scientific knowledge (ἐπιστήμη) as knowing "that the cause from which the fact results is the cause of that fact, and that the fact cannot be otherwise."[15] Following the thought of Aristotle, the schoolmen distinguished two essential principles of scientific knowledge: the active principles, which they called the *ratio formalis obiecti*, and the material principles of the intellectual habit, which they called the *obiectum materiale*.[16] The former designated the proper illuminating principles of the science; the latter represented any particular conclusion illuminated by the principles. Together they constitute the proper object of a science, for within that totality a truth is known (*scitum*) through its scientific causes. The radical modification, or configuration, of these essential principles gives to each science its unique character, so that truths known in mathematics or in ethics, let us say, have an entirely different character from those known in the natural sciences. This is the function of the intrinsic *modus* determined by objective reality. Because of this radically unique modality, mathematics, ethics, and natural science are specifically different scientific habits.

At this point it must be explicitly acknowledged that a given method or *modus* belongs not only to scientific knowledge already possessed but also to the acquisition of that science. In modern parlance the word "method" is more commonly used to designate the procedure or manner of acquiring scientific knowledge. But it would be a mistake to limit the concept of method merely to the acquisition of science,

---

[14] *Sum. theol.* I, 5, 5: "Utrum ratio boni consistat in modo, specie et ordine."
[15] Arist., *An. post.* I, 2, 71b10–12, trans. H. Tredennick, Loeb ed., p. 29.
[16] *Sum. theol.* II-II, 1, 1; 9, 2 ad 3. See also I-II, 54, 2 ad 2; *De virt.*, 13; *In I Post. Anal.*, lect. 41, n. 11.

since knowledge acquired continues to bear the seal of its origin. It is the same extrinsic "measure" which determines both the manner of acquiring and the manner of knowing scientific truths.

One further point remains to be clarified in order to understand the concept of method in general. We must examine the factors which actually determine the method of a particular science. These factors are complex. St. Thomas wisely observes that

the method followed in investigation must be appropriate [*congruere*] both to things and to us: for unless it is appropriate to the things studied, these could not be grasped, and unless it is appropriate for us, we could not comprehend.[17]

The appropriate method of a particular science, therefore, is determined both by the subjective requirements for comprehension and by the objective nature of the field to be investigated.

Among the subjective requirements of a fitting method there are at least three obvious determinants. The first is logic itself, since logic is the indispensable art or tool (*organon*) for acquiring all scientific knowledge. As an indispensable tool, it establishes a common method for all science, and for this reason it was antonomastically called "method" among the Greeks. The second determinant is the appropriate faculty of mind used; thus observation and reason are said to be the method of natural science, imagination the method of mathematics, intellectual intuition the method of metaphysics, introspection a convenient method of psychology, and so forth.[18] The third determinant is the knowledge already possessed by the investigator. Whatever is already known must be taken into consideration, since human knowledge must proceed from what is known to what is unknown. For this reason the teacher must choose examples carefully and present problems clearly in reference to the pupil's experience. There are perhaps many more subjective determinants of method, but these are sufficient for our purpose.

The objective determinant of method is also complex, but in a different way. The method of a science is objectively determined not only by the object studied as a whole, but also by its various parts. Scholastic writers commonly recognized that the objects studied in natural science actually exist in sensible matter and motion, and that consequently every definition in natural science must be in terms of

---

[17] *In Boeth. De Trin.*, expos. c. 2.
[18] Cf. *In Boeth. De Trin.*, q. 6, where St. Thomas examines Boethius's statement: "In naturalibus igitur rationabiliter, in mathematicis disciplinaliter, in divinis intellectualiter versari oportebit neque diduci ad imaginationes, sed potius ipsam inspicere formam."

matter and motion.[19] But it makes a great difference whether one examines this reality in general or in particular. For the basic problems of common experience, ordinary observation is sufficient; for the internal biology of animals, however, dissection is necessary; for chemical reactions, experimentation is required; and for random subatomic particles, a statistical method is called for. A similar latitude in methods is required in the moral sciences, mathematics, metaphysics, and even in history. Therefore, the proper method employed in the various parts of a single science depends on the type of thing considered.

In general we can say that the basic method of all speculative sciences is *resolutive*, or *analytic*, proceeding from a complex whole to its causes, principles, and elements. This common method of scientific knowledge is inevitably due to human logic. The proper method, however, is a further modification derived from the type of reality studied, both as a totality and as a complex whole made up of many different parts. This situation is similar to the case of the historical sciences. All the historical sciences use the "historical method." But this method is further modified and varied, depending upon whether one is doing economic history, political history, intellectual history, or the history of science.

With these preliminary observations in mind we can now consider three particularly notable stages in the evolution of scientific method: (1) the Aristotelian method, (2) the scholastic method, and (3) the Galilean method of the seventeenth century.

II. THE ARISTOTELIAN METHOD

In my preliminary remarks I have assumed that Aristotle's *Organon* is to be considered the general method of all scientific knowledge. Following the great Greek, Arab, and Latin commentators, I view the *Organon* as a single, complex tool of science, wherein discussion of the first and second operations of the mind (*Categories, Peri hermeneias*) is directed to an understanding of argumentation. The *Prior Analytics* discusses the formal structure of all argumentation, whether the argument be demonstrative, dialectical, or sophistical. The material structure of demonstrable matter, dialectical matter, and sophistical matter is then discussed in the *Posterior Analytics, Topics,* and *Sophistici elenchi* respectively. In this view, the *Posterior Analytics* is the principal

---

[19] Boeth., *De Trin.*, c. 2. Cf. St. Thomas, *In Boeth. De Trin.*, q. 5, a. 2; *In I Phys.*, lect. 1, n. 2; *In I De caelo*, lect. 1, n. 2; *In III De caelo*, lect. 3; *In VI Meta.*, lect. 1, nn. 1156–59; *In XI Meta.*, lect. 7, nn. 2256–58; *Sum. theol.* I, 84, 1.

part of logic and its crowning glory, since it deals with the acquisition of "scientific knowledge" strictly so called. For this reason St. Albert says: "Est ergo finis et perfectissima et sola simpliciter desiderabilis inter logicas scientias et sola nobilior et aliis certitudine probationum excellentior."[20] Scholastics generally, and Averroes, Grosseteste, St. Albert, and St. Thomas in particular, accepted Aristotle's *Posterior Analytics* as an authentic treatise in scientific methodology.

There are two modern views, however, which reject this scholastic interpretation. Some modern philologists and logicians claim that the *Posterior Analytics* is a disjointed, unintelligible hodgepodge of possibly distinct treatises. When it was recently pointed out to one such logician that St. Thomas, for one, had no difficulty in seeing the unity, the logician retorted, "But St. Thomas even saw unity among the letters of St. Paul!" It might have been pointed out to this logician that the two cases are not at all the same.

The second and more serious view suggests that the *Posterior Analytics* represents a beautiful Platonic ideal of science, but insists that it has nothing to do with the procedure Aristotle himself follows in actual investigation. John Herman Randall, Jr., for example, believes that "this Aristotelian conception of science, as set forth in the *Posterior Analytics*, is still the Platonic Idea, the ideal, of our modern scientific enterprise."[21] But he maintains that the work was never intended to be a description of scientific method. For Randall, Aristotle's actual method of scientific investigation is to be found in his scientific treatises. This method is seen to consist of five steps:[22]

1. "to determine the object of investigation," for example, the soul in *De anima*, natural motion in the *Physics*, human happiness in the *Ethics;*
2. "to examine previous opinions or hypotheses as to the best way to understand the subject matter in question";
3. "to undertake a dialectical examination of proposed *archai* or *endoxa* . . . to bring out all the difficulties and problems";
4. "to find the relevant facts"; and
5. "to explain the subject matter, to exhibit the intelligible structure of facts."

The obvious scholastic reply to Randall's view is that the very purpose of the *Posterior Analytics* is to analyze steps 1, 4, and 5 for any science whatever. Steps 2 and 3 are dialectical preparations for

---

[20] Albert, *Lib. I Post. Anal.*, tr. I, c. 1, ed. Borgnet, II, 2b.
[21] J. H. Randall, Jr., *Aristotle* (New York, 1960), p. 42.
[22] *Ibid.*, pp. 51–55.

scientific knowledge, and they are governed by the general principles of the *Topics*. Therefore, logic does discuss and offer the general method for all scientific investigation, as we have been saying.

After describing Aristotle's actual scientific method Randall goes on to say:

Why then did Aristotle not only fail to make discoveries that seem to us through long familiarity obvious; why did he make positive mistakes? He had a fruitful method, what most scientists would still today call the "right" method. . . . The answer is clear: Aristotle was too much of an empiricist. He was clearly the greatest observational scientist until the nineteenth century; and our modern scientific enterprise was born in the rejection of such "empiricism" for some form of "rationalism"—in the rejection of trust in sheer observation for faith in mathematical demonstration.[23]

Whatever may be said of Randall's enthusiasm for mathematical demonstration, one can find much wanting in his presentation of Aristotle's *Posterior Analytics*.

Undoubtedly there are many obscurities in Aristotle's *Posterior Analytics*, as even Themistius discovered.[24] For John of Salisbury, the book "contains almost as many stumbling blocks as it does chapters."[25] However, the essential points of Aristotle's work are not impossible to understand; at least they were not beyond the comprehension of the schoolmen. At the risk of oversimplifying, I would like to summarize the essential points in three paragraphs.[26]

First, scientific inquiry consists in asking questions—in asking the right question at the right time. The answer to the question can be found, not by remembering (Plato), nor by the addition of another fact (Sophists), but by investigation of the matter in terms of the question asked. One does not ask a scientific question unless one has a scientific problem: some contrariety of fact, view, or opinion. In every question the inquirer already has some knowledge. He knows at least the existence of and probably some definition of the subject, and presumably the predicate conveys some meaning, otherwise he could not and certainly would not ask the question. Furthermore, the questioner knows the basic truths of human intelligence. Therefore, the questioner does know a great deal when he asks about what he does not know. Of course, he does not yet know the answer or the reason

[23] *Ibid.*, p. 56.
[24] Themistius, *Paraphras. in lib. Post.*, praef., ed. M. Wallies, Comm. in Arist. Graeca, V, 1 (Berlin, 1900), p. 1; trans. by Gerard of Cremona, ed. J. R. O'Donnell, C.S.B., *Mediaeval Studies* 20 (1958), 242.
[25] John of Salisbury, *Metalogicon* IV, c. 6, ed. Webb (Oxford, 1929), p. 171.
[26] For a more detailed presentation, see my commentary on the *Posterior Analytics*, entitled "Aristotelian Methodology" (pro manuscripto), River Forest, Ill., 1958.

for the answer, but these can be found only in the light of what he knows. In other words, an answer to a scientific question is not found in spite of the question but precisely in terms of the question and the problem. We know scientifically when we know not only the correct answer but also the *precise reason* for that answer, and that there is no other explanation. Thus, whether we are right or wrong, we claim to have scientific knowledge "when we believe that we know (a) that the cause from which the fact results is the cause of that fact, and (b) that the fact cannot be otherwise" (*An. post.* I, 2, 71b10–12).

Second, there are only four scientific questions: *An sit? Quid sit? Qualis sit?* and *Propter quid sit?* While it is true that the principal concern of scientific investigation is the answer to *Propter quid sit?*, the ultimate answer cannot be found except within the nature, essence, or *quod quid est* of the subject responsible for the phenomenon under investigation. For this reason the cornerstone of Aristotle's scientific method is the search for definitions which can serve as the middle term in a scientific demonstration. Just as the entire force of a demonstration lies in the middle term of the syllogism, so the ultimate explanation of a phenomenon lies in the nature of the subject. Clearly it is not just any definition which will serve this purpose. Plato had already given the two basic methods of finding definitions, namely, by division and by comparison. These are merely the starting point for the discovery of "demonstrative" definitions: *propter quid* definitions of the predicate (phenomenon or attribute) involving the subject as cause. Once this kind of definition has been found, perhaps after much research, one need go no further. Such a definition is itself an implicit demonstration, "differing from demonstration in grammatical form" (*An. post.* II, 10, 94a12–13).[27]

Third, and most important, proper and adequate demonstrations can be found—if they are to be found at all—only within the proper subject matter of the science. For Aristotle, arguments drawn from

[27] Critics have often complained that there are few syllogisms in Aristotle's scientific works. However, the formal expression of the syllogism is not necessary for true demonstration; the main thing is to discover the middle term, the reason for asserting the conclusion. In *propter quid* demonstrations this middle term is nothing more than the causal definition of the property in question. "Et sic ex ipso *quod quid est* noto per sensum vel per suppositionem, demonstrant scientiae proprias passiones, quae secundum se insunt generi subiecto circa quod sunt. Nam definitio est medium in demonstratione propter quid" (St. Thomas, *In VI Meta.*, lect. 1, n. 1149). Critics have also complained that there are relatively few real demonstrations in Aristotle's works. But every scientist realizes that perfect and complete answers are hard to come by; often, despite much research and speculation, one must fall back on the opinions of others, on probabilities, possibilities, and hypotheses. These are steps in the direction of demonstrations not yet reached.

common sense or from common principles are not scientific demonstrations, although they may be highly indicative, that is, dialectical. Of great importance is Aristotle's insistence that arguments drawn from another area cannot be properly demonstrative. In other words, the answer to a mathematical problem must be found in mathematics, and not in ethics or in history. The solution to a problem of natural science must be found in the realm of natural science, not in theology, metaphysics, or mathematics. Here is the rub in the history of scientific method. For Aristotle, a mathematical middle term could not give the *propter quid* answer to a problem in natural science, for that middle term belongs to another area of study (τὸ γένος τὸ ὑποκείμενον). The application of mathematical principles, or middle terms, to natural phenomena could, at best, bring into being a new area of research, called a middle science (*scientia media*) between pure mathematics and natural science. It could not give adequate explanations of natural phenomena.

Here I have sketched only the scientific method discussed by Aristotle in the *Posterior Analytics*. I have said nothing about the principles of the dialectical method so necessary in solving scientific problems; these principles are discussed in the *Topics*. Nor have I said anything about the historical method used by Aristotle to introduce his scientific problems. Nor have I discussed the proper method (*modus proprius*) of Aristotle's natural sciences. Such an undertaking would be too vast and not really indispensable for an understanding of the scholastic method.

III. THE SCHOLASTIC METHOD

The scholastic method is one of the great glories of the Middle Ages; yet its history has not yet been written, and its nature has not yet been adequately explained.[28] What is commonly known as "Scholasticism" must not be imagined as a "body of doctrine." Neither was it essentially "a point of view regarding faith and reason," as it is sometimes claimed. Nor was it "the systematic use of reason in theology." This last expression, however, comes closer to the truth than any of

---

[28] A most valuable beginning is the incomplete work of M. Grabmann, *Die Geschichte der scholastischen Methode*, 2 vols. (Freiburg i. Br., 1909–11). See also "Die scholastische Methode und Literaturformen," in Ueberweg-Geyer, *Grundriss der Geschichte der Philosophie*, 12th ed. (Basel, 1951), pp. 152–57; G. Paré, A. Brunet, P. Tremblay, *La Renaissance du XIIe siècle, Les écoles et l'enseignement* (Paris-Ottawa, 1933); H.-D. Simonin, "Qu'est que la scholastique," *Vie intell.* 10 (1931), 234–42; M.-D. Chenu, *Introd. à l'étude de s. Thomas d'Aquin* (Paris, 1955), pp. 51–60.

the earlier, but it is not sufficiently accurate to satisfy a medievalist. Scholasticism is essentially a method of inquiry (*modus inveniendi*) which arose in the schools of the Middle Ages and was universally accepted as the best method of teaching (*modus docendi*). For the schoolmen the best method of teaching was a reasonable re-creation of the original discovery. Thus the order of teaching (*ordo doctrinae*) was said to follow the order of discovery (*ordo inventionis*).[29] It is truly amazing how Aristotelian in spirit this method was even before the introduction of the "new Aristotle" into the Latin West. To appreciate the historical development of the scholastic method, we should distinguish the original elements of the scholastic method from the later influence of the "new Aristotle," particularly the influence of the *Posterior Analytics*.

From its earliest, obscure beginnings there were two essential parts to the scholastic method: the *lectio* and the *disputatio*. The disputation was certainly the more original and the more characteristic, but the *lectio* was its foundation.[30]

The basis of all medieval teaching was the master's lecture, or commentary, on the official text accepted as the *auctoritas*.[31] From the very beginning the Bible was the only official text in theology. In arts the *auctoritas* was Cicero for rhetoric, Priscian and Donatus for grammar, Aristotle for logic. In the thirteenth century the rest of the Aristotelian books were incorporated in the faculty of arts. The *Decretum* and other collections became the official text in canon law, and Avicenna's *Canons of Medicine* became the main text in medicine. The schoolmen were convinced that students should learn from the best masters available. The study of these "great books" of human knowledge, as we have said, constituted the basis of medieval teaching.

While commenting on the text, however, certain obscurities of the author would present problems. Even early twelfth-century masters would digress to state the *pro* and *contra* of the case before attempting a solution. By the middle of the twelfth century the occasional digressions became more numerous and elaborate, and collections of *sic*

---

[29] See M. A. Glutz, C.P., "Order in the Philosophy of Nature," *The Dignity of Science*, ed. by J. A. Weisheipl, O.P. (Washington, D.C., 1961), pp. 268–71.

[30] "In tribus igitur consistit exercitium sacrae scripturae: circa lectionem, disputationem et praedicationem. . . . *Lectio* autem est quasi fundamentum et substratorium sequentium. . . . *Disputatio* quasi paries est in hoc exercitio et aedificio, quia nihil plene intelligitur fideliterve praedicatur, nisi prius dente disputationis frangatur. *Praedicatio* vero, cui subserviunt priora, quasi tectum est tegens fideles ab aestu et a turbine vitiorum" (Peter Cantor, *Verbum abbreviatum*, c. 1; PL 205, 25).

[31] On the technical meaning of "auctoritas," see M.-D. Chenu, *La Théologie au XIIe siècle* (Paris, 1957), pp. 353–57.

and *non* authorities and arguments were made. Such was Abelard's famous *Sic et Non* in philosophy (assuming that Abelard was the author of this well-known collection). Doctors of canon and civil law likewise collected conflicting legislation and interpretations of law. Thus the problem gave birth to the question, the scientific question.

With the evolution of the *quaestio* came the disputation as a distinct part of the scholastic method, conducted at a distinct time of the academic day. Generally, the lecture on the text was given in the morning, and the disputation on some point in the text was held in the afternoon. Originally the order of questions to be disputed followed the order of the text. A text like the Bible, however, hardly offered an order which could be called systematic, but by the middle of the twelfth century masters had achieved a certain systematic ordering of the fundamental questions following the articles of the Creed. Similarly in the arts, problems were discussed with a certain semblance of order among the various questions, but here there was much to be desired, since the masters in arts were young men and the disputants were teenagers. However, the protocol of the disputation was firmly fixed and there was little opportunity to stray from the point under discussion.

The introduction of Aristotle's *Posterior Analytics* exercised an important and invaluable influence on the scholastic method once it was understood. This understanding, however, took about one hundred years to achieve. Around the middle of the twelfth century there existed three new translations of the *Posterior Analytics,* two from the Greek and one from the Arabic. By 1159 the text was known to the masters of Paris, but John of Salisbury tells us that there was scarcely a master willing to expound it because of its extreme subtlety and obscurity. John himself gives us what is probably the first Latin paraphrase in his *Metalogicon.* The first full-length commentary known is that of Robert Grosseteste, written between 1200 and 1209. But it is one thing to explain the scientific method found in the *Posterior Analytics,* and quite another thing to see it actually employed in the sciences. Consequently, it was not until the schoolmen saw this method applied in the other Aristotelian books that they could appreciate the nuances of Aristotle's scientific method. The Latin translation of Averroes' great commentaries (ca. 1220–30) aided the schoolmen considerably in this appreciation. The first to appreciate fully the scientific method of Aristotle was, without doubt, Albertus Magnus, who utilized it not only in his paraphrases but also in his own original and extensive investigations of nature.

The most sublime product of the Aristotelian method in the Middle Ages, however, was none other than the *Summa theologiae* of St. Thomas Aquinas. He wrote this handbook for beginners, because they were in need of a brief, systematic presentation of sacred doctrine. His purpose is stated clearly in the prologue:

Students in this science have not seldom been hampered by what they found written by other authors, partly on account of the multiplicity of useless questions, articles, and arguments; partly also because the things they need to know are taught not according to the order of learning [*secundum ordinem disciplinae*] but according as the plan of the book might require, or the occasion of disputing [*disputandi*] might offer; partly, too, because frequent repetition brought weariness and confusion to the minds of the students.

The order and plan of the *Summa* cannot be appreciated without a good understanding of the *Posterior Analytics*, for in the *Summa* St. Thomas consciously applied the scientific method to an entirely new field. The general plan, of course, is the ancient Creed seen as a sublime *exitus et reditus* of creatures destined for salvation.[32] But it is the order of questions and the order of articles within each question that reveals St. Thomas's profound appreciation of the Aristotelian method of scientific knowledge.

Many modern misunderstandings have arisen in the reading of St. Thomas because the reader or commentator failed to appreciate the kind of question being asked. Historically and scientifically, we can say that every article in the *Summa* has its proper place and purpose. A clear example of St. Thomas's use of the scientific method can be seen in the very first question of the *Summa*. The failure to understand this method has occasioned an infinite variety of confusing commentaries on this so-called introduction to theology.[33] The entire question deals with one subject, sacred doctrine,[34] and each article within the question is designed to lead the student to a better idea of the subject he is about to study. The question is divided into three essential parts: its existence (*an sit*), its nature (*quid sit*), and its method (*de modo eius*). Thus:

[32] Cf. M.-D. Chenu, *Introd. à l'étude de s. Thomas*, pp. 258–73.

[33] See G. F. Van Ackeren, S.J., *Sacra Doctrina* (Rome, 1952).

[34] The extent to which commentators have gone in refusing to accept the unity of this question is summarized by Van Ackeren, *ibid.*, pp. 19–52. Fr. Chenu even maintains that articles 9 and 10 appear in the first question only out of St. Thomas's deference to usage—the internal logic of his theory will eliminate them in the course of time! M.-D. Chenu, "La théologie comme science au XIIIe siècle," *Arch. d'hist. doctr. et litt. du M. A.* 2 (1927), 69.

a.1: whether sacred
doctrine exists

aa. 2–7: search for definition — generic
- it is knowledge
- it is intrinsically one
- it is both speculative and practical
- it is the highest kind of knowledge
- it is, in fact, the highest wisdom

specific determinant: its subject is God himself

aa. 8–10: its method
- is demonstrative
- is symbolic and poetic
- is pluralistic in meaning

The method employed within each article is the scholastic *videtur quod non* and *sed contra* familiar to every schoolboy of the Middle Ages. The problem embodied in the arguments "for" and "against" clarifies the precise question under discussion. Obviously, not every solution offered in the body of the article should be taken as a scientific demonstration. When it is a question of *quid sit*, St. Thomas uses the proper method for finding definitions. When it is a question of probability, he uses the best and simplest dialectical argument intelligible to beginners.

In his requirements for a true scientific demonstration, St. Thomas was perhaps more rigorous than Aristotle. A number of arguments presented by Aristotle as demonstrative are rejected by St. Thomas as inconclusive—for example, the eternity of the world and animation of the celestial bodies. True demonstrations are not too difficult to discover in sacred doctrine, since all the important ones are revealed or rest on divine revelation. In natural science, however, true demonstrations are much more difficult because of the complexity of the physical world. But even here, Aquinas insisted that true, proper, and adequate explanations of natural phenomena must be sought within the proper subject matter of natural science. For this reason he denied that a mathematical middle term could give a *propter quid* explanation of a natural fact.[35]

---

[35] St. Thomas, *In I Post. Anal.*, lect. 25, n. 6. See Cajetan's explanation of this passage of St. Thomas, *In I Post. Anal.*, cap. 13, § *Quomodo in diversis*, ed. Venice, 1599, fol. 131a–b.

St. Thomas realized that quantity is an attribute of the physical world, and that, consequently, mathematical principles are indeed applicable to physical phenomena.[36] But for Aquinas, as for Albert before him, mathematical principles are applicable only to the quantitative aspects of the physical world.[37] There are other aspects of reality, which for Aquinas are not quantitative, and consequently not explainable in terms of mathematics. Such aspects would include actuality, potentiality, finality, form, existence, and causality. To the extent that mathematical principles are applicable to the physical world, mathematical explanations of natural phenomena are considered to be demonstrations *"quia" per causam remotam* by Aquinas. Where mathematical principles are inapplicable, then true mathematical demonstration is impossible, even though considerable information and insight may be obtained about secondary aspects of the problem.

In the fourteenth century the area of phenomena considered capable of mathematization was considerably extended. Schoolmen such as Thomas Bradwardine, John Dumbleton, Richard Swyneshed, and Nicole Oresme considered such qualities as heat, color, sound, density, and velocity to be forms capable of a certain latitude of intensity which could be determined mathematically. For Bradwardine the degree of motion (velocity) is intensified (accelerated) according to determined laws of geometrical proportion.[38] Theoretically Bradwardine's mathematical law of proportionality was perfect, and it inaugurated a new move to find this kind of kinematic proportionality in all types of "qualitative" changes. Dumbleton tried to work this out for degrees of certitude, doubt, condensation, rarefaction, and light; his attempts, however, produced little of merit.[39] Nevertheless, the "new physics" inaugurated by Bradwardine was immediately received in the schools and widely disseminated. There is abundant evidence to show that the "new physics" of the fourteenth century influenced the scientific revolution of the seventeenth century.[40] Even Leibniz was

---

[36] *In Boeth. De Trin.*, 5, 3 ad 5 and 6; *In II Phys.*, lect. 3, nn. 6–9; *Sum. theol.* I-II, 35, 8; II-II, 9, 2 ad 3.

[37] See my article "The Celestial Movers in Medieval Physics," in *The Dignity of Science*, pp. 153–61, and Chapter VII above.

[38] Bradwardine, *Tract. de proportione velocitatum in motibus*, c. 3, ed. H. L. Crosby, Jr., as *Tract. de proportionibus* (Madison, 1955), pp. 110–16. On the meaning of Bradwardine's law, see A. Maier, *Die Vorläufer Galileis im 14. Jahrhundert* (Rome, 1949), pp. 81–110; J. A. Weisheipl, *The Development of Physical Theory in the Middle Ages* (New York, 1959), pp. 73–81.

[39] See my article "The Place of John Dumbleton in the Merton School," *Isis* 50 (1959), 439–54.

[40] Much evidence is presented by Marshall Clagett, *The Science of Mechanics in the Middle Ages* (Madison, 1959), pp. 629–71, and by Anneliese Maier throughout her *Studien zur Naturphilosophie der Spätscholastik* (Rome, 1949–58).

so impressed with the work of Richard Swyneshed that he seriously considered putting out a new edition of the famous *Calculationes.* Leibniz was under the impression that Swyneshed was "the first to introduce mathematics into scholastic philosophy."[41]

The new physics founded by Bradwardine was not a rejection of the scholastic method. On the contrary, he uses it throughout his works. The new physics was simply an attempt to apply mathematical principles to more and more phenomena in nature. In the classical sense of *modus,* Bradwardine did in fact use a new method for the study of natural phenomena. That method was the mathematical method previously employed in astronomy and in the other "middle sciences" between mathematics and physics. This method was more thoroughly exploited in the seventeenth century.

IV. THE METHOD OF GALILEO GALILEI

The scientific revolution of the seventeenth century is commonly summed up under the caption "The Downfall of Aristotle." Not infrequently this "downfall" is credited to a new scientific method based on observation and experimentation. However, some years ago Ernst Cassirer suggested that Galileo's method was really the Aristotelian *compositio-resolutio* employed by Jacopo Zabarella.[42] This view has recently been defended by J. H. Randall, A. C. Crombie, and N. W. Gilbert.[43] For the present I would like to pass over both of these views and direct attention to two methodological innovations of Galileo which can more suitably culminate our discussion of scientific method.

The first innovation to be considered is the very point discussed by Aristotle in the *Posterior Analytics* and in the *Physics,* namely, the value of mathematical middle terms in the explanation of physical phenomena. It was Galileo more than anyone else who was chiefly responsible for introducing the mathematical middle term as the *only* true, certain, and *propter quid* demonstration in natural science. This is implied in his famous panegyric on mathematics:

Philosophy is written in that vast book . . . the universe. . . . It is written in

---

[41] "Vellem etiam edi scripta Suisseti vulgo dicti Calculatoris, qui mathesin in philosophiam scholasticam introduxit." Letter to Thomas Smith (1696), quoted by L. Thorndike, *History of Magic and Exper. Sc.* (1923–58), III, 370.

[42] E. Cassirer, *Das Erkenntnisproblem in der Philosophie und Wissenschaft der neueren Zeit,* 2 vols. (Berlin, 1906–7).

[43] J. H. Randall, Jr., "The Development of Scientific Method in the School of Padua," *J. Hist. Ideas* 1 (1940), 177ff.; A. C. Crombie, *Robert Grosseteste and the Origins of Experimental Science* (Oxford, 1953), pp. 303–19; N. W. Gilbert, *op. cit.*

mathematical language, and the letters are triangles, circles, and other geometrical figures, without which means it is humanly impossible to comprehend a single word.[44]

The origin of this innovation can be seen vaguely in the mathematical ideal of Robert Grosseteste and Roger Bacon, as A. C. Crombie has pointed out.[45] It can be seen more clearly in the kinematics and dynamics of Thomas Bradwardine, as we have already noted.[46] It is even more conspicuous in the cryptic notebooks and drawings of Leonardo da Vinci, for whom "no human inquiry can be called true science, unless it proceeds through mathematical demonstrations."[47] But none of these current claimants as "precursors of Galileo" can adequately account for Galileo's unshakable conviction in the power of mathematics. The origin of this innovation must be sought elsewhere.

Historically and doctrinally, Galileo's basic conviction that he had discovered "an entirely new science in which no one else, ancient or modern, has discovered any of the most remarkable laws which I demonstrate to exist in both natural and violent movement"[48] must be traced to Copernicus. It must be traced to Copernicus's own conviction that he had found, not merely another way in which "to save" the phenomena of the heavens, but the *only* way. Osiander's preface not withstanding, Copernicus himself and many of his supporters were not content to consider the new system as a mere theory, a mere "saving of the appearances."[49] The real point was that Copernicus and many Copernicans, including Galileo, insisted that it was the *only true* system of the system of the heavens. This was the understanding of the Holy Office in 1616 when the *De Revolutionibus Orbium* was placed on the Index "until corrected." In order to prove the absolute truth of

---

[44] Galileo, *Il Saggiatore*, q. 6: "La filosofia è scritta in questo grandissimo libro . . . (io dico l'Universo). . . . Egli è scritto in lingua matematica, e i caratteri son triangoli, cerchi, ed altre figure geometriche, senza i quali mezi è impossibile a intenderne umanamente parola" (*Opere*, ed. naz. IV, p. 232).

[45] Crombie, *op. cit.*, pp. 91–127; 139–45.

[46] In an encomium which reflects Roger Bacon and reminds us of Galileo, Thomas Bradwardine says: "It is [mathematics] which reveals every genuine truth, for it knows every hidden secret and bears the key to every subtlety of letters; whoever then has the effrontery to study physics while neglecting mathematics should know from the start that he will never make his entry through the portals of wisdom" (*Tract. de continuo*, Erfurt, MS Amplon Q. 385, fol. 31v and Torun MS 4°. 2, p. 171).

[47] Leonardo da Vinci, *Frammenti letterari e filosofici*, ed. Edmondo Solmi (Florence, 1925), p. 83. See the pioneer work on Leonardo by Pierre Duhem, *Études sur Léonard de Vinci*, 3 vols. (Paris, 1906–13).

[48] Letter of Galileo to Belisario Vinta (1610), trans. by S. Drake, *Discoveries and Opinions of Galileo* (New York, 1957), p. 63.

[49] On this point see Edward Rosen, *Three Copernican Treatises* (New York, 1959), pp. 22–33.

the Copernican system, Galileo frequently resorted to sensible proofs, such as the motion of the tides and telescopic evidence of corruptibility in the heavenly bodies.[50] Nevertheless he was convinced that mathematics alone sufficiently demonstrated the necessary truth of the Copernican system.

But if mathematics could demonstrate so perfectly the true world system in astronomy, why not in terrestrial physics as well? Many factors led Galileo and his contemporary John Kepler to believe that terrestrial and celestial phenomena must be governed by the same mathematical laws of nature. Those factors need not concern us here. The important point is that for Galileo only mathematics could give true and certain *propter quid* demonstrations in natural science. The basis for this conviction was his conception of quantity, which was thoroughly Platonic. Instead of considering mathematical entities as abstractions from nature, as Aristotle and St. Thomas had done, Galileo conceived the ideal geometrical bodies as the true substrate of all reality. During the second day of the *Dialogue concerning the Two Chief World Systems* Galileo explains that there is no real difference between abstract and concrete geometric figures:

Just as the computer who wants his calculations to deal with sugar, silk, and wool must discount the boxes, bales and other packings, so the mathematical scientist (*filosofo geometro*), when he wants to recognize in the concrete the effects which he has proved in the abstract, must deduct the material hindrances, and if he is able to do so, I assure you that things are in no less agreement than arithmetical computations.[51]

Consequently Galileo considered quantity and quantified aspects to be not a "remote cause" of natural phenomena but the immediate, proper cause of everything that counts in objective nature: "size, shape, quantity, and motion, swift or slow."[52] For this reason the so-called secondary sense qualities—tastes, smells, sounds, colors, heat, etc.—were eliminated from Galileo's objective world and reduced to individual sensations; they "are nothing more than mere names, and exist only in the sensitive body."[53]

[50] Cf. A. C. Crombie, "Galileo's Dialogues concerning the Two Principal Systems of the World," *Dominican Studies* 3 (1950), 105–38.

[51] Galileo, *Dialogue concerning the Two Chief World Systems*, trans. by S. Drake (Berkeley, 1953), p. 207. On Galileo's Platonism see A. Koyré, "Galileo and Plato," *J. Hist. Ideas* 4 (1943), 400ff., reprinted in *Roots of Scientific Thought*, ed. by P. P. Wiener and A. Noland (New York, 1957), pp. 147–75.

[52] Galileo, *Il Saggiatore*, q. 48; *Opere*, IV, 333. The full text is translated and discussed by E. A. Burtt, *The Metaphysical Foundations of Modern Physical Science*, rev. ed. (London, 1932), pp. 73–80.

[53] On the subjectivity of secondary qualities in Descartes and Hobbes, see Burtt, *ibid.*, pp. 111–13, 122–27.

However, if we overlook Galileo's Platonic view of quantity, and if we discount his optimism in the matter of demonstration, we must admit that he did discover a new method, a new *modus*, namely, the mathematical way to nature. Because this method is determined by the objectively measurable aspects of physical phenomena, he did indeed discover "an entirely new science." This "new science" was, in fact, an extension of celestial mechanics, the ancient science of astronomy, to the world of terrestrial phenomena.

The method of this new science is still the analytical or "resolutive method" of Aristotle, as Galileo himself states on the First Day of the *Dialogue*.[54] We should not have expected anything different, since mathematical physics is a speculative science, requiring the general method of all speculative knowledge. The special characteristics of the *modus proprius* are determined by the objective measure. Among the more important characteristics are:

1. the indispensable role of mathematics in all demonstrations of measurable quantities;
2. the impossibility of dealing with anything but measurable quantities;
3. the need to search for more and more suitable hypotheses to account for the facts, as did the astronomers of old; and
4. the necessity of experimentation (a) to obtain the necessary measures and (b) to verify or falsify the hypotheses proposed.

Historians of seventeenth-century science, I think, would admit that these characteristics were universally recognized and enthusiastically praised by the founders of classical physics.

The second innovation in seventeenth-century science need only be considered briefly to establish a very important point concerning the "new science." It is generally recognized that the seventeenth century gave birth not only to a new mathematical physics, but also to a new *mechanical philosophy*.[55] What is not so clearly recognized is that there is no necessary connection between these two. There was no necessary connection between these two even in the seventeenth century. The foremost proponents of the mechanical philosophy, namely, Descartes, Gassendi, Francis Bacon, and Robert Boyle, can hardly be listed as mathematical physicists. However, like Galileo, these philosophers recognized only two first principles in natural science—

[54] Galileo, *Dialogue concerning the Two Chief World Systems*, ed. cit., p. 51.
[55] On this, see the many writings of Marie Boas Hall, especially her "Establishment of the Mechanical Philosophy," *Osiris* 10 (1952), 412–541, and her "Matter in Seventeenth Century Science," in *The Concept of Matter*, ed. E. McMullin (Notre Dame, 1963).

matter and motion. Like Galileo, they recognized no motion in nature other than mechanical. The truth of the matter is that in the seventeenth, eighteenth, and nineteenth centuries there was a comfortable compatibility between a mechanical philosophy and mathematical physics. To use Whitehead's felicitous phrase, we might say that they were oblivious to "the fallacy of misplaced concreteness."

The essential feature of this mechanical philosophy was the rejection of φύσις, or nature, as an explanatory principle in natural science. With this rejection also went potency and act, substance, formal and final causality, and even the ontological reality of true causality. In their place, as is well known, the seventeenth-century philosophers substituted quantified matter (corpuscular, atomic, or continuous), mechanical agencies (like impulse, attractions, repellents, adhesive forces, and various energies), and local motion. But the important point is that these substitutes for the concept of nature were, in fact, principles proposed for a new *natural philosophy*. They were not the principles of the new mathematical physics actually discovered by Galileo. The principles of the new physics were and still are mathematical. In other words, the "new science" discovered by Galileo, and developed by Newton and perfected in our own day by the theories of relativity and quantum, can be recognized as a legitimate science in the Aristotelian sense of the term. At the same time we can reject the mechanical philosophy which happened to predominate in the seventeenth, eighteenth, and nineteenth centuries.

If we have presented a fair estimate of the evolution of scientific method, then we must say that this evolution did not consist in rejecting the old for the new. Rather, it consisted in the addition of new methods and discoveries to the still-valid ancient methods and discoveries.

XI

MEDIEVAL NATURAL PHILOSOPHY AND MODERN SCIENCE

Up to about eighty-five years ago, scientists and would-be historians of science blandly assumed that all modern science began with Galileo and Descartes in the seventeenth century, and that before the seventeenth century there was no science as we know it. That is to say, modern science, particularly physics, represented a complete break with earlier thought. When it was pointed out by historians of thought that some scientific notions existed in antiquity, particularly in biology and astronomy, this was shrugged off as of little importance compared to the science par excellence of physics. The view persisted that there was no continuity between ancient and modern science. Above all, there was nothing of interest in the "scientific night of the Middle Ages." This assumption of discontinuity prevailed especially among physicists, chemists, and astronomers, while biologists and allied scientists preferred to see some kind of continuity.

The pioneer work of Pierre Duhem (1861–1916) some eighty-five years ago opened the whole field of medieval science and made research in the area of medieval science respectable. Recently Stanley L. Jaki appraised the work of Pierre Duhem as follows:

Singlehanded he destroyed the legend of the "scientific night of the Middle Ages." Before him, the phrase was a hallowed shibboleth of a self-styled Enlightenment. After him it has become the sign of an inexcusable ignorance which unfortunately lingers on.[1]

Duhem proposed the notion of continuity between medieval and modern, or classical, physics. For him the discovery of impetus theory by the fourteenth-century Parisians Jean Buridan, Albert of Saxony, and others, led to the principle of inertia introduced by Galileo and

[1] Pierre Duhem, *To Save the Phenomena: An Essay on the Idea of Physical Theory from Plato to Galileo,* trans. E. Doland and C. Maschler with introd. by Stanley L. Jaki (Chicago, 1969), p. xvii.

Descartes as "the first article of the creed of science," as Whitehead calls it.[2] Following Duhem, a whole generation of historians grew up defending the new view of continuity.

On the popular stage of controversy the debate between the view of continuity and the view of discontinuity found its followers over the past thirty years, and there could be found as many defenders of the one as of the other.

In our own day, the late Anneliese Maier (1905–1971), by far the most illustrious historian of medieval science, not only reviewed the arguments of Duhem but contributed a vast amount of new material to the field of medieval scholarship. But instead of defending the continuity thesis of Duhem, she proved to her own satisfaction that there was no continuity between the qualitative aspects of medieval science and the quantitative character of modern physics. In fact, she maintained that there were certain basic views inherent in medieval physics that made development of modern physics impossible. In her view, one basic flaw in medieval physics was the principle "Omne quod movetur ab alio movetur." Until this fundamental principle was rejected in the seventeenth century, there could be no classical physics.[3] In other words, not only did Anneliese Maier reject Duhem's thesis concerning impetus and the principle of inertia, but she insisted that the medieval principle "Omne quod movetur ab alio movetur" is repugnant to the principle of inertia. Once the medieval principle was rejected by Galileo and Descartes, classical physics could begin. In the generation now growing up, we can expect to find ardent defenders of Maier's view of the basic discontinuity and opposition between medieval and modern science, notably physics.

However, the debate over continuity and discontinuity cannot be resolved solely on historical grounds. What is needed is a philosophical analysis of the true character of Aristotelian physics and the true character of modern science. In fact, the problem facing us is confused and almost lost by historical considerations, because, as Yves Simon has noticed, "When the historic conflict between the Aristotelian physics and the new physics opened, both sides were equally convinced that this was a conflict between two philosophies of nature."[4] That is to say, proponents of the two views debated as though they were talking about the same thing, whereas in fact they were talking at cross-purposes. An exclusively historical consideration

[2] *Essays in Science and Philosophy* (London, 1948), p. 171.
[3] Anneliese Maier, " 'Ergebnisse' der spätscholastischen Naturphilosophie," *Scholastik* 35 (1960), 161–87, especially 170.
[4] Yves Simon, *The Great Dialogue of Nature and Space* (Albany, 1970), pp. 4–5.

would lead us to believe that Aristotelian natural philosophy was completely disproved by the new physics. The physicomathematical science founded by Galileo and Descartes was taken by its proponents as a philosophy of nature and indeed as the only authentic one. The truth of the matter is that both were right and both were wrong. They were both right in seeing the novelty of the new physics. They were both wrong in seeing it as in opposition to Aristotle's natural philosophy.

Of course, there were whole areas where Aristotle had to be corrected by new evidence, but this process of correcting Aristotle had been taking place since the fifth century and was nothing new to the seventeenth. St. Thomas Aquinas himself corrected and reshaped much that was in Aristotle's natural philosophy. What I am proposing is the objective validity of both Aristotle's natural philosophy in its main structure and the new mathematical-physical consideration of nature that, for all practical purposes, prevailed in the seventeenth century.

To establish this view there are a certain number of preliminary points to be noted. First of all, the expression "modern science" is an equivocal term designating a vast assortment of fundamentally different types of knowledge cultivated today. There is nothing esoteric in being modern. Everything we accept today can be called modern, even though we have known it from antiquity. The problem is with the word "science." In all modern languages the term for "science" is equivocal; it stands for an amorphous type of knowledge that purports to be "scientific" or technical. The Greeks had no problem; when they used the word ἐπιστήμη, they meant knowledge of a thing or an event through its causes. It was clearly distinct from τέχνη, νοῦς, σοφία, or the like. When Aristotle called natural philosophy ἐπιστήμη, they all knew he meant a rational type of knowledge of nature through its sensible causes. The Latins, however, didn't fare so well. When St. Thomas called *sacra doctrina* a *scientia*, the commentators thought he meant scholastic theology, whereas he plainly meant *sacra doctrina*.[5] Nevertheless the Latin scholastics generally reserved the word "science" for knowledge through one or more causes of a thing or event. More than that, they distinguished *scientia* from art, prudence, technology, and intuition. Today too much is included in the word "science." Ideally, modern sciences are predominantly mathematical in character and experimental in practice. But it must

[5] See James A. Weisheipl, "The Meaning of *Sacra Doctrina* in *Summa Theologiae*, I, q. 1," *The Thomist* 38 (1974), 49–80.

be admitted that there are many modern sciences which are neither mathematical nor experimental. Anthropology, paleontology, botany, much of psychology, and the various life sciences continuously fail to be completely mathematicized. That is to say, modern physics is a radically different kind of science from, let us say, modern biology or anthropology. This radical difference lies in the fact that modern physics, like modern astronomy, is formally mathematical in structure and method, whereas modern biology is formally sensible (*sensibilis*, or *naturalis*) in structure and method. Jacques Maritain was one of the first modern Thomists to insist on this difference between physics, which is mathematical and empiriometric in structure, and biology, which is natural and empextrioschematic in character. Unless some such distinction is made between the two ends of the modern spectrum of science, there will be endless confusion. For purposes of this paper, the expression "modern science" will be taken to mean knowledge of the physicomathematical type exemplified by physics in all its branches and astronomy. We are not including the life sciences or the social sciences.

The second point to be noted is that knowledge of the physicomathematical type was not unknown to the ancients. The most highly cultivated science of this type was astronomy, especially in the hands of Ptolemy. But long before Ptolemy, Plato had posed the problem to Eudoxus of discovering the mathematics of the universe. In Simplicius's commentary on *De caelo* we find the Platonic tradition formulated in the following way:

Eudoxus of Cnidos was the first Greek to concern himself with hypotheses of this sort, Plato having, as Sosigenes says, set it as a problem to all earnest students of this subject to find what are the uniform and ordered movements by the assumption of which the phenomena in relation to the movements of the planets can be saved [σώζειν τὰ φαινόμενα].[6]

That is to say, the astronomer's problem is to discover all the hypotheses necessary to save the phenomena of planetary motion. Even the unsophisticated astronomy of Eudoxus and Callippus was considered distinct from natural philosophy by Aristotle. What would he have said about the epicycles and eccentrics of Ptolemy? Among the "more physical of the branches of mathematics," Aristotle lists not only astronomy but also optics and harmonics.[7] The scholastics recognized not only the astronomy of Ptolemy and the optics of Euclid, Alhazen, Pecham, and others as belonging to this category of the "more physi-

6 Simplicius, *In II De caelo* XII, comm. 43 (Venice, 1548, fol. 74r–v).
7 Aristotle, *Physics* II, 2, 194a8.

cal of the branches of mathematics," but also statics (*scientia de ponderibus*) and mechanics, the latter largely due to the mathematician Archimedes.

St. Thomas calls this type of intermediate knowledge *scientia media*, i.e., a type of knowledge that is intermediate between pure mathematics and straight natural philosophy.[8] In more specific terms, *scientia media* is a knowledge of nature based on mathematical principles. The clearest example of this kind of knowledge is, of course, Newton's *Principia Mathematica Philosophiae Naturalis*, where the very title reveals the precise nature of the work. But for Thomas the clearest example was the *Almagest* (the *Mathematical Syntaxis*) of Ptolemy. For Thomas it is clear that astronomy is a part of mathematics, "pars mathematicae"; the problem is how Aristotle can then go on to say that it is *magis naturalis quam mathematica*.[9] This is exactly what Moerbeke's translation says, and it is a legitimate translation of the Greek: τὰ φυσικώτερα τῶν μαθημάτων.[10] Aristotle had just finished talking about how such sciences abstract from motion, and consequently from sensible and natural matter: "abstrahit a materia sensibili et naturali."[11] To answer the apparent problem, Thomas says:

Although sciences of this type are intermediate between natural science and mathematics, they are nevertheless said by the Philosopher to be more natural than mathematical, because everything is denominated and specified by the term [*a termino*]. Hence, since the considerations of these sciences terminate in natural matter [*in materia naturali*], even though they proceed through mathematical principles, they are more natural than mathematical.[12]

The only way Thomas can resolve the problem is by saying that the subject matter is ultimately the same, i.e., both sciences ultimately study the same material universe. Thomas does not here say that the ultimate goal of astronomy and the other intermediate sciences is to know the ultimate natures of things. That is a different matter altogether. Rather, astronomy and natural philosophy can be said to study the same material object, although the *ratio formalis obiecti* through which the conclusion is known is specifically distinct, as Thomas says in *Summa theologiae* II-II, q. 1, a. 1.

Modern translations of the *Physics*, such as the one by Hardie and Gaye, avoid the problem by rendering Aristotle's phrase as "the more

[8] Thomas Aquinas, *In Boethium De Trinitate*, q. 5, a. 3 ad 5 and ad 6; see also *In II Phys.*, lect. 3, n. 8; *Sum. theol.* II-II, q. 9, a. 2 ad 3.
[9] Thomas, *In II Phys.*, lect. 3, nn. 8–9.
[10] Arist., *Phys.* II, 2, 194a7–8.
[11] Thomas, *In II Phys.*, lect. 3, nn. 5–7.
[12] *Ibid.*, lect. 3, n. 8.

physical of the branches of mathematics."[13] However, the Loeb translation of Wicksteed and Cornford interprets the phrase as Moerbeke did, namely, "those sciences which are rather physical than mathematical, though combining both disciplines."[14] Charlton's translation seems to be quite satisfactory. He translates it as "those branches of mathematics which come nearest to the study of nature, like optics, harmonics, and astronomy."[15]

The point I am trying to make is that Thomas was perfectly aware of that peculiar type of knowledge intermediate between mathematics and natural philosophy. He called the type *scientia media*. As far as I have been able to determine, no other writer in the Middle Ages used the expression *scientia media* in that sense. It seems to be unique to Thomas.

The next point is that while knowledge of the *scientia media* type was not new, the application of mathematical principles to the entire range of nature was indeed new to the seventeenth century. The great originality of the seventeenth century, as I see it, was the unification of celestial and terrestrial mechanics through mathematics. Perhaps the idea was not new, but the fact was new. Much has been said about the dreams of Robert Grosseteste and Roger Bacon in the thirteenth century. We are all aware of the strong language used by Roger Bacon against the neglect of mathematics. He says, for example:

The neglect [of mathematics] for the past thirty or forty years has nearly destroyed the entire learning of Latin Christendom. For he who does not know mathematics cannot know any of the other sciences.[16]

But Bradwardine in the fourteenth century was even more disconcerting:

It is [mathematics] which reveals every genuine truth, for it knows every hidden secret and bears the key to every subtlety of letters; whoever, then, has the effrontery to study physics while neglecting mathematics should know from the start that he will never make his entry through the portals of wisdom.[17]

I think Thomas Bradwardine, more than anyone else in the Middle Ages, saw the possibility of a unified dynamics for celestial and terrestrial motions. In the fourth and last chapter of his *De proportione*

---

[13] Oxford Aristotle in *The Basic Works of Aristotle*, ed. Richard McKeon (New York, 1941), p. 239.

[14] Arist., *Phys.* II, 2 (London, 1963, p. 121).

[15] *Aristotle's Physics I–II*, trans. W. Charlton (Oxford, 1970), p. 26.

[16] Roger Bacon, *Opus maius* IV, 1, 1 (ed. J. H. Bridges [Oxford, 1897], I, 97–98).

[17] Thomas Bradwardine, *Tractatus de continuo*, MS Erfurt Amplon Q. 385, fol. 31v.

velocitatum in motibus of 1328, he actually sought some foundation for comparing terrestrial and celestial velocities. For Aristotle, these diverse motions are incomparable, for there is nothing in common between rectilinear motion of a body and the circular motion of a sphere. Bradwardine, however, found it in the fastest moving point of the sphere considered or imagined as a straight line. As Anneliese Maier expressed it, Bradwardine "would have wanted to write the *Principia Mathematica Philosophiae Naturalis* of his century."[18]

But these were only dreams. It was not until the seventeenth century that the principle of inertia acquired the force of "the first law of nature." Giovanni Benedetti (1530–1590) in the sixteenth century had already insisted that every body, naturally falling or projected, tends to move in a straight line. But it was Galileo (1564–1642) who first formulated the principle of inertia. In his *Discourses on the Two New Sciences*, the Third Day, he assumes that the momentum of a given body falling down an inclined plane is proportional only to the vertical distance and independent of the inclination; from this he concludes that a body falling down one plane would acquire momentum which would carry it up another to the same height. Thus Galileo says, "Any velocity once received by a body is perpetually maintained as long as the external causes of acceleration or retardation are removed, a condition which is found only on horizontal planes."[19] Although Christian Huygens (1629–1695) had a clearer idea of the principle and formulated it as a "hypothesis" for his work on the pendulum, it was Descartes (1596–1650) who extended the principle to cover the whole of natural philosophy by making it "the first law of nature."[20] The principle of inertia reached its classical formulation in Isaac Newton's *Principia:* "Every body continues in its state of rest or uniform motion in a straight line, unless it is compelled to change that state by forces impressed upon it" (Law 1). In the seventeenth century the principle of inertia served wonderfully as a working hypothesis to "save the phenomena." On such a hypothesis the mathematics of the universe could be calculated.

To put the matter in another way, the narrow limits of *scientia media* in the Middle Ages as applied to astronomy were expanded to include the whole realm of nature, now known mathematically. We have come

---

[18] Anneliese Maier, *Studien zur Naturphilosophie der Spätscholastik*, I (Rome, 1949), 86, note 10.

[19] Galileo, *Discorsi . . . intorno a Due Nuove Scienze*, Giornata Terza, prob. 23, scholium (*Opera* [Padua, 1744], III, 123).

[20] René Descartes, *Principia Philosophiae* II, 37 (*Oeuvres*, ed. Charles Adam and Paul Tannery, VIII [Paris, 1905], 62).

to call this extended knowledge of nature through mathematics "modern physics," the structure and method of which is physico-mathematical, i.e., it is a *scientia media* in Thomas's sense of the phrase. Just as the epicycles and eccentrics of Ptolemy were convenient hypotheses for "saving the appearances" of celestial motions, so the principle of inertia was a convenient and fruitful hypothesis for saving the unity of locomotion in the heavens and on the earth.

Speaking in the context of Ptolemaic astronomy, St. Thomas says:

It is not necessary that the various hypotheses which [the astronomers] hit upon be true. For although these suppositions save the appearance, we are nevertheless not forced to say that these suppositions are true, because perhaps there is some other way men have not yet discovered by which the appearances of things may be saved concerning the stars.[21]

The same view was expressed by Thomas some six years earlier in his *Summa theologiae* when he says:

There are two kinds of argument put forward to prove something. The first goes to the root of the matter and fully demonstrates some point; for instance, in natural philosophy there is a conclusive argument to prove that celestial movements are of constant speed. The other kind does not prove a point conclusively but shows that its acceptance fits in with the observed effects; for instance, an astronomical argument about eccentric and epicyclic motions is put forward on the ground that by this hypothesis one can show how celestial motions appear as they do to observation. Such an argument is not fully conclusive, since an explanation might be possible even on another hypothesis.[22]

The point is that the hypotheses of astronomy, in this case Ptolemaic astronomy, are significant in that they may account for all the phenomena without forcing the mind to acknowledge their physical certainty. Speaking specifically about the movement of the earth, Thomas says that the appearances could be saved either by holding that the earth is stationary and the heavens are moving about it, or that the heavens are stationary and the earth is moving within, or that both the earth and the heavens are moving. These are different hypotheses—in the classical sense of the term—that can all "save the appearances," σώζειν τὰ φαινόμενα, i.e., render systematic intelligibility to all the known facts.

One of the most fruitful hypotheses devised in the seventeenth century was the principle of inertia. We have already noted that the late Anneliese Maier insisted on seeing a radical opposition between

[21] Thomas, *In I De caelo,* lect. 3, n. 7.
[22] Thomas, *Sum. theol.* I, q. 32, a. 1 ad 2.

the medieval principle of "Omne quod movetur ab alio movetur" and the seventeenth-century principle of inertia. The radical incompatibility of these two "principles" for Maier leads, of course, to the inevitable view of discontinuity between medieval and modern classical physics.

In two studies previously published,[23] I have tried to show that Maier completely misunderstands the medieval principle "Omne quod movetur ab alio movetur." Or more precisely, she understands the medieval principle solely through the eyes of Averroes, whose interpretation was explicitly rejected by Thomas Aquinas, Albert the Great, and many others in the thirteenth century. For St. Thomas the principle—which for him was demonstrated by Aristotle with *propter quid* certainty in Book VII of the *Physics* and proved inductively in Book VIII—does not mean that every motion here and now requires a mover, a *motor coniunctus,* to explain its continuation here and now in time. That is to say, the principle does not mean that everything here and now moving is moved here and now by something else. For Thomas, once a heavy body is generated, i.e., brought into existence, it spontaneously falls to the ground, if there is no obstacle, without any other cause moving it.[24] The efficient cause of this free-fall of heavy bodies is none other than the agent which generated the body in the first place. From one point of view, the position of Aristotle is much more sophisticated than Averroes and Anneliese Maier give him credit for. On the other hand, Anneliese Maier and the seventeenth-century philosophers like Galileo, Descartes, Beeckman and others were too hasty in accepting as "the first law of nature" a principle that can be nothing more than a hypothesis in the classical sense of the term.

I say that the principle of inertia is no more than a hypothesis because it is neither self-evident nor demonstrable. It is a likely extrapolation, which is not a proof. Terrestrial motions known in human experience all come to an end; they do not proceed in a straight line; and they are not uniform—they are rather accelerated or decelerated. Furthermore, celestial motions are neither straight nor uniform, but they are perpetual. If celestial motions ever came to an end, it would be disastrous for the universe. But all this proves is that celestial

---

[23] James A. Weisheipl, "The Principle *Omne quod movetur ab alio movetur* in Medieval Physics," *Isis* 56 (1965), 26–45; "Motion in a Void: Aquinas and Averroes," in *St. Thomas Aquinas 1274–1974: Commemorative Essays* (Toronto, 1974), I, 467–88; reprinted as Chapters IV and VI above.

[24] See Thomas, especially *In III De caelo,* lect. 8, n. 9; J. A. Weisheipl, *Nature and Gravitation* (River Forest, Ill., 1955).

motions, unlike terrestrial motions, are not designed to come to an end as to a final cause. That is to say, the causalities involved in terrestrial and celestial motions are somehow different.

It is commonly claimed that the greatest triumph of the seventeenth century was to rid the celestial spheres of spiritual movers and to effect a unification of celestial and terrestrial mechanics. As Herbert Butterfield puts it, "The modern law of inertia, the modern theory of motion, is the great factor which in the seventeenth century helped to drive the spirits out of the world and opened the way to a universe that ran like a piece of clockwork."[25] This is quite true. But it must be noted that the crux of the solution rests on the principle of inertia.

For Descartes, who first suggested the universality of the principle, the principle of inertia is founded on the conservation of momentum, measured by mass times velocity. Descartes contended that in the beginning God created not only matter but also a determined *quantitas motus*, which could be neither increased nor decreased, for otherwise God would have to continue creating motion, which would be contrary to his immutability![26] Throughout the entire universe the "quantity of motion" remains constant so that when one body is at rest, another is in motion; when one moves twice as fast, another moves half as fast as previously, and so on. Change then was to be explained as the transference of momentum from one body to another through impact. Thus for Descartes, as for Spinoza after him, the principle of inertia was based on the conservation of momentum (mv), and conservation was thought necessary because of the immutability of God.[27]

Leibniz, however, pointed out that momentum is not constant in the universe, for it cannot be shown that every body imparts the same quantity of motion to some other body.[28] Furthermore, Leibniz maintained that it is not momentum which accounts for movement but a certain *vis viva, lebendige Kraft,* which is measured not by mv but by

---

[25] Herbert Butterfield, *Origins of Modern Science* (London, 1951), p. 7; see also Charles Singer, *A Short History of Science* (Oxford, 1943), pp. 212–17.

[26] Descartes, *Principia Philosophiae* II, 36 (*ed. cit.*, VIII, 61).

[27] *Ibid.*, II, 37 (*ed. cit.*); see Spinoza, *Renati Des Cartes Principiorum Philosophiae Pars I et II More Geometrico Demonstratae* (*Opera*, ed. J. Van Vloten and J. P. N. Land, 3d edition [The Hague, 1914], IV, 159).

[28] Principally in his *Système nouveau de la nature*, ed. C. J. Gerhardt, *Die philosophischen Schriften von G. W. Leibnitz* (Berlin, 1890), IV. For the controversy between the followers of Descartes and Leibniz on this point, see W. H. B. Joseph, *Lectures on the Philosophy of Leibniz* (Oxford, 1949), pp. 27–54.

mass times velocity squared (mv^2).[29] Thus for Leibniz the principle of inertia is based on the conservation of energy (mv^2), instead of on Descartes' momentum. However, as Leibniz denies any real interaction between the unextended monads which make up the real world, the conservation of energy is a *phenomenological principle* which depends upon "pre-established harmony" in which God alone is the true cause. For Leibniz the phenomenological world may be described through mathematical and mechanical laws, but the real world and even the foundation of mechanical laws are to be found in realms beyond mechanics.[30] Thus the conservation of *vis viva* in the world depends upon the will of God.

Although a much more satisfactory presentation of the principle of inertia is to be found in Sir Isaac Newton's *Principia*, it must be noted that Newton does not attempt to demonstrate it but assumes it without offering any philosophical or theological foundation. It is in this latter context that Newton says, "Hypotheses non fingo," that is to say, Newton was unwilling to offer metaphysical causes for the principle but insisted that such principles of nature must be true. In other words, the whole structure of the universe for Newton presupposes the validity of the principle of inertia.[31] Newton, furthermore, discovered or devised a hypothesis which had far greater power than the basic law of motion, namely, the hypothesis of universal gravitation, or attraction. With these two fruitful hypotheses Newton could present the system of the world.

Pierre Duhem was so struck by this hypothetical feature of ancient astronomy and of modern physics that he developed his own philosophy of science, which refused to project mathematical hypotheses and mathematical entities into physical reality. For Duhem, scientific laws are not extramental laws in nature but mere conventionalism (*commodisme*), mental constructs temporarily accepted by scientists as useful expressions of reality, much like the conventional use of grammar among peoples of a particular group. The purpose of "physical theory," Duhem insisted, is to save the appearances, σώζειν τὰ φαινόμενα. Perhaps Duhem went too far in thinking that all physical laws are hypotheses, but he was not wrong in his appreciation of what a hypothesis really is. It would seem, however, that modern physics as

---

[29] On the importance of the squared velocity in Leibniz, see Joseph, *Lectures*, pp. 41–61.

[30] Leibniz, *Système nouveau* (*Philosophische Schriften*, ed. Gerhardt, IV, 444).

[31] For a clarification of the true foundation of the principle of inertia, see Weisheipl, *Nature and Gravitation*, pp. 48–64, and Chapters II and III above.

well as ancient astronomy has the right to concoct as many hypotheses as may be necessary to "save the appearances," to make sense out of the known facts.

With this in mind, I would like to make my next point. Just as the structure of Ptolemaic astronomy as a *scientia media* could coexist in medieval education and thought with Aristotle's natural philosophy, so too can modern physics, which in my view is a *scientia media*, coexist with a structured natural philosophy which is not a *scientia media*. I am talking not about details but about basic structure, method, and principles.

One of the characteristics of modern science is sometimes thought to be experimentation and prediction, verifying the theory or hypothesis. But experimentation as such does not distinguish the sciences, not even controlled experimentation and prediction. What distinguishes the sciences is the content, or modality, of the concepts, definitions, and the middle term of the proof. By modality I mean type of materiality and immateriality involved in the concepts, definitions, and proofs. Experimentation or the "tempting" of nature is common to all natural sciences in varying degrees. One might even go so far as to say that some kind of experimentation is involved in every human knowledge, even in politics and economics. There is, of course, a radical difference between experimentation in modern physics and experimentation in Aristotle's physics. In modern physics the intrinsic value of experimentation is taken as its ability to yield a numerical content of knowledge, i.e., a mathematical number, ratio, or symbol, which makes up the equation. Experimentation for Aristotle is revelatory of the physical structure or its physical causes. This is not to say that these two types of experimentation are contradictory, but only that they are radically different in content and goal. The modern physicist and the Aristotelian could be interested in the same experiment, but they would each get something different out of it.

The philosophy usually considered to be congenial to the new physics is "mechanical" or "corpuscular" philosophy, such as developed in the seventeenth century. But, it could be argued, this is only a first impression. Nature is not mechanical. Therefore it cannot be justified in a mechanistic philosophy. The dynamic character of φύσις, or *natura*, requires its justification in a philosophy that recognizes natural principles, causes, and elements. Such a philosophy would be based not on mathematical principles, legitimate as they are, but on principles that are truly "natural," i.e., active and passive principles of movement and rest in those things to which they belong *per se* and not *per accidens*.

Once the basic structure of the physicomathematical sciences is understood, it becomes clear that there is no radical opposition between modern science and a philosophy of nature such as devised by Aristotle and St. Thomas. Such a natural philosophy is not only valid but even necessary for the philosophical understanding of nature itself. That is to say, there are realities in nature that are not accounted for by physicomathematical abstraction, realities such as motion, time, causality, chance, substance, and change itself. The definition of motion, for example, given by Aristotle[32] may be of no use to the modern physicist, but it is the only definition that can be given without including the thing to be defined in the definition. To define motion as "the change of a body from one position to another" is not to define it at all. The measurement of time is well known to the physicist, but as Bergson pointed out a long time ago, the reality that is time itself escapes him completely.[33] The physicist is concerned with the length of time, not with the time that is always passing away. The physicist needs mechanical causes, such as matter and force, but the nature of causality as such is beyond mathematics, where even final causality is out of place. Concepts such as potency and act, matter and form, substance and accident, quite useless to the modern physicist, are established in a realistic natural philosophy.

The aforementioned concepts are not established in metaphysics, and in this connection it is important to stress the differences between metaphysics and natural philosophy and to indicate the nature and relationship of each. Whereas modern physicists tend to reject natural philosophy as an unwelcome part of metaphysics, it is interesting that many modern Thomists tend to reject outright the validity of natural philosophy and to put in its place modern physics. The former confuse natural philosophy with metaphysics as the latter confuse it with modern physics. The result has been to overload metaphysics with innumerable problems and areas of concern that rightly belong to the natural philosopher. This is a perversion of metaphysics as understood by St. Thomas. We wish here, not to justify natural philosophy against the claims of the modern Thomistic metaphysician, but rather to point out the relation between modern science and a realistic natural philosophy which is quite distinct from any metaphysics, even from Thomistic metaphysics. To amalgamate natural philosophy and metaphysics is to exaggerate the one and disparage the other. The

---

[32] Arist., *Phys.* III, 1, 201a10–11.
[33] Henri Bergson, *Essai sur les données immédiates de la conscience* (Paris, 1911; his doctoral dissertation presented in 1898).

whole structure of human knowledge is thus perverted and nothing is rightly understood.

This point can be put in another way. For Thomas Aquinas metaphysics presupposes natural philosophy for at least two reasons. First, it is natural philosophy that discovers the existence of separated substances, i.e., some nonmaterial being, and thus establishes the subject matter of a new science, namely, the science of being as such. In Book VI of the *Metaphysics* Aristotle says: "If there were no substance other than those which are formed by nature, natural science would be the first science; but if there is an immovable substance, the science of this must be prior and must be first philosophy."[34] Thomas not only comments on this clear statement but repeats it twice more in his commentary.[35] Thomas puts it this way:

If natural substances, which are sensible and mobile substances, are first among all being, then natural science would be the first among all the sciences. . . . But if there is another nature and substance besides natural substances, which is separable and immobile, it is necessary that there be another science about the very *esse* of that thing, which would be prior to the natural.[36]

But for St. Thomas there are two ways to establish the existence of such a substance separate from matter and motion. The first is through a consideration of physical motion, such as Aristotle undertakes in Books VII and VIII of the *Physics,* where he demonstrates that the cause of all physical motions in the world must itself be immaterial and immovable. The second is through a consideration of human intellection and volition, such as Aristotle gives in Book III of *De anima,* where he demonstrates that the human intellective soul must be immaterial and immortal. Even if the existence of only one such separated substance is proved, there is the foundation of a new science. Actually Aristotle thought that there were a great number (if not an infinite number) of separated substances. But only one is sufficient to constitute a new first philosophy in which is studied not only this one separate substance but also all those terms which are analogically applicable to both material and immaterial being.

This brings us to the second reason why natural philosophy must precede metaphysics. This is demanded by the nature of analogous concepts. Analogous concepts are not abstracted but constructed by

---

[34] Arist., *Metaphysics* VI, 1, 1026a27–31.
[35] Thomas, *In VI Metaph.,* lect. 1, n. 1170; see also *In III Metaph.,* lect. 4, n. 398; *In XI Metaph.,* lect. 7, n. 2267. Cf. *In IV Phys.,* lect. 1, n. 1.
[36] Thomas, *In XI Metaph.,* lect. 7, n. 2267.

the human mind. The prime analogue of our concept of "being," or "thing," is the sensible, material, concrete reality of things around us. The moment we realize that there is at least one thing that is not sensible, material, and movable, we break into the realm of analogy. From that moment on, terms such as "thing," "being," "substance," "cause," and the like are no longer restricted to the material and sensible world. We thereby stretch and enlarge our earlier conceptions to make them include immaterial reality. Such are our analogous concepts of being, substance, potency, act, cause, and the like. Such terms are seen in metaphysics to be applicable beyond the realm of material and sensible realities. The prime analogue *quoad nos* of all these concepts is material, sensible, movable being, which is the realm of the natural philosopher.

Thus, for St. Thomas, natural philosophy is prior *quoad nos* to metaphysics. Natural philosophy establishes by demonstration that there is some being which is not material. This negative judgment, or more properly, this judgment of separation, is the point of departure for a higher study, which can be called "first philosophy" or metaphysics. Consequently this new study is "prior" and "first" in itself, i.e., according to nature, but it is not first *quoad nos.*

Whenever Thomas presents the proper order of learning for philosophers or even for the learned man, he always lists natural philosophy before ethics and metaphysics. Thus Thomas says in his commentary on the *Ethics:*

The fitting order of learning, therefore, will be that boys are first instructed in logic, because logic teaches the method for all philosophy. Second, that they be instructed in mathematics, which neither requires experience nor transcends the imagination. Third, [instruction] in natural science, which even though it does not transcend sense and imagination, requires a great deal of experience. Fourth, in morals, which require experience and a soul free from passions, as was pointed out in the first book. Fifth, however, [instruction] in wise and divine things, which transcend imagination and require a strong intellect.[37]

That is to say, natural philosophy is indispensable to ethics and metaphysics. That ethics presupposes psychology is easier to see than the equal truth that metaphysics presupposes natural philosophy. A Thomist who rejects the valid and legitimate area of natural philosophy distinct from modern science and from metaphysics does so at

---

[37] Thomas, *In VI Ethic.*, lect. 7, n. 1211; see also *In lib. De causis*, prooem., ed. H. D. Saffrey (Fribourg, 1954), p. 2.

great peril. Not only does he lose the right to speak in the name of Thomas, but more important, he loses the foundation for every valid metaphysics.

If a realist natural philosophy is valid as a study becoming to man, then surely its value lies in the unique kind of knowledge provided, a knowledge distinct from the physicomathematical knowledge supplied by modern physics and astronomy. The value of natural philosophy lies not in pointing the way to new scientific discoveries but rather in supplementing one's basic knowledge of reality. Nature cannot be exhausted by any one type of knowledge. The totality of nature cannot be boxed in an equation. Natural philosophy, therefore, is not only valid but also valuable in giving us another avenue to understand the physical world.

The natural philosophy of which I speak not only includes the entire area of what Aristotle called the *libri naturales,* extending from a general analysis of motion and its causes in the *Physics* to detailed information about the structure, generation, and classification of plants, animals, and minerals, but would also include what today has come to be known as the history and philosophy of science. The critiques scientists themselves give of their work, principles, assumptions, and hypotheses properly belong to the realm of philosophy, specifically to the realm of natural philosophy. The critiques of such men of science as Duhem, Eddington, Jeans, Plank, Poincaré, and Whitehead are works of philosophy and pertain not to metaphysics but to natural philosophy in its properly critical role. The history of science, too, belongs to natural philosophy in this same role. Thus the extent of natural philosophy, as I see it, is truly vast. No one man can possibly know it all. But even some acquaintance with it is better than nothing at all. The point I have been trying to make is that natural philosophy is a valid study of the sensible world, one to which St. Thomas Aquinas contributed heavily. Such a philosophy is not only valid but also valuable; and its value lies in the kind of knowledge natural philosophy (side by side with modern physical science and metaphysics) can provide for modern man.

In Memoriam
The Very Reverend James A. Weisheipl, O.P.
1923–1984

"... And never let me be parted from You."

James Athanasius Weisheipl, a priest of the Order of Friars Preachers, died on Sunday, 30 December 1984 in Saskatoon, Saskatchewan. He was sixty-one years old and had been a priest for thirty-five years. He would want us to remember that he died on the Feast of the Holy Family because the rhythms of his life were so closely tied to the liturgical life of the Church. The Dominican ideal of the intellect in the service of God was the animating principle of his life, for there was no part of his life which was not directed to his vocation as a Dominican priest. Those who attended his Masses could not help being impressed by the intensity with which he celebrated the Eucharist. I was always struck by the joyful solemnity in which, with the consecrated bread and wine before him, he prayed:

> Lord Jesus Christ, Son of the living God, by the will of the Father and the work of the Holy Spirit Your death brought life to the world.
>
> By Your holy body and blood free me from all my sins and from every evil.
>
> Keep me faithful to Your teaching and never let me be parted from You.

The final sentence of this prayer captures the core of Fr. Weisheipl's life. His life had a center and a goal, namely, Christ, and in all he did he sought to discover and to proclaim God's truth to others so that he and they would never be parted from that Truth. He was not a priest who happened to be a scholar, but one for whom the disciplined life of the mind was an essential characteristic of his priestly vocation.

He was a superb historian, philosopher, and theologian—and each of these disciplines was for him a way to know, to love, and to serve

God. He earned doctorates in philosophy from the Angelicum in Rome and in the history of science from Oxford. And in 1978 he was honored by the Dominican Order with the degree of Master of Sacred Theology. He published widely in all three fields. Whether it was in Dominican *studia* in England and the United States, or at the Albertus Magnus Lyceum near Chicago, or for the past twenty years as a Senior Fellow of the Pontifical Institute of Mediaeval Studies in Toronto, or in his frequent lectures at colleges and universities throughout North America, Fr. Weisheipl brought to his teaching and writing those intellectual and moral virtues which elicited the respect and love of his colleagues and students. He served as President of the American Catholic Philosophical Association and Councillor of the Medieval Academy of America. He was the founder and first director of the American section of the Leonine Commission for the critical editing of the works of Aquinas, and he was one of the contributing editors of the *New Catholic Encyclopedia*. In addition to his position at the Pontifical Institute, Fr. Weisheipl was also a member of the faculties of the Graduate Centre for Medieval Studies, the Department of Philosophy, and the Institute for the History and Philosophy of Science and Technology of the University of Toronto.

Nature and Gravitation, The Development of Physical Theory in the Middle Ages, Albert the Great and the Sciences: Commemorative Essays, and more than thirty articles in scholarly journals throughout the world offer eloquent testimony of his contributions to the history of medieval science. It is his biography of Thomas Aquinas, however, first published in 1974, which brought him the greatest acclaim. Now in four different international editions, and with a second edition recently appearing in North America, *Friar Thomas d'Aquino: His Life, Thought, and Works* is the definitive book on the life of Aquinas. Prior to his death he was compiling material for a companion volume on the life and works of Albert the Great.

With Albert the Great and Thomas Aquinas, his confreres in the Order founded by St. Dominic, he believed that there is no hostility between faith and reason. He recognized the appropriate autonomy of each of the human sciences, but he knew further that the truth is one and God is its Author. He did not fear that the disciplined search for truth could ever lead one away from God. Revelation and science, faith and reason, grace and nature are complementary, not contradictory, orders of reality. Indeed, with Aquinas he affirmed that *sacra doctrina* is a science, although different from the other sciences in that its first principles are not known by reason alone. Fr. Weisheipl's analysis of the first question of the *Summa theologiae*, especially his explanation of the distinction between *sacra doctrina* and scholastic theology, provides a key for the further study of Aquinas's major work.

Like Albert and Thomas, Fr. Weisheipl lived in the world of the university. But also, like Albert and Thomas, at the university, Fr. Weisheipl was a constant witness to a spirituality which is truly otherworldly. His commitment to prayer and contemplation as the foundation of an active career was evident to those who knew him well. He often noted how much he depended upon the prayers of others, especially the Dominican Sisters of Lufkin, Texas. And he once remarked that were he to become a bishop, the first thing he would do would be to establish a convent of cloistered religious dedicated to praying for the diocese. As he saw no conflict between faith and reason, so he also saw no conflict between the roles of pastor and professor. He met weekly with students to pray the rosary and meditate on its mysteries. And he brought to his pastoral role that sharp and discerning intellect which won him international acclaim for his scholarly accomplishments. His intellectual apostolate included monthly meetings of the St. Thomas Society of Toronto at which students and professors discussed selected texts of Aquinas. In his introduction to the volume of essays *Albert the Great and the Sciences,* he noted that the major reason he undertook to edit these various essays was that modern scientists needed to be aware of the greatness of their patron saint so that in the face of the dilemmas and temptations which beset the scientific world the intercession of Albert might serve as a powerful resource.

As a result of years of study and reflection, Fr. Weisheipl thought as Thomas Aquinas thought: not in some abstract ahistorical sense, nor with that historicism which leads to a sterile relativism. Rather, his was an assimilated Thomism which is a part of a living and growing understanding of nature, human nature, and God, and which finds its sources in the first principles of reason and of faith. He recognized that the best way to understand St. Thomas was to study his life and thought in historical context. The medieval university was the setting for most of Aquinas's work, and Fr. Weisheipl was an expert on the structure and curriculum of the great universities at Oxford and Paris. As a philosopher and theologian, as well as a historian, he understood the intellectual context of the debates in natural philosophy, metaphysics, and theology which occupied the attention of university masters such as Albert and Thomas. Yet history, including the history of ideas, was for Fr. Weisheipl always propaedeutic. He would heartily reaffirm Thomas's observation that the final goal of study is not to know what men have thought, but what is the truth of things. Several years ago, he remarked to me that a teacher is a window to the truth and that his own goal was to be the means by which others could discover that truth. As a result of his profound and sympathetic study of Aquinas, Fr. Weisheipl contributed significantly to our understanding of his thought. The explanation of nature and motion—the subject of the essays collected in this volume—is a particularly good example of how Fr. Weisheipl's insight into the life and thought of Aquinas has aided in our knowledge of the broad continuities in the history of science. What is especially important in this respect is Fr. Weisheipl's explanation of the continuing and fundamental role of a science of nature, distinct from both metaphysics and the modern mathematical natural sciences. As a realist in the tradition of Aristotle, Albert, and Thomas, he was convinced of both the possibility and the value of a knowledge of the world of motion and change in terms of true causes.

He was a great teacher who instilled in several generations of graduate students a profound appreciation for the study of Thomistic thought, in general, and of natural philosophy, in particular. Much in the tradition of the medieval *magister*, he was the center of a thriving academic family with members in Canada, the United States, and Europe. At the Pontifical Institute of Mediaeval Studies he taught two year-long seminars on Aristotle's *Physics* and *Posterior Analytics* in the Latin Middle Ages. In these seminars he examined the development of natural philosophy in the context of the intellectual history of the Christian West from the early thirteenth to the seventeenth centuries. Nature, motion, time, the continuum, infinity, concepts of causality, the role of mathematics in understanding physics, the kinds of demonstrations in the natural sciences, and related questions constituted the substance of his courses. Such topics were, for Fr. Weisheipl, intimately a part of his Dominican vocation of the intellect in the service of God. He knew that the study of nature is a prerequisite for natural theology.

In recent years he focused his attention on the Christian doctrine of creation *ex nihilo*, examining the discussion in the twelfth and thirteenth centuries concerning creation and the eternity of the world. There is no better example of the brilliance of Aquinas's understanding of the relationship between faith and reason than his analysis of the philosophical and theological doctrines of creation. As Aquinas encountered the scientific heritage of Greece in its most sophisticated form, i.e., in the thought of Aristotle, and on a subject, creation, which unites physics, metaphysics, and theology, he forged an enduring synthesis of reason and faith. In particular, Fr. Weisheipl thought that Aquinas was correct in arguing not only that creation is rationally demonstrable but also that Aristotle's god was a *causa essendi,* that is, a first efficient cause of being. And at his death, Fr. Weisheipl left unfinished a brief outline for a new book: *Philosophy and the God of Abraham.* The book was to demonstrate that one did not have to choose between Athens and Jerusalem, between reason and faith. He always rejected the view that there is an inherent conflict between science and religion. In fact, as noted above, he would be the first to maintain that reason and faith support one another. His academic career, as well as his private life, exhibit the complementarity of the intellectual habits of philosophy and theology. Every day in the celebration of the Eucharist, Fr. Weisheipl expressed liturgically this complementarity as he united all he did with Christ to Whom he prayed: ". . . and never let me be parted from You."

On the ring he received as a sign of his office of Master of Sacred Theology, Fr. Weisheipl had inscribed the words Thomas Aquinas addressed to Christ. When St. Thomas was asked what reward he should receive for his devotion to Christ he replied: *Non nisi te Domine.* May the request of James A. Weisheipl, O.P., be granted.

WILLIAM E. CARROLL

Selected Bibliography of the Works of James A. Weisheipl, O.P.

BOOKS:

Nature and Gravitation (River Forest, Ill.: Aquinas Library, 1955; reprint, 1961).

The Development of Physical Theory in the Middle Ages (London and New York: Sheed and Ward, 1959 and 1960).

The Dignity of Science: Studies in the Philosophy of Science Presented to William Humbert Kane, O.P. (editor) (Washington, D.C.: Thomist Press, 1961).

Friar Thomas d'Aquino: His Life, Thought, and Works (Garden City, N.J.: Doubleday, 1974; reprint, Washington, D.C.: The Catholic University of America Press, 1983).

Albertus Magnus and the Sciences (editor) (Toronto: Pontifical Institute of Mediaeval Studies, 1980).

Commentary of St. Thomas Aquinas on the Gospel of St. John, Part I (general editor and translator with F. R. Larcher, O.P.), with "Appendices Historical and Theological" (Albany, N.Y.: Magi Books, 1980).

ARTICLES:

"The Concept of Nature," *The New Scholasticism* 28 (1954), 377–408; reprinted in *Nature and Gravitation*.

"Natural and Compulsory Movement," *The New Scholasticism* 29 (1955), 50–81; reprinted in *Nature and Gravitation*.

"Space and Gravitation," *The New Scholasticism* 29 (1955), 175–223; reprinted in *Nature and Gravitation*.

"Aristotle on Natural Place: A Rejoinder," *The New Scholasticism* 30 (1956), 211–15.

"Albertus Magnus and the Oxford Platonists," *Proceedings of the American Catholic Philosophical Association* 32 (1958), 124–39.

"The Place of John Dumbleton in the Merton School," *Isis* 50 (1959), 439–54.

"The Celestial Movers in Medieval Physics," *The Thomist* 24 (1961), 286–326; reprinted in *The Dignity of Science*.

"The Concept of Matter in Fourteenth Century Science," in *The Concept of Matter*, edited by Ernan McMullin (Notre Dame University Press, 1963), 319–41.

"The Evolution of Scientific Method," in *The Logic of Science*, edited by V. E. Smith (New York: St. John's University Press, 1964), 59–86.

"Roger Swyneshed, O.S.B., Logician, Natural Philosopher, and Theologian," in *Oxford Studies Presented to Daniel Callus* (Oxford: Oxford Historical Society, 1964), 231–52.

"The Curriculum of the Faculty of Arts at Oxford in the Early Fourteenth Century," *Mediaeval Studies* 26 (1964), 143–85.

"The Principle *Omne quod movetur ab alio movetur* in Medieval Physics," *Isis* 56 (1965), 26–45.

"Classification of the Sciences in Medieval Thought," *Mediaeval Studies* 27 (1965), 54–90.

"Developments in the Arts Curriculum at Oxford in the Early Fourteenth Century," *Mediaeval Studies* 28 (1966), 151–75.

"Galileo and His Precursors," in *Galileo, Man of Science,* edited by Ernan McMullin (New York: Basic Books, 1967), 85–97.

"Ockham and Some Mertonians," *Mediaeval Studies* 30 (1968), 163–213.

"Quidquid movetur ab alio movetur: A Reply [to Nikolaus Lobkowicz]," *The New Scholasticism* 42 (1968), 422–31.

"The Concept of Scientific Knowledge in Greek Philosophy," in *Mélanges Charles De Koninck* (Quebec: Laval, 1968), 487–507.

"Motion in a Void: Aquinas and Averroes," in *St. Thomas Aquinas 1274–1974: Commemorative Studies,* edited by Armand Maurer, C.S.B. (Toronto: Pontifical Institute of Mediaeval Studies, 1974), I, 467–88.

"The Parisian Faculty of Arts in the Mid-Thirteenth Century: 1240–1270," *The American Benedictine Review* 25 (1974), 200–217.

"The Meaning of *Sacra Doctrina* in *Summa Theologiae* I, q. 1," *The Thomist* 38 (1974), 49–80.

"Thomas's Evaluation of Plato and Aristotle," *The New Scholasticism* 48 (1974), 100–124.

"The Commentary of St. Thomas on the *De caelo* of Aristotle," *Sapientia* 29 (1974), 11–34.

"Alberti Magni, *Problemata determinata,*" in *Opera Omnia Alberti Magni* (Cologne: Aschendorff, 1975), XVII/1, 45–64.

"The Relationship of Medieval Natural Philosophy to Modern Science: The Contribution of Thomas Aquinas to Its Understanding," in *Science, Medicine, and the University: 1200–1550. Essays in Honor of Pearl Kibre,* *Manuscripta* 20 (1976), 181–96.

"Albertus Magnus and Universal Hylomorphism: Avicebron," *The Southwestern Journal of Philosophy* 10 (1980), 239–60.

"The Axiom *Opus naturae est opus intelligentiae* and Its Origins," in *Albertus Magnus Doctor Universalis: 1280/1980,* edited by Gerbert Meyer and Albert Zimmermann (Mainz: Matthias-Grunewald, 1980), 441–63.

"The Specter of *motor coniunctus* in Medieval Physics," in *Studi sul XIV secolo in memoria di Anneliese Maier,* edited by A. Maierù and A. P. Bagliani (Rome: Edizioni di Storia e Letteratura, 1981), 81–104.

"Approaches to Nature in the Middle Ages," in *Papers of the Tenth Annual Conference of the Center for Medieval and Early Renaissance Studies,* edited by Lawrence Roberts (Binghamton, New York: Center for Medieval and Early Renaissance Studies, 1982), 137–60.

"The Interpretation of Aristotle's *Physics* and the Science of Motion," in *The Cambridge History of Later Medieval Philosophy,* edited by Norman Kretzmann, Anthony Kenny, and Jan Pinborg (Cambridge: Cambridge University Press, 1982), 521–36.

"Galileo and the Principle of Inertia," lecture delivered at the Catholic University of America, Washington, D.C., December 3, 1982.

"Science in the Thirteenth Century," in *The History of the University of Oxford*, 1: *The Early Oxford Schools*, edited by J. I. Catto (Oxford: Clarendon Press, 1984), 435–69.

"Ockham and the Mertonians," in *The History of the University of Oxford*, 1: *The Early Oxford Schools*, edited by J. I. Catto (Oxford: Clarendon Press, 1984), 607–58.

"Athens and Jerusalem: The Spirituality of St. Thomas Aquinas," *The Canadian Catholic Review* 3 (1985), 23–28.

Index